The Sacred Pentagraph

A Craft Work
In Five Volumes

A Craft Application of Wicca
as an Occult Lodge System
and Craft Coven Organization

Tarostar V°

LEFTHANDPRESS
A subsidiary of Black Moon Publishing LLC
Cincinnati, Ohio USA

Black Moon Manifesto

It is the Will and misssion of Bate Cabal/Black Moon to effectively manifest unique and insightful occult Works for the esoteric community in a manner that is unfettered by commercial considerations.

BlackMoonPublishing.com

blackmoonpublishing@gmail.com

Left Hand Press is a subsidiary of
Black Moon Publishing, LLC

Design and layout by
Jo Bounds of Black Moon Publishing

Illustrations and photos by Tarostar.

ISBN: 978-1-890399-89-4

Contents

Book I: The Covenant

Book II: The Book of Beginnings

Book III: The Book of Lights

Book IV: The Book of Elders

Book V: The Cornucopia

Come one, come all on the road to Wych Cross.
Let life and good cheer burn out the dross.
Honour the Old Gods with Cup and Knife.
Wed in the Circle to drum and fife.
Call down the Moon, when She be Full,
That Witches Lore on thy heartstrings may pull.
Send out the call, gather the Covens from afar,
For on the horizon there is a new Star.
Up the Old Gods, down with the cross.
We shan't feel any pangs of loss.
Aquarius marks the Age of the Witch!
Leave the Christians to kvetch and bitch.

– Tarostar

The Sacred Pentagraph

Book I

The Covenant

Introduction

There are five secret books, which contain the complete way of life for the Wicca. These books are always kept at the Covenstead in the charge of the High Priesthood of the Craft.

Recording in them may be done by either the High Priest, High Priestess or the selected Coven Scribes.

Each new Coven shall have its own copy of *The Sacred Pentagraph.*

In the event of dissolution or voiding a Coven, the books shall be turned over to the Elders of the district; the Magister Sacrorum or the Queen Mother, who are Elders V° and overseers for all Covens in their district.

Coven members may consult the books in the Common Library at the Covenstead for any reference needed from them.

Revisions in the books may be made by any High Priest of High Priestess for the purpose of modification of improvement.

However, the original must be kept for a Century before it can be relegated to obsolescence.

A modification must be approved by a Council of Elders before it can be put into effect, and must bear their signature and seal and notation explaining reason for such and date of revision.

The following is a list and description of the five books known as:

The Sacred Pentagraph

Book I: The Covenant:

The Eunomia: Herein are all the Tenets and Redes of the Faith with the Laws of Wicca and Coven rules.

It expresses the conditions under which one enters the Faith and is accepted into the Craft and Coven.

The Covenant also contains the rubrics of Coven Worship.

Upon entrance into a Coven, all new members will read, sign and seal their names therein.

Therein is also The Log where all important Coven ceremonies and magic works are recorded. It also contains The Tree, which is the genealogy of the members and vital statistics of the Coven.

Book II: The Book of Beginnings:

Herein are the Initiations where the ancient ceremonies of rising in the Degrees of the Craft are explained and given for use. All spiritual ceremonies that mark the beginning of a new phase in the total life experience of a Covener are found therein.

Book III: The Book of Lights:

Section I: Works of the High Priest – Herein are the Coven Sabbat worship for the four Solar/Celestial Sabbats of the year.

Section II: Works of the High Priestess – The Coven Sabbat worship for the four Terrestrial Sabbats of the year.

Section III: The Manual of Exorcisms – Rituals to banish negative entities.

Section IV: Book of Elders – Concerning the Council of Elders and the Mystic Coven of Seven.

Book IV: The Book of Esbat: Herein are all the Coven Magics in full ceremony. It contains all the Full and New Moon Esbats.

Book V: The Cornucopia: Herein are all the Low Magics with the Arts of Spellcraft and Divination along with the basic study course outline for teaching the Craft and development of the powers of the mind for aspirants to the Craft.

Tenets of the Faith
(Speculum Doctrinale)

I : Let the Great Gods be called by whatever names they may be identified by the observer to be. A God or Goddess by any other name is still the same.

Since Ancient Times we worshipped the One Supreme Being who manifests to the children of the world as Light and Darkness; Heat and Cold; Male and Female; Death and Life. These are but some of the faces of the Great God and Goddess of all creation. Out of one comes the other, which returns again to its opposite.

Life is a spiral leading ever onward toward perfection as perceived or imagined, by the Creator. This goal of the Unmanifest Supreme Being transpires through the agency of Manifested Forces we call God and Goddess, each in cyclic turn, but each containing and retaining part of its opposite. Therefore, that which is active must also be passive, and that which is passive, must also be active.

Every man is a potential God, yet deep within him, he carries the gentle essence of the Goddess. Every woman is a potential Goddess, yet she bears the seed of the God. Therefore, let not man strive to rule woman, and let not woman seek to dominate man. For only in the mutual and harmonious exchange of spiritual essences can we follow the path toward progress and perfection.

II. In Ancient Times, the peoples of all parts of the world celebrated the eternal exchange of forces at the Four Quarters of the year when the "Times" change. To them were added the Festivals of the Cross Quarters (Seasonal Theme Celebrations).

Man planted his crops, tended them, harvested his labor's reward, and consumed their life force into his being, according to the cycles measured off by the Great Festivals or Sabbats.

To these, the Tides of the Moon were added as times for using the power of the Gods to work the group Will of the Coven community. These are the times for expansion of Human Consciousness. A drawing close to Divine Being and manifestation of Human Will were celebrated on those nights.

Therefore, It Has Been Ordained of Old that at the Quarter Days we observe the changing of the Tides/Times of life, and as the Cross Quarter Days we celebrate the life and death (Manifestation and Rest) cycles of the Earth's Rhythms/Seasons. At the Full and New Moons, we experience a joyous communion with ourselves and our Gods, using the power generated for common problems, to better ourselves as Human Beings and refine our spiritual essence.

In marking the Tides and Cycles of Nature, we harken to the progress of our own lives.

III. In earlier times the worship of the Goddess was widespread among mankind. Divinity was perceived as the Spirit of the Earth, as Pro-Creator of all living things and later was symbolized by the Moon. The Goddess was seen as Mother and Matrix of all life and the binding force of ecstatic love personified as the eternal Nymph.

The worship of the masculine aspect of Deity came into acceptance in a later cycle and was personified as God of the Hunt (Provider in the barren months), then as the God of Death because during His reign the days became shorter, and all seemed to be shrouded in cold and darkness, the season when many succumbed to the harsh elements and lack of nourishment.

Later, the male Deity was symbolized by the Sun, which displayed positive force, vitality and majesty. The Solar Myth then became worldwide in tradition.

Many abandoned the old ways to worship a God cruel and terrible, whose proponents preached love, but spread hate and terror.

They visited with fire and sword upon those who perceived the passive and active roles of manifestation in the nature of Divinity. They brought "The Burning Times" to harass the children of The Old Religion.

Yet, like the Goddess, and the renewal of the Earth, we always return to proclaim: "The cycles change, the tides turn, everything comes around again, but on a more evolved level. The circle that is an unending spiral moves ever upward."

Even those who would torture and persecute us will one day know the truth and behold the two-fold countenance of the One Supreme

Being, who is our Heavenly Father God and Earthly Mother Goddess through whose eternal embrace all creation will one day return to its source.

Therefore, It Has Been Ordained of Late by the Elders of the Craft, for the benefit and as the request of the High Priesthood, Keepers of the Flame, that the antiquated Tenets that were in force from the Burning Time until the cusp between the Ages of Pisces and Aquarius be revised and renewed.

The message of Aquarius will be The Human Mind, Seat Of Conscious Awareness, Is The Greatest Gift Of All From the Gods. We Must Develop Its Potential, That We May Perceive the Divine Essence In All Things.

The keynote of Pisces was Peace and Brotherly Love, which was exemplified by the stern but just Roman Empire, preached and enforced by the Medieval Church and upheld by moral ethics and dogma perpetrated upon peoples and nations in recent times.

However, peace carries within it the seed of its opposite – strife. So the Age of Pisces was marked by periods of harmonious progress and discordant warring.

In the same manner, Aquarius will not be a golden age of "good." We can expect times of harsher philosophies. But its theme of Fraternity and Sorority along with expansion of the Human Mind Potential can make it a far more pleasant age than Pisces.

To this end, the age old doctrine of wisdom needs to be re-written to lead it forward into times ahead. So Be It Ordained.

IV. Although the dangers of the Burning Time have ceased, the proponents of bigotry and prejudice may yet prevail.

While the hidden children of the God and Goddess may now seek the light of religious freedom that other Faiths have declared, they must ever be mindful that no Civil Law or Ordnance be violated in the practice of their Faith. Nor should they draw attention to any acts or practices of the Craft, which are viewed by opposers as "unusual" or "extraordinary". Anything that is distasteful to those outside the Craft, or of opposing Faiths, should be done with utmost Discretion. Many operations may have to be disguised to escape the cutting barbs of the heavily prejudiced.

We must invoke respect and reflect it, if we expect to earn it from ill-informed nations.

V. To the forgoing extent, those of the Craft shall seek to establish in themselves a BALANCED LIFE. All things in the manifested Universe are composed of the same energy in differing proportions. We must seek a harmonious existence between all parts of the Cosmic Whole.

VI. One of the old entrance rituals into the Craft Circle states: "There is no part of me that is not of the Gods." This means that everything in Nature, everything that responds to the Creative Life Force, is as much a part of the individual as is his/her body, mind and spirit.

All things exhibit the harmonics and rhythms of Life. THEREFORE, NOTHING IN NATURE SHALL BE CONSIDERED UGLY OR UNHOLY. Those of the Craft maintain harmony with life by accepting all things in their proper perspective.

VII. The Craft places great value on Perfect Love and Perfect Trust. This does not mean that the Wicca shall love freely and trust haphazardly. After careful observation of all facts and conditions in a relationship, where trust is indicated love will surely be found. Without one, the other will surely perish. Misplaced love or trust will bring aborted efforts. Therefore, it is a violation of the Law of Conservation of Energy. Wasted energies are causes of unbalanced living.

VIII. Humility is not a virtue to be worn on the sleeve, as is the custom among certain highly respected religious orders. It is not an attitude toward life, nor a pious servitude, but a realization of the nature of things. That which is best for the group, or which benefits the greatest number, is more important than progress for the individual. Knowing that life springs eternal and that no one entity is indispensable to Nature's plan overall, gives those of the Craft a universal outlook.

That which one is, and accomplishes (or not, as the case may be) is returned to the Universal Flux, to be picked up and resumed, or improved upon at a later time by another entity.

Let not a person of the Craft make vainglorious statements of self, nor harsh judgements regarding another being. Just as Saints and Sages reincarnate among Humanity for its education and betterment, so do Conquerors, Oppressors and Dictators for its testing and retraction.

Biding by the tides and doing that which is on service to one's fellow beings without demand for egotistical recognition is what is meant by true Humility.

IX. Misunderstanding and ignorance can be read in the words and on the faces of many people. Those of the Craft are ever patient with the ones who have not established harmonious accord with the world around them, and with those of other opinions or persuasions.

Never shall one of the Craft blaspheme or defame another's religion, for all doctrines contain an essence of the truth and it is the improper interpretations of the individual, which is their detriment.

X. Living is a process of learning. One should never cease to acquire more knowledge. The Craft is a religion of learning. Craft members should cultivate and seek to understand in all branches of metaphysical and natural sciences, from the nature of the Supreme Being, on the highest spiritual planes, and the potentials of the Human Mind, to the deepest secrets of inert Matter. They must acquaint themselves with the Kingdoms of Nature and seek harmonious co-habitation on Earth with other life forms.

XI. The spiritual essence of any entity, as a spark of the Fire of Divine Life Force, continues to exist, inhabiting body after body in a course of successive lives, gathering spiritual strength through knowledge applied to life experiences, in each incarnation, until it no longer needs the lessons of the school of matter and it rises to a new level on the Universal Spiral. All that has been involuted will of necessity evolve and ever strive to return to its source.

Each successive incarnation is a progression. One is always better off than one was in a previous life, on one way or another. Nothing ever regresses, nor is any punishment meted out as a "Divine Retribution" for previous acts or deeds. One can only stagnate at a certain level and repeat the same life circumstances until they are mastered.

XII. Individuals by application of free will in the Law of Cause and Effect create their own rewards and punishments, according to their words, thoughts and deeds. (Kyklos Geneseos)

All Faiths that accept Reincarnation and abide by the Golden Rule are sister Faiths to Wicca. One must always strive to do good for oneself and for others. What goes around comes around. We attract to ourselves only that which we have been willing to give, and as the spiral accelerates, our deeds return to us threefold.

XIII. We shall experience in the interim cycles between incarnations that which we have created from spiritual thoughts deeply impressed on the inner depths of our beings. (De Integritate)

Those who thought into existence the fundamental concepts of "Hell" and the "Devil," will unfortunately, likely meet with such on the other side of the veil. For these are their own making and LIKE ATTRACTS LIKE on the spiritual levels as well as the physical.

Man must ever be mindful that "Seeking God" does not mean we shall create jealous, vengeful, condemning or greedy Gods in our own image.

The Wiccan Affirmation of Faith

Therefore it is reaffirmed that the children of the God and Goddess of Wicca shall accept a belief in the ideals of a balanced life; the philosophy of Harmony among Nature's Kingdoms; an outlook of Perfect Love and Perfect Trust; an attitude of Humility; a patient tolerance for those less evolved; an obligation of learning and the application of Knowledge toward Wisdom.

These will bring advancement to better levels of life, according to the Law of Progressive Evolution, in a series of successive life cycles.

So Be It Ordained.

THE LAWS OF THE CRAFT
The Rhetra

[A] IT WAS ORDAINED OF OLD that *The Book of the Covenant* should contain the Laws of the Craft for the guidance of Coven needs and responsibilities.

It is in keeping with this tradition that the Laws are here set down by the Elders of The Craft. They are hereby passed down and offered to all who serve the Craft and Her worshippers as High Priest and High Priestess.

It therefore behooves every truly initiated member of the High Priesthood to see that these Laws are kept.

Only then may the Craft be re-knit together and gathered from far and wide whence it scattered at the onset of the Burning Time.

Certain of the Elders, acting under Divine Guidance, have been given the task of calling the far-flung Covens of authentic initiatory tradition back together.

It is the Will of the Gods that their "Hidden Children" once again take their place amidst Humanity's spiritual heritages.

[B] SO BE IT ORDAINED: The God and Goddess are Co-equal and Co-eternal. So it is in the affairs of men and women of the Craft. Each person is an expression of the Divine and has a voice in Coven affairs.

No person may be denied access to the Craft who earnestly seeks true knowledge of the same and who has successfully completes both Neophyte and Probationer status. (He/she must be given I° Initiation; anything beyond is optional.)

The Craft shall not exclude any of the God's children for reasons of Race, National Origin, Sexual Orientation or Previous Religious Background.

[C] IN TIME OF OLD, the words and wishes of the High Priest and High Priestess were Law in the Coven. NOT SO TODAY!

1. Both are subject to the decisions of the Council of Elders, of which they both are members. Both are subject to the group will embodied

in the Coven Council, which makes decisions as to Coven policy. (The Apella.)

2. The High Priestess must at all times strive to be a worthy representative of the Goddess. She is due all respect as the living embodiment of the feminine principle in Nature.

3. She must be knowledgeable in most aspects of Craft Lore and be able to act as Mother and Spiritual Advisor to all Coveners.

4. Following the guidelines in *Books III and IV*, she may interpret and conduct Coven worship.

5. She will act as assistant to the High Priest during the Solar/Celestial Sabbats as he assists her during the Terrestrial Sabbats.

6. She is ever to be watchful among the younger women of the Craft for those who possess the necessary talent to be trained as a Hand Maiden III° and eventually be elevated to the rank of High Priestess.

7. The High Priestess must supervise the conducting of classes to all those of the Coven aspiring to obtain higher Initiations. (An Artisan II° may assist her as teacher.)

 a. The classes should be in keeping with the guidelines from *Book V.*

 b. The initiations should always be in the tradition of *Book II: The Book of Beginnings.*

8. She may interpret the Will of the Gods as she functions in her capacity as High Priestess within the Circle, but she can in no way speak for the Gods either within or without the Circle.

9. The Craft recognizes no so-called "Kings and Queens of all Witches" and no authority below the Elders.

10. The creeds and precepts of *Book I: The Covenant* should always be the only guide in dealing with affairs of and within the Coven for this Tradition.

[D] The High Priest is to augment and implement the traditions of the Craft along with the High Priestess.

1. He is a teacher and spiritual guide to all members of the Coven.

2. He must at all times seek to be a worthy representative of the God. He is the living embodiment of the masculine element of Nature and due all respect as such.

3. The High Priest must follow the Coven Worship as outlined in *Books III and IV.*

4. He must prepare and train those from among the young men of the Coven who have been properly initiated and who have the talent as aspirants to the rank of Practicus III° who may eventually become High Priests.

5. His is the duty and obligation, as Father of his Coven, to see that classes are conducted to lead Coveners to the higher Initiations.

a. An Artisan II° may assist him as teacher to relieve him of heavy duties should the Coven be large with a full schedule.

b. The Class Outlines in *Book V* should be his teaching guide.

c. It is further his duty to see that only valid Initiations according to *Book II* are given. He will be answerable to the Council of Elders for this, as a Father must bear the responsibility for his children. It is the duty of the Elders to see that the Craft is handed down with a valid tradition.

[E] The Craft takes its example from Nature around it. Wicca must be progressive or it dies.

1. So Be It Ordained: At least once each 10 years a High Priest and High Priestess, serving a Coven Circle, must elevate young members to hive off and form new Covens.

2. High Priests and High Priestesses who do not perpetuate the Craft thus, do not become eligible to become Magister Sacrorum or Queen Mother V° and may not seek higher Initiations from the Elders.

3. The Practicus and Hand Maiden who are properly elevated to the High Priesthood will be provided with a complete set of *The Sacred Pentagraph* and sent out by the Coven Council to organize new Covens in other parts.

4. Those of the High Priesthood must ever seek to maintain a loving and harmonious atmosphere among all members of the Coven group. Only thus may a Coven work at Esbat and Worship at Sabbat be fruitful and elevating.

5. A Coven that is marred by disharmony may be called to account at the yearly Council of Elders at the Full Moon of July, which may advise that the Coven be voided and the High Priesthood take a sabbatical to renew studies in Craft Tradition before a new Coven should be formed.

6. The Two Scribes and the Summoner, as Officers of the Coven Council, acting in unison, for and in the best interests of their Coven, do have the Right of Appeal to the Council of Elders against oppressively

arbitrary decisions of the High Priesthood.

7. The Council of Elders then acts as a Board of Arbitration for the airing of grievances, and tries to draw a fitting compromise in the best interests of all concerned, not as a legislative body passing Laws. In this way Elders try to bring a more democratic character into the affairs of Covens in their Districts.

The Ancient "Lord of the Manor" mentality of the Craft from bygone eras is not fitting to Modern Man. So many big frogs in little ponds have caused much strife among various Covens in recent years. Wicca must reflect the character of the world around it, or it becomes an obstruction to the God's Universal Order of Progressive Evolution and must fade out.

[F] It Was Ordained of Old that the High Priesthood were allowed to be absent from Coven duties for a year and a day, before they could be voted out of office. Times are such, in this day and age, that an absence of so long a nature may not be allowed.

1. So Be It Ordained: Knowing that temporary absences for short periods of time are unavoidable, an absence of one full Season of the year's complete cycle may be allowed. In which case a properly trained Practicus and/or Hand Maiden may assume an office of the High Priesthood temporarily.

2. If the situation of a member of the High Priesthood alters so that long absences are unavoidable, he/she must call a Coven Council and formally resign. Whereupon the Coven Council will invest the next person in line to assume the vacant office, provided that person soon will be initiated to the IV°, or an Elder may be asked to be the Officiant until suitable persons can be trained.

3. A Practicus and/or Hand Maiden III° only may assume the office of the High Priesthood temporarily, but must seek the proper Initiation from the Elders to that level before being allowed to continue in that office.

4. The Elders will allow a period of six months for the Initiation elevating temporary officiants to be taken. If such is not done, the Elders will assume the office of the High Priesthood until proper persons are installed.

5. It is the duty of the Coven Council to see this continuity of office is maintained.

[G] It Has Ever Been a tradition within the Craft that members of a Coven who find difficulties in effectively working under a particular member of the High Priesthood were told to "Get Thee Hence." The Craft realizes some individuals are incompatible and makes no judgments as to right or wrong.

1. So Be It Ordained: Let the one wishes to quit the Covenstead for such a reason first seek the proper Initiations elevating him/her to the High Priesthood, and remove to another district to form a new Coven, in other words, making a valid Hive Off.

2. The High Priesthood of the Coven from which such a person wishes to depart, should gladly act as sponsor to assist said person in obtaining the valid Initiations to raise him/her to the proper rank allowing a valid Hive Off.

3. In this way the spirit of peace and fraternity will exist between all groups of the Covendom and within the Craft.

4. It has been much to the Craft's detriment of late for some members of the High Priesthood to pontificate and rule their Covens in an absolute fashion. Many unprepared individuals have split off from their own groups and have not had the level of Craft Knowledge and/or experience to be worthy as a Mentor to the Gods' children. The result has been chaos and has spawned aborted efforts, which is an abomination in the sight of true Craft Elders.

5. The High Priesthood will issue Credentials of Introduction for all Coveners who must move to other areas leaving their own home Coven. The Credentials will state that the bearer has been properly initiated into his/her rank or grade according to *Book II* in order that the Covener may join a new Coven in the new city or area.

6. The Credential will be signed by both members of the High Priesthood and be notarized.

7. Most other legal matters pertaining to the Coven from the preceding year should be attended to by the High Priesthood around the Full Moon of January. Six months later, at the Full Moon of July, the High Priesthood must report to the Council of Elders the outcome of such and what may still be pending.

[H] Concerning The Pact. In times of old, an Initiate's measure was wrought of a clipping of hair was taken by those conferring the Initiation in order to magically ensure that the Initiate would be true to the ways of the Craft.

1. So Be It Ordained: At the Initiation of persons to the rank of High Priest and/or High Priestess IV° let the Elders present them with a document for their signature. The document will state that the individual being elevated to the High Priesthood accepts his/her duties and responsibilities to the Craft according to *Book I: The Covenant.*

2. The Elders will keep the original of said document and the Initiate will keep a copy.

3. Thus may the Elders sanction each High Priest and High Priestess as valid and true Practitioners of the Craft and rightful High Priesthood of Wicca. The Elders wish to settle disputes concerning validity, which have plagued the Craft because of insecure claims by some of the High Priesthood.

[I] Organization Of The Coven.

So Be It Ordained:

1. Those who have reached the Third Level of Initiation, which constitutes the First Degree, are allowed to attend Sabbat Festivals and participate in Coven worship. This is the stage of the Craftsman I°.

2. With the Fourth Level of Initiation, the Craftsman becomes a Covener and is required to attend all Sabbats, Esbats and Coven Council meetings. He/she has a full vote in all Coven matters.

3. The Fifth Level of Initiation brings the Second Degree in the Craft, the stage of the Artisan II°. The Artisan is, therefore, a Priest or Priestess of the Craft, and may practice the Craft without a Coven affiliation. He/she may also teach Neophytes and Probationers the ways of Wicca, but only under a proper High Priest or High Priestess in a Coven group. (Licentio docendi.)

4. The Artisan takes the Sixth Level of Initiation and assumes the Third Degree in the Craft. This is the level of the Practicus and Hand Maiden III°. They are apprenticed to the High Priesthood and must learn all Sabbat Ceremony and must serve at all Esbat Circles.

5. At the Seventh Level, the Fourth Degree (IV°) is assumed and it bestows the High Priestly Office. The High Priesthood officiates at all Sabbat and Esbat Circles. This Degree confers the power to form new Covens. (De propaganda fide.)

6. With the Eighth Level of Initiation the Fifth and final Degree in the Craft is taken. This is the Magister Sacrorum and Queen Mother

V°, who are the true and active Coven Elders. They may or may not participate in Circle activities. They supervise the working of the two or more Covens they have helped to found in their districts.

7. Those of the First and Second levels of Initiation are Neophytes and Probationers and do not take part in Coven affairs. The Ninth Level is the honour of the retired Elders of the Craft – the Philosophus and Oracle V°, who do not participate in Coven business, but may attend Worship at Sabbat or work at Esbat at whatever Coven they choose to honour.

8. All those below the Fourth Degree are simply called Coveners. Those of the Fourth Degree compose the High Priesthood and those above compose the Elders.

9. All Coveners, excluding Craftsman, of the First through Fourth Degree compose the Coven Council.

10. The Coven Council will meet formally at least once every six months, and more often as needed to discuss any important Coven activities.

11. The Coven Council will decide upon the business of the Coven and any fundraising activities as may be necessary, and determine Coven policy, orientation and Coven Magic works.

12. The Coven Council elects the Officers, the two Scribes and the Summoner, who serve a term of one year. They may be re-elected of changed as the Coven Council sees fit.

[J] Duties Of The Coven Officers – The Ephors

1. Concerning the Scribes. Scribes must be individuals of the highest integrity and be at least II°.

2. One Scribe shall be known as the First Scribe and will handle all secretarial duties of the Coven. He/she will record all minutes and proceedings of Coven meetings and attend to any correspondence as may be necessary. (Magister Epistolarum.)

3. He/she must have a clear and legible handwriting so that anything recorded in the Log and the Tree for future generations may be clearly read.

4. He/she will also record any gifts and donations to the Coven.

5. He/she will also act as Coven Librarian and keep track of all books and teaching aids used by Neophytes and probationers.

6. He/she will vow to keep secret all Coven affairs and to never

make or keep unauthorized copies of Coven property.

7. He/she will handle all votes by roll call during business meetings of the Coven Council.

8. The Scribes may wear a feather quill pen as insignia of office in their cingulums or cinch belts during ceremonies of a formal or semi-formal nature.

9. The other Scribe shall be called the Second Scribe. He/she will act as Treasurer to the Coven. (Actor Summarum.)

10. He/she takes charge of all collections and gifts for proper recording by the First Scribe.

11. He/she will be responsible for depositing the annual Coven dues collected at the Autumnal Equinox Sabbat.

12. He/she will co-sign all cheques on the Coven account with a member of the High Priesthood.

13. He/she will keep an up-to-date balance of all Coven income and expenditures and be able to present it in Coven Council when called upon.

14. Section J:6 is also binding on the Second Scribe.

a. To Keep Coven Records

Why would anyone, or any institution keep records?

We must learn from the past. It gives us a continuity of Tradition.

Coven records avoid disputes and show what is what, as far as Coven property is concerned.

Have you ever been to a Craft ceremony, where someone got into a snit and said: "Well, if it's not my way, I'll take my magical Altar Cloth and leave!"

Ritual Altar equipment would be listed in the Log, in the Covenant, and recorded as to whether it was a gift to the Coven, or just on loan from an individual.

The Log would also record the Real Property rights, movable property rights, when a donation of cash, labour, tools etc. was procured by the Coven and from whom.

It would also be the place the periodic Financial Statements would be kept which were presented to review by the Coven Council.

The Log records the ceremonies of Sabbats, Esbats and the

minutes of the Coven Council meetings.

The results of the Coven Magics and the prognostications of the Coven Seers would also be set down.

This way the Coven shows itself as a growing spiritual entity.

The Covenant also contains the Tree, which is the vital statistics of the group. It records the membership, the births and the Coven Necrologia for the members who passed the veil.

The Register of Seals contains the signatures of the Coveners when they enter the Coven as Covener I0 and thereby agree to the duties and obligations of membership in the Coven Family.

The First Scribe, as Coven General Secretary, would be under obligation to keep the Register, the Log and the Tree current and up to date.

When done faithfully, the Craft and its Covens and Traditions will not have to suffer a dearth of recorded references for times in the Future, as was the case with many Occult and Old Religion practices in the Past.

As you can see, running a Coven is much, much more than going to periodic Mountain Meets. It demands time, effort, sweat and tears.

b. Coven Funds

As we have stipulated before, a functioning Coven ought to be run and organized along the lines of an Occult Lodge with Corporate status and procedure.

We make provision for an annual dues required of all members of I0 through to those of IV° participating at Sabbat, Esbat and Coven Council. The dues may be determined by the Coven Council, and which according to The Covenant, do not exceed $100 per member each year.

It does take time for a Coven to grow to its full membership of 12 duly initiated members, so the process begins very slowly.

As soon as possible, the Officers are elected and handle the necessary duties of corporate association.

The dues are collected each year at the Autumnal Equinox Sabbat and placed in a bank account, administered by the Second Scribe and one of the members of the High Priesthood.

They should be the co-signers on the account.

As the Coven Council may vote to change the individual

holding the Office of Second Scribe periodically, naturally, the bank would be kept informed of new officers andarrange a change on one of the signatures necessary to activate the funds and function the account.

Ideally, with a full Coven, $1,200 yearly would be invested into the account. From that amount necessary expenses for Coven needs and Craft supplies would be obtained. The costs of Sabbat meals, incense, candles, robes etc. etc. would be paid for from the Common funds.

A regular up-to-date Financial Statement is presented to the meeting of the Coven Council every six months, as stipulated by The Covenant.

Unusual expenditures would also have to be cleared by authorization of a majority vote.

Should a member of the High Priesthood, for some reason, leave the Coven, who is one of the co-signers, again the proper transfer of a signature with the bank would be made.

The new member of the High Priesthood, assuming Office, may take over that position, or the right to sign may be transferred to the other member of the High Priesthood, who did not quit the Coven, as the Council so decides.

Once a Coven is established, it becomes its own reason for being, as any living corporate entity. The individual personalities of the founders take a back seat to the Will of the Coven Council.

Continuity in Office and maintaining the group, considering the dictum the greatest good for the greatest number, becomes paramount. A Coven is a family by choice. All are to be considered.

Its funds are administered for the benefit of the whole.

15. The Ancient Tradition Of The Black Ball. How the Scribes handle the Secret Ballot.

Decisions of the Coven Council of other than a business nature, requiring a vote by all Coveners, such as decisions to admit a Craftsman to the Circle of the Coven Family, decisions to censure one not paying dues, or a decision to cast a Covener out of the Coven Family, must be held by both Scribes.

a. The First Scribe will pass out to all present voting both a white and a black marble, or pebble. He/she will then bring the proposition before the Coven Council. He/she will hold discussions on the matter and allow each Covener to present his/her views.

b. At the time for voting, the Second Scribe, blindfolded, will pass among the Coven carrying a small cloth bag. Each

Covener will deposit one or the other of the marbles or pebbles into the bag.

c. Both Scribes will then count the votes before the assembled Coven.

d. If the Coven is in agreement on the matter, all the marbles or pebbles should be white. One black ball means more investigation and discussion is needed. The balloting will continue until the Coven is of one accord.

e. If the decision is to admit one into the Coven, one black will forbid such until objections can be rectified, or the Coven votes to reject the candidate.

f. If the vote is to cast one out of the Family, all balls should be black. One white means to have the Coven re-examine its harsh position and try to reconcile to offender to the Family. If such is not possible, a majority decision will stand. The Covener under censure may speak on, but may not vote on his/her own behalf.

Reasons for Coven Censure:

1. Public acts, which bring the Coven group into disrepute.
2. Habitual failure to live up to Coven obligations.

g. A vote of such a serious nature requires the permission of the High Priesthood. It may not be lightly done.

h. The Coven may vote to censure, but the High Priesthood will determine the penalty, if any, to be imposed.

16. The Summoner. The Covener elected as Summoner shall be of at least I° status. He/she must be able to contact all Coveners personally.

17. The High Priesthood will give all pertinent information regarding Sabbats and meetings to the Summoner to inform all other Coveners. No use of mails may be employed to send word of Coven meetings.

18. The Summoner acts as Sgt. At-Arms for all Coven Council meetings, and may assist in Circle if no III° persons are present.

19. The Summoner will have the respect of an Officer, but shall always enter the Coven Circle or Meeting last in line to show all

expected are present.

20. COMMUNICATIONS LIAISON OFFICER.

a. In the old Lore of the Craft, some writers speak of the Summoner as the man who was the Secret Link between the Coveners and the High Priesthood.

During the Dark Times of the Witchcraft persecutions, messages affecting the needs of a Coven and calls to Sabbat would be sent to the Folk by word of mouth.

Covens were not always free to hold a Sabbat or Esbat as the Tides and Times would indicate. Sometimes, due to a particular pressure in an area by a Witch Burner, Covens would go into hiding and not practice the Faith.

Years may go by before the Witches could once again gather to hold an Esbat or Sabbat.

When times were rather safe, a High Priestess, or a High Priest would send the Summoner throughout the territory to visit the farms and households of all principal Clans in the Covendom.

He was known by his dress, or by the style of song he sung, if he went as a wandering minstrel.

Perhaps he could not speak openly of a Sabbat or Esbat, but his verses would be picked up by the folk who would know a gathering of Witches was planned at the local grove or hill-top.

"Ride a Cock Horse to Banbury Cross, to see a fine Lady upon a white horse. With rings on her fingers and bells on her toes, she shall have music wherever she goes!" would be an example of a Summoner's song as he traversed an area.

That was the call which went out over the territory in the days of my childhood, I remember.

The folk would take the refrain and repeat it far and wide in the district, so all the Witches would know the Lady or Lord were to hold a gathering.

b. In more dangerous times, when Coven had to gather for some form of Spellcraft, the Summoner would simply be dressed in black and appear in the local village, but say nothing. He would be seen only as a wandering Pilgrim, perhaps, but those who knew him would then repair to the secret meeting at night.

Not as many would be gathered for works of Spellcraft as were summoned to Sabbat.

c. Today, many Covens still have a Summoner, but do not employ him/her in the same way. With the relative freedom Covens have to worship, the secret gathering is not performed. Telephones are used to call Witches. Mail and newsletters and internet are used to notify of gatherings.

d. That is fine in decent times, but we must not allow the Office of Summoner to fall by the way side. There may be times ahead when that method of summoning may once more be necessary.

At Circle of Starmeadow, we still use the Summoner to notify the Witches of a meeting, be it Coven Council or Sabbat or Esbat.

The Summoner receives everyone attending and only those he/she contacted are admitted to the Covenstead.

e. The Summoner also acts as Sgt. At-Arms for times when meetings of the Coven Council get heated. He/she has the right to restore order to the proceedings. The Coveners, by consensus of all, agree to his/her authority in those matters.

21. Exactly What Are The Officers Of The Coven Council? (Notitia Dignitatum)

We commented on the Summoner and clarified his/her position within the Coven. Therefore, let us just briefly explain the duties and office of the First and Second Scribes.

a. The First Scribe acts as Secretary for the Coven Council. He/she would keep all minutes up to date and handle records of Coven properties. Also, the First Scribe would officiate at any legal ceremony for the Coven and act as "Major Domo/Seneschal" for the group.

The necessary supplies and needs of the Coven would be his/her domain. He/she is presiding officer at the Coven Council, and would handle all matters pertaining to votes and voting procedures for the group.

The First Scribe acts always in the best interests of the Coven as a corporate entity, to see it functions as it should.

b. The Second Scribe is the Coven Treasurer and keeps all financial records up to date to be presented at Coven Council meetings, where a financial statement is called for. He/she assists the First Scribe in the operation and logistics of the Coven.

c. It is never recommended to allow the offices of Secretary and Treasurer to be combined. Control of records and finances in one pair of hands make too much of a concentration of powers. One acts as a check on the other.

d. Together, the three Coven Officers, the Scribes and the Summoner, act as a sort of Board of Directors for the Coven Entity. The rest of the twelve Coveners attend the Council meetings and discuss and vote matters of import to the group: 1 person, 1 vote.

e. The High Priesthood, at Coven Council meetings, acts as mere members and not as religious officiants. However, as mother and father of the Coven, their views may be given consideration the same as any parents to a family.

f. The Officers are elected to terms of office, prescribed either by The Covenant, or by individual group consensus. The members of the Coven's High Priesthood may run for the Offices, as any other individual Covener may. Those duties, however, they would fulfill in addition to their proper religious office at Sabbat and/or Esbat.

g. In this way we have a democratic Pagan Republic in the best of ancient tradition. It also allows the Coven to function as a Lodge, more or less.

h. Corporate organization and structure give legitimacy to Craft efforts that seem lacking in many groups. To instill responsibility to the group and require one's best efforts be applied for the Faith and benefit of the Coven as a Family by choice.

Such is the Craft in the Way of the Wise.

[K] Of Dues And Offerings: All that which is given, whether it be money or goods, shall be blessed and considered as a token of one's willingness to share. All shall be considered as an offering towards the Coven work. The receiver shall accept them with the humility of a servant of the Gods. Remember, that when one serves the Gods, they shall provide all needs in their own way. De Monete:

1. At each Initiation Ceremony, the Initiate shall bring a dowry to cover the expenses of the Ceremony (I - IV°).

2. Coveners should share the burden of running the Coven and bring periodic gifts of candles, incense, oils and refreshments to serve after the Ceremonies.

3. All Coveners of I - IV° will share the Coven costs by paying Coven Dues of $100 per person, per year, or as the Coven Council stipulates, but not to exceed the above amount.

4. The Dues are collected at the Autumn Equinox Sabbat when they are placed in the tambourine during the Ritual. No Covener shall be guilty of constant negligence, or chronic excuses, as that imposes a burden upon the others. It is better to deny oneself, than to deny one's brothers and sisters and the Gods.

5. No one shall partake without giving in return. If there shall be such a one, then, by agreement of all; *Sec. J:15,* the shirker may be banished from all important workings until such a time as willingness and ability to assume a share of responsibilities can be shown. A weak limb will sap the strength of the tree. It must be removed.

6. Every Covener's dowries and fair share of Coven maintenance will be determined by the Coven Council.

[L] THE COUNCIL OF ELDERS – DEFENDERS OF THE FAITH (The Gerousia):

1. All persons of the IV - V° in the Craft constitute the Council of Elders. Those serving as High Priests and High Priestesses IV° are junior members. Those of the V° are senior members. All matters of the Ancient Traditions in the Craft are their domain.

2. The Elders V° act as advisors to all of the High Priesthood within their Covendom or district. Those of the IV° act as advisors to all Coveners within their respective Covensteads.

3. The Magister Sacrorum V° acts as trustee for any Coven properties for the two or more Covens he has helped to found. The Queen Mother V° is the Matriarch of the two or more Covens she has helped to found, and is the arbiter for any points of Craft Tradition which may be obscure. The heart of Wiccan Worship is in her keeping.

4. Once each year, better it be at the Full Moon of July, the High Priesthood, the Magister, Queen Mother and/or Philosophus and Oracle, if there be any in the Covendom, convene to discuss the state of the Faith within their district.

5. This yearly conclave is a formal meeting that can determine

the policy of the Covendom for the coming year. Any pending legal questions such as Civil Permissions to perform Marriages, or Coven Corporate Tax Exempt statuses are discussed and determined.

6. All appeals and petitions may be presented to the Elders at this time, from the respective Coven Councils, in writing, by the First Scribes, through certified mail.

7. The minutes and decisions of the Council of Elders will be copied and distributed to all Covens represented for their consideration.

8. Those unable to be represented by their respective members of the High Priesthood, are to submit their reasons for absence, by certified mail, and will also receive copies of the minutes and decisions.

9. Our Faith does not make tyrants of men. Therefore the Council of Elders must maintain good will and harmony with all Covens everywhere. The Council is not a Law-making body, but a Clearing House for that which is considered to be the best of Craft Lore and Tradition. Via Compromissi.

10. Let all Covens thus organized under The Covenant so abide.

THEREFORE, IT HAS BEEN ORDAINED OF LATE by the High Priesthood of the Ancient Craft of Wicca, in the Way of the Wise, to accept these foregoing precepts as governing rules for Craft and Coven.

[M] USES OF CRAFT POWER. Heretofore, the Laws of *The Book of Shadows* have bound those of the Craft from the use of the "Art Magical" for any but the most pressing emergencies.

HENCEFORTH, the power of the Ancient Craft of the Wise need not lurk in the "shadows." Let the true Wiccan Works of the Craft now seek the light. For this reason, *Book IV: The Book of Esbat* will be made available from the Elders.

SO BE IT ORDAINED: Conclusiones Magicae:

1. The Magic Circle must always be properly constructed and kept pure of any adverse vibrations.

2. Ritual Flagellation must never be practiced, either before, during or after any Circle Ceremony. Even lightly done it raises energies of pain and may carry previous associations of medieval torture chambers and life under the dominance of our good friends the Christians.

3. The Sabbat Ceremonies of the Quarter and Cross-Quarter days are devoted to pure worship for the Gods. No Magics are worked at Sabbat.

4. The Circle must always be entered with Perfect Love and Perfect Trust in our hearts for our Deities, our Brothers and Sisters of the Craft and for ourselves.

5. Each Sabbat bears a theme to help us elevate our spiritual natures and to better ourselves as Human Beings.

6. HENCEFORTH, let the Full Moon of October be known as the Grand Sabbat where one Coven will host another with an "Oktoberfest" and good cheer. (Should Hallowmas fall on that day, Hallowmas will take precedence.)

7. The power raised by the Magic Circle is the principle of the cyclotron. The Circle Dance widdershins attracts and invokes the power called. Spiral or Snake Dances may be good for post-ritual party, but do not raise power.

8. The power is directed, after it is raised, by the mental concentration and prayer "in one accord" of all the participants.

a. Prayer in one accord brings the power of many minds to concert on the object of the spiritual problem at hand.

b. The power is directed by the prayers of the Officiant, following the Circle Dance, as explained in *Books III and IV* for each Sabbat or Esbat Ritual.

9. The Esbat Rituals of the Thirteen Full Moons and the New Moons are devoted to the true Craft Work. They are not times of worship, but ceremonies for spellcasting. They are devoted to constructive purposes such as healings, Talismanic Magics, material increase, etc. etc. as explained in *The Book of Esbat.*

10. In the years when thirteen New Moons fall, the Thirteenth shall be known as the Grand Esbat. This is when more than one Coven joins together to concentrate on magical themes affecting large groups, or the Craft as a whole. (Should a regular Sabbat fall on that day, the Sabbat will take precedence.)

11. It is permissible to use the "Art Magical" for our collective well being and/or protection.

12. It is permissible to use the "Art Magical" to confound the enemies of the Craft.

13. It is permissible to use the "Art Magical" in any manner, which serves a constructive purpose.

14. It behooves members of the Craft to learn and practice the Arts

of Low Magic for their own well being and for the benefit of others.

15. It is permissible to accept financial gain from the employ of the Art provided the matter is constructive and part of the proceeds go to the Coven Common Funds.

16. It is NOT permissible to use the "Art Magical" to debase or degrade Human Consciousness or to lower spirituality to a degenerate level.

17. It is NOT permissible to practice diabolic magics.

18. The use of sexual practice in Craft Ritual is not permitted.

a. The true Craft understands sexual connotations to be on Cosmic, rather than physical levels.

b. Only the Great Rite preformed after the Midsummer Sabbat, in private, by the two delegated to act as God and Goddess, is allowed. (See *Book III.*)

19. Only the Rituals and Rites of *The Sacred Pentagraph* are valid for those practicing this Tradition. Rites and Rituals from other systems may be done, to provide variation, but would not be held as "traditionally" valid.

20. No more than 12 Wiccans should practice the Craft in any one Esbat Coven Circle Ceremony. THE THIRTEENTH PARTICIPANT MUST ALWAYS BE THE UNSEEN PRESENCE OF DEITY. Any additional Coveners must act as observers outside the Circle, but may join in the prayers and recitations. Sabbat Circles could be larger than 12.

21. When a Coven grows to such a large number, those eligible to be elevated to the High Priesthood, should be initiated as soon as possible and sent out from the Covenstead to form a new one elsewhere, taking any excess Coveners, who will, with them. Thus the Craft will ever survive.

HENCEFORTH, let these precepts of permissible uses be sealed upon those who practice the Ancient Craft of Wicca, in the Way of the Wise.

Until such time as the state of conditions in the world, or the tides in the affairs of Mankind, be such as to warrant major changes in this emphasis and structure of the Craft, SO BE IT HENCEFORTH AND EVERMORE! BLESSED BE!

THE WAY OF THE WISE

How one enters the Craft and is accepted into the Faith can be easily accomplished, or can be made a long and lengthy process, depending on one's desire to learn, and willingness to apply one's instruction.

The High Priesthood will begin to organize a Coven by offering classes in the Craft for all who may be interested. Adults seeking contact with a Coven must approach a member of the High Priesthood and request to be dedicated to the Craft.

The High Priest and High Priestess will discuss the person and then decide if Pre-Initiate status is in order. This is the stage whereupon it becomes necessary to study the 47 Precepts of Cosmic Order from *The Book of the Wise I* (These instruction books are in *Book V: The Cornucopia*), which will be taught by the High Priesthood on a one-on-one basis.

When the High Priesthood feels that the Pre-Initiate is ready to become a Neophyte, to therefore begin studies for the I° in the Craft, they set the date for the First Initiation. It is customary to initiate Neophytes and Probationers at the Vernal Equinox Sabbat.

The candidates are summoned to the Covenstead on that night, but do not see, nor participate in Sabbat Ceremony. They wait outside the Ritual Chamber until the main part of the Sabbat is concluded and the Summoner and their Sponsor(s), at least a I° Wiccan, fetch them.

Their Initiations are given and they are removed from the Chamber before the Sabbat Circle is closed. They may, however, join in post-Ritual festivities.

The Neophytes and Probationers compose what is called the Outer Portico of the Temple. It is customary to remain in Neophyte status for one year. The Neophyte uses that time to learn magical principles. He/she may be taught in classes given by either the High Priesthood or an Artisan II° from *The Book of the Wise II*.

At the next Vernal Equinox, if the Neophyte has successfully mastered the lessons of that grade, he/she is given the Second level of

Initiation and becomes a Probationer.

The Probationer then is to apply and master the Consecration Rituals for his/her Magical Tools from *The Book of the Wise III.*

When the High Priesthood and any Artisans, who may have taught the Probationer, agree that the work has been mastered, the Probationer is told to prepare for the Third Level of Initiation, the attainment of the First Degree (I^0) in the Craft.

The First Degree can be given at any time or season and need not take a year as the Neophyte status does. However, it must not be hastily done. Allow at least Six Months to master the grade of Probationer.

On becoming I^0, one is still only half way between the Outer Portico and the Coven Circle. This is the grade of the Craftsman. He/she is allowed to attend Sabbat Ceremonies only.

The High Priesthood will take the Craftsman under scrutiny and seek to know if said individual would be compatible with the rest of the Coven in works of Magic at Esbat Circle. If not, the Craftsman will only be summoned for Sabbat.

If, however, the Craftsman will enhance and meld harmoniously at Esbat, and the Coven Council agrees, he/she will be told to begin study of Esbat Ritual, the Laws of the Covenant and magical procedure to the Coven.

When sufficient time has elapsed for these things to be mastered, the Craftsman will be initiated to the Fourth level and become a true Covener. He/she signs and seals *Book I: The Covenant.*

Henceforth, the Covener is a member of the Coven Family Circle and will be required to attend all Sabbats, Esbats and Coven Council meetings.

As any further advancement in the Craft is optional from this point, all particulars for the Initiation Rituals will be found in *Book II: Book of Beginnings.*

Let not those of the I^0, but not accepted Coveners, feel that there is anything amiss, or that there is anything wrong with themselves. Each working Coven must be of one accord in works of the Lunar Tide at Esbat Circle. Not all individuals will blend correctly with the group for successful spellcasting of that nature.

The Craftsman may stay on as a dues-paying member attending

worship at Sabbat or quit the Covenstead, with proper documentation, and be recommended to other Covens and/or various Traditions in the Craft.

The Ideal Functioning of a Coven

From what we gather, listening to other Traditions and Covendoms, it would appear groups grow and evolve, break-up, disband, re-form and start again. There does not appear to be an overall blueprint for the eventual goals.

Covens are living entities, just as any other group or association. Allowed to evolve, expand and go up and down, as sort of a natural evolution, is in actuality, a chaos of sorts.

That is not how God/Goddess nurtures the Cosmos. They project the Archetype held firmly in Divine Mind and allow the plastic substances of the various planes to flesh it out. That is true Evolution. Without the vision of the archetypal perfection, nothing would move to bring it about.

We must do very much the same in building a Coven.

The Universe needs a Father and Mother. The Coven needs the High Priest and High Priestess; co-equal, co-officiant.

The parental elements would, upon their elevation to the High Priesthood, go into new territories to establish a Coven.

Having gathered three more persons, whom they have brought to I° status, they would Center the Cone, which is a ritual act of birthing the Coven Spirit. The Covenstead is than set up and the group may begin to attract other people interested in Wicca.

The Celestial and Terrestrial Sabbats are properly celebrated and the Esbat cycle may be practiced as best the group is able.

All the while trying to bring the membership to 12 persons. The thirteenth member should be Deity/Coven Group Spirit.

Also the Initiations above I° are being sought by the members and training in the Outer Portico for Neophytes and Probationers continues.

The High Priesthood would be seeking those they could train in the Craft beyond II° status, bringing them to III°.

At the proper time, those III° persons would be brought before the Elders of the Covendom and given the IV°, making them High Priesthood. Assuming, of course, they progress in their training and lessons, as they should, in order to qualify. Initiations are earned, not given.

The elevated members then hive off to become the parents of their own Covens in due course.

Meanwhile, the Coven has formed its Coven Council to handle its business and legal affairs.

It is also properly practicing the worship of the Old Gods at Sabbat and working its constructive magics at Esbat.

A Coven is a unit, operating in one accord, to bless the community with the employ of the Art Magical for collective wellbeing. It uses the High Magics of the Craft and combines its energies for positive purposes.

Eight times a year the Sabbat Round is celebrated. The New and Full Moons are used as the times for the group to evoke its own forces and powers in works of Spellcraft and Magic.

Thus we have the basic idea as to what a properly functioning Coven should be and do.

Without the ideal, held as a goal toward which to strive, proceeding to that ideal as best one is able to embody it, nothing worthwhile would ever come to be.

This way we create as the Gods themselves. First the Idea, then the Desire, then the Will, then the Action equals the accomplished fact.

That is how the Universes come into being. Can we do otherwise?

The Ordeal: Ars Magna

Pre-Initiate

Must study the 47 Precepts of Cosmic Order from *The Book of the Wise I.*

Neophyte

Master lessons from *The Book of the Wise II.*

Probationer

Master the Rituals in *The Book of the Wise III.*

Craftsman I°

Must cast a Magic Circle using own Tools in full Coven.

Assumes the Bell and blue cord.

Covener

Must study, sign and seal *Book I: The Covenant.*

Assumes the book and the green cord.

Artisan II°

Must cast a spell or consecrate a talisman in full Coven.

Assumed the candle and yellow cord.

Practicus and/or Hand Maiden III°

Must give a 10-minute talk on Craft Lore and perform Witches Banishing Ritual of the Pentagram without notes in full Coven.

Assumes the sword and red cord.

High Priest and/or High Priestess IV°

Must expound on Wiccan Law and sign the Pact before the Elders.

Assumes the Great Wand and/or Broom and gold and/or silver cord.

Magister Sacrorum and/or Queen Mother V°

Must have founded two or more full working Covens.

Assumes the purple sash and/or green garter with a silver Pentagram for each Coven founded.

Philosophus and/or Oracle V°

Must prepare writings of own Craft experiences and magical

and occult knowledge to pass on to younger Wiccans.
Assumes a bejeweled scimitar and/or Moonstone pendant.

A Wiccan born need not undergo the Neophyte and Probationer stage. 60 days after birth he/she is presented at the Covenstead to the High Priesthood and proper notation made in the tree.

At age 10 the symbols of the Craft are presented and explained by the parents. At age 15 he/she studies *The Book of the Wise I.*

At age 20 he/she may take the I° Initiation, if desired.

The Wiccan Born should have been raised in the Craft seeing his/her parents in Circle at Sabbat and Esbat, so much of the religious practice need not be studied in depth up to that time.

Initiations are earned and not merely given.

Lady Charmaine's Charge To The Craft – 1979 ce

Wicca is more than a Magical Philosophy. It is a way of life enhancing, strengthening and enriching the Human Experience. Its aim is to bring about fulfillment to each individual, without penalizing any other being, or destroying Nature's balance.

Wicca is a firmly embedded religion, which offers as a bonus the gift of magical powers. The latter is gained as an effect of the former, through practices, hard work, study and application.

The lesser magics must never be pursued bypassing the Religion, otherwise, the individual must brand him/herself "Sorcerer, Black Magician or Wizard," rather than Wicca. For these endeavors are truly not "wise" as they lead not to "wisdom" but to an actual annihilation of a part of the Self, if not totally.

True Magic requires a finely developed vehicle tuned by training in the Craft discipline, which is necessary for the individual to be in touch with the different Kingdoms of Nature and the total environment. One can not hope to master, or even to make contact with forces and powers beyond the Human if one does not possess knowledge of their being and conditions. Such knowledge and power may be touched upon through books and from teachers, but can only be ratified by personal experience.

Only a fool will mistake an induced hallucination for a true "psychic" experience.

But the Wise will, undoubtedly, know that there are much greater things to be encountered, and will forego the momentary pleasures of such trivia in favor of expansion of his/her limitless potentials by the slower, but more correct natural methods of spiritual growth. Therefore, the Wicca disavow the use of psychedelic hallucinogens.

The Wise will safeguard his/her physical, emotional and mental health at all costs, and avoid over-indulgence in any kind of excesses, while not denying the self of pleasures and luxuries. These things are put before us to enhance, not to destroy life. They should be taken gently, always considering the cost, whether immediate or long term. Therefore, the Wicca lead a life of moderation in all things, avoiding extremes.

Let each Brother and Sister seek out the nurturing of his/her own temperament and strive to develop one of the particular Arts or Crafts to the degree of excellence.

All are not suited to officiate at the High Ceremonials, therefore, let one excel at Seership, another at healing with herbs, another by touch, another might make and charge oils and Talismans. One or more will find their work in teaching. Some, who are slower in manifesting the psychic or "magical" powers, may excel at cooking, sewing the robes or maintaining the Coven properties.

Let no task be considered humble, but each a particular challenge which requires the very best effort possible. The strength of the Coven lies in the combined qualities and resources of its members.

Therefore, let each accept whatever task one may be called upon to do. The Wicca know all things are necessary in their own way and at their present level.

–Lady Charmaine Dey, QM V°
A.O. of B.B. & C.

Formal Coven Ceremonies

This is the way in which a Coven may be initiated, maintained in continuity, and voided if necessary.

How The Wicca Found A Coven

"Centering The Cone"
Ex Instituto

This ceremony is the ritual act of creating the collective thought-form that will grow as the "Spirit of the Coven," the Mystic Thirteenth Member, the Presence of Deity.

A valid High Priest and High Priestess together are required in order for a Coven to be properly founded in balance.

The High Priesthood begins by organizing classes in Craft Tradition and Occult Lore in an area where they wish to form a Coven.

When they have gathered at least three more persons and have initiated them properly to the First Degree in the Craft, and all express the desire to form a Coven, they all meet at the next New Moon.

Therefore, at least five Coveners, including the High Priesthood, are necessary in order to center the cone.

On the Night of the New Moon, the five shall meet at the Covenstead, in the place that is to be their Ritual Chamber.

An invoking Pentagram is marked out on the floor, large enough for a person to stand in each of the five points. Its top point should be to the North and have enough room for the participants to move around within.

In the center of the Pentagram on a black cloth on the floor stands a Chalice of Water, a dish of Salt, a Thurible for Incense and live coal and a small votive candle purple in colour. With these items is a string of 27 beads (13 black beads strung between 14 white ones).

The Ritual Items in the Center of the Pentagram are arranged in a deosil fashion according to the diagram to follow thus:

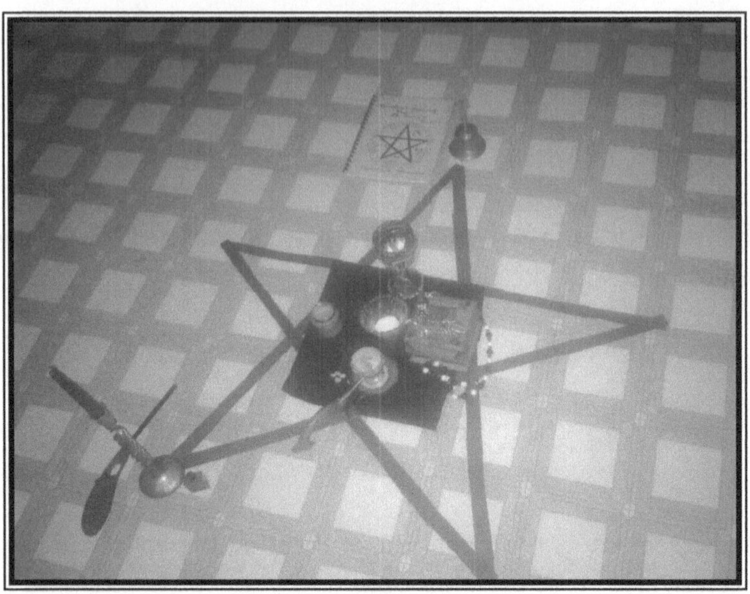

The High Priest is the officiant for this ceremony and the High Priestess takes the part of the Second Covener. The other three Coveners take their places either by seniority or alphabetical order.

The Officiant stands at the North facing the center holding the Covenant and a bell.

The Second Covener holds a vial of Sacred Oil (Rosemary and Lemon Verbena Sabbat Oil) and a lit purple taper candle.

When all is thus prepared, the officiants sounds the bell five times: * * pause * pause * pause *.

With the sounding of the bell, all take their places around the Pentagram. The officiant speaks:

The Moon stands new. This is the night of new beginnings, and for the inception of ideas.

Good Brothers and Sisters, though we be but five, the force we initiate this night will grow and draw to us the Sacred Number of Thirteen.

Thirteen souls to worship in the Old Way, thirteen souls to tred the Ancient round. Thirteen Children of the Craft led by perfect love and perfect trust to find in their hearts the perfect peace profound.

A new Coven is born this night, a new branch of the old tree planted in far distant times by the Wise Ones from Ages of Ages. We summon the Ancient Ones to bear witness to our Work.

He sounds the bell once for the God and twice for the Goddess: * pause * * and continues:

Hear us, O Ancient Ones, out of the mists of time and space we summon thee.

Out of the Shadows of Darkness, out of the Blinding Light of the Higher Planes; assemble to us. Ascend to us. Descend to us. Meet and conjoin in this Holy Place.

As our Will, so be it done.

The Second Covener moves to the center of the Pentagram and kneels down over the items arranged there upon the cloth. She draws an invoking pentagram over them with the flame of the taper and lights the votive saying:

In this place of Earth, by this purple flame of spiritual authority and power, we begin the founding of a Coven. We intitiate a body of worship.

Setting down the vial of oil, she takes pinches of salt and sprinkles them to the five points of the Pentagram in invoking order from the North. She then recites:

May the Earth bring power to us. May she guide the steps of Wiccan souls seeking a home. May she bless and sustain this newly born Coven. Hear me, O Ancient Ones, and let it be.

She then takes oil on her fingers and places a dab in the center of the spiral near the dish of salt. With the candle in her hand, she describes a widdershins spiral in the air over the objects in the center as she says:

The waves upon the sea, the sounds carried in the air, the flickering of light with the currents from the Earth, let this force draw in from all quarters aspects of love and light until it calls out to the whole world and touches the hearts of true believers of the Old Gods.

She then unfastens her cinch cord and rings the objects with it on the floor. One end is looped around the five items and the cord reaches up between her thighs and is held close to her mouth at the other end. She blows 13 breaths upon the cord and says:

Form from the Earth, spirit from the sky, to a Cone of Power we now give birth. Blessed be.

She refastens her cinch cord and stands up. With the oil she steps to the northern point of the Pentagram and bends down and places a dab of oil before the feet of the officiant. She anoints all points in turn in an invoking movement around the Pentagram. She then places a second dab at the North after the other points have been anointed and returns to her place to stand.

The officiant sets down the bell at the North and moves to the center. He takes up the chalice of water and says:

Waters of creation, Mother of all Life, mediatrix of feelings and reflections, purify this Holy Place and make it a pleasing and fit recepticle to receive the Spirit of new beginnings.

He sprinkles water to the five points in silence. Putting down the chalice, he places some incense of Olibanum on the live coal in the Thurible and draws an invoking pentagram over it with the right thumb as he says:

Air of sweetness, air of fragrance, cleanse and consecrate this Holy Pentagram, symbol of the rule of Spirit over matter. Make it a Sacred and blessed dwelling for the Spirit of new beginnings.

Taking up the Thurible, and holding *The Book of the Covenant* beneath it, he begins to walk in a deosil spiral slowly expanding outward as he says:

Around and out, around and out, forces of the elements attend. Around and out, around and out, from the center a call we send. Hear us, Ancient Ones, and help us grow as the spiral's forces outward flow.

Setting the Thurible back in place, he moves back to the northern point, takes up the bell and stands.

The Third, Forth and Fifth Coveners move into the center, and take up the string of beads. Placing their right hands upon the beads, they chant in unison:

Five we be, but more we see. Five to summon, five to call. Twelve of us and one for Spirit shall it be, from five to thirteen souls in all.

Let this be a Sacred Talisman, let this be a binding ring, let this be a Magic Bond that will into our Circle seven more bring.

The Third Covener then ties the two ends of the string of beads together to form a circle and sets the beads back down on the floor in their place. The three Coveners then return to their places at the points of the Pentagram.

The officiant and Second Covener then pray:

Hear us, O Ancient Ones, a new entity is born. Send to it the Spirit of new beginnings and nurture it to grow.

We name this entity the Coven of__________ and swear before the Gods of the Ancients that it will prosper.

Upon our honour as the High Priesthood of the Craft of the Wise, let it be so.

Holding *The Book of the Covenant* high above his head, the officiant then says:

Holy Oil, Book and Bell, summon the forces to work this spell. The Coven of__________ needs their aid. Come ye as the call is made.

Holding *The Book of the Covenant* high above his head, the officiant then says:

Holy Oil, Book and Bell, summon the forces to work this spell. The Coven of__________ needs their aid. Come ye as the call is made.

He rings the bell 13 times (nine * pause and four *). Then all five recite this prayer:

Gods of our most Ancient Faith, hear us! The Holy Lamp, the Bell and Book open the Path to Sacred things. We speak a blessing upon our common efforts this night.

We dedicate and consecrate our Work to the Ancient Craft of the Wise.

May the Spirit be summoned by the sound of the Bell, may the Laws and Lore be taught by The Book, may our traditions be continued in the Candle Flame of the Sacred Light. So we will it. Blessed be.

The five may then step out of place and clear everything away. The candles are left to burn themselves out.

The rind of beads is secluded away by the High Priesthood as a link of dedication and kept locked up until such a time as the Coven may need to be voided. All may discuss the needs of the new Coven and record its particulars in the Log. (Date, place, name etc.)

The Elders in the district should be notified soon thereafter so they may note the inception of a new Coven of the true Craft.

Should a Covenstead ever have to be moved, the Cone must be centered again in the new location.

The Stranger (non-Wiccan) must never know of the existence or whereabouts of any Covenstead.

Formal Resignation of a Member of The High Priesthood From a Coven

(Se magistratu abdicare)

It may happen that a member of the High Priesthood must quit the Covenstead. Whatever the case may be, this procedure is followed in full Coven:

The Summoner assembles all members at whatever time the one resigning designates (betimes emergencies arise unexpectedly).

The Practicus holds the bell and the Hand Maiden a lit black taper candle. They stand on opposite sides of the one (or both) resigning.

The one resigning holds *The Book of the Covenant* facing the Coven with back to the altar, which is draped in black.

The First Scribe asks why the Coven was assembled at this time. The one resigning explains the nature of the problem forcing this action. After all have heard and understood, the Wiccan Farewell is given thus:

The Practicus rings the bell thrice; the Hand Maiden moves the candle nearer *The Book of the Covenant.* The person (persons) resigning opens it and reads:

Brothers and Sisters of the Craft, grieve not for me as I leave this Loving Circle. I hold you in my heart and will carry the Spirit of Love and joy through the cycles of the seasons. Blessed be.

Keep well the Ancient Faith we have shared together. Honour the Gods from of Old for they love you in all ways. Blessed be.

May the Power that bides in the Earth, the Fire, the Wind and the Sea sustain you and prosper your Works. The Ancient Craft of the Wise is an honourable tradition. I pray the Gods that you continue to grow with it in perfect love and perfect trust. Blessed be.

The Covenant is closed and held to the breast of the one (or both) resigning. He/she speaks a word of personal farewell, such as:

Bide well in the Craft. I go knowing that others will follow and take up where I leave off. If our paths should cross again, may the same spirit of fellowship we have wrought in this Coven rekindle for us.

If both of the High Priesthood are to depart, they place the keeping of the Sacred Flame[1] into the hands of the Hand Maiden, as she will most likely be elevated to replace the High Priestess. A Magister will then take charge of all properties.

If only one member of the High Priesthood is to resign, the one remaining will handle all properties.

With Covenant held tight, he/she (or both) bows the head as the Hand Maiden leads the way from the Ritual Chamber and the Practicus tolls the bell mournfully. The Coven is to then observe a period of mourning until a new member of the High Priesthood is installed.

How The Coven Installs A New Member of The High Priesthood

(Bene constitutum)

In the event a member of the High Priesthood must be replaced following a resignation, the Coven must be certain that the candidate(s) assuming the office has/have been properly initiated. That means an Elder of the Craft must assure the Coven Council that such is the case, as Elders only would have been present at initiation to the IV°.

At the next New Moon the Coven is to assemble prior to the regular Esbat Ceremony. (In the event a Full Moon Esbat or a Sabbat falls between the vacancy and the new Moon, the remaining member of the

1 See *Sacred Flame in Book III: Works of the High Priestess.*

High Priesthood will officiate alone. In the event both members of the High Priesthood have resigned or removed themselves, the Practicus and Hand Maiden will officiate.)

This formality must be observed before the regular New Moon Esbat is celebrated.

The Candidate(s) with an Elder as voucher stand before the full Coven. The Elder speaks:

Coven of__________, it has reached us that your Council has decided to accept_______ (and_______) as your new High Priest (and/or High Priestess). Is that true?

The First Scribe answers affirmatively and the Elder continues:

As an Elder of the Fifth Degree, I verify that_________ (and______) has/have been duly elevated to the Fourth Degree according to the Sacred Tradition of the Way of the Wise. Will you accept him/her (or both)?

The First Scribe answers again affirmatively. The candidate(s) kneels before the altar and all Coveners move forward to place a hand on the shoulders of him/her kneeling.

Both Scribes and the Summoner recite for all:

The God and Goddess bless you. The Spirit of this Coven fills you. The Light of Divine Guidance inspires you.

We accept you to be our High Priest (and/or High Priestess) and place our faith in your rule. Be our teacher, be our gentle and loving parent(s). You bring the Mysteries of the Gods into our Circle. We empower you with our perfect love and perfect trust. So be it done.

The Candidate(s) rises and receives a kiss for all Coveners. The regular Esbat Ceremony may then begin with the new official(s) officiating.

The Ritual of Bell, Book and Candle To Cast a Covener Out of The Coven

In the initial stages of a person's contact with the Craft, he/she is under direct observation by the High Priesthood, as teachers, or with the lower Priesthood, the Artisans II°, teaching under a High Priest or

High Priestess.

Also, being only admitted to the outer Portico of the Temple, the rest of the Coven group, coming and going, see and observe him/her.

This is sufficient opportunity for evaluation to be made as to the aspirant's character to be an asset to the Coven.

Those who do not advance in the successful mastery of their lessons are simply not enjoined to return and continue with their teaching.

That is handled by the teachers; the High Priesthood and teaching Artisans in collective decision. No formal declaration of disassociation of such an individual from the Coven is made.

When a properly initiated member becomes a disrupting influence in the effective running of a Coven group, more formal procedures need be handled.

In the Laws of The Covenant, those things which may result in Coven censure are discussed. The disruptive problems may be brought before a meeting of the Coven Council and handled as the collective Will would warrant.

After the offender's case has received a thorough airing and the voting by Black Ball has determined the results, and the case is to cast the offender out of the group, not being able to reconcile to the Coven Family, the First Scribe will take up a hand bell, the Second Scribe will open The Covenant to the Register of Seals, with pen in hand, and the Summoner will hold a lighted black or purple candle.

Ringing the bell once, loudly, the First Scribe will announce:

All Wicca attend! We ruefully regret we may not reconcile this Brother/Sister to the Coven. We bid this one be gone from this Coven Circle, this Hearthfire of the Old Religion. Let the God and Goddess guide him/her to other ways and other Hearthfires. ________, get thee hence.

The Second Scribe will scratch out the name of the offender from the Register of Seals and the Summoner will snuff out the candle upon that spot in the Covenant and cast the candle forcefully to the floor.

The First Scribe will ring the bell a mournful 13 times.

From that hour, the Coven will never mention that person's name, nor will any Covener speak to him/her. He/she no longer exists in the Coven's Hearthfire, the Coven Family Circle. Nominare non permittit.

It is not in the best interests of the Craft to not have the offender present at the airing of his/her offense. He/she should be able to see the collective Will of the Coven in action. This may, in many instances, bring about a sincere effort to reconcile to the Family, before matters come to casting out by Bell, Book and Candle.

It should not be done without the offender being able to speak on his/her behalf, although he/she may not vote in the Ritual of the Black Balls.

Above all, there are to be no cursings, nor pronouncements of any anathema. The offender is a duly Initiated Member of the Craft. A Brother/Sister in the Faith. That can not ever be taken from him/her. Let him/her seek out other places and other Covens and/or Traditions.

Should an offender be unwilling to attend such a meeting of the Coven Council, it may be taken as an unwillingness to reconcile and seek an amicable solution.

In that event, by consensus of all, according to The Covenant, the offender may be considered cast out.

The three Officers must then take the symbols to the public street outside the offender's dwelling and by Bell, Book and Candle, perform the ceremony to disassociate the Coven from the offender.

The High Priesthood would not participate in such a distasteful task. They would consider such an eventuality as a failure on their part to have properly taught the values of the Ancient Wisdom to the individual coming under such a Coven censure.

They should mark the time with a brief period of mourning and seclusion from the Coven to seek the cause of the failure and the resolution to not have such happen again. One of their children in the Faith has been cast out.

If it does become possible to reconcile the offender to the Family, but the offence still warranting a Coven censure, the Coven Council should turn the offender over to the High Priesthood, with recommendation for a penalty to be imposed.

The fine, labour penalty or penance to be imposed, will be determined by the High Priesthood, as they are the parental elements of the Coven and must correct their own children.

The Coven Council will be able to see that the necessary penalty has been carried out, and will accept it as valid and full compensation for the offence, accepting the offender back into the Family.

We must try as we can to avoid casting our Brothers and Sisters out of the Coven and be able, as much as possible, to maintain harmony and balanced effort within the Coven Circle.

Bell, Book and Candle is the absolute last resort.

Alternate suggestions are offered for some Coven use in the *Appendix.*

The Coven method of holding Court, the matter of Banishment from the Coven and the High Solemn Excommunication before the Elders are given in detail, for those who may find such useful.

How To Void a Coven: Banishing The Spirit
Oliganthropia

The Elders must ever seek to maintain peace and harmony within the Craft, favouring neither one person of Coven nor the other. If a Coven seems inflicted with discontent and internal strife, in no way should its members enter a Magic Circle together. Such would create a foul and putrid aura to bring before the Gods. The Elders in such a case, should recommend the Coven be voided.

It may happen that attrition of members reduces the Coven to less than the original five. When all efforts to revitalize the Coven entity have proven fruitless, the Coven must be declared void and a new one centered at a more propitious time.

The remaining members of the Coven with the High Priest and High Priestess meet at the next Full Moon. In the Sanctum Niche (see *Book III*) rests the Sacred Flame, a chalice of Water and a dish of salt. With them stands a Thurible burning a live coal and next to that a bell.

The High Priestess acts as officiant for this ceremony and the High Priest takes the part of the Second Covener.

She brings out the ring of beads that was secluded after the Coven's inception and steps to the Sacred Flame in the Sanctum Niche. All remaining Coveners gather around as she drapes the circle of beads around the glass containing the Sacred Flame.

No words are spoken by any save the officiants. She places some incense of Patchouli on the coal and draws a banishing pentagram over it with the left thumb as the incense begins to burn.

She takes up the Sacred Flame and beads, the Second Covener takes up the salt and water. The Third Covener carries the Thurible and the Fourth the bell.

All proceed in that order to circumambulate the Ritual Chamber deosil 13 times as the bell is rung mournfully once for each circumambulation. Then, in silence, the officiant places the Flame in the center of the altar. She then says:

Spirit of this Coven Body, return, return to Summerland, quit this plane of Earthly woes.

The Second Covener places the dish of salt over the glass of the Sacred Flame so that is slowly smothers out.

The Officiant picks up and unties the string of beads and all then proceed out of doors.

Turning deosil to the Four Quarters, the Second Covener pours the water from the chalice out upon the ground.

The Third Covener censes deosil to the Four Quarters and then scatters the remaining ashes to the North Wind as the Fourth rings the bell 13 times once again.

The officiant scatters the beads to the Four Quarters as all silently bid farewell to the Spirit of the Coven.

All Coven properties are then turned over to the Elders to keep until a New Coven needs to be outfitted. The Elders will exorcise them of previous associations.

Left over funds will be given to the Elders so they may help any active but needy Covens in the district.

So Be It Ordained.

Why Is It Important To Void a Coven?

Very few do. When a group falls into disarray, members leave, bad mouth flies around, hard feelings exist between individuals and things become nasty and even childish.

Why is that? People invest a tremendous amount of energy into group or Coven efforts and place their good Will and hopes on the functioning of the collective.

Once having put out money, work, time and personal soul into a group entity, it becomes very hard when the inertia of non-participation begins to erode the group.

Whichever the reason may be for the break-up, the resulting chaos will continue to reverberate on the Ether and on the Physical unless the Group Spirit has been properly sent back to the Inner Planes.

A properly centered Cone or Coven creates an entity composed of all the emotions and mental auras of those working in it. That is the etheric body for the Spirit of Deity to inhabit during the collective Coven Works of Sabbat, Esbat or Council.

With time, it will seem to take on a momentum and grow and evolve, as the individuals within it also mature in God/Goddess. At times it can be highly felt and at others just barely perceptible. Be that as it may, each working group emits its own collective Vibration/Aura into the Spiritual Ethers. Its positive or negative bent is seen and/or felt. Persons sensitive to atmospheres can tell the health of any Coven group just by being around it.

Once a Cone has been centered and an embryonic Group Spirit conceived on the Ether, gaining its sustenance from the participation of the group members, it has to be recognized just as any "physical" member. Its feelings, its joys and sorrows, its existence must be considered in all acts affecting the Coven as a whole. It is the channel for the manifestation of the Divine Spirit through which God/Goddess communes with the Coven worshipers.

Very few Covens today invest sufficient energy to correctly establish a true Group Spirit. I even doubt that, in many instances, the Craft is being practiced. It seems most of the High Priesthood do not understand the esoteric meanings of these important considerations.

To create an open channel to Deity is not easily accomplished, but is the heart and core of Craft Coven Worship.

Therefore, when a group effort does not grow and bear the fruit of its labors, it should be voided by ritual to cut the links each member has to it on the Inner Planes. It must not be left to dangle halfway between the Worlds by all members just going off in all directions at will. It would be like leaving a child in a busy bus station and walking away. There would still be a pull on the emotions.

If a Coven, after it has ceased to function properly, is left and just abandoned, its Spirit decomposes to a clump of Astral Compost which still can fester and infect one's future efforts along those lines.

Be responsible enough to send back to the Gods what they helped one create after it has shown itself not progressive and growing. Then start over again, learning from the mistakes of the past.

To All Who Sign And Seal The Covenant

It, hereby, becomes binding on all Coveners of the I°, II° and III° of the Craft to learn all Sabbat Ritual and Esbat Ceremonial practices, to be able to make the proper responses that any ritual or ceremony requires.

The chants of the Circle Dances in raising the Cone of Power should be memorized and reviewed before each ceremony.

All should be attentive to what proceeds during any Craft ritual or ceremony and let the import of the charges and blessings sink into the deep mind.

Only in this way may a Coven work in one accord so that the combined will of the group may manifest its magic and bring about the desired results of the true Witches Will.

Each Covener is potentially a High Priest or High Priestess. Therefore, each should prepare him/herself for the day when asked to study for the higher initiations.

Always arrive at the Covenstead prepared for the ceremony of the day as instructed by the Summoner.

Do not be irritated when asked to show Grade Signs and/or give the Coven's yearly Watchword. All is part of the discipline of advancing on the planes of being.

Above all, never neglect an opportunity to learn more of Craft lore and tradition.

When you set your signature herein and kiss the book to seal it, you enter into an ancient and venerable Order that has survived lo these many centuries against persecution, death and Holy Terror.

Always, therefore, strive to be a worthy member of the Coven in honoring the Gods from of Old, in pressing onward toward your ultimate spiritual perfection and being of service to your fellow beings and co-creatures on this Earth.

Bide Well In The Craft.

Tarostar ✯ V°
Magister Sacrorum Circle of Starmeadow
Ancient Order of Bell, Book and Candle

The following is a list of Sections and information that should be posted in the Coven's Book of Records:

Register of Seals

Herein are written the names of all Coveners of the 1° called into the true Coven Family of the Ancient Craft in the Way of the Wise. The Craftsman will sign his/her name and kiss the page to seal it.

So Be It Ordained.

All signing herein assume the Grade of Covener 1°.

To Wit: Entering into the Coven of ______________

Communio Jurata:

1.

2.

3.

...

We, the above signed, enter into this Coven Family, this Hearth-fire of the Old Religion, of our own free will and accept the Ancient Craft of Wicca in the Way of the Wise, according to the tradition of *Book I.*

So Be It Done!

The Log

Herein are recorded all rituals and ceremonies of the Coven; their purpose, officiants, date, time, astrological conditions and results (recorded later).

Prognostications by the Coven Seers may be recorded and signed and witnessed. Results would be added and recorded at a later date.

Herein is also a listing of gifts and offerings and donations to the Coven with date and donor.

The Tree

Herein is recorded the Geneology of the Coven, previous affiliations of members, dates of Initiations, births, deaths and Coven vital statistics.

Appendix

This addenda pertains to *Section J* of *The Laws of the Craft (pg 22)* and may offer some elucidation and deeper, more comprehensive method of practice. It is offered as a suggestion only, as the "ideal" method, but with full knowledge that sometimes ideals have to be modified to suit actual situations.

Coven Secret Ballot

Whenever a secret "Yay or Nay" vote is required by the Coven Council, it is traditionally accomplished by the Ritual of the White and Black Balls.

Required are:

2 opaque containers, possibly velvet bags; one bag for the vote and one for the discard. They should be of different colours.

An equal number of white and black balls to the number of voted to be cast (marbles are usually ideal).

This excludes Coven matters of business, which require roll call votes handled by the two Scribes.

This ritual is presented for truly serious affairs where absolute secrecy is desired in the ballot.

Procedure begins with the distribution of two balls, one white and one black, to all voting participants.

Each voter is to keep them concealed so that only he/she knows which one is cast as a vote and which one is to be placed in the discard.

For the application of the Craftsman (1^0) to become a Covener (1^0) and admitted into the Coven Family, the vote should be unanimously positive; all white balls.

If one black ball shows up among the votes, the candidate may apply again at a later date, determined by the High Priesthood. (See *Sec. J: c, d, and e.*)

If several black balls appear, the High Priesthood, or the First Scribe, should ask for a discussion of the reasons for rejections, which shall be a secret discussion, voters not identifying themselves.

When the First Scribe calls for the vote, the Second Scribe will carry the bags; one for the vote and one for the discard among the assembled Coven, as each deposits his/her white or black ball in the vote bag and the discard in the other. Or they may file past him/her and deposit their votes and discards.

For section *J: f,* matters of suspension of a Covener from the Coven Family, the procedure is the same, however a majority of black balls is necessary.

For matters involving a censure, *Sec. J-H, the High Priesthoods* should determine the penalty and terms of suspension, such as fines, labour, penances etc.

Concerning matters of banishment from the Coven: Covenant, this is a suggested method for which the Coven Council may conduct its Court, the Apella.

The accused is called before the Coven Council to defend his/her actions. He/she may not vote.

The First Scribe acts as Judge, the Second Scribe acts as Recorder and the Summoner is Sgt. At-Arms.

The accuser speaks first and must call forth at least one witness to verify the claims of wrongdoing on the part of the accused.

The accused is given an opportunity to make a statement in defense and may call witnesses for the defense. (Witnesses need not be Coven Members, or even of the Craft, since the alleged offense may be in the nature of unethical practices outside the Craft, which may jeopardize the Coven and/or Craft.)

Non Crafters, as witnesses, will not be in the room during discussion and voting, but are called in at the proper time for their testimony.

Each side will be given an opportunity for rebuttal and cross-questioning, in order to establish or reveal possible extenuating circumstances.

After all testimony has been given, and both sides have concluded their arguments, the voting proceeds in this manner:

The Summoner votes his black or white ball, and passes the vote bag to the Recorder, who votes, then the Judge and then the members of the High Priesthood. Finally the vote bag is passed to the remaining Coveners.

The discard is then collected and set aside.

One, as a voter, keeps the ball being cast tightly in the fist, so it can not be seen and reaches deep into the vote bag to deposit it. None may see which ball is being cast by any individual voter. The same with the discard balls, so no one knows which vote an individual has cast.

The counting of the votes will determine the outcome.

To count the votes, the Recorder and the High Priesthood will retire from the room where they count the tally.

The results are written down and handed to the Judge, when they return to the room.

If the vote is unanimously negative; all black balls, the Judge will announce that the Coven desires banishment.

He/she will then advise the accused that appeal may be made before the next Council of Elders at the forthcoming Full Moon of July. (The appeal to the Council of Elders can be made as an alternative to the Ritual of Bell, Book and Candle at the discretion of the Ephors, the Coven Officers, should they feel the harshness of the B B & C Ritual is not necessary in an individual case.)

Should there be even one, several, or all white balls, the accused would be given a chance to redeem him/herself, from the accusations made and substantiated, by accepting whatever punishments the High Priesthood may impose; such as demotions in rank and status, exclusions from social activities for stipulated periods of time and/or extra work loads, or fines paid to the Coven Common Funds.

Should the course of the trial, before the vote, bring out the accused has been wrongfully put upon, and that the accusations bear no weight, the accuser must formally apologize and the Court will acquit the accused.

The appeal must be in writing giving the accused's reasons why he/she feels re-instatement would be in order. It also contains the reasons for the Coven's desire to banish, in the first place and the results of the vote tally.

(Any possible re-instatement is always accompanied by demotion to a lower level in the Craft, determined by the High Priesthood, at the direction of the Elders, taking into consideration the gravity of the offense. The re-instated individual should be placed at a level where he/she may re-learn the lessons he/she obviously disregarded.)

Procedure of Appeal

The High Priesthood shall present the complaint and written statements of the accused/one to be banished to the Scribe of the

Council of Elders. He/she will present the matter to the Elders in collective at the next formal meeting/Full Moon of July.

At that time the accused and the High Priesthood will attend the Council Meeting for this particular part, not for the entire meeting, except as the High Priesthood are junior members.

This means the accused remains outside the Council until his/her matter comes up on the agenda.

One member of the accused's High Priesthood will speak for the Coven and represent the complaint. The other member will represent the accused and speak for the defense before the Elders. The accused does not speak.

This is an open forum where each Elder present may question the complaint and defense.

When all has been heard and the Elders satisfied, the Scribe of the Council will call for a motion and a second, to consider the vote.

Whereupon, the accused must leave the room to await the decision.

News of re-instatement would be carried out to him/her, and the matter goes back to his/her High Priesthood, as stated before.

Should the Elders feel removal from the Coven, but not the Craft, is in order, the accused is summoned back into the room and a decision given by the Scribe of the Council of Elders:

Your Elders have seen fit to remove you from the Hearthfire, protection and comraderie of your Coven Family, henceforth and forevermore. Your are reminded the Coven retains your Oath and Seal. Therefore, since you have erred against them, rather then they against you, you are well advised to depart in peace and live in peace, seeking spiritual advancement in other covens and other traditions. You may remain either within or without The Craft as destiny may guide you. So mote it be!

Should the Elders have decided on banishment from the Craft in toto, they are prepared to enact the Ritual of High Solemn Excommunication, the Ceremony of Formal Banishment. (Excommunication was a Druidical practice ere it ever became a rite of the Medieval Christian Church.)

All Elders present will be formally robed and bearing their status symbols.

Two Elders step forward and flank the accused on both sides. The High Priesthood moves off into the background and stands among the remaining Elders.

On a small table or podium shall be placed one white candle burning, plus an open copy of the Covenant showing the Register of Seals, which the accused had signed as Covener (1°), also a large harsh sounding, low-toned bell.

The Elders flanking the accused remove his/her Athamé and place it on the table across the book.

The Scribe of the Council says:

You are guilty of the most gross offenses against your Brothers and Sisters of the Craft, who have given you their perfect love and perfect trust.

For having made a mockery of that love and abused that trust, let your Symbol of Power be forever divested of its virtues!

Each Elder present, from the most senior on down will file past the open book and place his/her right hand on the accused's Athamé and say: SO BE IT, LET IT FOREVER BE SO!

During this procession of Elders, the Scribe will toll the bell slowly and harshly.

The Athamé of the accused is handed to the High Priest of his/her Coven to be returned to him/her later.

A pen with black ink is brought forward and the Scribe of the Council writes "Banished" across the accused seal in the Covenant. The book is then forcefully slammed shut.

Finally, the Scribe takes the lit candle from its holder and holds it upside down to burn reversed, as he/she declares:

You are no longer our Brother/Sister! No radiance eminates from your tarnished soul, for you have violated our most Sacred Trust. You shall no longer merit the perfect love and perfect trust of the Wicca!

The Scribe brings the reversed flame down forcefully on the podium or table, snuffing it out and casts it contemptuously to the floor.

The two flanking Elders, produce a blindfold and place it over the accused's eyes.

The Scribe continues:

You will no longer be able to see or communicate with the Divine Beings in the world known only to those who are able to see the Astral Light.

One of the flanking Elders takes out a Bolline blade and cuts off the accused's cingulum cord and casts it down and stamps it under foot.
The Scribe continues:

You are hereby cut loose from the comraderie of your former Brothers and Sisters. Your name is forever anathema to all Wicca!
Let that flameless torch, cast upon the floor, be the symbol of your soul grasping in the darkness forever!

All present respond:

So Mote It Be!

High Solemn Dismissal

All Elders and members of the High Priesthood turn their eyes away, as the Scribe of the Council pronounces this dismissal, as the bell slowly tolls:

You are hereby disarmed and divested of all your Powers. Should you attempt to regain the use of them, let all your Workings be aborted, all of your prayers and petitions shall be sterile, bearing you no fruit, for as we close your Third Eye, and seal your Inner Ear (one of the flanking elders makes several passes over the accused's forehead and ears) *you will be unable to communicate with those who dwell in the Pure Light.*
You are naught but a piece of decaying flesh, and your soul, after abandoning it, shall never find a place in the beautiful Summerland, but wander aimlessly in limbo – unless you find solace or salvation on some other path.
For you there shall be no peace, only a restless, helpless kind of inertia, the frustration of which may help you break away from your aimless existence, and seek a satisfying way of life. Begone! Depart!

The banished one is lead out from the room and taken to the door of the Covenstead and thrust out, as the door is slammed shut behind.
The two flanking Elders who have ejected the banished one return to the room as the Scribe continues:

Blessed Lord and Lady, we petition thy forgiveness for our weakness in being unable to bring thy lost child to the maturity of his/her full potential.

It is within thy domain to open for him/her a new path, in order that the good which may be in him/her, but beyond our range or sensitivity, may develop, rather than being wasted adrift in the outer sphere.

We hold no malice, and pledge our forgiveness to the one in exile, even though we have found it necessary to mete out a punishment befitting his/her misdeeds, in order to avoid further injury to thy Sons and Daughters of the Craft and to protect the Sacred Mysteries from any profanations.

The deed is done, and we ask thy blessing upon us and upon all. Blessed be!

From this point, there will never be spoken any word concerning the one banished.

The Council of Elders would dismiss or move on to other business.

Should the accused not appear for the formal proceedings stated above, the matter can be handled by Banishment in Effigy, where a doll would suffice for the accused, and the formal ritual carried out as above.

In the modern age, how are you to get someone to stand still for such abuse?

If the ritual has to be done in effigy, it must be kept on its high Druidical level and not allowed to degenerate to the level of the common Sorcerer; by allowing the doll to be mutilated.

There is to be No Mutilation, Sewing Of The Mouth, Binding Of The Hands Or Feet, Nor Immolation.

Should Elders of the Craft participate in such low forms of sorcery, they defeat their own raison d'etre, and should not be Craft Elders.

Therefore, it is suggested the ritual be done by proxy, so the full ceremonial implications can be brought into effect. Each Covendom would have to work the particulars out for themselves.

End of The Covenant. ☆ So Mote It Be!

The Sacred Pentagraph

Book II

The Book of Beginnings

Initiations in the Craft

Rites of Passage

This is the volume of the valid Rites of Passage for those of the Ancient Craft in the Way of the Wise and the true Initiatory Tradition handed down from the Elders, who have secretly preserved the old ways, and modified them to be in keeping with the spiritual needs of modern Western Man.

All rituals marking the inception of new phases in the total life experience of the Wicca are found herein.

Preface

The Ancient Craft of the Way of the Wise presents the traditions of Wicca as a total life commitment and discipline, which demands responsibility, and integrity of its members.

It is a method of rising on the planes of consciousness in the material world, as we know it. It is an initiatory process elevating the total person from birth through death in a series of successive grades to master the ordeals of life by application of Craft religious ideals and philosophical outlook.

Nothing is ever gained without expenditure of energy and application of will power. Nothing worthwhile comes from faint-hearted efforts. Nothing is given without a compensating value in return.

This inductive method of advancement in the Craft presents an 11-fold path of learning and spiritual guidance from 0-10, birth to death, in a guided, step-by-step process marking the levels of knowledge and gathered experience and wisdom as they are met on life's journey.

This Craft Tradition encompasses the individual from birth through the higher levels of Elder status and on to the elevated cycles when crossing the veil to help perfect his/her spirit essence and aid the individual entity in returning to this world in a more perfect and spiritual aspect.

Each level demands applications of self-discipline and learning, which assist the Initiate in everyday life as well. Each level adds to that of the previous one an accomplishment and acquired abilities, which stimulate soul growth. Each level leads to the development of the spiritual process of an entity, fine tuning powers of Occult Wisdom.

From infancy to old age and beyond, the Initiates of this path develop into forces for good, whose minds and spirits are capable of directly affecting the world around them.

Adepthood of this nature is not an easy task to accomplish, nor is it lightly bestowed on the unworthy. No short cuts to "Magical Powers" will be found herein. We may be able to have instant mashed potatoes or coffee, but there are no "10 Easy Lessons to the Great Work."

There are, however, 10 difficult and demanding steps to power, which the true Craft can teach. The Great Work lies in perfecting oneself. Only the powers of the Wiccan Craft can bring about that transformation.

By the volumes of *The Sacred Pentagraph*, the work of the true Magical Will and tradition of valid instruction and induction into the Craft are brought forth. If this discipline is faithfully followed and its ordeals successfully mastered, one is well on the way to the crown of spiritual adepthood; the Great Work is being accomplished.

The one binding requirement, however, is that the development of these powers must accompany the balance given by the Craft as a religion. To seek and pursue them without the Old Gods, leads to the abyss and the spiritual annihilation of the works of Sorcery. The totality of one's being is at stake.

If Thou Hast The Will To Work The Way, Read On. If Not, Close This Tome And Depart In Peace, The Works Of Witchery Be Not For Thee!

Introduction

The previous volume, *Book I: The Covenant*, may have presented concepts new to some in the Craft. This is because; the Elders bringing forth this information on Wicca have kept this tradition and refined it over the years to produce a workable system.

It is an Initiatory Occult Society, giving cohesiveness to Wicca as The Old Religion and bringing forth its inner doctrines and ideals.

The Sacred Pentagraph is not a collection of occult curiosa one can just thumb through and take a bit here and a bit there, without reading and understanding the system in toto. It is designed to be worked through form one level to the next, from on degree to the next, step by step.

If you are looking for "Pagan Dress Up" and the dumb "Fun and Games" one usually finds in certain Pagan Circles, this is the wrong place to be. Those things one may find elsewhere, but not in Wicca, as is practiced by this system; as is being brought forward in its original intent.

The Old Religion/Wicca very definitely has a doctrine of religious belief and practice and a body of philosophical view that has not been properly studied, nor applied by even those who claim to be longstanding Wiccans.

With the revival of Wicca in the present day, the Craft has passed its infancy and is now ready to embark on its adolescent development by expanding its consciousness and its image of Self. It has a deep body of spiritual knowledge to give Humanity, as is felt by many who are attracted to Wicca. Now is the time to begin to develop that inner essence and bring forward suggestions for an "ideal" practice of the Craft. To this end these volumes are offered to the Craft and its diverse Traditions.

Because of the fact the Initiatory Process of the Ancient Wisdom is complicated and not easy to grasp in a short article, I will present an outline of the system, grade-by-grade, describing each and listing the requirements necessary.

Before going into the Rituals, the system and its purpose must be fully understood, or else they appear confusing. That is necessary, as it deflects the uncommitted and the thrill seeker. The exoteric possesses blinds and confusions to eliminate those not willing to invest time, energy, effort, sweat, money and personal integrity on any path of Occult Philosophy.

The esoteric core, however, becomes clear the deeper one gets into an occult system and brings forth its pearls of wisdom, helping the Initiate become an Adept.

If you are not willing to work on the Self, in the perfecting of Being, the Occult itself is not your path. *The Sacred Pentagraph* is no place for sissies and requires the serious Occultist.

If, however, you are seeking the esoteric inner core of the Craft/Wicca/Old Religion, this system is for you.

Why The Sacred Pentagraph?

First and foremost, the Gods will it.

In the mid 70s the Craft was in disarray. Witchcraft and Pagan groups were spawning in every which direction. So-called Witches and Occult Wonder Workers were creeping from under the rug everywhere.

Books, supposedly on Craft rites and ceremonies, flooded off the press and each muddied the view of Wicca according to the author's personal bias.

Works of Wizardry and Magic, Sorcerers and Seeresses, Occult systems ad infinitum were touted as part of the Old Religion.

Persons of Pagan persuasion joined groups and Circles and so-called Covens in almost every part of the globe. The revival of interest in the old ways was, however, the only saving grace of that time of chaos.

Out of chaos comes cosmos.

People coming to the Craft were; in general, drop outs from the vapid and shallow mainstream faiths. They wanted the Love and Light of the Old Gods, but were tainted with the Judeo-Christian ethic. Those purporting to be leaders of the Craft fell into the same mold as power hungry Bible-thumping bigots. They caused more harm than good to the Craft.

High Priests and High Priestesses were seen as people with more Ego than knowledge. One-upmanship by supposed Crafters in the fields of Occult lore, caused strife and bickering, backbiting and hard feelings. Splinter group after splinter group broke away and set up their own so-called validity. The Craft as a working system of occult attainment fell into disrepute even among dedicated Witches.

But out of chaos comes cosmos.

During that sorry state of affairs, one small group, who had kept to themselves, not making public Craft contacts, but who were the Keepers of a valid system of occult Craft Initiations, were singled out by the God and Goddess. That small group was composed of Witches who had been in the traditions of the Craft since birth. They were Witches and children of Witches whose roots in Craft religious works went back to old Bohemia under the Hapsburg Empire, and from the State of Hesse in the Kaiser's time. The tradition stretched back into time in Central Europe.

By the late 70s, only a few Elders remained of the Ancient Order of Bell, Book and Candle. They had preserved faithfully the ways of Witchery and kept a small spark of the true Craft intact.

The Ancient Order of Bell, Book and Candle was in Medieval Times, composed of those who were cast off by the power elite of that day. They were those who thought for themselves and would not accept the ignorance of Holy Church. Remnants of that Order have survived to this day. Bell, Book and Candle means that Holy Church consigns one's soul to the outer darkness. The outer darkness of Holy Church is, however, the Light and Love of the God and Goddess.

To those few Elders at the Circle of Starmeadow, the Gods gave a mandate: To bring forth the tradition of Craft worship and learning. Craft Works and Laws, and present them in modern form to those in the Craft who still seek a true and valid path to the Old Gods.

Some of them have passed on and not been able to complete the task. Others carry on the work as best they can. The era of the "pop-Witches" is on the decline. Let the Way of the Wise now seek the light.

Out of chaos comes cosmos. Blessed Be.

"But, My Lord Elder, you have so many rules and regulations! Are they all necessary?"

The Sacred Pentagraph is an ideal system of functioning an Occult

Group or Society.

It is one of many.

It does not say, you, specifically, have to follow it.

However, if you are going to work any System of Occult Philosophy, work it ideally, from beginning to end, or not at all!

Part I - Major Rites of Passage

Section I

Outline of The Grades On The Levels of Initiation

Initiare

As the Latin word indicates, Initiation means to begin, with the implication of into the Mysteries. However, Initiations begin nothing, they confirm the level of spiritual awareness an Initiate has already gained by study and induction into the esoteric Wisdom Lore of the Ancients.

An Initiation Ceremony is not undergone until the Ordeal of Mastery has been successfully experienced. It must be earned and shows the Initiate to be qualified to be considered an Initiate of a specific Level or Grade in the Craft.

If one is asked to undergo a Ceremony, first, before one may study the Craft, or Wicca, the process is being worked backwards. When one studies first and attains a certain body of knowledge and then is given the Initiation Ceremony, as a Confirmation of that level of lessons, one can be assured the true Occult Wisdom Tradition is being worked.

Also, one would not be asked to perform acts, or engage in activity unworthy of a serious body of knowledge. If, one as a Candidate for Initiation, would be asked to place one's body, for sexual use by the Guru, on the line before one could be "initiated", know right away, the true Craft/Wisdom/Tradition/Old Religion is not being taught by such a Guru or group.

It is best for a person to go into the Occult with the eyes wide open and the feet firmly on the ground. It is the Spirit, which is being cultivated through a true Wisdom Channel, not the momentary pleasures of the physical.

This in no way makes the Craft dour and prudish, but it has a definite responsibility to those who come to it seeking true knowledge of the Occult and the Craft Magical Powers.

Inexperienced persons, or rather those new to Occultism and unaware of the esoteric core, at times seem to display starry eyes and willowy minds and allow themselves to be talked into engaging in all sorts of fun-and-games "party" activities, under the guise of being Wicca.

Often they are not told what would be expected of them in the Initiation until the very last minute and to back out then would cause a loss of face and personal prestige.

If a suggestion of any act or activity deemed initiatory, goes against one's personal inner feeling of propriety, there may be something wrong with the entire system and most definitely wrong with the person or persons urging one to undergo it.

An Initiation Ceremony is to be studied and rehearsed beforehand by they Initiate and the one conferring the Initiation, so the Candidate knows what is expected and what words of response would be required to speak. If all has to be kept hush-hush and deep dark secret before one performs the Ceremony, perhaps the entire system is suspect of not having a true depth of spiritual value to teach.

Secretiveness is a part of the discipline in the Occult System, not a cover to keep the outer World from knowing what is going on in the Coven. Nothing should be going on in a Coven activity that the serious-minded person could not be allowed to know.

With the above in mind, *The Sacred Pentagraph*, as an Occult System, puts herewith, the Initiatory Process and the Rituals down on paper for the benefit and edification of those who will find them helpful.

Blessed Be!

0° Level of Initiation - The Wiccan Born

Naturally, as the saying goes, the place to start is at the beginning. Let us first take the two paths allowing entry into the Craft - that of the hereditary one of those born into a Craft family and that of those from among the Stranger who enter the Faith through choice.

When a Wiccan couple give birth to a child, it should be taken out under the stars, as soon as it is old enough to be out of doors.

The Father should take it up in his arms and hold it to the Four

Quarters; North, West, South and East, saying at each Quarter:

Hear me, O Ancient Ones, and Watchers from the Times of Old; a new entity has come forth into this world! Bless him/her and keep him/her ever in thy heart!

Should the newborn only have its Mother, in a one-parent family, she must also do this for the infant (Aunts, Uncles, and/or Grandparents may also do it, if the infant is orphaned).

When the infant is 60 days old, he/she should be taken to the Covenstead and presented to the High Priesthood. The High Priest will take the infant in his arms and anoint its forehead with an Invoking Pentagram in Oil of Frankincense, as he says:

Child of love, child of light, may the God sustain thee with all his might. Blessed be!

He kisses the infant and passes it to the High Priestess. She holds the infant to her breast and sprinkles a few drops of water on its head as she says:

Child of light, child of love, the Goddess bless thee from above.

Unwrapping the infant from its blankets, she will touch its feet with a handful of Earth and say:

(Name), May the Goddess, who is Mother of this world's creation, guide thy footsteps all the days of thy life. Blessed be!

She also kisses the infant, wraps it back up and hands it back to the Mother.

Proper recording should then be made in the Tree to mark the birth (see *Book I*) and notation of this Dedication Ceremony, date and time, placed in the Log, by the High Priesthood.

From that time on, the child is allowed to grow and be raised, as the parents are able, given the best care possible. The child should receive the proper education the Society of the Times indicates.

At the Tenth Birthday, the child should be given a boiled egg, which represents the basic idea of a cell of life, a large coin, which stands for the Wealth of the World, a loaf of homemade bread, which shows the sustaining bounty of the Goddess, and a lit candle (white if male, black if female), which symbolizes the Craft, the Light of Knowledge. These items are presented and explained to the child.

Between the tenth and fifteenth year, the child should acquire his/her Four Basic Tools of the Craft: the Athamé, the Chalice, the Thurible and the Pentacle.

He/she should not be allowed to play with them, but only collect them and keep them and understand their proper meanings, so they may be employed at a later date, when the child may enter the Craft at I^0 status.

With the fifteenth year, the child is given *The Book of the Wise I* to study and understand the 47 Precepts of Cosmic Order (see *Book V: The Cornucopia,* for the teaching guides).

When it is felt the child has a fair knowledge of the Precepts, he/she is told he/she may choose to pursue The Quest of the Wiccan Born.

The Ancient Tradition of sending the young on a quest is sadly lacking from this modern world.

In Times of Old, the young person had to achieve some dangerous fete in order to be called "adult" and accepted into the group.

The Wiccan Born should be encouraged to develop a responsibility with an ethic of work, labour or struggle to produce something from its raw material form all the way through to its finished product.

Considering place and circumstances, one may choose to raise a goat and see it through all its necessary phases into adulthood, milking and eventually make cheese. One may choose to spin wool into thread, weave material and produce a finished garment. One may choose to plant a grapevine, tend it for the necessary years and make wine from its grapes. Another may choose to grow herbs or mushrooms for sale.

The idea being that the young person begin, continue and see the project through to its finished product, unaided by adults. If a young person's job is necessary to pay for it, so much the better.

Let the child take the raw material and learn the entire process of producing a finished product or craft totally on his/her own from scratch.

The "Quest" is to teach the young person an appreciation for the values of the old handmade Arts and Crafts and as to how the ancestors had to labour for their produce.

The project should be geared to reach its conclusion between the eighteenth and twentieth year.

If a child does not choose to take the Quest, he/she foregoes the chance of entering the Craft at 1° status. The young person may enter the Craft later, but would have to undergo Neophyte and Probationer Grades.

With the successful completion of the Quest, the child should be formally told by the adults of the family that he/she has now reached Manhood or Womanhood. The Father, Uncle or Grandfather, or lacking those, the High Priest, should make this a formal and family occasion for the male child. The Mother, Aunt or Grandmother, or lacking those, the High Priestess, should do the same for the female child.

It is very important in the development of a young person to be told the elder members of the same sex that he/she has finally passed the childhood phase and is now a full-grown man or woman entitled to group approval in the mysteries of his/her gender.

Having been raised in the Craft, seeing his/her parents at Sabbat and Esbat, (as an observer outside the Circle), he/she would be familiar with religious observances and Magical Works. He/she should, however, be taught not to confide in the Stranger about the inner workings of the Craft.

At the twentieth year, he/she may be presented at the Covenstead so the High Priesthood may set the date for the 1° Initiation, as a Craftsman. All other advancement in the Craft is optional.

Even though parents like to see their children follow in the Faith, Wicca does not automatically force such compliance, as do other religious persuasions.

The Wiccan Born may enter the Craft, or not, as a matter of conscience.

Neophyte 0° – First Level of Initiation

Let us say, for instance, a person was initiated Neophyte on the Vernal Equinox. It took, however, perhaps 14 months to master the year of study. He/she would still have to wait for the following Vernal Equinox to be elevated to Probationer, having missed the one when he/she should have taken the Grade. At least, that is, if we are going to go by the tradition. It lends for good discipline. However, as we have seen, the High Priesthood would have the final word in this matter. Each case would have to be judged on its own merits.

The second path into the Craft is for those of rational age, who come to The Ancient Wisdom by choice and conviction. Let us hypothetically follow an Initiate through the Grades of the Craft.

Adults seeking to join the Craft should be brought to the High Priesthood by a Wiccan of at least 1°, (if the Coven is operational), or may come via the notices of classes in the Craft put out by the High Priesthood in the process of forming a new Coven.

The 1° person introducing one to the High Priesthood, would, generally, thereafter, act as Sponsor for the said individual later at the Neophyte and Probationer Initiations.

However, never allow the Stranger to see or attend at the Covenstead, once the Cone has been centered. Individuals meeting with the High Priesthood for the first time should do so elsewhere at some public or distant spot away from the Covenstead. Always must the center of Wiccan Worship be kept safe from the prying eyes of the uninformed.

The High Priesthood would need to sponsor the first ones they initiate through Neophyte, Probationer to Craftsman 1° status. Thereafter, the first Craftsman could sponsor the other two, until the proper five are present to Center the Cone. (See *Book I: The Covenant.*)

Before the Neophyte level can be assumed, the individual is considered a Pre-Initiate.

Upon meeting with the approval of the High Priesthood, he/she will be given a copy of *The Book of the Wise I*, (from *Book V*), and told to meditate on each of the 47 precepts of Cosmic Order and write a short paragraph in his/her own words, as to what he/she feels each precept means.

There are no rights or wrongs, as these universal precepts mean something different to each individual, in his/her understanding of the workings of this universe.

Neither is grammar or literary style that important. The main point being that the Pre-Initiate will complete the Ordeal. The idea of intellectual discipline and the willingness to complete a project, is what is the most important consideration.

Give the Pre-Initiate whatever amount of time he/she may need to complete the ordeal. If it is not completed, nor even attempted, stamp the dust off your feet before him/her and walk away. That person may not be thereafter a candidate for any association with the Ancient Craft, in the Way of the Wise.

It is traditional to initiate persons to Neophyte status and to elevate them to Probationer status during the Vernal Equinox Sabbat. However, the Initiations may be given at the discretion of the High Priesthood, when they feel a case warrants. It may happen a Coven could have persons scheduled to be initiated to Neophyte and to Probationer status on the same Vernal Equinox, and the length of the night's ritual could, therefore, become quite long. For that reason, the High Priesthood must be given more flexibility in these matters.

We will assume, however, for the purposes of this book, that we will follow the tradition.

After the successful completion of the Ordeal of the Pre-Initiate, that person may attend at the Covenstead to learn more about the Craft and what would be expected of a Neophyte. (They are not to attend any worship ceremony of the Sabbat cycle, nor any magical works of the Esbat cycle.)

On the night of the Vernal Equinox, he/she is summoned to the Covenstead.

The Pre-Initiate does not see, nor in any way participate in the regular Sabbat Ceremony. He/she waits outside the Ritual Chamber until the Summoner and the Sponsor come to fetch him/her into the Chamber.

He/she is admitted to the Circle, initiated, then removed from the Chamber by those who admitted him/her, before the Sabbat Circle is closed.

The Sabbat Ritual is rather short for Vernal Equinox in order to allow more time for Initiations. (See *Book III: The Book of Lights.*)

The newly initiated Neophyte may join in post-ritual festivities and enjoy the Coven good cheer and party atmosphere, which is traditional after worship of the Old Gods.

From this point on, the Neophyte is to take the year long course of instruction from *The Book of the Wise II,* given at the Covenstead under the direction of the High Priesthood and any Artisan II°, who may assist them as teachers.

It is mandatory to remain in Neophyte status for a year to seek out and acquire the Four Basic Tools of the Craft.

This gives sufficient time to master the monthly lessons and complete the two Research Papers required by the Grade as the Ordeal of the Neophyte.

It also allows the High Priesthood and any teaching Artisans to evaluate the Neophyte as to willingness and ability to complete the assignments of the Grade.

Should he/she fall by the wayside during the year, no further association will be allowed that individual with the Ancient Craft in the Way of the Wise. However, circumstances may force one to delay his/her study. It may take longer than a year.

Upon successful completion of the Ordeal, the Neophyte will be summoned to the Covenstead on the following Vernal Equinox to be given the Second Level of Initiation, becoming a Probationer.

Thus we have seen the two main branches from which persons enter the Craft. That is, for persons either born into a Wiccan Family, or coming of their own accord.

For the Tradition of *The Sacred Pentagraph,* the Ancient Craft of Wicca in the Way of the Wise, there may be others coming to it, from various Craft Covens and groups from other traditions. They may enter this Tradition at the next point on the initiatory level we will be discussing - Probationer. Those with previous Craft affiliation may begin at the Second Level, as if they had just been given the Probationer Ceremony.

Probationer 0° – Second Level of Initiation

One year from the night of the Initiation to Neophyte status, presumably the next Vernal Equinox, the Neophyte is summoned to the Covenstead.

He/she must again wait outside the Ritual Chamber to be fetched by the Summoner and Sponsor.

After the main part of the Sabbat has been completed, and after any Pre-Initiates there may be for that year, have been elevated to Neophyte status, the Neophyte, to be elevated to Probationer, is taken into the Ritual Chamber and given the Initiation to that Grade.

He/she is again removed from the Ritual Chamber before the Sabbat Ceremony is closed.

The new Probationer may also join in the post-ritual festivities, but is given a toast by the High Priesthood and any teaching Artisans under whom he/she studies, as to having completed the Year's Ordeal.

From this point on, the Probationer is given at least six months to take *The Book of the Wise III* and perform the simple Consecration Rituals for his/her own Magical Tools.

This is the Ordeal of the Probationer: To be given a set of instructions and be able to follow them out to their logical conclusions, totally on his/her own.

He/she must follow the rubrics and perform the Rituals and report the successful completion of each to the High Priesthood, or any teaching Artisans with whom he/she is studying.

He/she is also continuing in the classes on Magical Methods being given by the High Priesthood and/or Artisans.

When the High Priesthood, having discussed the Probationer with the teaching Artisans, feels the Ordeals have been mastered, they tell the Probationer to prepare his/her Formal Coven Robe and to make the blue cingulum cord (see *Book V: The Cornucopia*) and to learn the method of casting a Magic Circle (see Circle of Initiates in Craftsman Ceremony).

The Coven Council will provide the Hand Bell which will be given the Initiate at the Ceremony, initiating him/her to I°.

Do not pressure the Probationer into mastering the Ordeal. He/she has six months to do it. The Grade of Probationer may, however, take longer, Should the Probationer take a lot of time to complete the Ordeal, it may mark against him/her, later on in the Craft, should he/she wish to advance above Craftsman I° status.

As can be seen, I am presenting the process of advancing in the Grades of the Craft in an orderly, logical, precise system of inductions. It may sound tiring, but is the only way to present the Ancient Wisdom Tradition in an uncomplicated manner. Only in this way do we avoid overlooking important details, which prove helpful later on in the Craft.

The Sacred Pentagraph is meant to be studied, then applied. It can work for the individual in no other way.

Craftsman I° – Third Level of Initiation

It is the Ordeal of the Craftsman to be able to cast and banish a proper Magic Circle within which the Mysteries may be assumed, or Spells cast, or Ceremonies performed etc. etc.

This must be done in full view of the assembled Coven, either at a regular meeting of the Coven Council, or at a New or Full Moon Esbat, when the Coven is present, before the regular ceremony.

This must be done by the Probationer using his/her own Magical Tools to erect and banish the Circle, without use of ritual notes. Therefore, sufficient time must have been allowed the Probationer to master the skill (see Initiation to *Craftsman Ritual* in *Section II*).

The Probationer will cast the Circle, the High Priesthood will enter. They will then require the Probationer to recite the Resolves of the Craftsman I°. They will then bestow the blue cord and Bell and declare the Probationer to be a Witch I°.

They then exit the Circle, with the proper seal being made behind them, and the new Craftsman will banish the Circle properly.

Afterwards, the Coven may proceed into its regular meeting or Esbat. The new Craftsman may observe from outside the Esbat Circle this one time only, as to how the Coven functions its Magical Works.

Thereafter, the Craftsman will only be summoned for Sabbat and become a dues paying member of the Coven.

From this point, the Coven takes the Craftsman under observation and evaluates his/her potential to be an asset to the Coven's Magical Works at Esbat.

They would bring the matter up at a regular meeting of the Coven Council and vote by secret ballot to admit the Craftsman as a Covener (see *Book I: The Covenant, Sec. J:15*). How much time would be needed for a proper observation, must be left to the Coven Council.

The allowing of a Craftsman to observe the Esbat ceremony, should he/she be initiated on a Night of the New or Full Moon, would, however, be a decision of the Coven consensus itself. Perhaps the ritual for that night may be something not for the eyes of one inexperienced in Magic.

Under no circumstances would the Craftsman be allowed to participate. By being allowed to observe, maybe his/her interest will be sparked to want to delve further into the Occult aspects of the Craft.

In any event, the entire group must be in accord on the Craftsman's presence. Otherwise, after his/her elevation to I° status, he/she must quit the Covenstead for that night, taking his/her Magical Tools.

Thus we see three levels of study, personal application and hard work bring an Initiate into full status as the First Degree in the Craft. Three is the mystic number of creation; a thing done in threes is symbolically done an infinite number of times. The Initiate, therefore, is of Wicca forevermore.

The actual Initiation Rituals, in the second section of this volume, will flesh out the process and give all particulars needed to accomplish the full Initiations.

As stated in The Covenant, all further advancement in the Craft is optional to the individual Initiate and to the Coven itself.

Covener I° – Fourth Level of Initiation

Civitatem aliqui donare

When both the High Priesthood and Coven Council agree that the Craftsman would be able to harmoniously blend into the Esbat Works as positive force, which would enhance the Coven body, he/she is told to make the green cingulum cord for his/her robe.

The robe of the Craftsman had been made according to the instructions in *Book V*, by hand. Now, to be a Covener, he/she needs a better robe with a hood, to be like the other Coveners. That is, to have the uniform Coven Robe. This robe should be professionally made, black in colour and may bear any insignia on the breast the Coven uses to identify itself.

The Craftsman is told to procure the uniform Coven Robe to go with his/her green cingulum cord.

Now, the Craftsman is allowed to study the Esbat procedures peculiar to the Coven itself, so he/she fully understands the object and reasons for particular Magic Workings at each Lunar Tide.

The Coven will purchase the blank book to be given the Initiate as symbol of the Covener Grade. (As Craftsman, he/she took the bell. At Covener, the book is assumed. At Artisan, the candle will be taken to complete the symbols in the assumption of the venerable Order of Bell, Book and Candle.)

The blank book is the Covener's record of his/her own Magical Journey, to be a personal diary of both successes and failures in the Art Magical.

Allow for sufficient time for the above stipulations to be carried out, so the Craftsman has had thorough background in Esbat Lore. The Craftsman is also to be given The Covenant to study the Craft Laws, so he/she fully understands his/her obligations to the Craft and the Coven.

By being given The Covenant, does not mean he/she takes it home away from the Covenstead, but to study the Craft Laws at the Covenstead, so he/she may ask the High Priesthood or the Coven officers to explain any particulars, which may seem obscure.

The official acceptance ceremony, taking the Craftsman into the Coven Family as a Covener I°, is done at a New Moon Esbat, just prior to the regular Esbat ceremony for that night. (See *Ceremony for a Covener* in *Section II.*)

He/she must be familiar with the Laws of the Craft and be willing to accept his/her obligations to the Coven thereunder. By signing and sealing the Covenant, he/she has a duty to the Coven from then on.

Should the Craftsman choose not to become a Covener, he/she may stay on in the Coven as a dues paying member, and only be summoned for Sabbat. Or, he/she may quit the Covenstead and take the Document of Introduction, from the High Priesthood, which has been notarized (as per *The Covenant, Section G:5-6*) confirming his/her First Degree status, to seek entrance into other Covens and Traditions in the Craft elsewhere.

A copy of any Document of Introduction is always entered in the Log by the First Scribe, to provide verification of such an individual's Craft status, according to this tradition.

This precludes individuals showing up later in the Craft, claiming status this Tradition has not granted.

One must never feel one is forced to comply with the Way of the Wise. All is done by choice and Free Will. However, once a choice is made, one must stand by it. A Would-be-Wiccan of weak and vacillating Will, would not have reached Craftsman status in the first place.

Artisan II° – Fifth Level of Initiation

Rising beyond I° status is optional in the Craft. Being accepted as a Covener is also optional. However, I° persons, not accepted as Coveners do not become eligible to take higher Initiations of the Ancient Craft of Wicca, in the Way of the Wise.

Advancing to II° must also be optional for the Covener.

Should a Covener wish to take the next Initiation, he/she must prepare for it totally on his/her own. The obligation of fostering a person along, by the High Priesthood, is finished once the Craftsman becomes a Covener. They may not lend further aid as teachers.

The Covener is to take upon him/herself the study of Spellcasting and the making and consecrating of Talismans. (Some basic methods may be found in *Book V, The Cornucopia,* as suggestions.)

When the Covener feels and knows he/she is able to successfully cast spells and consecrate Talismans, he/she approaches the High Priesthood and the First Scribe together and claims the right to undergo the Ordeal of the Artisan II°.

The High Priesthood will scoff and gently rebuff such presumption.

The First Scribe will issue the Witches Challenge (Should a Coven be new, without a FS, the High Priesthood will challenge):

Oh Covener, boast not what ye can do, lest the Gods reduce thee a notch or two.

To prove thy boasting be no myth, I lay this charge upon thee forthwith:

At full moon next be ready to show thy witchy works to us of the

Priesthood, both high and low!

In issuing the Witches Challenge, the First Scribe stands forth, drawn up to his/her full height, pointing his/her quill pen at the Covener and speaks forth the above words in a deep foreboding manner.

Then the Covener immediately quits the Covenstead to prepare for the Ordeal of the Artisan II°.

He/she must make the yellow cingulum cord and acquire the Lamp of Art. There must be allowed enough time prior to the next Full Moon to be able to consecrate the lamp properly (see *Ceremony for the Artisan in Section II*).

He/she should prepare a spell or a Talisman to be cast or consecrated before the entire Coven using full ceremonial: 1) Circle of Initiates; 2) the spell or consecration; 3) banishing the Circle.

This would be done just prior to the Coven's Full Moon Esbat on the next Full Moon, as the challenge stipulated. (The spell or Talisman to be cast or consecrated would, however, be discussed with and approved by the High Priesthood before it is performed.)

Upon the successful completion of the Ordeal, the High Priesthood will bestow the yellow cingulum and bless the Initiate with the Lamp of Art.

All Coveners below III° will give a bow to the new Artisan and offer him/her a toast as a Priest/Priestess of the Art Magical, after the usual Esbat ceremony.

This Ordeal has shown the Artisan to be fully competent to practice the Art Magical. He/she has reached full status in the Craft.

If he/she is suitable as a teacher, Neophytes and Probationers may be given him/her to help train, under the supervision of the High Priesthood.

This is also the level where one may practice the Craft as full-fledged Wiccans without Coven affiliation, should such eventuate in the Artisan's life.

He/she, however, may not teach the Craft, in this Tradition, outside of a Coven group not under a valid High Priesthood of the Ancient Craft of Wicca, in the Way of the Wise.

This will be seen to, as now the Initiate, at II° status, comes under observation and scrutiny of the Elders.

Thus with five complete levels of Initiation, an Initiate is brought into full status in this Wiccan Tradition.

The system has produced a person with an adamant Magical Will, who is advancing on the Road to Adepthood.

This may be as far as most individuals would care to advance, due to obligations of job, family or other considerations and demands on time and attention.

The Initiate may rest from his/her labours at this level for as long as he/she wills.

Practicus and/or Hand Maiden III° Sixth Level of Initiation

The first five levels are called "the Basics." That may be as high as most persons may wish to aspire in the Craft.

All those persons of II° are given a tough scrutiny by the High Priesthood and the Elders in the district or Covendom.

Those who possess a talent for ritual and display the abilities to lead and organize, may be asked by the High Priesthood to prepare for III°.

This decision rests heavily upon the High Priesthood, as III° persons become acolytes to attend upon the High Priesthood at Esbat ceremonial rituals. There should be a closeness and almost a "flesh and blood" relationship as if the Acolytes were the children of the High Priesthood.

These levels above Second Degree are called "the Vocationals" and once these are taken and accepted, the Craft becomes almost the primary concern in one's life. Total dedication, as much as possibly can be given, will be required by the needs of the Craft.

Persons should not be pressured to proceed, if their personal and/or home life make more important demands. However, later in life, should circumstances be different, they may wish to advance. A candidate is always given free choice.

When the Artisan accepts the call to advance, he/she will seek the sword as symbol of office (see *Ceremony for III° in Section II*) and perform the proper consecration ritual for it.

A candidate aspiring to III° must learn all needed responsibilities for Esbat Ritual and study all Sabbat Ceremonial should a Hand Maiden or Practicus ever have to fill in for a member of the High Priesthood.

Then the preparation for the Ordeal of the Acolytes must be made. The Ordeal consists of preparing a 10-minute talk on some aspect of Craft Lore, which is to be presented before the entire Coven on a night marking the anniversary of the Centering of the Cone in the founding of the Coven (see *Book I: The Covenant*).

This anniversary party should be a festive occasion, as it marks the fact that the Coven is evolving as it should in preparing younger persons to assume office and "Hive Off", perpetuating the Craft in other parts.

The 10-minute talk is but the first part of the Ordeal. The second part consists of the Candidate being able to perform, without notes, *The Witches Banishing Ritual of The Pentagram*, using the Sword of Art.

On the night appointed for the ceremony, the candidate appears at the Covenstead in formal Robe, but without the cingulum of II°, and carrying the sword held across the arms.

The Summoner will proceed in procession clearing the way and calling the Coven to order.

The High Priesthood will stand forth in full regalia of office as the Coven takes positions around the outer corners of the Ritual Chamber.

Before the assembled Coven the candidate presents the talk on Craft Lore and performs the Ritual from beginning to end.

The High Priesthood will bestow the red cingulum and the minor jewels and declare the Ordeal to be finished. This is a proud moment for the High Priest and High Priestess, as they are seeing one of their fledglings take flight.

The Coven will then celebrate its anniversary with a festive party honoring the new III° person(s) with the seat of honour at the party table. Always remember, Wicca is a joyous Faith celebrating life and its beauty.

The new Practicus and/or Hand Maiden are now apprenticed to the High Priesthood and must fulfill their duties to the Altar of Wicca. To learn the Worship of the Old Gods is the primary task of the III°.

Those of this Degree are to prepare themselves for the time when the Elders may call them to begin to study for the IV°.

The Craft Elders will determine the time when a Coven should elevate new High Priests and High Priestesses and send them out to other parts among the Stranger where no Coven exists to form new ones.

This III° level, in most other Craft Traditions, would normally qualify for the High Priesthood. However, we feel it should be an intermediary stage where the Initiate devotes his/her time and effort to acquire a complete foundation in the forms of Sabbat Worship and Esbat Practice.

This is to preclude situations where unprepared individuals take a little from here, there and every which where and call it Wicca. We feel a solid background in Coven organization and practical theory is necessary before one could qualify as a valid member of the High Priesthood.

A person coming up through the ranks, in a Coven organized under *The Sacred Pentagraph,* would have participated in study, Coven group activity, Coven Council and Craft Ritual Ceremonial. This process builds the inner strengths and co-operative spirit necessary to draw the best efforts from an individual. It teaches how to gain the co-operation from others in a group effort.

Because a Coven is a Family by choice, the attitudes of little Hitlers would not make for the cohesion necessary in building an edifice, or a Coven group of which one could be proud.

That is why the long process of qualification, here outlined, would be essential to a valid member of the Craft Hierarchy.

From this point on, the higher Initiations would be handled by the Craft Elders of the Covendom or Tradition. No one of any Degree lower than III° would view an Initiation to the High Priesthood or to Elder status beyond.

Normally, at an elevation of a Practicus/Hand Maiden to High Priesthood, the only III° person present would be the Initiate being elevated him/herself. All others would be members of the High Priesthood from throughout the Covendom and the Elders themselves.

The reason being, the "Vocationals," above the first five levels of the basics, concern those who have devoted and those who are willing to devote total commitment to the needs of the Craft and Coven.

This point puts the Initiate on the path toward eventually being able to assume High Priesthood status and, hopefully, to become an Elder and work in the Mystic Coven of Seven, the Inner Temple of the Craft.

The High Priesthood IV°
Seventh Level of Initiation

This is the office of the Keepers of the Flame, of those who mark the Times and keep the Seasons, of those who mediate the Mysteries of the Old Gods in the lives of Coveners. This Office confers the power to form new Covens.

The Elders will keep those of the III° under close observation to see which are able to conduct rituals with effective intensity, thus being able to mediate the intention of Sabbat worship and help those of lesser evolution experience the joys and Mysteries of the Old Gods.

Those who are able to inspire others with their deep-set Faith and are able to channel higher forces down to Earth Level as a benefit to bless lesser beings, may be considered for advancement to IV°.

The Power Hungry and Seekers of Ego Gratification are not to be considered. The ill tempered and argumentative, the faultfinders and the petty should have fallen by the wayside long before III°.

However things may be with any Coven group, those adverse negative qualities will disqualify any person from being entrusted with the responsibility for the evolution and advancement of learning souls eagerly seeking the true light of the Ancient Wisdom.

The High Priesthood assumes the responsibility for the consequences of thought and action of those they foster in the Faith. The Elders bear the responsibility for those they send out into the World as a valid High Priesthood. The Coven itself bears the responsibility for its individual units.

All are under the Law of Compensation in the Course of Cosmos, as ordained by the Gods.

Those of the III° whose positive qualities stand forth and who fully understand the Law of Compensation in the Plan of Divine Justice, may be considered worthy of elevation to the High Priesthood.

The Ordeal should be undertaken and mastered only in the presence of valid members of the High Priesthood and Elders.

A Practicus and/or Handmaiden should, therefore only be elevated to the High Priesthood at the Full Moon of July, when the Elders of the district or Covendom hold their annual Council, after the official Meeting is finished.

Prior to this night, the Elders will have sent a summons to the High Priesthood of the Coven whose III° members have been chosen. This will have been done well enough in advance to allow the candidate(s) to procure and consecrate the Coven Broom and/or Great Wand. (See *Ceremony for the Fourth Degree, Sec. II.*)

The High Priesthood will order the two Scribes and the Summoner to cancel the regular Esbat Ceremony for that Full Moon, but to assemble the Coven and await word from the High Priesthood.

The sponsoring High Priesthood, bringing their Practicus and/or Hand Maiden to be elevated, appear before the Elders.

III° persons, being elevated, wear the formal Coven Robe, but without jewels, cingulum or sword. They do carry, however, either the Coven Broom or Great Wand they have newly consecrated.

The High Priesthood, in full regalia and symbols of authority, stand on opposite sides of their candidate (s).

The candidate(s) will undergo the Ordeal which is an oral quiz prepared by the Elders and all High Priesthood present from *Books I - IV.*

The quiz will be questions concerning the beliefs from the Tenets, the modes of Coven Worship at Sabbat and work at Esbat and points of Craft Law and Coven organization.

Each Elder and member of the High Priesthood present will ask the candidate(s) a specific question, which, when answered in a straightforward manner, unaided, will show the candidate's understanding of his/her responsibilities as a member of the High Priesthood in the Way of the Wise.

Then the candidate(s) will recite the Resolves of the IV° and sign the Pact.

The Elders will then bestow the gold/silver cingulum and the sponsoring High Priesthood will invest the candidate(s) with the High Priestly jewels. The cingulum and jewels are provided by the candidate(s) own home Coven.

The candidate(s) are then declared, by all present to be IV° and the Council of Elders is closed.

The sponsoring High Priesthood will notify their own Coven of the elevation and return to the Covenstead with the newly elevated one(s). The Coven will greet them with a party and good cheer.

Soon afterwards, the Coven Council will prepare a copy of *Books I-V* to bestow upon the new members of the High Priesthood and bid them farewell as they "Hive Off" from the Covenstead for new parts.

The older remaining members of the High Priesthood should then set about preparing others to raise to III^0 status.

The Full Moon of July is the traditional time to elevate to the High Priesthood. However, other times may be necessary to replace a resigning High Priest of High Priestess from the Coven. (See *Book I: The Covenant.*)

In this manner the Craft will ever survive. It will be able to draw upon a pool of properly trained members of a valid High Priesthood, in all parts of the Country, operating an entire Occult Lodge System with similar emphasis on the Sabbat Cycle of the Old Religion.

Magister Sacrorum and/or Queen Mother V^0 Eighth Level of Initiation

The work of a High Priest and High Priestess consists in forming a full working Coven and elevating those to "Hive Off" to form their own.

The one that has hived off is considered to be of the Covendom of the Coven from whence it came. When the new Coven has properly been founded it may look to the High Priesthood from which its own High Priesthood came as Grand Dame and Grand Peré. They aid with sage advice where they can.

When a hived off Coven hives of a Coven on its own, then Grand Dame and Grand Peré become eligible to be considered for advancement to Elder status.

A High Priest and High Priestess do not only rely on one hived off Coven to successfully prove worthy of their tutelage. They ideally should successfully hive off new Covens at least once every 10 years.

Elders must have two or more Covens to their credit.

A successful High Priest and High Priestess with the minimum two Covens, their own and a full working hived off one, do not automatically become Elders. They are junior members of the Council of Elders, due to their IV° status, but that is not yet the V^0.

The hiving off process to make one eligible for V^0 is this:

A valid High Priest and High Priestess must work together. When one alone is elevated to IV^0, he/she may not hive off until another of the same home Coven is elevated of the opposite sex to be able to function as the complimentary parental element.

Or, he/she may seek out and find a valid member of the IV° from some other Covendom who will be able to harmoniously act as the other parent to form a Coven. They must then decide to which Covendom they will then belong.

It would be best if a working Coven were able to train its III° persons simultaneously and have them compatible to work together. Such is not always the case.

A newly elevated IV° person would hive off only when an opposite parental element may go with him/her into new territories. They must then set about the labours of forming a new Coven. When they have attracted and trained the other necessary three persons, they will Center the Cone. (See *Book I: The Covenant.*)

Should both of them come from the same home Coven, their original High Priesthood then become Grand Dame and Grand Peré, to act as advisors, but not active officiants in the new Coven.

Should the two of the High Priesthood come from separate home Covens, both sets of original High Priesthood take the Grand Parent status.

When the hived off Coven, over a period of time, has the full capacity of Coveners to function in Sabbat and Esbat Circles, that is twelve for Circle Ceremonies and possibly more, and has elevated at least one III° person to IV°, who is waiting for the right to hive off, him/herself, then and only then do Grand Dame and Grand Peré become eligible to be considered for V° status.

When a valid High Priest and High Priestess have been able to meet with the requirements of the above, the Elders V° will decide among themselves the time to bestow the next Initiation.

Due to the fact this level involved only the Elders themselves, it has been decided to remove this section concerning elevation to Elder status and put it in *The Book of Elders,* which can be found as *Section IV of Book III, The Book of Lights.*

All matters pertaining to the function of the Elders in the Ancient Craft of Wicca, in the Way of the Wise, will be found therein.

There have been requests for a clarification as to who and what may constitute the Elders and to why and how they function as arbiter of Craft Lore. Therefore, it has been found more expedient to place all available information in the Way of the Wise pertaining to Elders in one tome.

Philosophus And Oracle V⁰ Ninth Level Of Initiation

When an Elder wishes to retire from active participation in Craft affairs, he/she informs all other known Elders of that fact and calls together the High Priesthoods under his/her tutelage and formally announces he/she wishes to retire. His/her reasons may be personal, or they may be forced by time and age. They will be accepted and respected by all High Priesthoods who have grown in the Faith under the guidance of that particular Elder.

The many Covens associated with that particular Elder would then set about obtaining the bejeweled Scimitar for the Philosophus, or the Moonstone Pendant for the Oracle. They should each contribute some funding to it.

There is no ceremony of elevation to this rank, but a formal Testimonial Dinner is given by the Elder's Covens at an appropriate time at the convenience of all concerned.

How that is done must be left to the ability and substance of the Covens. It should, however, be made as formal and expensive as possible. The Covens may pool their financial contributions to this effort, or each individual Coven may foot the expense for different parts of the Elder's retirement bash.

At the announcement of retirement, the Elder will take the resolves of this grade before his/her assembled High Priesthoods:

Before all of you. My gathered children and grandchildren. I, as an Elder V⁰ do hereby resolve to always be available to grant the benefit of wisdom of experience to others in the Craft. To teach worthy seekers. Within the Craft of the Ancient Lore that it may never perish. To pass on to worthy members of the Craft Magical Tools used by myself in my life's Work and to prepare my manuscripts of Magical Lore which the Elders will keep in the Codex of Craft Tradition for the benefit of all.

At the Testimonial Dinner, Witches from other traditions, who may have known, loved and worked with the retiring Elder may come to pay their respects.

The insignia of rank is bestowed upon the Elder by the ranking High Priest or High Priestess present.

Thereafter, the retiring Elder may, health-permitting, function only with the other Elders at the Yearly Council of Elders and/or in the higher Magical Rites of the Mystic Coven of Seven (see *The Book of Elders*). He/she may also attend Sabbat and/or Esbat at any of the Covens he/she has worked with over the years.

The retirement should be made as comfortable as possible. He/she may be sought out for advice, but he/she should not be expected to work in the difficult tasks of furthering Coven organization. Allow the Elder to set the key to his/her own pace in these matters.

Section II

Initiation Rituals For The Grades In The Craft

Initiation of A Neophyte

At the Vernal Equinox Sabbat, selected for this Initiation, the Pre-Initiate will arrive at the Covenstead in clothing showing good taste. We will always come before the Gods in the best we have. Jeans and T-shirts do not honour the God and Goddess in Circle.

The assembled Coven, however, will be in their formal Coven robes with cinch cords of rank.

The pre-Initiate waits outside of the Ritual Chamber as the Coven holds its Vernal Equinox Sabbat. He/she must not see any of the ceremony.

According to the instructions in *Book III: The Book of Lights*, a small credence table is set to the side of the Altar for the Vernal Equinox Sabbat. This table will contain the items necessary for Initiations to be given on that night.

For the Neophyte, a stick of floral or herbal incense will be set to burn before the Pre-Initiate is brought in. There will also be a small chalice of water, a small white votive candle burning and a small dish of salt.

There is also the Holy Sabbat Anointing Oil of Rosemary and Verbena in a small vial near the candle.

After the main body of the Sabbat Ritual has been celebrated, the High Priesthood will inform the Summoner and the Sponsor to fetch the Pre-Initiate.

He/she is escorted in and brought to the Northeastern door of the Sabbat Circle. (The Summoner and Sponsor will have made the proper openings in the Circle barrier when they exited to fetch the Initiate.)

The Initiate is not blindfolded nor bound in any way. One enters the Craft of free will and by personal choice.

The High Priest issues a challenge:

Summoner, what have you brought before us?

The Summoner says: *A Postulant seeking the Light of the Ancient Wisdom, my Lord.*

The High Priestess responds: *Does the Postulant come of free will and by personal choice to this Temple of the Old Gods?*

The Sponsor answers: *Yea, my Lady, he/she does.*

High Priest: *Know, O seeking one, that only by your mastery of the Ordeal of the pre-Initiate have you been summoned here. Is it your wish to accept the other ordeals and disciplines necessary to seek the Love and Light of the Old Gods?*

Initiate: *It is my choice and desire, my Lord.*

High Priestess: *Enter this Sacred Grove, this Holy Place, this Temple of Light and be blessed.*

The Summoner and Sponsor bring the Initiate into the Circle and stand him/her before the Altar facing the High Priesthood. They then step back to their places in Circle. (The Circle is not closed behind them, for Initiates on this level are not full Wiccans and may not be totally enclosed in Circle with the true Brothers and Sisters of the Craft.)

The High Priest takes up the candle and incense and passes them around the head of the Postulant and says:

The Air element and the Fire are the symbols of your rightful Spiritual Father. They inspire and empower. Keep always faith with them.

The High Priestess takes up the Chalice of water and a pinch of salt. She says:

The Water and the Earth are the symbols of your Rightful Spiritual Mother. They emote and sustain. Keep faith with them and your Works will prosper all your days. A sip of water and a taste of salt are given.

The symbols are replaced on the credence table. The High Priestess takes up the vial of oil and puts a dab on her strongest hand.

The High Priest places his hands on the Postulant's shoulders.

The High Priestess says as she anoints the brow of the Postulant:

By the power of the Old Gods' love, I dedicate this putified vessel to the way of the Wise, the Ancient Craft of Wicca and the ways of Witchery.

The High Priest says: *This charge we lay on you: to perfect your being in knowledge and labour to learn the lore and wisdom you will be taught in the Outer Portico of the Temple. We dedicate you a Neophyte to the Ancient Craft in the Way of the Wise. Blessed be.*

The Summoner and Sponsor now step forward and escort the new Neophyte from the Ritual Chamber. He/she must wait again outside.

The Summoner and Sponsor return to the Circle, enter and seal the opening and step back into place. The Sabbat Ceremony continues.

When the Circle has been formally closed, the Neophyte may join the Coven for refreshments.

Initiation of a Probationer

During the year's course of study required by the Grade of Neophyte, he/she has gathered the four basic Magical Tools of the Craft.

These Tools are given over to the Covenstead so they will be put on the credence table to be used during the Initiation Ceremony when they are explained and presented to the Initiate. They must be virgin; that is, not used by anyone for magical purposes prior to that time.

On the night of the Vernal Equinox, one year hence from becoming a Neophyte, he/she is summoned to the Covenstead and should be in a well-dressed and tasteful set of attire.

After any Pre-Initiates, there may be for this year, have been given the Grade of Neophyte, the Neophyte to be elevated is fetched into the Ritual Chamber by the Summoner and, if possible, by the same Sponsor.

Again he/she comes unbound and of free will.

This time the Summoner and Sponsor set the neophyte at the Northeastern gate of the Circle and step in and take their own places in Circle.

The High Priest says:

We see you have mastered the Ordeal of the Neophyte and come before us to be fostered further in the Faith. Is that your wish?

Initiate: Yes, my Lord, it is.

The High Priestess: *Your path from this point will become more difficult and demanding. Is that also your wish and desire?*

Initiate: *Yes, my Lady. The Gods guide my way.*

The high priestess: Enter, then, and be welcome at the Altar of Wicca.

The Initiate steps into the Circle and stands before the Altar.

The High Priest takes up the Initiate's Thurible off the credence table, passes it over his/her head and says:

As you progress to Mastery in the Ancient Craft in the Way of the Wise, as you one day become a Witch in the valid Tradition of the Ancient Order of Bell, Book and Candle, command of the Powers of the Element of Mystic Intuition and that known as "Air" will be your aim.

This Censer is the tool of that element. It will burn the sufummigations to invoke the positive powers. It will burn the censes to drive out the negative forces. I lay the charge upon you to learn the Lore of the Censer.

The Thurible is replaced and he takes up the Athamé and continues:

The Weapon of the Witch, this Blade of Art. Never is it to be drawn against human entities. Never blood of mankind must it taste. In its Spiritual Consecration it makes you Master of the Fire Realm, the weilder of an adamant Will. With it Will is imposed on persons, places and things. With it banishings of evil are properly employed. Be charged, therefore, to learn the Lore of the Blade and be the Ruler of the Fire Power.

The High Priest then sets the blade back down and steps aside.

The High Priestess steps forward and takes up the Chalice. She says:

This Cup of Life stands for the Mother Goddess. It will contain the Waters and Lustrations and the pure emotions of a Blessed Being. From the Goddess you came and to Her you will go. Take this charge to learn the lessons of love.

She replaces the Chalice and takes up the Pentacle:

This is the foundation of the other three. This is the solid world of form and firmament. This is the Mystical Shield and defense of your Magical Power. Take the charge to learn the Lore of the Earth Element.

The Pentacle is replaced on the table and she steps aside. The High Priest says:

By the Four Fold Blessing of the Mystical Forces, you become elevated to the grade of Probationer. Blessed be.

The new Probationer now steps out of the Circle and leaves the Ritual Chamber. The Circle is sealed behind him/her and the regular Sabbat Ceremony is concluded.

Now the Probationer is to embark on the real work of becoming a Witch. His/her Magical Tools are returned to him/her after the ceremony, so that the work of the Ordeal of the Probationer may begin from that point.

Initiation to Craftmanship I°

Upon becoming a Probationer, the Initiate must continue the classes given by the High Priesthood and/or any teaching Artisans II°. These classes, however, teach the meat of magical Ritual Methods. The Probationer will be taught all necessary correspondences and astrological connections for the Art Magical.

He/she will also set about figuring the proper times for the minor consecrations for the magical Tools. The basic robe is also made.

One is admonished not to rush the Probationer, but to allow him/her to proceed at his/her own rate and speed. A period of at least six months should be sufficient to remain as a Probationer. This allows sufficient time to master the knowledge on a basic level of Magic and Occultism.

The best time to initiate a Probationer to Craftsman status would be on a day or night just before a regular meeting of the Coven Council. That way, the majority of the Coven will be present and have an opportunity to see the Craftsman perform.

It may also be given on a night just prior to a New or Full Moon Esbat. However, after the Initiation, the Craftsman is to either leave the Ritual Chamber, not to see the Coven Esbat works, or may be allowed to observe outside Circle this one time only as to how a Coven works its will on magical matters. This is left to the collective decision of the High Priesthood and the Coven Council as to whether or not they wish a non-Covener to see the Esbat works.

At the time set for the ceremony, the Probationer appears at the Covenstead in robe, without hood (as per instructions in *Book V*).

He/she has also made the blue cingulum cord, but does not yet wear it. The Coven has provided the hand bell, which will be bestowed on the Initiate as a gift for having successfully mastered the Ordeal of the Probationer.

A small Altar has been set in the center of the ritual space with a blue candle burning at the center. Around it rest the Probationer's Thurible burning a Mercurial Incense, his/her Athamé, Chalice and Pentacle. (The Initiate must set the Altar for him/herself, as the Tools are by now consecrated to him/her.)

The Chalice holds a bit of salted water and the Pentacle holds salt.

The Summoner calls the Coven to order thus:

Coven of ________, hear me. Attend upon this Ancient Rite. A Postulant to the Craft seeks thy presence. By mastery of the Ordeal of Probationer, he/she has that right.

The Probationer then proceeds to Casting The Circle of Initiates:

Standing at the Altar, the Postulant says:

I build a Temple. I make a Holy Place in the manner of the Ancient Faith from long ago. Blessed be.

Taking up the Athamé, the Postulant moves to the North of the Altar facing out. Pointing it to the North Quarter, the Postulant declares:

Come, O Powers of the Witches Will, I arouse thee from slumber. Attend to me and build my barrier at this Mystic Gate.

The Athamé, held high is carried around widdershins to the West Quarter and pointed as the same call is made. Then the same at the South and East. Finally a salute with the Athamé is made at the North to complete the Circle.

The blade is replaced on the Altar and a bit more incense set to burn.

With the Thurible held high, the Postulant again walks to the North. An invoking pentagram made in the air at that Quarter with these words:

Come the Old Gods. Comes the Power to create the Sacred Circle of Wiccan Lore. Blessed be the Ancient Faith.

The Postulant moves around widdershins with the incense, drawing the Invoking Pentagram at each Quarter and repeating the call, from North to North again. The Circle is complete.

Returning to the Altar, the Incense is replaced on it. Taking up the Athamé once again, the Postulant moves to the Northeast of the Circle and cuts a doorway in the air at that point. He/she steps back and bows the head.

Both the High Priest and High Priestess have been waiting at that point. He with the hand bell, and she with the blue cingulum cord.

They both step into the Circle and move to stand before the Altar facing the Postulant. (Again the Circle would not be sealed behind them, because the Probationer, becoming a Craftsman, is still not a full member of a Coven family. A true Witch would never be completely sealed inside a Magic Circle except with those of the Coven Family to who he/she would trust his/her own life.)

The High Priest says:

Postulant, you have learned well. A Temple of the Old Gods has been erected in the Ancient Way. In it you are able to receive and mediate the Mysteries of the God and Goddess. In it the Works of your true Witches Will may manifest in the Arts of Spellcraft and Witchery. Assume then this Bell to command the Spirits as is the right of the Craftsman I°.

He rings the bell once for the God and twice for the Goddess and hands it to the Postulant.

He continues:

Recite the Resolves of the First Degree.

The Postulant recites:

Within this Circle, before this Company and the Spirit of the Ancient Gods, I, hereby resolve...to honour the Faith in the Way of the Wise. To dedicate myself to living the balanced life of the Thirteen Creeds and the Precepts of Cosmic Order. To accept the Religious Rubrics of the Craft and study the Sabbat Rituals in order to properly contribute my part in the worship of the Old Gods at the Eight Holy Days of the year. Blessed be.

The High Priestess now speaks:

By thy own Oath, O Postulant, thou hast bound thyself to the Ancient Craft in the Way of the Wise and begun to assume the symbols of the Ancient Order of Bell, Book and Candle. Should thy path lead thee away from this Coven Family, thou still hast our love and respect as a Brother/Sister Witch. The Blue Cord of the Air Element is the rank of thy status.

She binds the cord around the Postulant's waist.
Both the High Priesthood proclaims:

Thou are forever a Witch in the rightful way of the Ancient Faith. Thou art Craftsman 1°.

The high priestess continues:

Craftsman, complete thy Ordeal.

The High Priesthood depart the Circle and the Craftsman takes the Athamé and draws a barrier cross at their point of exit (NE) sealing the Circle.

The new Craftsman must now properly banish the Circle.

Returning the Athamé to the Altar, he/she takes up the Chalice of Water. Moving to the North Quarter, the Chalice is elevated to the North and a Banishing Pentagram is drawn at that point with these words:

Spirits and Powers of Witchery's Ways, let be peace between me and thee. Return to thy place in time and space. Blessed be and blessed be.

The same is done at all points at the Quarters moving deosil from North to North.

The Chalice is replaced on the Altar and the Pentacle with salt taken up. A sprinkling of salt is made at the four Quarters around the Circle in silence moving deosil.

Then the Craftsman steps to the altar and says: IT IS DONE.

He/she rings the bell thirteen times to clear the atmosphere and snuffs out the candle.

The Coven then greets and honours the new Craftsman I°.

His/her Magical Tools must then be put away and taken from the Covenstead by the Craftsman when he/she departs.

Ceremony For a Covenor

How long one is to remain in Craftsman status is to be determined by the Coven Council in their observation of the person. They are the ones who will be working in Magic Circle together and work their will in one accord to accomplish the Arts of Coven Spellcraft at Esbat. They must have only those who would be a harmonious asset to them.

When they feel the Craftsman is right for their family, they will inform the High Priesthood of that decision. The next New Moon Esbat the Craftsman will be summoned to the Covenstead. That is the first indication he/she will have that the Coven has accepted him/her.

He/she will be told to begin to study the necessary Esbat rituals peculiar to the Coven and to take the Covenant and study the obligations of Craft Law. He/she will not be allowed to attend the New Moon Esbat on that night. He/she must make or buy the formal hooded Coven robe.

One month hence, at the next New Moon, this formality is observed prior to the Esbat Ceremony:

The Craftsman arrives at the Covenstead in hooded robe carrying his/her green cingulum cord. The Coven Council has provided the blank book to bestow on the Initiate as a Magical Diary, to be kept from this time on.

The cord is given over to the Second Scribe.

The Summoner calls the Coven to order: *Coven of________, by Will of all. We have summoned a Craftsman to enter the family. Give ear to the proper rite.*

The First Scribe presents the Coven copy of the Covenant along with pen and ink.

He/she says: *Craftsman. It is our Collective Will that you be accepted as a member of this Coven Family. Is it also your Will and Choice?*

The Initiate says: *It is my Will. Blessed be.*

The First Scribe then says: *Recite then the Resolves of the Covener.*

The Initiate: *As a Covener I resolve...to honour and abide by the Laws of the Covenant. To contribute the best possible effort as a harmonious unit within the Family Circle of the Coven. To study and learn the Esbat Rites of the Coven and be able to meld properly therein. Blessed be.*

The First Scribe then offers the pen to the Initiate. He/she signs his/her legal name into the Register of Seals in the Covenant. He/she then kisses the page to seal it. The First Scribe steps back and the Second Scribe steps forward and says:

You belong to us and we belong to you. Your seeking soul has now found its place at the hearthfire of the Old Religion. Take the cord of green, the fertile verdure colour of our living Mother the Earth and take the book to record the wisdom your journey in life in the ancient faith will teach you. He/she binds the cord around the Initiate and hinds him/her the book.

The Summoner then says: *We salute you Covener 1°.*

Then the new Covener may join in the Esbat Ritual after all Coveners have greeted him/her with an embrace.

Should a Coven be new, without a full contingent of Officers, the High Priesthood will bestow the Initiation.

In the deliberations to determine the acceptance of the Craftsman as a Covener, the High Priesthood would of course be included in the decision. However, they act as individual members of the Coven Council and not in the power and prestige of High Priesthood.

The Coven Officers will, if at all possible, carry the task of presenting the good points of the Craftsman to the Coven for deliberation. (See *The Covenant, Laws of the Craft, Sec. J:15.*)

Those Craftsmen not accepted to the Coven as a whole, are still

Brothers and Sisters in the Faith, and in no way unworthy of respect and consideration as such.

He/she may at all times be acceptable to worship the Old Gods at Sabbat, according to the Covenant, and accept a fair share in Coven maintenance.

It may be that one's life circumstances make it impossible to devote more than Craftsman participation in the Coven. Let the Craftsman determine for him/herself the wish to advance beyond that status.

Should the Craftsman wish to depart for other parts or other Covendoms, the proper documentation per Covenant, Laws (*Sec. G:5-6*) will be issued.

It may happen, after one has been accepted as a Covener, that an incompatibility with other Coveners and/or members of the High Priesthood may arise. Rather than allow such a thing to mar the proper functioning of the Coven and its effectiveness as a working unit, the incompatible one will be told by the collective will of the Coven members to "Get Thee Hence." The incompatible one will then seek the proper documentation from the High Priesthood to rightfully depart. This applies to Coveners of I° status only.

Should such an irreversible incompatibility develop after one has advanced above Covener I° status, that is the II° or III°, who are under the scrutiny and observation of the Elders, the High Priesthood of the Coven the incompatible one wishes to depart, take him/her before the Elders of the District or Covendom and discuss the matter thoroughly.

Artisans II° are true Priests and Priestesses of the Craft, and the Hand Maidens and Practicuses III° are Acolytes to the High Priesthood and may not be lightly treated. They deserve consideration before the Elders.

The Elders will try, from their sage wisdom, to eliminate the causes of friction so the Coven may function properly.

If such can not be done, the High Priesthood, in the interests of fairness to those who have advanced so far in the Craft, will act as sponsor to train and elevate them and see their proper Initiations bringing them to the IV° in the Craft, so they may rightfully "Hive Off".

In this case, the II° and III° persons must temporarily bide their time and set about the proper studies to qualify them for the IV°.

This will eliminate any unprepared persons from splitting off and giving out claims of High Priesthood status that the Elders have not declared.

The Lamp of Art

Consecration Ritual for Coveners I° soon to become Artisan II° in the Craft.

When the High Priesthood feels the time is right, and the Covener knows he/she has mastered the necessary requirements for II°, the Lamp of Art is purchased and dedicated thus:

On a Night of Mercury, as the Moon waxeth, the lamp is set in a ring of salt. A purple candle is set to burn in it. As it burns, the Covener says:

In the flickering candle light the Old Lore has been taught for many a year. The light that comes from darkness is the symbol of the Craft. As I prepare to take the vows as a priest/priestess of the Old Gods, let me find illumination in my heart, inspiration in my mind and light in my life to always walk in fairness with my Coven and my faith. If I be called as a teacher and guide to lesser ones, let the Lamp light my path and those for whom I am responsible. Blessed be. Let the candle burn out. The Lamp must rest in the ring of salt for three days. Then it is cleaned and set aside until the time for the II° Initiation.

Whenever the Artisan teaches a class to any Neophytes or Probationers, he/she carries the lit lamp into the class and keeps it burning during the lessons. The act of dispersing illumination is the province of the Artisan.

Ceremony for the Artisan II°

On the Night of the Full Moon, set for the Initiation for the Artisan, the Initiate arrives at the Covenstead in formal Coven robe but without cingulum of Covener status. The yellow cingulum and the newly consecrated Lamp of Art are carried by the Initiate.

The Altar is set with the Initiate's Magical tools as for the ritual to Craftsman status, but with a yellow candle. The items necessary for the Initiate to cast a spell or consecrate a proper Talisman are also there. An incense proper to the spell is burning in the Thurible.

The Lamp of Art and the yellow cingulum are given over to the High Priesthood.

The Summoner calls all to order: *Witches attend! One who has demanded the right to undergo the Ordeal of the Artisan II° bids your leave.*

The Initiate then, without further ado, casts the Circle of Initiates, as for the I° ceremony, casts a spell and banishes the Circle in proper fashion.

Before beginning, however, the First Scribe, or the one who had laid the Witches Challenge upon the Initiate, sets an hour glass, which would measure at least a half hour, upon the Altar and says:

Thou has boasted of thy Witchy ways to us of the Priesthood both high and low. Ere the sands of time run out, this spell must be completed without a fault. So be it done.

The Initiate must complete the task in that allotted time, however, he/she is not to speedily rush and do a sloppy or haphazard job. (This is to ensure that the Initiate has learned and rehearsed the ritual job to perfection.)

When the Ordeal has been mastered, the Coven gathers around the Initiate as the High Priesthood step forward. The High Priest carries the yellow cingulum and the High Priestess carries the Lamp of Art burning a purple taper.

He says: Well done, Postulant. We see the Craft is honoured by thy works. Recite now the resolves of the Artisan II°.

Initiate: Surrounded by my Coven Family, I resolve...to use the Art Magical and the Craft of the Faith only for the benefit of the Coven Family and for individual well being. Not to practice the Arts and Crafts of the Faith on a debased level. To help and aid the High Priesthood to teach the fundamentals of Wicca to aspiring souls. Blessed be.

The High Priest continues:
The yellow shade of cord about the waist shows the Priest/Priestess of the Ancient Craft. Accept it now and bless thyself with the Rite of the Water Element. (He girds the yellow cinch cord about the Initiate.)

The Initiate takes up his/her Chalice from the Altar and sprinkles a bit upon him/herself with these words: *May my forceful Witch Works of Will be yet tempered by feeling and compassion. Let me walk in the Old Gods' love and light. Blessed be.*

The High Priestess now steps forward and circumambulates the Initiate with the burning Lamp of Art thrice with these words:

Thou hast taken the Bell and the Initiation of Air; thou hast taken the Book and the Initiation of Earth; thou now takest the Candle and the Grade of the Water Element. The venerable order of Bell, Book and Candle is now satisfied in thee. (She hands the Lamp to the Initiate, who is still holding the Chalice of water.) *Balance what thou hast in thy hands; the Light of Knowledge and the Womb of Compassion. Know when and where to use them. Thou are Artisan II°.*
Shouldst thou seek the higher grades of Fire and Spirit, the Elders may call thee. For now rest from thy labours and serve the Craft and all her children as a Priest/Priestess of the Art Magical in the Ancient Craft in the way of the wise. Blessed be.

The Coven may then move to its regular Full Moon Esbat.
The Magical Tools used by the Initiate are his/her own and not to be handled by any other. He/she must see to their proper care and put them away to take home after Esbat.

The Sword of Art

Consecration Ritual for those who will soon become III° in the Craft.

When the High Priesthood tell the Artisan II° to begin to study for the III° Initiation, he/she must then search out, find and purchase a suitable sword, a ring with a red stone and a red leather belt if one it to become a Practicus – or a necklace of red beads and a red garter, if one is to become a Hand Maiden. Those are the insignia of the Witch III°.

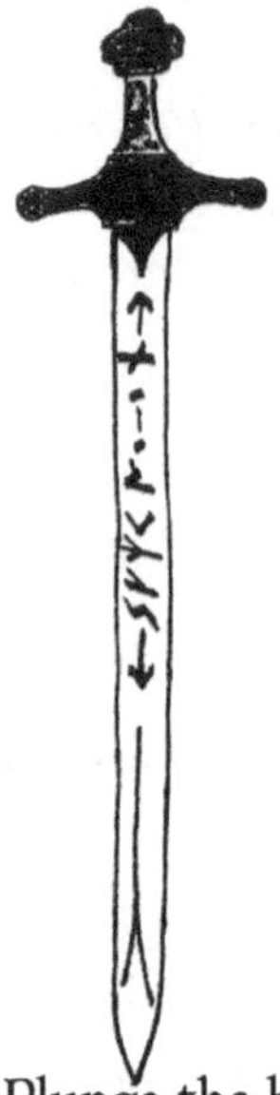

The High Priestess will fashion the red cingulum to be given the candidate at the Initiation Ceremony. The cingulum will thereafter be worn whenever the Coven Ritual prescribes formal robed attire for the Hand Maiden or Practicus.

The ring and belt, or beads and garter will thereafter be worn by the III° Witch with any casual attire daily out in public. Thus other Witches will know and recognize the III° as aspirants to the High Priesthood.

Ceremony of the Sword

On a Day of Sol, at the rising of the Sun as the orb of the Moon be on the increase, just prior to the III° Initiation, the blade of the sword must be symbolically forged in fire.

Set a brazier (BBQ type) alight with glowing coals. Plunge the blade deep into them until it becomes quite hot.

Have a barrel or large container of water nearby. The blade is heated and plunged into the water thrice. The water must hiss from the heat. (Be careful, however not to damage the blade by making it too hot.)

Heat the blade, whisper a secret name over it and plunge it into the water thrice.

Pass the blade then through the smoke of Frankincense as you silently dedicate the Sword to the Works of Witchery and your own power in the Craft.

Clean the blade and set it away to be used at the Initiation Ceremony. Thereafter, never let any other person touch or wield your blade.

Should the Sword ever need to be carried into a house where Wicca abides, let it enter hilt first, rather than blade first, so it is not seen as a weapon of hostile intent.

Elevation to III°

Prior to the Ceremony the High Priestess has fashioned the red Cingulum for the Initiate(s). The Minor Jewels have been procured and are in the keeping of the High Priest until the Ceremony.

At the appointed time, the Summoner calls the Coven to order:

Coven of _________, attend to me. An Artisan II° has chosen and been called to seek the Higher Paths. Give ear and respect to one who will be dedicated to the Craft to serve at the Altar of the Old Gods. Blessed be.

The Coven gathers around as the Initiate gives a 10-minute lecture on some aspect of Witchcraft he/she has researched (without notes or briefing aids). One must know the lore of Witchery well enough to disclaim it at length when needed.

Then the second part of the Ordeal begins:

The Witches Banishing Ritual of the Pentagram

This is a ritual act of creating a consecrated space in the midst of space and time to banish and drive forth any adverse and/or negative activity from around and in the affairs of an accomplished Witch. It builds the Fortress of Witches Will to forcefully withstand the possible onslaughts from those we term enemies of the Faith, those called Sorcerers and Black Magicians, from the Workers of Darkness and Servants of Chaos and Old Night.

When the spawn of Evil be abroad in the land, a Witch of at least III° will be sent out by the Coven to seek out its source. He/she will build this fortress and resist the Evil and block its progress. With the sword, a barrier is laid upon the direction or place from whence the Evil comes to bar the way and send it back to its point of origin. The Witch will remain in this circle resisting and forbidding further progress of the Works of Darkness until it dissipates and flees back to feed on the mind and body of its sender.

It is an eternal Law of the Cosmos, of the Ancient Path of the Old Gods that no matter how strong and powerful Negative Evil may seem to be, when the Positives are invoked and properly directed, the

Negative must always give place. The key is in being strong of heart and persevering of nature to win out in the long run.

For the ritual, the Coven will provide a consecrated Thurible to burn Frankincense and Myrrh, a powerfully charged Athamé dedicated to banish ill, a consecrated Chalice to contain salted water and a Pentacle of wood or metal 10 inches across bearing a white Pentagram on a black background.

These are set at their respective Quarters around the area to be used by this ritual creating a Circle space of at least 9-foot in diameter. (Normally these Hallows will be wrapped in a sack to be carried by III° to the place needed and set out when the ritual is to begin. However, for the purposes of this Initiation Ceremony, they are already in place.)

When this ritual would be used in actual practice by a Witch of at least III° he/she would wear proper cingulum and jewels of rank. For the employ of it in an Initiation, he/she has not yet been declared III°, and the ritual is only conducted to show mastery of the skill.

When all is ready the Initiate takes up his/her sword and steps to the North Quarter of the ritual area by the Pentacle. The Sword is pointed to the earth and its point is pulled along the floor or ground straight across the Circle to the Athamé at the South Quarter, drawing a line and held firmly in mind by the Initiate.

He/she moves to the East and does the same, drawing a line with the point of the Sword across to the Chalice in the West.

This produces a Solar Cross to mark off the space encompassed by the Circle. As it is being drawn from Quarter to Quarter, the Initiate says:

North to South and East to West. This world of cosmos is pure and blessed.

Moving to the North again, the Sword is held out and pointed to that Quarter. A large Banishing Pentagram is inscribed in the air with it and these words spoken:

From the Northern Gate of Ice, be thou barred O Works of Darkness.

Moving Deosil to the East another Pentagram is inscribed with these words:

By the Light of the Gates of Dawn. Thou art shut out O Spawn of Chaos.

Moving to the South and pointing the Sword and inscribing another Banishing Pentagram these words are spoken:

The Fire Castle of Flaming Power guard against all evil will.

Moving to the West the Pentagram is again drawn and this spoken:

The Great Barrier Sea prevents thy passage. O ye Serpent Wiles of Old Night.

The Initiate again continues around to the North to complete the Circle and draws a barrier cross at that Quarter and says:

The Seal and Bonds of the Old Gods be upon thee. It is done.

The Initiate then goes to the center of the Circle and sits down and lays the Sword across the knees and faces the East. He/she invokes thus:

God and Goddess, Lord and Lady, Light and Love, Powers of the Cosmos and the Forces of Positive Mien, give me thy might and strength to keep vigil at the edge of the Abyss. Aid me to defend the world against that which would spread chaos and evil. I shall persevere in the Old Gods' Love. Blessed be.

(Normally the Witch would then keep vigil inside this Astral Fortress and work whatever spells and banishings as may be needed to continue to resist and weaken the dark forces. He/she would have any candles and censes and other necessary items to break and send back whatever powers were being resisted.)

For the purposes of the Initiation, however, nothing else is necessary. The Initiate has erected the proper barrier and sits immovable within.

When employed in actual combat against dark forces, the barrier would never be torn down. The Witch would be a sentinel at that point for as long as it takes to win out.

Standing in the path of approaching evil, this barrier will block it. The negative will rush upon the walls of the barrier and create an astral storm that the Witch will feel. The walls will shake but hold and the evil will slip back to its own darkness pulling the barrier seals with it, thus locking itself up to return to its sender. The Witch may then safely leave the area.

For the purposes of the use of this ritual in an Initiation to III° status, a Covener will now ring the hand bell 13 times to astringe the atmosphere of the Ritual Chamber and allow the Initiate to leave the area where the barrier was erected. The Ordeal is over and mastered.

The High Priesthood now steps forward as the Initiate sets down the Sword and stands before them.

The High Priest says: *In ancient times the grade you now earn was that of Exorcist, nowadays it is called Acolyte to the Altar of Wicca. We invest you with the minor jewels of rank.*

He hands the ring and belt to the Initiate if he is a male or the beads and garter to the Initiate if she is female.

He continues: *Recite now the Resolves of the III°.*

Initiate: Called to serve at the Altar of Wicca, I resolve: to edify the Old Gods in all my works. To obey the High Priesthood in all matters concerning worship at Sabbat and Craft Works at Esbat. To learn continually in order to one day assume the leadership of a Coven of the Faithful as a worthy parent and guardian. Blessed be.

The High Priestess now speaks:

We have trained you and elevated you in the Faith. We have spoken for you before the Elders. Be then worthy of our trust in you. From this day/night, your duty is to spread love and light to all those who worship at the Altar of our God and Goddess. Remember, not all the Gods' children and creatures are as exalted as you. Be patient and restrained with those of lesser degree, be at peace and in good faith with those who are your equals. Stand firm against the evil doers and resist the pull of the dark side of things. Accept the Red Cord of Fire and be Practicus/Hand Maiden III°.

She girds the cord around the Initiate and says: Blessed be the road you embark upon. The Craft now becomes your only concern in this life.

The Coven anniversary celebration may now begin.

The Coven Broom

Domestic Symbol of the Authority of the High Priestess.

This is a broom made in the old way. It can be fashioned by the Hand Maiden herself, when called by the Elders to prepare to become a High Priestess, or it may be purchased for her by the Coven.

Standing in her full robes and regalia, with the broom in hand, the High Priestess represents the will of the Coven, the authority of the Goddess and the spiritual power of Wicca. All will bow or curtsy before this powerful figure.

Ceremony for the Broom

On a Day of Luna as she waxeth, the soon-to-be High Priestess must use the Broom to sweep 20 copper pennies from outside into the center of the Covenstead floor. Symbolically insuring prosperity for her reign.

On a day of Luna, as she waneth, the Broom must be used to sweep clean the entire Covenstead and push the dust out the door. Symbolically banishing things unwanted.

Then on the next Day of Luna as she waxeth, these words must be spoken over the Broom:

Frick and Frack, forward and back, let there never be blight or lack. Banish the wolf from before the door and be a blessing to both rich and poor.

The Broom is then set aside by the Hand Maiden until the day or night of her Initiation to the IV^0.

At that time, she appears before the Elders in formal Coven robe, without cingulum, but with Broom in hand.

Thereafter, she carries the Broom at Esbat Ceremony in processional. She does not carry it at Sabbat. She stands with it in hand when she must make pronouncements of import to the Coven. Bush upward if the tidings are dire, and downward if all is well.

The Coven Great Wand

Domestic Symbol of the Authority of the High Priest.

The Great Wand is a staff at least as tall as the High Priest himself.

Standing in his robes and regalia, with the Great Wand in hand, he represents the total will of the Coven, the authority of the God and the enforcement of the Laws of Wicca. All will give honour and deference to his imposing figure.

When a III^0 person is called by the Elders to prepare to become a High Priest, he will go out into Nature and seek a suitable staff.

Consecration of the Great Wand

On a Day and Hour of Mercury, as the Lunar Orb waxeth...

The Wand is to be sprinkled with salted water and passed thrice through the smoke of Benzoin as the soon-to-be High Priest says:

Staff of the Prophet, Staff of the Shepherd, Rod of Power, Imposer of Will, all these be thy domain. Blessed be.

The Wand is then put aside until the next Day and Hour of Sol when it again sprinkled with salted water and passed six times through the smoke of Frankincense as these words are spoken:

Be my symbol of the Laws of the Ancient Craft in the Way of the

Wise. Let me lean my weariness on thee. Guide my footsteps to foster the Faith. Bar the gate to the stranger and deciever, but admit the seeker true of heart.

The Wand is then laid on the floor with upper end to the North. A magnet is placed at the North and South with the Wand resting between them. It is to lie thus for six days.

When the Initiation to the IV⁰ is to commence, the candidate appears before the Elders in formal robe, without cingulum, but with Great Wand in hand.

Thereafter, the Great Wand is carried by the High Priest at all Esbat Ceremonies in processional. He does not carry it at Sabbat. He stands with it in hand at all times when he must make official pronouncements concerning Coven affairs.

Ceremony to the IV°

The decision to elevate a person to High Priestly office rests heavy upon the Elders themselves. It would depend on the needs of the Coven which has qualified persons of III° and which is growing in the Faith as it should so that a valid "Hive Off" can be made.

Other particular considerations are given in the *The Book of Elders, Section IV, Book III: The Book of Lights.* (*The Book of Elders* was written in answer to a need by certain Crafters to know the inner workings of the Council of Elders and the occult traditions of the Mystic Coven of Seven.)

At the Council of Elders held at the Full Moon in July, after the regular business of the Council is concluded, these waiting to be elevated are brought forward and into the presence of the Elders by their own High Priestess and High Priest. (Perhaps several Covens are having members elevated on a particular Full Moon in July and an orderly process of one at a time should be arranged. Perhaps by age of the sponsoring Coven, or by alphabetical order of the Initiates themselves.)

The Elders will face the High Priesthood who stand flanking their candidate. The one acting as Scribe of the Council of Elders will ask:

By thy manner and mien as thou standeth before us, we see thou hast brought forth a Child of the Gods. Dost thou vouch for him/her?

The High Priest will answer: *We vouch for all our Coven Children – this one in particular.*

The Scribe of the Council of Elders: *Upon thy honour as the rightful and valid High Priesthood of Wicca in the Way of the Wise dost thou verify thy candidate to be properly qualified to be elevated as an equal to thyself?*

High Priest: *Not as equal in our Coven, but as equal to rightly hive off in the Faith. He/she is qualified to be a mentor to other Children of the Old Gods.*

Scribe: *Candidate, dost thou come of thy own free will to the responsibility of this degree in the Craft?*

Initiate: *Lord/Lady Elder, it is my will.*

Scribe: *Let the Ordeal begin.*

Each Elder and Member of the High Priesthood (even those from other Covens present) will pose a specific question to the Candidate on any point of Coven and/or Craft Law, or on points of Sabbat Ritual, or on points of Esbat practice from *Books I-IV.*

The questions are not to be obscuritanist in nature to trap the Candidate, but to show, when answered, that the Candidate understands the duties and obligations of a High Priest and/or High Priestess.

When the Ordeal is finished, the Scribe of the Council of Elders says:

Thou hast mastered the Ordeal. Recite now the Resolves of the IV°.

Initiate: Before thee, Lords and Ladies, Elders and High Priesthood and before my Spiritual Mother and Father in the Faith and before my God and Goddess I hereby resolve: to teach the Way of the Wise to all true seekers. To lead fairly and justly with consideration and compassion for all. To expand the Faith by founding Covens and properly elevating deserving initiates. To ever act as a worthy representative of the Old Gods and properly mediate between spiritual things and the needs of humankind. Blessed be.

The Scribe of the Council of Elders now brings forth the Pact. He/she says:

In days of old and initiate's measure was wrought to insure fidelity to the Coven and protection of the Brothers and Sisters in the Craft. If one fell into the snare of the witchburner, one would ratehr die than expose others to danger and face the magical wrath of the Coven. It is in keeping with that ancient tradition that ye who aspire to the High Priestly office assure the Elders of thy fidelity to the Craft. Sign then this Pact with us in the Faith.

(Format of the Pact:

I, __________, vow before the Elders and High Priesthood, that I will execute my duties to the Craft according to the guidelines in *Book I: The Covenant.*

Signed and sealed this ____ night of ___ in the year _____ of the Current Era.

__________; ___________ – Signature of two Elders to act in lieu of Notary.)

The Initiate signs and two Elders step forward and also sign.

The Scribe continues: *Prepare Now for Thy Spiritual Consecration*

The Initiate sets his/her Great Wand or Coven Broom before him/herself on the floor or ground and kneels before the Elders.

The Scribe of the Council of Elders has been officiating heretofore. Perhaps another Elder may step forward and continue the ceremony from this point. (If not, the Scribe will continue.)

The Elder brings forth a vial of Sacred anointing Oil of Frankincense and Myrrh and anoints an Invoking Pentagram on the Initiate's nape of the neck, on the throat and on the forehead with these words:

Accipe potestatum offere sanctificum. Accipe potestatum absolvere delictum. Accipe potestatum facere sanctum.

Thou art now set apart from the rest of mankind. Thou art now a spiritual force for good. Thou art now a holy vessel unto the Old Gods. Blessed be.

The Elder steps back. The sponsoring High Priesthood help their candidate to rise and again take up his/her Great Wand or Broom.

Another, or perhaps the same Elder, comes forward with the gold/ silver cingulum cord of rank and girds it around the candidate with these words:

With this High Priestly Vestment goes a heavy yoke of responsibility under the Law of Compensation in the Law of Cause and Effect. Thy path will not be at all times easy. We of the Elders will ever stand ready to aid thee where we can with our wisdom of experience. We will not, however, make thy load lighter. Only thou canst do that thyself by overcoming and perservering.

The Candidate's High Priest defended him/her at the beginning of the Ceremony; his/her High Priestess will now bestow the blessing and the jewels.

For a male candidate, the home Coven has provided a headband with an amethyst set in gold, which will sit in the center of his forehead. For a female Candidate the home Coven has provided a tiara bejeweled in the shape of a Crescent Moon or a Pentagram to wear atop the head.

The High Priestess will place the jewels upon the head of the Candidate and say:

Thy Crown has been attained. my child, thy work well done. Take Blessing in the Faith to other parts of this world. As thou hivest off and becomest a Mother/Father of thine own Coven. May what thou hast learned at our hearthfire inspire thee all thy days. Blessed be.

All Elders and High Priesthood draw and raise their Athamés high in salute to the Initiate, proclaim in unison: *Thou art High Priest/High Priestess IV*^{0}.

The sponsoring High Priesthood and the newly elevated ones leave the presence of the Elders.

Crossing the Veil

Ceremony For a Covener

(10th Level of Initiation)

In Coven Communities of old, it was part of Women's Mysteries to mark the coming and going of life in this world. The Priestesses of the Old Religion were also the Midwives and herbal practitioners for the Coven.

Theirs was the duty to see life in by assisting at the births of the Wiccan born. Theirs was also the duty to sit with and keep vigil by the dying to see life out of this world and send it on its way to the Gods and to spiritual progression.

It is in keeping with this age-old tradition that these ceremonies and observances are here set down.

A Craftsman I^0, not yet part of the Coven family, who passes on, should be given a candle dedicated to his/her memory on the 30th, 60th and 90th day after death.

The High Priestess will mark this observance with a prayer of dedication to joyfully elevate the spirit of the departed to the realms of the Gods.

Wicca is a religion, which respects and avows life. Wiccans know that the thing we call death is the gate to a richer life on higher planes of being.

Wiccans do not sit Shivah as the Jews, nor do they make a public display of sorrow and mourning as Christians are expected to do. Wiccans remember the deceased with smiles of love and joy, for they have gone on to better things. Wiccans do not glorify, nor "Egyptianize" the fact of death.

A Covener I^0 to IV^0 (IV^0 as being a High Priest/ess who have not yet become Elders V^0), who is active as a member of a true Coven Family, must see to it by a legal document, that his/her relatives, who may be among the Stranger (Non-Wiccan) will respect and allow the Wiccan Faith to be observed in matters of death.

As the hour for Crossing approaches, the Coven women take over the task of tending the dying. The High Priestess and women of Artisan

II°, as Priestesses of the Craft, sit with the dying to tenderly care for his/her needs in the final hours.

Relatives, visitors, spouses and lovers may come to attend and should be allowed their final respects, but under the watchful eyes of the Coven women.

A large white candle must be kept lit in the room of the dying and all mirrors should be draped with a dark cover. (Mirrors are doors to deeper, darker dimensions, and we must not allow a soul of a departing loved one be trapped in them.)

It is important that a Covener not be left to cross over alone and unattended. The High Priestess and/or female Artisans II° should be there at that time to hold the hand of the dying and give words of loving encouragement as the soul departs.

Once the crossing over has been made, never are the male members of the family or Coven to touch the body. The women's work now begins.

The body must be washed and dressed in its formal Coven Robe. Four white candles are set at the Four Quarters around the body and a silver Pentagram laid upon the breast. A small wooden dish of salt is set upon the solar plexus and the High Priestess or an Artisan II° will anoint a pentagram upon the forehead with Sabbat Oil.

The High Priestess or Artisan II° in attendance will then speak these words:

Brother/Sister, the Old Religion commends you into the Fellowship of the God and Goddess. Go now to greet them with our blessing. May you find in them perfect love and perfect trust. Blessed be.

A male member of the Coven of at least I° will then come into the room and stand beside the body. He is the "Sin Eater" to drain off the karma of any left over compensation of a negative nature that may linger to the spirit of the departed.

He carries a chalice of water and a small loaf of bread. These items he passes over the body three times in silence. He pours a few drops into the dish of salt and says:

I cleanse the Earthly remains of all that which may hold you to this realm. Be blessed and pure in the Gods' loving light.

He then eats a bit of the bread and says:

We of the Coven take to ourselves all the dross of your earthly life. Let this Alchemy of Love transmute the bad into the good. Be blessed with the Old Gods' love. Return to a loving Coven in a future day in a more perfected state of being. Blessed be the Ancient Way.

The "Sin Eater" departs and the Coven Women leave the body to lay alone. There is nothing more of the deceased in the room. The body is left to await transport to the Crematorium.

When it has finished the legal requirements, the body is to be again dressed in the formal Coven robe with the wooden dish of salt on the solar plexus. With cingulum of Craft rank coiled on the breast, the body is consigned to the flames.

The ashes are then to be given to the family to dispose of out in Nature as they see fit.

The Coveners Magic Tools must them be exorcised by the High Priest of the Coven and kept as a memento of the departed Brother or Sister, but never again used by any of the Craft, unless the deceased stipulated otherwise.

His/her writings and magical diaries may be added to the Coven library for future use.

Again, the High Priestess will mark the 30th, 60th and 90th day after death with a candle dedication and joyful prayers to help elevate the spirit of the departed.

Thus do members of the true Craft in the Way of the Wise Cross the Veil.

Should a Covener have an accidental or violent death, the same attention must be given to the body as stated above before burning.

Should the body be in a mutilated state and therefore unavailable for the proper rites, a tag lock such as a clipping of hair or a piece of garment may be used over which the rites may be given. In either event, the act of the "Sin Eater" must not be left undone.

Ceremony For a Craft Elder

An Elder of the Craft, would be totally dedicated to the Old Religion, and would see to it that these observances be done for his/her last remains.

The same vigil and ceremonies as for a Covener will be done by the High Priestesses of the two or more Covens the Elder has helped to form. These women will attend to the Elder's body.

The High Priests, of the Elders Covens, will go out into Nature, upon the death of the Elder, and seek out a high place far away from human habitation and control by the civil authorities.

They will clear a space from any bushes and undergrowth and erect a pyre of wood.

The Elder would have stipulated that his/her remains be turned over to the High Priestesses after the legal documentation of death has been handles by the civil authorities.

The High Priests, when they have prepared the high place, will contact the High Priestesses and inform them where the body is to be brought.

The High Priestess, along with all Coveners who are able, will accompany the body to the area.

The body will be placed on a bier. It will be dressed in the Elders white robe, with black cingulum cord coiled upon the breast and the dish of salt on the solar plexus.

All Coveners in attendance will wear the black formal Coven robe with insignia of rank. Hoods will be drawn up.

The male Coveners will carry the bier; the female Coveners will carry flowers and garlands.

The High Priestesses will precede the bier in procession to the high place with lit torches.

Songs and chants of joy and happiness may be sung by the procession as it is carried up to the high place. They will take it and place it on the pyre.

All Coveners will then stand in a circle around the pyre. The women will scatter the flowers and garlands onto the body.

The High Priests, standing to the South of the pyre, will speak these words:

True to the Old and Venerable Ways of our Faith, we come to this high place, under sky and in the sight of the God and Goddess to send the final essence of our beloved Elder and teacher on its final journey. Be He/She blessed forever and a day.

A male Covener will then soak the pyre with a flammable liquid to facilitate the immolation.

The High Priestess will then circumambulate the pyre thrice with their lit torches as they speak these words:

Beloved Elder, as your spirit has gone forth to the Gods, we now commit your last remains to Nature's loving embrace. May we meet again in some future known only to the mysteries of the Gods. Blessed be.

They then set the torches to the pyre.

All Coveners then bid final farewell to the memory of the Elder as the flames accept their due.

More wood may be added as needed to make a thorough burning of all remains. When finally the fire is out and the Coveners have all paid their last respects with feelings of love and tenderness for the Elder, the High Priestesses will take the cold ashes and scatter them to the four winds some distance from the pyre.

Larger bones not thoroughly burned, will now be taken by the High Priests and buried far away further out in Nature.

From that time, never is a Stranger to know the resting place of an Elder of the Craft.

The modern world being as it is, the practices of Wicca may not be understood by the civil authorities and they may not want to allow the ceremony of the Elder. The High Priestesses should see to it that all objections to the practice of our faith in this respect can be rectified.

Perhaps the high place could be on a Covener's private land, or that all can be done quietly without intervention by public officials. An attorney may be necessary to clear the way.

Perhaps the high place will have to be set up in a completely "wilderness" area and an expedition mounted to that place. The body of the Elder may be kept in a sealed wooden coffin in that event.

However it is done, we must not allow the world to force a compromise in the expression of our religious observances. Follow the *Tenet IV* from the *The Covenant,* so as not to offend the Stranger, but honour the Elders in this respect as much as possible given the abilities of the Elder's Covens.

It may happen that the body may need to be burned in a

Crematorium, but the procession and observances may still be done to take the Elder's ashes to a high place and formally scattered by the Covens which owe their existence to the life's work and dedication to the craft by the deceased Elder. The Elder's Coven should try as much as humanly possible to observe the tradition.

Should a Covener or member of the High Priesthood die before reaching Elder status, be it assumed that their souls have been purified as much as possible in the time they have been allotted. They will one day return to a Coven tradition, but their real work of advancement will not begin until they have again reached the level where they broke off in a previous life span. Therein lies an Arcanum of the Gods, ponder it.

Part II – The Minor Rites of Passage

The Rite of Handfasting

In some communities a religious minister is allowed to perform a marriage ceremony and have it recognized by the civil authorities as legal and valid. Other communities require a minister to first be licensed by the county.

The Coven entity should as soon as possible, establish corporate status under the statutes of the state to be able to qualify the High Priesthood to function as recognized and/or licensed ministers able to perform a legal marriage.

An Elder V° will act as a corporate officer, along with the members of the High Priesthood to establish legal corporate status to qualify before the laws of the State as a Church or religious institution. Normally, this task would fall to a Magister, but in the absence of one, a Queen Mother may also assume this duty.

Prior to legal acceptance of the Coven as a bonafide religious institution, a Civil ceremony, by the JP may first be necessary. Before the Wiccan Handfasting is performed to establish a spiritual foundation for Craft weddings, the legal situation of the Handfasting couple should be seen to by the High Priesthood.

Another alternative may be to allow the couple to enter into a partnership creating a form of contract setting forth the rights and obligations of the couple to each other and have it notarized or properly witnessed and filed with the County Recorder or Clerk. In this way a Civil Wedding is not needed and the Handfasting may be done to formally spiritualize the union.

Contracts of Partnership in the Bonds of Holy Union by Rite of Handfasting may be drawn up by the High Priesthood. The contract should state the reason that the couple wish to dedicate their lives to one another and to share their life and love with each other in common.

That they agree to be a mutual helpmate to one another and share any commonly accrued property.

Stipulations should be made for the care and support of offspring, should such eventuate.

There must also be a provision for the dissolution of the Partnership should the couple come to the Rite of Handloosing.

In this way a Wiccan Handfasting is more binding than a traditional Marriage in the usual accepted sense. No format for the Contract can be given, but should be made personal to the couple and hold the agreements they feel are best for them. Some will have very strict provisions, while others may have looser ties.

In the event the couple wish to terminate their partnership, they must then seek out a valid High Priest and High Priestess of Wicca and draw up a legal paper to dissolve the partnership. It should state what each is to receive from the years spent together and what is to be done with accrued property. The consideration for offspring must be seen to in order to accommodate their well-being.

When an amicable agreement has been reached, the High Priesthood will give the Rite of Handloosing. The legal paper will then be notarized and/or witnessed and filed with the proper Civil Office.

These duties to the men and women of the Craft place the High Priesthood in the center and heart of those receiving the Rite of Handfasting in the true Craft of the Wise. They therefore become involved in the well being of the Couples they foster in the faith. They have an interest to see that the union will survive in the best interests of all, and most important, the interests of the Wiccan Born. They become a family confidant, not favouring the man or the woman in family disputes, but who strives to correctly counsel their Coveners in family problems.

In the event of a Handloosing, the High Priesthood are to champion the rights of the offspring and see that they are not deprived of the mutual love and support of their parents. They should always strive to bring about an amicable parting of the ways when a union is not able to continue.

Always remembering, a Coven is a family on an extended level, of those who choose to associate for common religious purposes. Therefore, abuse and/or neglect of one member or another, becomes the concern of all.

Ceremony of Handfasting

In the Way of the Wise, the Seasons of Beltane is the traditional time to celebrate the union of two elements of Love. It is the Season of Wine and Roses, when the joy and beauty of Spring and the potential of future promise is celebrated.

The Coven may schedule Handfastings to follow the Beltane Sabbat Ritual. In such a case, however, no non-Wiccans would be allowed to attend. Should the Handfasting couple wish friends and relatives to be guests, then the Handfasting may be given at any other time and season outside and away from the Covenstead. (Perhaps on the Night of Beltane at a private home or rented hall after the regular Sabbat at the Covenstead.)

Weddings can be simple or elaborate, as the substance of the Couple would permit. For the purposes of tradition, however, only the basic essentials for a valid Wiccan Wedding will be given. They may be modified and expanded as individual couples wish. The basics would not, however, be neglected.

The High Priesthood is to co-officiate. As in everything else in this Cosmos, a Male and Female element is required to bring it into manifestations. The Gods are not sterile and one may not exist without the other.

The High Priesthood would wear full regalia for a Handfasting.

The couple would wear white robes with garlands of flowers in their hair. Each would carry a piece of Wedding cake, cut prior to the ceremony. His cut in the form of a triangle, hers cut in the form of a small square.

On the altar the Coven ceremonial Chalice would hold a rich red wine. Beside it the Groom's Athamé would rest. Nearby a binding cord of gold cloth and the rings to be exchanged.

A floral incense would be lightly scenting the room, and a large white candle would be burning in the center of the altar.

No one gives a Witch Maiden away, for she comes of her own free will. The young maids of the Coven, or friends of the Bride may act as the Bride's Maids to escort the couple scattering flower petals to the altar.

The young men of the coven, or the Groom's friends flank the path to the altar, forming an arch with their arms held high through which the couple will walk.

As the couple steps into the room, any music or love songs may be sung or played as a prelude to the ceremony.

As they pass by the assembled Coven and/or guests, each person will smile and say Blessed Be.

The Maidens will pass through the arch of the Groom's attendants and scatter the flower petals in the path. They will then flank to the sides near the two officiants.

When the Bride and Groom pass through the arch, the men will step back and flank to the sides beside the Maidens.

The Bride and Groom stand before the High Priest and High Priestess. They each place their slices of cake on the altar near the Chalice.

The High Priest will issue the Challenge:

________ and____do you come of your own free will to be joined in Holy Union by Rite of Handfasting according to our Ancient Faith?

The couple responds: *We do.*

He continues: *Is there any reason to object to this union of two souls?*

There is a slight pause and the couple will then answer: *There is not.*

The High Priestess then speaks:

________and______, thy two hearts have consented to join in a bond of mutual love before the Gods and this Coven Family. Love is the power that holds creation in firm and forward motion. It is the joy and warmth of the Gods from of Old.

Be a comforter, a help mate, a companion and a lover to the other. There will be times of joy and times of stress. Let love guide thy path together. Love gives and love shares. Love uplifts and love inspires. It clings not. Nor is ever insecure. Where love abides, trust will also be found. One heart trusts itself to another. Be thou ever mindful of that intimate responsibility. True love never causes the beloved pain.

The High Priest then blesses the two rings by drawing an invoking Pentagram over them with his right thumb.

He gives hers to the Groom and his to the Bride. He says:

Take these symbols of the eternal love of the God and Goddess and give that love one to the other.

The Bride and Groom exchange rings and exclaim *Blessed be* to each other as they do.

The two officiants now step to the sides of the altar as the Bride and Groom step closer to stand at the altar.

The bride takes up the Chalice of wine and her square of cake. The Groom takes up his Athamé and his triangular piece of cake.

She holds the Chalice beneath his Athamé.

He dips the point of the blade into the wine in the Chalice thrice.

She feeds him her piece of cake and recites whatever vows of love she wishes to say to him.

He feeds her his piece of cake and speaks whatever vows of love he wishes to say to her. (The vows are personal and composed by the couple for themselves.) The Chalice and Athamé are then replaced on the altar and the couple steps back to their places.

The High Priesthood resume their places before the couple.

The High Priest takes up the binding cord as the couple joins hands. He then binds the Bride's and Groom's joined hands together with these words:

By the rights of our Ancient Faith we bind thy two hearts and souls in holy union. May this joining sustain and nourish thy lives all thy days together. Blessed be.

The High Priestess takes up the Chalice of wine and offers a sip to the High Priest and then sips from the Chalice herself. She says:

________and________, the God and Goddess bless thy love and life. May their eternal joy and renewal of creation always guide thee.

She offers a sip to the Groom and then to the Bride. She then drains the Chalice herself and sets it back on the altar.

She takes up the Incense burning sweetly and the candle burning brightly from the altar and circumambulates the couple thrice widdershins as she blesses them thus:

O God and Goddess bless this union. May the thoughts and vows and deeds invested in love bear a fruitful and prosperous harvest. Blessed be.

She returns the items to the altar.

The High Priest places a hand on the head of both the Bride and Groom as he says:

These two are one. These hearts beat as one. These lives are now one. According to our Ancient Faith the couple ______ and ______ are now wed in the embrace of the God and Goddess. Blessed be.

The Bride and Groom may now embrace and kiss.

They recess from the altar and a traditional wedding party may now ensue. The Coven and/or guests celebrate with much joy and good cheer.

The High Priestess' Coven Broom has been set before the door to lie in the couple's path. They must both jump over it to the cheers of the Coven to inspire domestic prosperity before they retire from the party.

In times of old, the Handfastings were more of a community fertility rite to insure the perpetuation of the Clan. The couple used to consummate their union in Circle.

For the purposes of historicity the ancient formula is given, to inform of the traditions of the ancient ancestors. That is why the ritual gesture of the Chalice and Athamé is preserved in the true Craft ceremony.

The assembled Coven would wear full capes over their robes. The couple would be skyclad save for their garlands of flowers.

After the rings would be given and before the binding of hands, the Coven would form a circle around the couple and turn their backs on them as all spread their capes and joined hands facing outwards.

Such an act created a barrier of a solid wall around the couple so they could consummate their union as the coven chanted prayers of love and sang songs to the Gods. No one would look behind upon the rite being engaged in by the couple.

This ancient rite was for a time when virginity was prized and the idea of property and clan honour and purity were much more important.

In this day and age, however, we have evolved beyond the old Pagan value system and virginity is no longer to be esteemed as clan honour.

The symbolic act serves to comply with the tradition of *Book I: The Covenant; Uses of Craft Power, sec. 18,* where the spirit of the cosmic union of God and Goddess is understood in the ceremony.

By Handfasting, the Craft in the Way of the Wise joins two hearts, two persons, two elements of love, who wish to share their lives in common. Therefore, the Craft will not deny the joining of those of the same gender whose orientation is of that nature from being Handfasted. All the Gods' children should be allowed to find fulfillment in love as their nature may lead them. Witches, least of all, judge others harshly.

In that case, however, the Chalice and Athamé gesture would then be eliminated from the ceremony.

The Witches Houseblessing

When a newly Handfasted Witch Couple, or a Witch Solo, are to take up residence in a new house or apartment — even those freshly built and previously unlived in, a general blessing should be done to bring the Spirit of the Old Gods to abide in the home.

Should an adverse feeling linger from the presence of previous occupants, a bit of Frankincense should be burned in the center of the building and the door frames should be anointed with Verbena Oil to rid the unsettling vibes.

On the New Moon, or as close thereto as possible, the head of the household must carry a bit of bread and a dish of salt into each room and offer them at the four Quarters widdershins to invoke the powers. As that is being done, these words are spoken at each Quarter by all the family present:

Blessed be this happy home. may the love of the Gods abide within.

From that time on, it may be assumed that Wicca abides in the house. Brothers and Sisters of the Craft, worthy of one's love and esteem, should always find welcome and shelter from the world, when necessary, if at all possible.

When, for any reason, the Witch Couple, or Solo Witch, must move out of the house or apartment, a proper banishing should be done.

A raw egg is passed around all the door frames and windows to absorb the essence of the Witches who have dwelt there. A bit of Sulphur is then set to burn in the center of the building or apartment after all traces of the Craft have been moved out.

The egg is carried to the new dwelling and buried near the front door. If the new dwelling is inside an apartment complex, a potted plant may be set outside the apartment door and the egg buried in it after it has been carried around in the new dwelling to bless the place.

Thus may the spirit of the Craft and the Old Gods remain with the Witch at all times.

Handloosing

The Craft knows that people grow and evolve their own emotional natures and their spiritual outlooks as time goes by. We are not always the same person at 25 that we are at 40.

For this reason Craft Handfasting is not necessarily a life long commitment as other Faiths view a marriage. It is hoped that two souls are able to find a spiritual companion in each other and will spend their lives together, but the Craft knows that in many instances a relationship may change as the individuals evolve themselves.

A Handfasting is entered into by free will and choice. A Handloosing must also be allowed to be the same.

The High Priesthood, as father and mother to their Coveners, will try to see that a Handfasting, marred by disharmony, be worked out. If it may not be, then they are to do what they can to create an amicable parting, to the best interests of all concerned.

The couple, wishing to be Handloosened, come to their final agreement and seek out the High Priesthood in private.

They come before the High Priesthood with hands bound together as for the Handfasting.

On the altar rests and empty Chalice. Beside it the Groom's Athamé. One black candle is burning beside the Chalice.

The High Priest asks:

________ and _______, do you come to this parting of the ways of *your own accord and desire?*

The couple answers affirmatively.

He continues:

I charge you to always keep a warm love in your hearts, one for the other, even though you have been drawn to a parting of the ways. Know, above all, that bad feeling and rancor draw pain in their wake. Wish each other only the best of all that is good, as you begin a life on separate paths.

He unfastens the binding cord around their joined hands in silence.

The woman takes up the Chalice and turns it upside down to rest on its rim. The man takes his Athamé and rests it crosswise across the upturned bottom of the Chalice. They both say: *Consummatum est.*

The High Priestess takes up the black candle and passes it down between the parted couple with these words:

The Gods do not require that we remain in an intolerable position. Perhaps in their wisdom they are to lead you to understanding and fulfillment in other ways and other places. We know that you have learned from each other in the time you spent together. Go now your own ways in the Light the God and Goddess lead you. Blessed be, our children, blessed be.

She blows out the candle and snaps it in two. Each of the couple takes a half of it and leaves the altar.

In this way are the spiritual bonds of a Wiccan Handfasting loosened.

Should the couple have had a civil wedding prior to the Handfasting, the civil divorce then must take its course.

If they had entered into a Partnership filed with the county offices, the proper paper of dissolution will then have to be filed and its provisions enacted.

Perhaps one of the loosened couple would not find it possible to continue at the Covenstead to worship at Sabbat and work at Esbat with the other. One may wish to quit the Covenstead for other parts.

The High Priesthood will prepare the proper documentation to commend such a one to other Covens elsewhere. (See *The Covenant, Laws of the Craft, Sec. G, paragraphs 5-6.*)

It can be seen we have hypothetically traced an individual's journey through an ideal application of the Ancient Craft of Wicca, in the Way of the Wise.

It is up to the individual to embody the ideal as best he/she, or as best as his/her group is able. The ideal is not to be made subservient to the individual.

The Cosmic Principles we call God/Goddess expend a tremendous amount of energy just to bring about the physical manifestation of but one single living entity in physical creation. Are we, as Initiates of their Sacred Mysteries, to do anything of less worth and value?

Wicca/The Old Religion contains many Traditions and modes of Craft expression, which range from the highly hierarchical to the most loosely organized. That gives Wicca a beauty, but not a strength.

The craft needs a basic doctrinal and liturgical identity, which should be common to all aspects and Traditions. It has a common background and common Mysteries, so; therefore, it should have an ideal common mode of expression.

In that way, Wicca/The Old Religion would be able to be recognized as a viable Faith and a deep body of philosophical value. It would be seen and recognized in all parts of the world where it is being practiced. Wiccans could then be able to seek out others of their Faith and be able to share the common bond of belief in the Old Gods.

As stated earlier, *The Sacred Pentagraph*, as an Occult System, is to be studied and applied. We receive back from the Cosmos what we are willing, as individuals and as collectives, to invest into it. Blessed Be!

Those who would only play at being a Witch would see themselves washed out by the Initiation Ordeals and would dismiss these Tomes rather discourteously.

A very few, however, will see the value in the system and choose to work it through. Those are the real Witches. A.O. of B.B.C.

The Sacred Pentagraph

Book III
The Book of Lights

Sabbat Ceremonies

Heed the Ancient Elements Four
And eschew not the Wisdom from of yore
For-sooth the Old Ways shall return.

– Tarostar ✯ V°

This is the volume of the worship of the Old Gods at Sabbat Time of the eight Holy Days in the Cycle of the Year.

These are the true Works of the High Priest and the High Priestess of Wicca in the Ancient Craft in the Way of the Wise.

Preface

The Ancient Order of Bell, Book and Candle

Under the auspices of the Chiefs of the A.O. of B.B.C., the works of Tarostar ✯ V° are authorized to provide an open access to the Ancient Wisdom Tradition through the exoteric forms of Coven worship which are to help true and dedicated seekers to eventually aspire to the esoteric core and the development of Adepthood in the Great Work.

To those few who persevere through the System of the Craft, as taught by the Tomes of *The Sacred Pentagraph,* from Craftsman I° to Elder V°, the road to Adepthood in the Field of Occultism is certain.

As Aquarius dawns upon the horizon, the Mystery Schools of the Temples of Antiquity will be re-established in the inner and outer Porticos of the true Coven Temple Ceremonies and teachings. To this end these guidelines in *The Sacred Pentagraph* are made public and hereby granted approval by the Chiefs of the order as the Craft of Wicca in the Way of the Wise and therefore true and valid.

Given under our Seal this day of Saturn, the 10th, November, in the 1,984th year of the current era, Sol in Scorpio, Luna waneth in Gemini.

Council of Elders, Circle of Starmeadow, A.O. of B.B. & C.

Introduction

In the 1,976th Year of the Current Era, the Mysteries of God/ Goddess came to the last surviving Elders of the Ancient Order of Bell, Book and Candle. The small Coven of Circle of Starmeadow drew down the Goddess and She spoke.

The Coven Oracle was the medium for that memorable experience. Those of us who were there will never forget it.

In essence, this is what the Goddess said:

The revival of the Ancient Craft is in its infancy. Its birth pangs pained us sorely. But now, O Faithful Ones, the charge you were given many centuries ago, to keep the heart of the Old Ways, is now to be fulfilled.

The call went out across the world to re-affirm the Ancient Faith. A new age comes, a new star is on the horizon, the order of the world moves on. The necessary astringing of the human mind under the Piscean dispensation has run its course.

The world will know that God is both Father and Mother. A sterile masculine trinity can not create a cosmos. And yet, my children, do not worship me as Goddess only. As Goddess I also need the potency of God. As God I must have the form giving love of Goddess.

For the New Age dawns, bring forth your order's rituals and tenets and revitalize them. Those who seek us as true God and Goddess will find the way. Blessed be and blessed be!

From the time of that Full Moon Esbat we have worked where we can to advance to Faith. The inception of the idea of *The Sacred Pentagraph,* a work in five volumes, to contain the basic essentials of true Craft worship was brought forth.

Dedication

Much has been written of late concerning the Sabbat Festivals of the various traditions of Wicca. Articles and commentary in books delve deeply into the supposed ancient pagan Nature Religions. To try to link the modern Craft with the pre-Christian beliefs of by-gone eras produces much confusion for the contemporary student. Chaos and disorientation result from such attempts.

The Universe is a spiral flow of Time and Space. That which was, is again, but on a higher level. So many changes have occurred in the world of human ideas and ideals since the Ancient Wisdom Religion was clouded over by Ecclesiastical Christianity, that any attempt to recreate or return to ancient sources is futile. Thick mists of time and temperament have obscured the exoteric form of The Old Religion. The only things that remain certain are the eternal Divine Verities inherent in the Cosmos in which we live. Those, the Craft worshipped and celebrated in time of old. Unto these verities the Craft adheres. True practitioners of the craft see much which is chaotic and scattered, purported to be Wicca. Wicca worships the Divine Order of the Universe, yet many of Her followers seem to show no such order within themselves, nor within their religious practice.

It is with this in mind that the few true practitioners of the Craft left in the world today, wish to make public this comprehensive liturgy of worship for the modern day follower of the Ancient Craft of the Wise.

No claims of unsevered links to pre-Christian times are made for these rituals. The rituals that follow are for the contemporary practitioner of the Craft who have attained the level of High Priest or High Priestess. Yet the rituals contain the essence of the age old cycle of birth, life, death and regeneration; the Divine Verities that were much the part of the Ancient Craft of previous ages.

A High Priest or High Priestess assumes the responsibility to teach and spread the Craft wherever fertile ground can be found. It is unto these dear souls who have undertaken a very difficult road to spiritual attainment, that this tome is dedicated. For those who assume the role as spiritual mentor to humanity in teaching the Craft; for those, who by their attainment of the grade as High Priest or High Priestess in this age, to bring order out of chaos and to show the Ancient Craft of the Wise to the world in it's true light.

Both in their personal and public lives must the modern practitioners be exemplary and manifest the precepts of the ancient and venerable Earth. This requires a consecration to spiritual purpose.

May yours be such a path.

Blessed Be!

R.G.B. Magister Sacrorum
A.O. of B.B & C.

Understanding the Sabbats

There are two cycles, which interconnect and compliment each other in a Cosmic Whole. Previous Ages did not draw the correlation between the two systems.

Some orientations were for the God and followed the Solstices and Equinoxes in the configurations of the Heavens. The masculine potency represented by the God ordained the Times, as the Sun seemed to pass in its stations as the years rolled by. This God Power stood for the Order of the Cosmos in the determination of Time.

Other cultures followed the passing of the Seasons, in devotion to the Goddess, as She established the form taken by the World in relation to and response to the Times set by the God.

The interdependence of the two was not always clearly seen by previous cultures. Peoples and Nations generally were devoted to either one or the other of the two halves of the Great All, which is God/Goddess.

Therefore, at times, either the Gods or the Goddesses were given precedence by the established authorities of different cultures and societies.

Where and when, either one of the other was held supreme, the other would assume a lesser role, or almost even disappear from general lore.

The God represented stability and Order. As the unified World of the Classical Age passed into Chaos, with the Fall of Rome, appeal was made to shore up the decline and God/Male Paternalistic forms took the lead in religious thought.

Goddesses were not accepted as potent enough to prevent the descent into darkness, as barbarian chaos swept Rome away.

The God's observances, maintained by the Clergy of the Exoteric, allied to the State, began to eliminate all other forms of religious expression.

That is why those remaining loyal to the Old Religion seem to place a heavy emphasis on the Goddess. Even, at times, to the exclusion of the God.

The Cross-Quarter Days, of the seasonal changes became much more important to the Old Religion, with the Solstices and Equinoxes being left to the State Religion, espoused by the Clergy.

It created the Jesus Solar Myth and used those Times for its major celebrations: Easter - Vernal Equinox; St. John's Day - Summer Solstice; St. Michael's Day - Autumnal Equinox and Christmas - Midwinter Solstice.

Hallowmas, Candlemas, Beltane and Lammas were the major celebrations to honour the Lady.

Both the solar celebrations and the seasonal rites existed side by side throughout most of the Medieval Period and well into Modern Times. The pull of the influence of the Goddess was much too strong for the exoteric Clergy to eliminate all together, so the days were observed, but as lesser themes, for Folk-Fests, rather than "Holy Days."

Officially, the Crown, the Priesthood and the Secular Authority observed the established Sun God Cult - Christianity.

Popular Religion, however, was still attached to the unofficial Lady Worship of the Goddess. She ruled the Seasons, upon which Human Life depended for its sustenance and livelihood.

In most records, pertaining to the conflict between the Lady Cult and the Official Sun Cult, the Cross-Quarter Days, generally were turned into demonic observances by the exoteric Clergy.

The Witchcraft Mania was a feature of that conflict, as the Official Sun Cult sought to weed out and eliminate other forms of religious rites and orientations.

Control of the records and archives and of the education system allowed the official Clergy to program and document only its own "official" guidelines, so that later generations came to accept the official view as standard and acceptable.

The old lore went into abeyance and became obscure, observed by only a very few.

The spiritual upliftment of the Lady Cult was reversed by the Clergy and made to look sinister. Halloween, for instance, a very Holy Sabbat in the Old Religion, degenerated into spooks and goblins and hags on brooms.

Candlemas, had to be incorporated into the official Church as Lady Day, and given to the Mary Cult within the acceptable norm.

The folk, however, would not give up their old Pagan lore, so the Church had to sanctify aspects from the Goddess and make them Christian. It had to allow the Midwinter Revels, where the official Church and Clergy were spoofed and paraded around as buffoons. The Lord of Misrule became the symbol, indicative of the break up of life in Winter's thrall.

The Goddess remained, but was reduced to Folklore, and rural seasonal celebrations.

The yearly cycle of the eight Sabbats compose a grand drama of action and reaction. These are four Celestial (or Solar) Sabbats and four Terrestrial. The four Celestial Sabbats are called 'The Times'. These are the inexorable changes in the celestial tides which move ever on, and effect Mankind and all life around him. His is lent to accept and co-operate with the Divine Will. "The Times" are a cosmic symbol of the birth, life, death and regeneration rhythm of and for this planet and all life thereupon. They are the basic inspirational rituals commemorating the four Spiritual Elements and the wisdom teachings represented by each one.

The four Terrestrial Sabbats are the mutable tides, or the 'Seasons Between The Times'. They are the response of the Earth and reaction to the Solar Tides. The Earth and all her abundant creation answer back to the changes in the life cycle. They are the basic Earth rituals with themes of fertility and abundance linking past and future.

Today, in the late Twentieth Century of the Current Era, we have seen a revival of the Old Religion, called Wicca, or Gwydon. It has been named Witchcraft, but it incorporated Occultism and Spiritual Arts and Sciences from the Ancient Wisdom.

The revival has brought forward a resurgence of the Goddess side of the Great All, or Supreme Being and the official Sun Cult, in many ways is on the decline.

The power of the official Clergy has been broken and it has been removed from control of the education system and the influence in the minds and hearts of the people.

However, within the "Craft," as the Old Religion is called, a heavy emphasis was placed on the Goddess, in the early revival. Much of the necessary masculine half of the Godhead was not used. It became almost as one-sided as the official Sun Cult.

A sterile masculine Trinity can not create a Cosmos. A totally Goddess orientation would be equally unfruitful.

The Ancients knew the Hieros Gamos was necessary for the creation of Worlds and Universes. God and Goddess must create in harmony together, before anything could be.

This is why, those of us in the Craft who adhere to the Ancient Wisdom, understand we must unite the two systems of Solstices/ Equinoxes and Cross-Quarter Days for a harmonious blending of God and Goddess.

The yearly cycle of the eight Sabbats compose a grand drama of action and reaction. There are four Celestial Sabbats and four Terrestrial.

The four Celestial Sabbats are called "the Times." These are the inexorable changes in the Celestial tides, which move ever on, and effect Mankind and all life. His is but to accept and cooperate with the Divine Will. "The Times" are a cosmic symbol of the birth, life, death and regeneration rhythm of and for this planet and all life thereupon. They are the basic inspirational rituals commemorating the four Spiritual Elements and the wisdom technique represented by each one.

The four Terrestrial Sabbats are the mutable tides, or the "Seasons Between the Times." They are the response of the Earth in reaction to the Celestial tides. The Earth and all her abundant creation answer back to the changes in the life cycle. They are the basic Earth rituals with themes of fertility and abundance linking past and future.

Stations of the Sun; Solstices and Equinoxes, set the Times, That is, the God ordains and Order in the Cosmos, by configurations of the Heavens. The Goddess, as Executrix of the Order, establishes the Seasons, giving living form to the Order. Thus, life progresses ever onward upon the spiral flow of the Universe, as we know it.

The Sabbats alternate male and female around the course of the year's cycle. Four pertain to the God and four embody the potency of the Goddess.

Hallowmas, a female Sabbat, represents the darkness of Old Night, before living things were. Death is its theme. It symbolizes the descent into break up, or the Crossing of the Veil. It is a very Holy Sabbat in which Wiccans, or those of the Old Religion, commune with the Spirits of the departed.

It also looks ahead to the coming Tide of Life, as the New Year. Divinations are cast for Coveners and Covens on that Night.

Midwinter, the Solstice in the Dark Tide, is a rite for the God. The solar power is seen to begin its return out of the depths, bringing a new hope to life; A masculine Sabbat for the "Child of Promise."

Candlemas, a female Sabbat, responds to the Winter Solstice as the womb of the Goddess is symbolically prepared to conceive and bring forth living matter. Seeds are planted to ensure She of the Corn will give birth.

Vernal Equinox celebrates a masculine theme in the idea of youth and joy in life as it flowers. The major Tenets of the Faith are re-affirmed and new Initiates are accepted into the Craft.

Beltane, a female Sabbat, brings the feminine response to the Equinox with the glory of life in flower. The Maiden Goddess is seen as luck, life and pure joy. May Poles or Cauldron Rites to foster proper growth and maturity are the themes.

Summer Solstice is masculine and shows the God at His potent height. Fire Rituals to cleanse and purify are the usual observance. The Great Rite may follow upon this Sabbat, for those who are able to undertake its serious obligations.

Lammas is a female rite to bless the first fruits from the field and return to the Goddess something of her nature to ensure Her fertility.

Autumn Equinox is the masculine Sabbat of Judgement. The God sees us as we really are and we reap the dues of our own making. We eat the harvest we have prepared for ourselves, by our own inner beings. The Sabbat of Compensation; Judgement before the God; the All Seeing, All Knowing.

Hallowmas then begins the spiral road all over again.

Thus we see how the Sabbats of the Old Religion, both of God and Goddess compliment and reinforce each other as they alternate around the cycle.

They need each other to be, to create and to evolve. We need them to exist and they need us to express their creation. The Cosmos is a unified and interdependent whole. The whole affects the part and the part affects the whole. Thus says the Ancient Wisdom.

As can be seen, the Sabbats of the Craft are both solemn and festive as they alternate around the year.

The Works of the High Priest are solemn, ceremonial and impersonal to symbolize the Divine Order that progresses ever onward.

The Works of the High Priestess, however, are festive, relaxed and personal, just as the Earth Mother is personal to all beings.

These eight Sabbats are times of worship and communion with Deity. No magics are performed at Sabbat time.

Spells and Coven magic and the teaching of the Craft Lore are conducted at the Esbats of the Lunar tide. Esbats are both New Moon and Full Moon, and compose the actual working nights of any sincere coven. (See *Book IV: The Book of Esbats.*)

MIDSUMMER

Firing the Temple
MALE
The Great Rite (optional)
Purification by Fire

BELTANE
FEMALE
Bringing in the May

Season of Wine & Roses
(Handfastings optional)

LAMMAS
FEMALE
Blessing the First Fruits

Maturity of Bounty

The Male Times set the theme
and the Female Seasons give
expression to that theme.

VERNAL EQUINOX
Male
Affirmation &
New Beginnings

AUTUMNAL EQUINOX
Male
Compensation & Dues
Harvest Fruit

THE WHEEL
Thus the eternal cycle
alternates male-female
on the upward spiral of Life

Mysteries of Cybele
CANDLEMAS
Female
Waxing Light &
Making the Earth
Fertile

HALLOWMAS
Female
Season of Death
Dumb Supper & Coven
Divination

MIDWINTER
Male
Entering in of Death
Child of Promise

Preliminary Necessities

As can be seen from *Book I, The Covenant* and *Book II, The Book of Beginnings,* this Tradition in the Craft places much emphasis on detail and attention to ritual procedure. It is a complicated system of practice in the Old Religion, but well worth the effort to embody.

The Wheel, or the Yearly Round of the Sabbats, is a closed circle with only one point of entry on or off the Wheel. That point is the Vernal Equinox.

Beginning with that Equinox Sabbat, and following through the cycle, some element from each Sabbat is collected to be used in the Candlemas Sabbat, at the Rites of Cybele, by the Coven women. Thereby, causing a chain binding the year and the two Sabbat cycles together.

As a Coven, you would need to begin working the Sabbats at a Vernal Equinox and follow the system all around until the final usage of the elements from all the Sabbats are placed in the Earth just after the Candlemas Celebration.

Once the Wheel has been put in motion by a Coven group, it should be continued and not stopped until the Candlemas Season.

That means, even should the Coven not be able as a group to complete a particular cycle, the Officiants/The High Priesthood, should do it themselves. To start a round of Sacred Ceremonies, and not to finish, produces an incomplete Sacred Drama and would, very often, cause adverse spiritual and psychic reverberations for those just walking away and not fulfilling the cycle.

Sabbats require responsibility to self and to the Old Gods.

A lot of effort, sweat, tears, labour and financial output would be necessary to properly and correctly practice the Old Religion.

If those priorities are not in your make-up, as a Wiccan, I would advise you not to even attempt working any Occult System for Magical Attainment. You would not bring forth anything of value to yourself, nor your Gods.

I would prefer to discourage you from the start, than have you bring forth miscarriages of effort and abortions; wasted energy, and call it

Wicca/The Old Religion.

The Spirit embodied as Wicca is a deep abiding Faith, which has survived Fire, Sword, persecution and Holy Terror. Do it honour, or not at all!

THE TEMPLE – RITUAL CHAMBER

This is a room reserved exclusively for Coven work. It should be vacant, large enough to accommodate the Circle, and as private and sound proof as possible. The Circle may be permanently inscribes on the floor, if desired, but no symbols of any kind should be included in it.

Against the North Wall is a credenza type small Altar with a canopy, or curtain tracks overhead, and around which a sheer veil is drawn. This is the "Sanctum."

Overhead hanging on a hook, or installed on a wall fixture, or standing on the credenza is an ornate metal holder, designed to hold a ruby 7-day Sanctum Lamp, kept eternally burning by lighting a new one from its flame (using a taper) before the old one burns out. This is known as the "Sacred Flame" and represents the Holy Spirit.

The pilot lamps are kept upon the Sanctum Altar and are lit from the Sacred Flame to be carried into Circle as each ritual commences and from which in turn all candles used in rituals are lit. (See *Ritual of the Sacred Flame, Section II, Works of the High Priestess.*)

The High Priestess is responsible, as Keeper of the sacred Flame, to perpetuate it throughout the year.

The flame may be renewed twice each year, in the Midwinter Sabbat during the act of Bringing Forth the Child of Promise (when the High Priest produces the Earth Fire with Flint and Steel) and prior to the Midsummer Sabbat at Firing the Temple (which Draws Down the Sun). The High Priest produces the Flame and gives it into the keeping of the High Priestess.

The Ritual Chamber will also need a closet or cabinets with locks to accommodate all ritual equipment. The Consecrated articles must never be left lying around where they might be damaged or handled and/or desecrated.

The Altar

The Altar stands in the center of the Ritual Chamber and faces North before the Sanctum. It should be set properly for the ritual at hand and consecrated at each use before all Sabbat Ceremonies.

It may be something collapsible and folded away, or be a permanent fixture such as a coffee table or specially built Altar. Being the focal point of contact with the Deities and other higher spiritual energies, it must always be regarded with utmost respect and kept spotlessly clean and in perfect order.

It would not be proper, for instance, to ever sit or put one's feet upon this particular furnishing, nor to allow shoes or filth of any kind tossed upon it.

Therefore, if an Altar must double as a cocktail table between meetings, the host or hostess had best be tactfully alert. It is not an actual act of desecration unless something is intentionally or deliberately defiled, or carelessly allowed to become so. Accidents or unavoidable abuses by children or animals are not serious, unless brought about by neglect on the part of an adult.

Small, newly-formed Covens are not usually able to maintain a special Temple. However, a Sanctum should be kept and all other facilities simulated as closely as possible.

The Altar is draped in black for the Autumnal Equinox and Winter Solstice Sabbats and in white for the Vernal Equinox and Summer Solstice Sabbats. These are works of the High Priest and discussed in *Section I.* The High Priestess will set up the Altar and Consecrate it for these four Sabbats.

The four Terrestrial Sabbats are the works of the High Priestess and would have the Altar set according to the rubrics of *Section II.* The High Priest would then set up and consecrate the Altar at these times.

All objects used in Craft Ceremonies should be properly consecrated before they are brought into a Circle, especially if they are to be placed upon the Altar. (See *Blessing Altar Equipment, Section II*).

For Esbat Circle works of Craft magic the Practicus and Hand Maiden may set the Altar and have it prepared, but a member of the

High Priesthood should consecrate it.

Esbat work is co-celebrated by both members of the High Priesthood, so they may alternate turns in consecrating the Altar for New and Full Moon Rites. (A Practicus and Hand Maiden may be allowed to occasionally consecrate the Altar as part of their ritual training.)

Here follows a simple ceremony to consecrate the Altar:

NOTATE BENE, before we proceed, attention to detail may seem overly emphasized in this system. When things are done right and a faithful regimen adhered to, occult tools and ritual objects build up a powerful potency over a period of time. The positive energies invested by repeated ritual detail make one's magics and spiritual observances highly effective.

Thy works will prosper and thy road to adepthood will be more certain. If it seems too difficult, and half-hearted efforts made, expect only sterility of results and unfruitful or aborted magics. If Spiritual Adepthood be not thy goal, "Get Thee Hence" thou art not for the Way of the Wise.

Approximately two hours before the main body of the Coven is to arrive at the Covenstead for Sabbat or Esbat, the High Priestess lights a votive candle from the Sacred Flame and sets it aside for use at the Altar consecration. (From it also other lights may be taken to use on the Altar or in processional to the Altar depending on the Ceremony of the Day.)

The person conducting this ceremony then sets the Altar according to the season and places all objects needed for the Ritual on it.

He or she then retires from the room and vests in the robes needed for the Sabbat or Esbat later that night. It is best, at this point to read through the main ceremony to be conducted and recheck all that is on the Altar to make sure nothing has been overlooked.

When all is ready, the person conducting this Altar Consecration will stand outside the Ritual Chamber with either *The Book of Lights* or *The Book of Esbat* flat in his/her hand, so that the bell and vial of Sacred Anointing Oil may rest upon the book as though it were a tray. In the left hand is carried a taper candle in a holder which is lit from the votive taken from the Sacred Flame by the High Priestess (no one else, ever, should be allowed to take fire from the Sacred Flame - except a Queen Mother or an Oracle delegated by the High Priestess).

The bell is rung thrice and placed upon the book beside the oil. The taper is taken in the left hand and lit from the votive. He/she proceeds into the Ritual Chamber holding the candle high. This formula is recited approaching the Altar:

Ring the Bell. Light the Candle and open The Book of Lights/Esbat. Thus from of old it has always been and we of the Priesthood of the Ancient Faith do likewise.

When he/she reaches the Altar the candle is placed upon it with the left hand and the bell and oil are set down beside it. The book is opened to the Ritual of the Day (Sabbat or Esbat for later that night), and the bell is taken back up in the left hand. Then he/she begins to circumambulate the Altar thrice deosil, ringing the bell slowly, and reciting thus:

Banished be all previous forces from this Holy Spot. Banished be all adverse conditions from this Sacred Place. Banished and be gone. Banished and begone. Leaving what is bright, pure and clean.

Setting down the bell and the book on the Altar, he/she takes up the vial of oil and prays:

Supreme Being, God and Goddess, bless this Wiccan Altar of the Sacred Mysteries. Soon the Sabbat/Esbat Circle will be built. Soon the Ancient Round be trod.

From Ages of Ages we have called you from Altars such as this.

From Ages of Ages you have answered; the Goddess our Mother, our Father the God. Blessed be.

Taking a dab of oil on the right thumb, the four cardinal points of the Altar are anointed in silence.

The oil is set back down on the Altar and the open book taken up and held before the breast. He/she circumambulates the Altar thrice widdershins as this is recited:

Holy Oil, Book and Bell, summon the forces to work this spell.

Keep this Altar in the Goddess' name, love and light shine forth from its frame. Keep this Altar in the God's name, strength and purpose do the same. Holy Oil, Book and Bell, seal the Power of this Spell. Blessed be.

After the third circumambulation, the book is set back down on the Altar (open to the Ritual of the Day) and the candle taken back up. He/she steps softly from the Ritual Chamber and snuffs out the taper, leaving the Altar to rest in darkness and silence to await the time of Sabbat/Esbat.

Thus is an Altar made ready for Ritual Ceremony.

NOTATE BENE: Under NO, NO, NO circumstances shall matches of any kind be placed upon or struck within the vicinity of the Sanctum or Altar, or Consecrated Circle, or in areas where consecrated equipment is stored.

The tips contain phosphorus and brimstone - two substances associated in the evocation of Malignant Spirits, and would create a negative vibration which tends to destroy the psycho-magnetic field established through the use of Sacred Oils, Prayers and Ritual.

Purity of ritual essence is very important in the success of spiritual observances and magical rites.

That is the reason for the maintaining of a Sacred Flame in an active Temple. That is the reason at least a Sacred Flame should be kept by small Covens even without a proper Ritual Chamber.

All candles, lights and incense should be lit from the Sacred Flame in any magical rite, for whatever purpose throughout the year. It is produced by natural means twice a year and should be used for the spiritual and occult works.

Modes of Apparel

Informally Dressed – Anything clean and comfortable. No Craft weapons are displayed, but a Pentagram necklace may be worn. This mode is for the meetings of a Coven Council.

Informally Robed – Each will wear a ritualistic type garment of personal choice, such as a tabard, kaftan, long tunic or Alb (with hood down) of any colour other than black. Cingulums are worn of the colour designating one's rank. The Athamé, in sheath, may be worn on the cingulum. Jewelry may be worn, within the ethics of good taste. This mode is for private works of spellcasting and whenever a witch undertakes to employ the Art Magical for personal use, or for the benefit of Strangers or other Witches.

Semi-Formally Robed – Each will wear the formal black robe of the Coven, with hoods down. Cingulums of rank and Athamé in sheath. Each wears a Pentagram necklace, except Officers of rank who wear ceremonial jewels.

The High Priest wears his amethyst head-band and carries the Great Wand. The High Priestess wears her tiara and carries the Coven Broom. This mode is for the 26 Esbat Celebrations.

Formally Robed – All Coveners wear the uniform black robe with hoods drawn up over the head. The rules for cords and jewelry, as for semi-formally robed affairs also applies here. This mode is for all Coveners I°-III° for the eight Sabbats. (Craftsman I°, however, wear their handmade robe without the hood, see *Book V*).

The High Priesthood has their own mode for Sabbat Rituals.

For the Celestial Sabbats - The High Priest wears a black robe with gold cingulum and a white cope covering his robe for the Vernal Equinox and Summer Solstices, meaning that darkness is always encased in light.

He wears a white robe with gold cord and a black cope for Autumnal Equinox and Winter Solstice to show that darkness also contains light.

As he will be officiating at the above, he does not carry the Great Wand, but wears the head-band.

When he serves as assistant to the High Priestess at the Terrestrial Sabbats, he will wear his black robe with gold cingulum and band. In other words, formally robed as the other Coveners.

At the four Terrestrial Sabbats the High Priestess wears robes of a seasonal colour. For instance, at Hallowmas she may wear purple or black, at Candlemas blue, at Beltane mint green or rose and at Lammas rich dark green or orange or browns. To this she always adds her silver cord and tiara.

When she serves as assistant to the High Priest at the Celestial Sabbats, she should wear her black robe with silver cord and tiara.

For Esbat Rituals more diversity may be given. The Esbat works are co-celebrated and the High Priestess may wear whatever colour she feels is appropriate to the magical work at hand.

SKYCLAD – Meaning nudity. Some covens prefer such at celebrations. However, in the Way of the Wise, only the Great Rite following the Midsummer Sabbat is celebrated skyclad.

SHOES – All indoor ceremonies should be celebrated barefoot. However, if a coven elects to hold outdoor ceremonies, the area for the Circle should be cleared and packed down well. It would be best to walk barefoot upon Mother Earth. If the terrain is rocky, or just after a rain, then leather or chamois sandals may be worn. No synthetics should be between a Covener and Mother Earth.

NOTATE BENE: Have you not attended Occult Ceremonies, my Readers, where things were left in disarray? Wine left to corrode the bottom of Chalices? Wax dripped upon the linens? Dust among the candles? Spider webs and dust balls in the Ritual Chamber? Would you bring that before the Gods?

Such lack of care speaks volumes about the Practitioner of the Arts. So, continue on.

Proper Disposal of Elements Used In Craft Ritual Ceremony

Ashes from Censers and drippings from candles are cast upon the ground, to be consumed back into the Earth or dispersed by the wind. If there is no open ground in the immediate vicinity, a flower-pot or earthenware vessel or urn, filled with soil, shall be kept as an immediate receptacle. This must be always kept covered and consecrated to that purpose. It must be taken out to a proper place and emptied with a refill of fresh soil added periodically. This "casket" of soil shall be kept in a private place, preferably near Sacred Equipment, or in an atrium of living plants.

Any remaining blessed or consecrated fresh (unsalted) water which has been placed or left in consecrated vessels, must be given to some living thing, plants, grass, trees, animals, etc.

Any remaining salted blessed or consecrated water, must be returned to a moving body of water; river, lake or ocean, so as not to kill any plant or grass etc. A proper drain would also be permissible, as that is a moving body of water.

As each element is dispersed, it is important to bless it with the words: *Blessed Be!*

After removing all drippings, Altar candles must be cleaned, wiped with a linen or paper towel, wrapped in foil or wax paper and put away with other Altar Equipment for re-dressing and subsequent use. They must never be burned for any purpose other than Altar Ritual and prior to setting up, must have their tips trimmed with Bolline and be properly dressed each time. When too short for use, stubs may be taken out and buried with drippings and ashes.

Altar duties, such as the above, could be delegated by the High Priestess to a Hand Maiden, or other Coven women.

Notate Bene: Are you still with me, Reader? Perhaps there is hope for you yet! Do you still desire to be High Priest or High Priestess? There is much more yet to come. All is part of The Great Work.

To properly dispose of leftover wine and bread from Sabbat Celebrations, a few simple rubrics should be followed:

After Sabbat a clean linen cloth is taken out and set upon the ground. The plates containing the bread and the Sacred Chalice or Quaich upon that. Those are consecrated articles and may not be directly set upon the ground.

The Officiant faces North and digs a hole large enough to hold the bread with a spade or large spoon. Then the plate taken up and held to the North as this dedication is intoned:

Bless this Element, O Ancient Ones, we present to thee. Let Spirit fly to Spirit and Earth to Earth. Look kindly upon us and bless us in all ways.

Then the leftover bread is poured into the hole. The plate is set back down on the cloth and earth pushed in to refill the hole.

Then the leftover wine is raised to the North as this is said:

A libation we give the Earth to seal our blessings from the Old Gods.

A small drop is poured deosil to the Four Quarters (N.E.S.W.) in that order and the remainder poured upon the spot where the bread is buried, as this prayer is recited:

Hear, O Ancient Ones and Watchers from the Times of Old! Bless the Works and Worship of the Coven of ______ and prosper it in all ways to enliven the Ancient Faith in the hearts of all who seek her. Blessed Be!

Then the vessels and cloth are taken and returned to the Covenstead without looking back.

Any and all leftover food -stuffs from Hallowmas Sabbat are that which was shared with the Spirits at Dumb Supper. They should be quietly buried without any words spoken.

Some Preparations For the One or Both Officiating

1. Always observe a fast for at least 12 hours before any major rite.

2. Observe chastity for 12 hours before performing any major rite.

3. Observe a one-hour period of silence prior to any rite or ceremonial.

4. One hour before the rite is to begin, observe the proper ablutions and anointing: have a bath, shower or scrub. Hair must, of course, be clean. Anoint liberally with a proper Magical Oil.

5. Do not don robes to be worn in ceremony until immediately before the rite is to begin. It is in the best magical tradition to pray at the vesting. Rehearse mentally, (everyone should have their own certain duties in preparation; the non-officiating member of the High Priesthood, the Practicus and Handmaiden, the Scribes and Summoner). This eliminates any need of unnecessary conversation on the part of the one, or both, officiating.

6. All Ritual and Ceremonials should be well rehearsed in advance. However, should someone make a mistake, or forget lines, they must be lovingly directed by the High Priest or High Priestess, and No, No, No Negative Looks, Attitudes or Gestures Given, Which Would Cause The Entire Rite to Abort.

Tempestuous temperamentalities have no place in the Way of the Wise.

Section I

Works of the High Priest

These be the rites of the Minor Hierophant, the earthly representative of the Good God, the Teacher of the Faith, the Father of the Coven. He is the one who keepeth the Times.

The terms Minor Hierophant and Guardian of the Path best describe the duties and obligations of the Craft office known as the High Priest.

He should be a mature man between the ages of thirty and sixty. By age thirty he should have made a study of comparative religions so that he could fluently discuss or write upon any of this world's leading Faiths.

The High Priest must have an avocation for ceremonial magic and be able to draw upon his own resources in ceremonial methods to create and improvise ritual.

In order to have wisdom, his knowledge must be tempered with understanding. Above all, he must be guided by compassion for the less-evolved souls that he will guide along the way.

The High Priest is not a father confessor. He is first and foremost a teacher. That is why, before taking the initiation elevating him to office of High Priest, his training should have led him to study and digest all works available that pertain to magical development and practice.

Any Elders conferring such an initiation must be convinced as to the qualification of the candidate to High Priest.

Also, the High Priest must be thoroughly versed in the tenets of Reincarnation and Karma. He must have an exceptional knowledge of the purpose of human spiritual progression and social evolution.

These points are essential, because they are some of the chief tenets of the Faith that the High Priest in his role as Minor Hierophant will be called upon to explain.

Such are the wisdom traditions of all Mystic and Occult Faiths, and are what the High Priest is called upon to expound to all sincere seekers. In short, all teachings carrying theosophies and esoteric knowledge become his domain.

Furthermore, it is the obligation of the High Priest, as Guardian of the Faith, to ensure that each individual aspirant to higher knowledge undergoes the proper initiations.

His is to see, that, as each aspirant reaches a higher level of consciousness, the proper initiations are given as they are needed and that they are always in keeping with the best traditions of the Ancient Craft of the Wise, as embodied in *The Sacred Pentagraph* Tradition.

Such knowledge, duty and obligation entail heavy responsibility. No initiations may be lightly given. Such abuse could harm a soul unprepared.

Therefore, in official capacity, the High Priest should be stern and somber.

The Sabbats conducted by the High Priest mark the ebb and flow of the masculine element of Nature. His Sabbat rituals are designed to augment and commemorate the vital energy passing through the world at the "Times."

In the Spring and Summer his Altar cloths should be white. Any decoration on them such as solar crosses or pentagrams should be black (gold may be used as secondary choice). Conversely, in Autumn and Winter, the Altar cloths should be black with white embellishment (red may be a secondary choice).

Secondary colours are only for the solar crosses or pentagrams.

His vestments should also reflect this theme. In the Spring and Summer he should wear a black robe with a gold cinch cord. A white cope should drape over his shoulders to the floor. In the Autumn and Winter he should wear a white robe tied with a gold cinch cord over which is worn a black cope.

This is to symbolize, by dress, that all things contain their opposite.

Any crosses and pentagrams on his copes and robes may be either red or gold.

If the coven chooses to be skyclad, a simple cinch cord of gold should be enough.

The High Priest should possess chalices of gold, two in number; one for water and the other for red wine. He should also have two silver pattens; one for salt or earth and the other for the bread.

A sturdy censer and a votive glass for a pilot lamp either red or yellow, complete the list of Altar tools for the High Priest.

Wands, pentacles and magical tools, etc., are for spell casting and thus relegated to the realm of the Esbats, where works of magic are performed. (See *The Book of Esbat* and *The Cornucopia*).

However, the sword may be used in creating the Sabbat circle, if it is desired. Other tools may be used, but they are not essential.

Altar of The High Priest

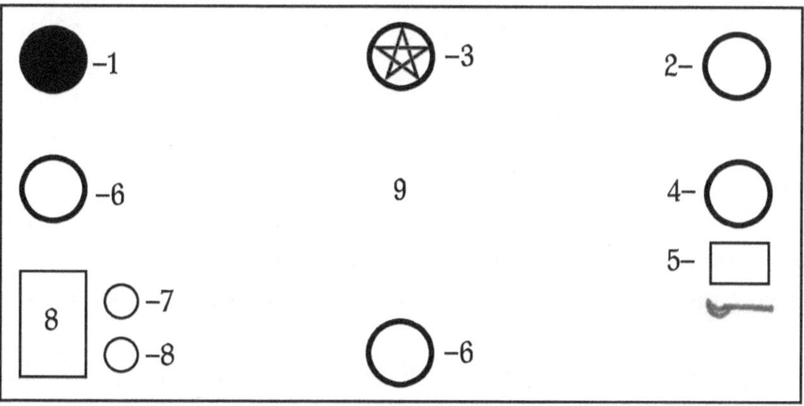

Altar Arrangements For The Celestial Sabbats

1. The left Altar Candle (black jumbo size), which represents the Temple column of Severity.

2. The Right Altar Candle (white jumbo size) to act as the Temple column of Mercy.

3. The Pentacle which holds a dish of Salt or Earth to stand as the Middle Pillar to balance the two.

4. The Thurible.

5. Extra incense and coals with small spoon. (The Thurible, burning the proper incense, is carried to the Altar, in processional.)

6. A small votive or taper, lit from the votive taken from the Sacred Flame is also carried to the Altar in processional.

7. The High Priest's #1 Gold Chalice to contain salted or fresh water.

8. Ritual notes.

9. The Center space to contain whatever items will be used in the

Ceremony.

10. The Bell.
11. Sacred Oil.

The High Priest would have his Altars set by the High Priestess. She would see that all is ready and that the Thurible and candle for him to carry to the Altar are in readiness outside the Ritual Chamber so that he may proceed in and cast the Circle with Air and Fire.

For Autumnal Equinox and Midwinter Sabbats the Altar drape should be black. For Vernal Equinox and Midsummer it should be white.

The High Priest should have two gold chalices. One as #1, which will hold only the Water upon the Altar, and #2 with a Silver Plate for his serving of the Sacred Bread and Wine.

All other particulars will be given in each ceremony as they are needed.

Sabbats are devotional services to the Old Gods and should be given our best efforts. Some covens have been in the habit of using the Sabbat times to consecrate Swords, or cast spells and works of the Art Magical.

Such works do not honour the Gods. All works of Coven Will should be relegated to the Esbat cycle.

Sabbats are times to invoke the Cosmic Power of the Ancient Deities for Worship and to celebrate a theme that helps to better us as Human Beings.

The Circle

As in the days of old, followers of the Craft worship in a circle. That is nature's most perfect shape, showing completion, and is a symbol without beginning or end. Life is a circle, as is the greater universe at large. It is a circle that is a spiral moving ever outward or ever inward from infinity.

The true temple of Wicca employs the theory of the cyclotron and both invokes and banishes depending on the circumambulations employed in erecting its walls on the mental and spiritual planes.

The movements counter-clockwise or widdershins are negative in aspect and correspondence. Negativity attracts to itself. It is of feminine nature in that it attracts and builds form.

For that reason, the circle is always cast widdershins as the Sacred and Holy Names of the Supreme Godhead are invoked.

On the other hand, a motion clockwise or deosil is positive and masculine of nature and therefore banishes or sends out. The circle is closed by motion in a deosil fashion around its rim as blessings are pronounced in a positive manner.

This is in keeping with the force of motion that occultists employ in using the invoking and banishing pentagrams.

The circle is invoked widdershins, filled with the energy of the ritual and then banished deosil releasing the energy.

As can be gathered from the foregoing, the circle can be a force both for good and ill. Whatever power is invoked in building the circle, lends its vibrations to the ritual or spell performed, thereby creating a power and force that is released out upon the world at large as the circle is banished.

It has always been the practice of true practitioners of Wicca to only invoke forces for good purposes and thereby bless the world with constructive and cosmic purpose and effort.

This is mentioned only to illustrate the fact that all power and force in the universe contains the opposite or the key to destructive purposes. With this in mind, true practitioners of the Craft must always assume responsibility for their works. The symbolic double-edged sword should be held in mind.

To Cast The Circle With Fire and Air

This is the preliminary or opening Rite before the main body of the Sabbat should be started. It sets up the vibratory purpose for the devotional work to follow.

The format should be that the High Priest opens the Sabbat by casting a Circle with the masculine elements Air and Fire, conducts the Sabbat Ceremony and closes the Circle with the feminine elements of Water and Earth.

The opening and closing observances are given first and the main bodies of the Sabbat Rituals, to be place between them will follow in their due course.

These opening and closing rites should be learned by heart, so they may be conducted smoothly and efficiently.

There have been requests for clarification about why the Circle should be built widdershins. Most systems cast deosil. The fact is that a widdershins motion is a negative gesture and negativity attracts that which is called. Deosil is a positive gesture and positivity banishes that which is already there.

The key is in the Pentagram:

An Invoking Pentagram produces a widdershins force flow. A Banishing Pentagram creates a deosil movement in the ether.

Therefore, to create a Magic Circle for any form of occult work which is to call and attract a specific Force, a widdershins motion should be started. A Circle or Ritual that is to cleanse or banish a Force or entity form an area requires a deosil movement.

An Invoking Circle cast deosil only cleans out the space within and prevents any force from being attracted to it. The Rite may be pretty and pleasing, but is only an act of the Officiant's will and does not bring in the power of the Gods.

Prior to the Sabbat, the Altar will be set and left in darkness with only the Sanctum Lamp burning in the Ritual Chamber.

The Thurible of the High Priest with coal and incense and a votive or taper, unlit, will be waiting outside the Ritual Chamber. (Their places on the Altar, 4 & 6, will be empty.)

The Summoner will have acted as Doorkeeper to admit all Coveners as each arrived at the Covenstead. He/she takes up position near the door to the Ritual Chamber when Sabbat is ready to begin.

NOTATE BENE: Coveners should arrive early and change into robes and regalia well enough in advance so as to be ready. Do not dress for Sabbat prior to arriving at Covenstead. In other words, one does not travel to Sabbat in robes and regalia on a city bus. Laugh not, my children, such has been known to happen.

The High Priest will approach the Summoner and show grade sign and give the Watchword (see *Hallowmas Sabbat*).

He then steps to the Thurible and unlit taper or votive. He lights the coal and the Incense and the taper or votive from the votive taken from the Sacred Flame by the High Priestess, earlier, before the Altar was consecrated. The High Priestess follows behind him in processional.

As each Covener passes the Summoner, he/she will give the proper grade sign of his/her rank to the Summoner and whisper the Coven's

Watchword into the Summoner's ear.

The High Priest carrying the Air and Fire, steps to the Altar and stands silently, allowing the Coven to follow into the Ritual Chamber and take up positions around the far edges of the room.

When all have entered and the Summoner has entered and sealed the door, he may begin:

Setting the Air and Fire upon the Altar in their places, he says:

It is Sabbat. The time of worship of the Old Gods begins. Blessed be.

He lights the Altar candles #2 and then #1 from the votive or taper. He says:

Attend to us, O Gods of the Ancient Faith and Watchers from the Times of Old. We kindle these Sabbat Lights in thy honour. Be with us now as we build the Temple in the custom of our Forefathers and Mothers since time before time. Blessed be.

He takes up the burning Incense in the Thurible and moves to the North Quarter of the Circle area (always moving widdershins from and to the Altar when the Quarters need be addressed).

At the North he holds the burning Incense before him and says:

By this Sacred Element, I call the Power of the Old Gods. The good God and the gracious Goddess draw in to us from all quarters of the Cosmos. blessed be.

He carries the Incense around widdershins to all other Quarters North to North again, repeating the words are each point. A slight bow is given when reaching the North the second time, and he passes around back to the Altar and replaces the Incense.

Taking up the white Altar candle into the right hand and the black one into the left, he moves again to the North.

Holding the lights high before him at the Quarter, he says:

By the power of the mighty Symbol of our Faith, the Pentagram of the Ancient Wisdom, we invoke the Gods. We offer our light and love to them as they have given same to us from immemorial time. Blessed be.

Bringing the candles down, he descends to the left knee and allows the bottoms of the candles to touch the floor. Coming up off the knee, he sweeps the candles up and across to the right as far as he can reach. Sweeping the candles across before him to the left as far as he can reach, he then descends to the right knee, drawing the candles down across to touch the floor at the right side. He rises off the right knee, to bring the candles back to their starting position.

(A large Invoking Pentagram has thus been drawn at the North. This act should be well rehearsed to flow smoothly and not put the candles out.)

The Invocation and gesture are repeated at each Quarter, moving widdershins around the area. At the North, he will give a slight bow to seal the Circle. He moves back to the Altar and replaces the Altar candles. The Psychic Barrier of the Temple is erect.

He unsheathes his Athamé and moves to the North East quadrant of the Circle area, where the Summoner should be standing, and draws an arch in the air with the blade. He re-sheathes the Athamé and returns to stand before the Altar, hands in the grade sign of his rank, facing North. He says nothing but should smile in blessing as the High Priestess leads the Coveners into Circle to take their positions around the area.

She stands near him to assist where needed during the Sabbat Rite to follow. Coveners should enter by seniority in the Coven, but the Summoner enters last and seals the Circle with his/her Athamé, by drawing a barrier Cross at the place the Arch was made and through which all have passed.

The High Priest now says:

O Lord and Lady of Light and Love thy Coven of _______ stands now before thee. Bless us this Sabbat night.

The regular ceremony proceeds from this point.

To Close The Circle By Water and Earth

After the Sabbat Rite has been concluded, the High Priest stands facing North across the Altar.

He takes up the #1 Chalice from the West of the Altar (position 7) and moves to the North of the Circle. The Coveners stand within the Circle and he circumambulates around behind them.

Holding the Chalice of Water to the North, he inscribes a Banishing Pentagram in the air with it at that Quarter. (It need not be as large as the Invoking one drawn with the Candles, see previous section.)

As the gesture is made, he says:

Hail and farewell, we bid the Spirit of the Old Gods depart. May their blessing remain in us as the Temple is taken down.

He moves deosil inscribing the Pentagram at each Quarter with the Chalice and repeating the words (continuing to move deosil from and to the Altar as the Quarters are addressed).

Back in place at the Altar, the Chalice is replaced and the Pentacle bearing the dish of Salt is taken up.

He once again moves to the North and holds the Salt before him and sprinkles a bit to the Quarter and says:

Peace, be still, this Sacred Space, banished be all beings and forces. let Earth return to Earth and stillness reign. Blessed be.

He moves around to each Quarter deosil the same and repeating the words. At the North again, he bows to the Quarter and returns and replaces the Pentacle in its place.

He snuffs out the Altar candles and says:

It is done. Sabbat has been kept

He snuffs out the votive or taper and all may now leave the area.

A party atmosphere to honour the Gods and the Coven may now commence.

Before the refreshments are served, the Coven robes are changed for normal street clothes and the Sabbat Altar equipment is cleared away.

The votive, from the Sacred Flame, burning outside the Ritual Chamber, is snuffed out.

Preliminary Rite For Midwinter The Entering In of Death

Three days before the Winter Solstice, the Ritual Chamber should be stripped bare and the Altar taken down.

All Coven ceremonial properties should be removed to another part of the Covenstead where they may be thoroughly cleansed and blessed by the High Priestess (see *Section II*).

The Sacred Flame is to be put out at this time, so that a new one may be kindled at Midwinter Sabbat.

The High Priestess has secreted away a spark from this flame to use later in Blessing the Tools, then it is also put out. (See *Works of the High priestess.*)

Before stripping the Chamber and Altar, the High Priest goes to the Sanctum and faces the Sacred Flame. He has a small, flat dish in his hand as he speaks over the Flame:

The Light of this world dies at this cold, barren season. Cruel winter's rule lays heavy on us. The times of joy are shrouded in bitter and desolate landscapes of dead and dying nature. (He knocks thrice loudly upon the floor with the Great Wand.) *The Lord of Death comes to us all. He stands before our very gates. We pray he will not take but his due. His time be now and he will not wait.*

The High Priestess opens the door to the Ritual Chamber and bows as she steps back to allow Death to enter.

The High Priest continues:

We greet thee Lord, in this cold and dying season. Into the bitter times we go, into the darkness of this night of time. We shroud our souls deep within us and hope for future day. Blessed be. Take, O Dark One, our Sacred Light as our offering to thee.

He places the small dish on top of the glass holding the Candle of the Sacred Flame, so that it slowly smothers out. He says:

All is gone. The rule of Death is upon us now.

The High Priestess tolls a hand bell 13 times as the flame dwindles out.

Both he and the High Priestess strip the Chamber and Altar in silence.

The Ritual Chamber will sit in dark and quiet for the next days until just before Midwinter Sabbat, then the properties are returned and the Altar set for the Sabbat Ceremony. If at all possible, no one should enter until the Day of Midwinter to dress and consecrate the Altar anew.

The High Priest and High Priestess speak not a word as they work. From the Sacred Flame being smothered out, and the tolling of the bell, silence must reign in the ritual chamber. When all objects have been removed, they walk out together and close the door.

The High Priestess may seal the door by drawing a barrier cross in front of the door with her Athamé. From that point on the ritual chamber is not to be entered until the Day of the Winter Solstice. The season of Dark, Death and Winter rule the world.

All the ritual tools should be cleaned and re-blessed by the High Priestess during these three days. (See *Works of the High Priestess.*) On the Day of the Winter Solstice she unseals the door by banishing the barrier cross with her Athamé and enters the chamber. The altar is now reset and all is prepared for the celebration of the Midwinter Sabbat.

Midwinter Sabbat
Bring To Us The Child of Promise

This is the first in the Cycle of the High Priest of the Solar or Celestial Sabbats to being the yearly Keeping of the Times. These of the Solstices and Equinoxes are celebrated in honour of the Good God who initiates the Law of the Cosmic Order from our vantage point on this Planet. (The practice of this system in the Southern Hemisphere, would, of course, be reversed.)

The Sabbats run active and passive, male and female, alternating around the order of the year. The God orders or initiates the Times and the Goddess fulfills the Order with a responding seasonal change six weeks later. The Agency of the Good God ordains the Law and the Agency of the Gracious Goddess gives form and meaning to the Law.

For the Sabbat the Altar and Ritual Chamber have been thoroughly cleaned and all tools and Coven religious properties rightfully blessed (see *Section II*).

The Altar will hold in addition to the needs according to the set up for the High Priest, a few necessary things for this season:

In the center space #8 will sit a Cauldron filled with Earth in which stands a large red candle. The Cauldron is flanked with seasonal sprigs of Holly and Pine with Cones. On the Altar will also be a taper candle for each Covener to participate in the Ceremony, red for a male, green for a female. The Incense should be of pine and spice, heavy and sharp.

The Ritual Chamber is dark, the Altar sits dark, as no Sanctum Lamp burns yet. The Covenstead is also in total darkness as the coven assembles outside the Ritual Chamber.

The High Priest holds the flint and steel to produce the Earth Fire, a modern cigarette lighter will do.

All stand in silence contemplating this deep Darkness of the Night of Time. The High Priest says:

De profundis clamavi ad te, domine, runs the Ancient call to God for aid. We stand wrapped deep within our souls in darkness and despair. The Rule of Death is upon us at this desolate hour. We have only our hope for future day to carry us through this cold time of trial. Blessed be. Hidden within the Goddess' womb stirs our joy of tomorrow, when the Light of this World returns to us.

All male Coveners chant: *Bring to us the Child of Promise.*

All female Coveners respond: *Io Evo Heh, the Lord of Life is born this night.*

The High Priest produces a spark with the flint and steel and puts it out. The Coveners repeat the chant and he does so again. On the third round of the chant he keeps the flame he has produced and lights a votive or taper.

All exclaim:

Blessed be! Cruel Winter's reign the Good God puts on the wane.

The High Priest will light his Incense and give grade sign and Watchword to the Summoner. All Coveners follow suit.

The High Priestess has been holding the Candle to go into the Sanctum. The High Priest lights the candle for her from his taper produced from the Earth Fire.

As the High Priest steps into the dark Ritual Chamber with his Incense and Candle he announces:

Flee all darkness, flee all despair, the Good God comes. Set aside all care.

The High Priestess follows him in and moves to the Sanctum to install the Sacred Flame in its place. (See *Section II.*)

The High Priest casts the Circle in his fashion with Air and Fire.

When the coven has assembled inside the Circle (see instructions in previous section of *Casting the Circle*) the High Priest lights the red candle in the center of the Cauldron of earth. He prays:

Our Good God, our Lord of Life, our Light of this World, Father of all being, bless us and keep us in times of trouble and in times of joy. Accept our act of devotion to Thee this Midwinter Sabbat, this joyous time of Yule. Blessed be.

He then says:

Out of the Great Mother's Womb has issued forth our hope for future day. The darkness of the Night of Time is banished. Light and love once more enter through the portals of this World. Let us tread the Ancient Round to raise the Cone of Power to aid the waxing Power of the God.

The High Priestess begins by taking the hands of the Coveners next to her and starts to move widdershins as all Coveners link hands and form a circle around the inner edges of the Circle area.

The High Priest stands at the Altar to be able to feel and sense the power as it is drawn in and raised.

The coven led by the High Priestess, circles around slowly at first, but increasing in tempo with steady measured form footsteps. As they move, they chant in unison:

God of Light, God of Life, cast out winter's tempest and strife. Wax with love, wax with will, in our lives all joy fulfill. Flint and steel have given thee birth, power from the Goddess' girth. No more darkness, no more despair, give us Thy goodness, as we tend thee with care.

The Circle Dance should move faster and faster and the chant become louder and louder as the Coveners circle widdershins until they are running and chanting as fast as they can.

When the High Priest feels the invoked power is at its height, he will shout:

Peace be still. The God here.

All Coveners stop and fall to rest on the floor, looking inward and catch their breath as they meditate to increase the power drawn by the dance.

The High Priestess will move to stand beside the High Priest at the Altar. They both face South with backs to the Altar.

He takes up the vial of Anointing Oil, she takes up the tapers off the Altar.

Each Covener then, one at a time, steps forward and receives an anointing on the forehead from the High Priest, and a dab of oil for his/her hands and a candle from the High Priestess. He/she will then step back into place around the Circle and sit down.

Each Covener, then has a candle, red for male, green for female, and they sit and dress that candle for whatever private intention they wish for themselves, drawing on the invoked power of the God in the Circle.

The High Priesthood also anoints their own private candles for their own request to the God.

When the candles have been given a thorough charging (at least five full minutes of intense, silent stroking with oil and will power) the High Priest will light his from the red one in the Cauldron. Each Covener will then follow suit to step forward and light his/her own and place it to stand in the Cauldron flanking the large red one.

The High Priesthood place theirs after all Coveners have done so and stepped back into place.

The High Priest prays to send the power:

Invoked Will of our Mighty God. We loose Thee into this world of man. Go Thee out to all corners, and bring us the results of our thought and deed. Work our private Wills for us as is most expediant and as best for our individual and collective well being. Blessed be, O God of Light.

Each Covener then draws his/her Athamé and holds it high pointing upward and all chant in unison:

O God of Witches' Power and Will. We bless thee to work thy might in light and love and works of wonder. Let thy light refresh us with love and good fellowship for all our co-creatures and fellow beings. Blessed be.

Athamés are re-sheathed and the coven meditates silently to bid the invoked power on its way. The Cauldron candles are to burn themselves out.

The High Priest will then close the Circle with Water and Earth.

After the ceremony, the High Priestess will bless the Yule Log, (see *Section II*) and a seasonal festive dinner should be celebrated with the traditional Old World Yule Time foods and beverages. This party should be joyous with ribald and lustful Pagan good cheer and revel. In the morning as many as can should go out to greet the Dawn.

And a good Yule to all.

Notes on the Sabbat Rituals Winter Solstice

1. It is the duty of the High Priest to ensure that all persons who participate in a Sabbat circle are well versed in the Sabbats meaning and are able to join the chants and responses. During the course of classes in Craft studies that the High Priest gives, he must see to it that those who have reached the First Degree (1^0) of Craft are familiar with all that any Sabbat Ritual may require them to do.

2. No Sabbat may have non- participating observers who have not taken the third level of initiation, which is the First Degree (1^0). It may be advisable to hold a special class in Sabbat practice for those in the third level where notes on the chants and responses may be given out for study.

3. The Four Watchtowers are not set up for Sabbat Ritual. They are used and employed at Esbat Time because the Esbat circle is used for working spells and magics.

4. If a New Moon or Full Moon falls within the three- day period at Sabbat Time i.e. the day before or the day after a Sabbat, the Esbat will be dropped and the Sabbat takes precedence.

5. The grade sign used by the High Priest in blessing each and every Covener during the Midwinter Sabbat, by anointing them with oil is a pentagram surmounted by a fire triangle indicating that the person

is at least of the third level of initiation. This is not the grade sign that is used upon entry into the circle. The grade signs showing levels of initiation are conferred at initiations and will be explained in their proper place in *Book V: The Cornucopia.*

Vernal Equinox Sabbat

This Sabbat is the traditional time Covens would initiate Pre-Initiates into the Outer Portico of the Temple. The Initiations to Neophyte status would be given and elevations of Neophytes as Probationers, who have successfully completed the one- year study course.

Those ceremonies are found in *Book II - The Book of Beginnings.*

The length of this Sabbat is shortened from some of the ancient rituals for this time of the year in order to facilitate a coven in the task of Initiations. Always remembering, Pre-Initiates being elevated to Neophyte and Neophytes being elevated to Probationer, do not see, nor participate in the Sabbat ritual. Arrangements for them should be made to wait outside the Ritual Chamber. The Summoner will see to it that they are kept occupied somewhere so not to be able to see the Craft Grade signs or rank as the Coveners entering the Ritual Chamber give them.

The Grade Sign is given to the Craftsman upon assuming that rank, and with each succeeding rank taken in the Craft, he/she assumes the proper one. (See *Grade Signs* in *Book V: The Cornucopia.*)

For this Sabbat a cauldron of sand or earth is set before the door to the Ritual Chamber, outside, The Incense should be a pleasant Benzoin with Mace.

The Altar would be set in the manner of the High Priest with a twig of leaves from a living tree and a blue taper candle for all Coveners participating in Circle. (Some covens may be large with more than the required twelve for Circle. Additional members may observe and join in the recitations from outside Circle.)

When all is ready, the High Priest casts the Circle with Air and Fire.

To begin the Sabbat he says:

It has always been the Ancient Way to reaffirm the Faith at this time in the cycle of the year. As the Good God gives the potency of Nature to reaffirm life this festival of spring, let us do likewise, to rekindle in our hearts the Ancient tenets of our Craft and chosen road to the Sacred Wisdom. Blessed be.

Let us call the God and raise the Cone.

He hands to the High Priestess a twig of leaves and a blue taper from off the Altar. She passes them around to each Covener in Circle.

The High Priest takes up Altar Candle #2 and moves around the Circle taking light to each Covener, lighting his/her taper.

Setting the Altar Candle back in place, he says:

This is the Night of the Balance of Forces, light and dark stand equal at this time. Let us balance them in ourselves.

The High Priestess begins to lead the Circle Dance. Moving widdershins the coven follows her. With light in one hand and a sprig of Life in the other, all lightly and lively tread around the Circle chanting in unison:

Hail the young Lord, proud and potent, affirms the Will of Creation's Flower. Light affirms life at this Equinox hour.

Balance we now our Will in this way. That love and light in our hearts shall stay. Blessed be, O God of Life.

The Circle Dance need not be long, nor need it raise a lot of Power. When the High Priest feels the drawn-in presence of the Gods, he says:

Peace, be still. The Good God is here.

The Circle Dance halts and each Covener faces into the centre of the Circle, holding his/her lit taper high before him/her, and the High Priest leads everyone in the recitation of the Litany of Creeds:

I. I believe in the Supreme Being known to Mankind as the God and Goddess, co-equal and co-eternal.

II. I believe in honouring the Gods at the Eight Sabbats of the yearly round.

III. I believe that the Human Mind is the greatest gift of the Gods. It will lead Mankind ever forward to perceive the Divine Essence in all living beings.

IV. I believe in observing discretion in all matters pertaining to the Craft communicated to the Stranger.

V. I believe in establishing within myself a balanced life in harmony with all other parts of the Manifested Universe.

VI. I believe that nothing in Nature is ugly or unholy.

VII. I believe in Perfect Love and Perfect Trust, tempered to those of good will and worthy.

VIII. I believe in walking in humility with my Gods and in relationships with all my fellow beings.

IX. I believe in being patient with and in giving understanding to those less evolved on Life's path.

X. I believe living is an eternal process of learning.

XI. I believe in the progressive spiritual evolution of the Human Soul through the process of successive life cycles on Earth and on Spiritual Planes.

XII. I believe in Cause and Effect and accept all Esoteric Religions as sister Faiths to Wicca.

XIII. I believe in holding my thoughts steadfast for the Good, so that I may experience only good in the interims between incarnations. Blessed Be, the Ancient Wisdom.

After the Litany, the Summoner and Sponsor for the one/s to be elevated step out of Circle, by creating the proper door, and fetch in the Initiate/s for Initiation. (See *Book II.*)

After the Initiations, the High Priest closes the Circle with Water and Earth.

The blue taper candles are deposited in the Cauldron as each Covener passes out of the Ritual Chamber. They are to burn themselves out.

The High Priestess will collect the twigs of leaves and secret them away for drying, to be used at next Candlemas (see *Section II*).

Notes on the Invocatory Circumambulation Led by the High Priestess

Thus far the Winter Solstice and the Vernal Equinox Sabbats have been described. As already mentioned, the High Priestess acts as helper and assistant to the High Priest. He is the celebrant for the Sabbat and conducts the pace of the ritual. She leads the Coveners in all chants and dances around the circle.

At the Winter Solstice the Coveners each light a taper from the Sacred Flame in the Cauldron and the High Priestess starts the dance. The Sabbat dances are symbolic of the Element corresponding to the time of year. They are movements widdershins to invoke the elemental power associated with the Sabbat. The ring of light created by the Coveners at the Winter solstice represents the first stirring and upward thrust of Spirit encased in Matter. The tred of the dance is slow and heavy. The movements must show or be indicative of the Earth Element and imitate a long climbing process. It is symbolic of one who is slowly and steadily climbing the stairs in a dark round tower, bearing a faint light to show the way. Weary persistence yet determined effort will eventually reach the top.

At the Vernal Equinox the theme is the gift of Spring and the balance of Light and Life. Each Covener carries those symbols in his or her hands. With a light in one hand and a twig of buds in the other, the dance is light and carefree. The movements are airy and rapid. An imitation of birds or the young forest creatures of Spring would be symbolic. The High Priest and High Priestess should work out the dances and instruct all Coveners who participate at Sabbat in their movements and meanings. The dances can be interpretive and vary from year to year. Coveners may have suggestions and interpretations of their own they may wish to share with all, as long as it is in keeping with the main theme of the Sabbat.

It is for this reason that Watchtowers are not erected at Sabbat Circle. The Watchtowers mark off a Circle from the rest of the world creating a space within space, to contain the power of a ritual until it is released with the closing ceremony. Sabbat time does not do this. It invokes the positive forces into the material plane and allows them to bless the world at large. Therefore, the Sabbat Circle may be crossed in and out as the dancers movements interpret the Elemental theme of the Sabbat.

At Esbat Time, the lunar tides for works of magic, the Watchtowers contain the ritual in the Esbat Circle. (See *The Book of Esbat.*)

During the dances, or the invocatory circumambulation of the coven, the High Priest stands as the ritual indicates and watches that all is done properly. He as observer, quiet and still, will be able to feel the presence of the in-drawing elemental forces. When he feels sufficient power has been gathered by the movements of the dance, he will signal the High Priestess, who will then begin to end the dance in order to bring the coven back to its place in Circle. More will be said on the dance later concerning the final two Sabbats of the Solar Cycle.

The Preliminary Rite For Midsummer Firing The Temple

The Altar and Ritual Chamber should be stripped and thoroughly cleaned prior to this ceremony.

The Sacred Flame, however, is not put out, but, being the Earth Fire, is should be allowed to die out of its own accord after the High Priest produces the Celestial Fire from Drawing Down the Sun, at this Rite to follow.

The Practicus and Hand Maiden may be allowed to perform this Rite as part of their ritual training. (They would take the part of the High Priest and High Priestess.)

Notate Bene: One may not always depend on the meteorological conditions to comply with the calendar. Should the day of the Midsummer Solstice be overcast, so that a Drawing Down the Sun is not possible, it is permissible to celebrate Midsummer some time within the Octave of the Season. That is within the eight-day period from the calendrical day. Perhaps it would be necessary to procure the Celestial Fire and then keep it set aside until the Temple can be fired before celebrating Midsummer. We will assume, however, for the purpose of this book, that all is well on Midsummer Day.

What is needed for this ceremony is a metal or brass bowl filled with earth, charcoal, straw or dry twigs and or wood shavings, a bit of Vesta Powder or Saltpetre, a large red or gold candle, an Incense of Frankincense and a magnifying glass, called the Sun Crystal.

The Ritual Chamber is cleaned and the Altar left bare. The only light is from the Earth Fire in the Sanctum, which was produced at Midwinter.

All things needed to dress the Altar for Midsummer have been cleaned and wait outside the Ritual Chamber.

At High Noon on the Day of Midsummer the High Priest is to Draw Down the Sun.

The charcoal is placed on the earth in the metal bowl and a sprinkling of Vesta Powder placed on that. The straw and twigs and wood shavings arranged around to take a flame. The large candle is kept handy and the incense with a coal kept by the High Priestess nearby.

The High Priest takes the bowl and the Sun Crystal out under the hot rays of the Summer Sun. He prays:

O Living God of this World's Light, give us of thy potent might.

Draw down to us this midsummer day and live in our midst in the Ancient Way. Blessed Be.

He focuses the rays of the Celestial Orb on to the charcoal and Vesta Powder. It will soon begin to smoke and smoulder. He may have to blow upon the spark to feed the process. When the combustibles catch, the flame will leap up. He should light the candle from it and take it back into the Covenstead.

Inside the Covenstead, he lights the coal for the High Priestess to burn in a Thurible for the Frankincense.

He then moves toward the Ritual Chamber holding the candle with the Celestial Fire high before him and she follows with the burning Incense.

At the open door to the Ritual Chamber he says:

Burn out the old, burn out the old! Behold the God of this World's Light enters in through Celestial Gold.

No forces of chaos, nor minions of Old Night may stand in the Good God's all embracing sight. Blessed be.

He moves to the Northwest corner of the Chamber and draws a large Solar Cross with the Flame. (The High Priestess follows him and does likewise with the Thurible of Incense.)

He moves back past his starting point at the Altar and passes to the Southeast Corner and does the same.

Moving back to the Centre, he pivots and steps to the Southwestern Corner and draws a Solar Cross. He moves back to the Centre and beyond to the North-eastern Corner and does the same. Back at the Altar he places the candle of Celestial Fire upon it and says:

To all the corners of this Cosmos, let our love and light shine forth this day. This Temple is a bastion of power to keep the darkness of chaos at bay. Blessed be..

The High Priestess sets the Incense Thurbile next to the Candle and says:

Air of sweetness; air of fragrance, exalt the Gods in this Fortress of Light. Blessed be.

The High Priest retires from the Ritual Chamber and the High Priestess sets the Celestial Fire into a new glass encased Candle in the Sanctum, so that it may take the place of the Earth Fire, which is allowed to burn itself out.

To keep the Spirit of a SacredFlame, she sets a small taper to light from the old Earth Fire, from Midwinter and touches the flame to the already burning wick of the Solar Flame, thus combining the two fires. Then the old flame can be allowed to burn out of itself.

She then sets about dressing the Altar and consecrating it for the Midsummer Sabbat to follow later that night.

Midsummer Sabbat

This is the Time when the potency of Life is at its height. The full and intense vibration of the growing Season is manifest. The Celestial Fire has been lodged in the Sanctum and the Temple purified with it.

Witches now use this Time to commune with the potency of the God and purify themselves with the Sacred Element.

Needed for this Sabbat after the Altar has been set for the High Priest, are: the #2 Gold Chalice of the High Priest filled with rich red wine; his Silver Plate holding Sabbat sweet cakes; three candles set in a row: one of red for strength and resolve, one of green for material things and one of dark blue or purple for spiritual problems. The Incense would be pure Frankincense. A brassen bowl of earth will set beside the candles.

As each Covener arrives for Sabbat, prior to the start of the Ritual, he/she will write either a problem or a request for personal needs on a small square of parchment. He/she will then place that parchment before one of the candles on the Altar. (The red one will be for healing and/or medical problems; the green one will be for financial or material things; the blue or purple one for any heavy spiritual problems a Covener may have.)

No one will read these parchments, folded before their respective candles, as they are personal and between the Covener and the Good God. They will be burned and sent to Him by the Cone of Power raised at Sabbat.

After the High Priestess has set the Altar and consecrated it, she takes a votive from the Celestial Fire and sets it before the Ritual Chamber door for the High Priest to use. The preliminary format should be familiar by now, see the previous Sabbat Ceremonies.

At the time for Sabbat the High Priest casts the Circle with Air and Fire.

To begin he says:

The Fire of the Velestial Orb illumines this Sabbat Circle. the Temple has been cleansed and properly fired. We worship not the Fire, but the Fire behind the Fire. The Good God, whose paternal potency keeps our ordered cosmos and sustains us by his light. Blessed be.

He prays:

O Mighty and Potent God of Light, thy Coven of______ would ask of thy might to bless us this Night of Nights.

He places his hands above the three candles and continues:

Read in the Parchments we send to thee, the needs and prayers of us, thy hidden children of the Ancient Way. Grant to each as is most expedient the fulfillment of these written words. Blessed be.

He takes up the #2 Altar Candle and lights the three candles on the Altar and sets the #2 Candle back in place.

He says: *Witches, call thy God and raise the Cone.*

The High Priestess begins to lead the Circle Dance, moving widdershins around the area. The coven follows her lead by joining hands and chants with her:

Around we go. around we go ever on the spiral flow.
Our thoughts take winged upward flight to the mighty God of Light.
Draw near, draw near, draw near to us, to us. give us thy ear.
We tred this Ancient Midsummer Round that thy power and might in us shall abound.

The dance must become faster and faster and the chant louder and louder, to raise as much potency and power as can be. Coveners must expend their energies to give to the Gods in order for the Gods to give of themselves in response.

When the High Priest feels the drawn-in power be at its height, he will shout:

Peace, be still before the Mighty One.

The Coveners should drop to the floor in place around the Circle and catch their breaths as they intently meditate, each one on his/her own parchment request.

The High Priest will take up each folded parchment and burn it in the flame of the Candle before which it lay. The burning brands he drops into the brassen bowl of earth to turn to spent ashes.

As he burns the parchments, he prays:

To thee, to thee, our only Good God, we send thy Coven's ardent desires. Manifest thy will in our ways as is thy Mystery of Light. Blessed be.

He then blesses the Wine and Cakes:

Wine is life matured by the Sun. Let it be our liquid of love that the Old Gods mature in our lives. Blessed be.

Bread is life nutured by the Earth to sustain our beings and build us in body. Let it be our food of love that the Old Gods share with all creation. Blessed be.

He takes up the #2 Altar candle once again and the High Priestess takes the #2 Chalice and the tray of Cakes. He steps to each Covener in turn placing a hand on his/her head and passing the flame around the Covener's head and says:

Be thou purified before the Good God of Light.

The High Priestess gives each Covener in turn a sip of the Wine and a bit of the Cake as she says:

Our Gods have blessed thee with abundant life and a loving Coven Family. Take of their love and commune with them. Blessed be, O Child of Wicca.

When all are communed the #2 Candle is placed on the Altar.

The High Priesthood commune themselves last as each Covener then meditates in silence with the Gods in the privacy of his/her own heart.

The High Priest, after a brief meditation, closes the Circle with Water and Earth.

The High Priestess takes a dab of the wine onto a ball of cotton and a piece of the cake wrapped to dry in a paper napkin and secrets them away for use after next Candlemas. (See *Section II.*)

The post Ritual party should be the most lively of the year.

The Great Rite

This is an optional rite to follow Midsummer for the Covens that feel they can accept and adhere to the collective responsibility this would entail.

Notate Bene: Hast thou wondered, my children, why such demands are made on thee for Ritual Purity and why we, the Elders, insist on their observance? This Rite may lead to the conception and eventual incarnation of a God's Child.

This be not a Rite for fun and games. This is not an excuse for sexual license. It be a doorway from Tomorrow that may bring a being into this world under the aegis of the God and Goddess. It would be a special child, a Sacred and Holy being raised and trained in the Craft by the collective of the coven community.

The Great Rite may not, therefore, be performed each and every year. Only when a Coven is in a financial and firm and sound foundation in the Faith, should the Great Rite be attempted.

The Coven Council will weigh the heavy responsibility entailed in this matter. It and only it will determine the Coven's ability and sincere commitment to the Faith to be able to undertake this work. It must be a total Community decision.

The needs are:

Dedicated Coveners of at least I° who will be delegated as God and Goddess for the Rite; the two parental Elements. They may or may not be a Handfasted Couple, however, such would be preferred.

Dedicated Women of the Coven skilled in midwifery, to see the possible conception to birth. The Herbal Arts and natural medications would be employed to bring forth a pure vessel of the Old Gods.

Dedicated men of the Coven to establish a financial nest egg for the raising and sustenance of the Child.

Dedicated legal commitment, should the Child be orphaned, to see that by proper documentation, the Coven Trustees become guardians.

Dedication of the entire Coven Community to rear the child in a loving family, although being allowed to be raised by its natural mother and father if they are hand-fasted, or at least by the Mother if not.

Dedication to train the child in the Arts of the Craft, to develop it in the ways of Witchery as an investment in Tomorrow.

Then and only then should the Great Rite even be considered by a Coven.

This is not the Ritual to Incarnate a God-form. That Ritual will be given to certain Elders to keep under key for the time in the Future, when Wicca as a whole is able and ready to bring forth an Avatar.

Considerations of the Utmost Importance

The background of the prospective Parental Elements should be thoroughly checked to provide the best possible strain, so that there should not be the slightest chance of birth defect or other genetic problems.

This means complete physicals for both Parental Elements (VD, Herpes etc.)

There must not be any drug history in either of the Parental Elements.

The female Element must have been off any contraceptive pills and/ or medication for at least six months prior to participation in this Rite.

She must be within normal childbearing years and not barren.

She must have a pre-determination pregnancy test and a fertility test prior to participation in this Rite, to preclude the coven taking on a child not conceived at the Great Rite.

Ideally, at the Time of the Great Rite, she should be in her fertile period (10 days prior to her expected beginning of menses, the ovulation period).

The Great Rite need not be done on the actual Night of Midsummer, but may be done at a propitious fertile time, according to the Female Element's lunar tide, between Midsummer and Lammas, but not after.

The Male Element must be free from having had a bout of Venereal Disease for at least nine months prior to participation in this Rite.

No contraceptives of any kind are to be used.

The Male Element must be either young and virile, or mature and potent. A proper sperm count needs to be made to determine potency.

He should, if at all possible, be circumcised and clean to prevent a possibility of cervical cancer in the Female Element.

A proper pregnancy test should be made two days and again one week, after the Great Rite, to be sure the conception has taken place.

Under NO circumstances is abortion to be considered. Even if it is known she is carrying a defective child. It is the Will of the Gods.

If the delivery would result in an optional situation of saving Mother or Child, the option is for the Child, if both cannot be saved.

In the event of multiple births, all children will receive the same considerations from the Coven. Primogeniture would not prevail.

It must be arranged for a Midwife of the Coven to attend and deliver at a proper Women's Pavillion in a hospital, in order to provide for any contingencies for the Gods Child/Children.

The New Born is to be looked to by a Medical Physician and attended by a Pediatrician. Male hands should not touch it as it issues forth.

In the event of a Male Child, he is to be circumcised surgically by a proper Medical Physician.

The foreskin, of a Male Child, and the Child's umbilical cord and placenta are to be given over to the Midwife, who will deliver them over to the High Priest for burning, to preclude an adverse occult link to the Babe.

In the event a Child is born with a veil, it is a sign of special Divine Providence, as an indication of the Gods singling out this Child as a Seer/ess. The veil will be given by the Midwife to the High Priestess, who will deliver it into the safe keeping of the Elders, to be dried and stored away.

Breastfeeding, if at all possible, will be given the Child by the Mother or a Coven Wet Nurse, or in lieu of such, Mother's Milk may be bought on the market. Cow's Milk should be avoided due to steroids, hormones and/or antibiotics given to cattle, which may tend to obesity and other health problems (anti-biotic resistant strains of Bacteria in cattle). Later the Child should be given Goat's Milk after weaning.

The Midwives of the Coven will see to it that Pennyroyal, herb and/or oil and Tansy or other abortifacients not be administered to the Female Element during pregnancy, or even come into contact with her.

Prescription medications and over-the-counter drugs contra-indicated for pregnant women must be avoided.

Normal activities during pregnancy are allowed, such as the Female Element's job (up until the reasonable time). Walking and proper exercise should be encouraged. Enrollment in a natural childhood class should be considered. Motorcycle and horseback riding are to be avoided.

The Coven Entity, itself, will see to the Female Element's spiritual, mental and emotional health during the pregnancy. The expectant Mother should practice the Craft teaching and discipline to make every effort to maintain a happy frame of mind, so as not to affect the growing foetus adversely.

In realising the responsibility in carrying such a Child, her mental and emotional balance should be maintained. She should consider herself as a consecrated vessel unto the Gods, for the duration of the pregnancy.

She should not actively participate in Treading the Round to raise the Cone during Sabbat and Esbat while pregnant. She should, however, be given an honoured place outside Circle, possibly free from Incense fumes.

In the event of a disaster or catastrophe of any kind, the Coven will see to her safety and the Child's safety after birth. A Covener, who does not have family responsibility of his/her own, will be assigned to go directly to the Mother's or Child's aid. This Covener is known as the steward/ess of the Gods' Child.

To avoid disputes over the Child's welfare, Coveners are to act as "Aunts and Uncles" rather than as parents.

Should the biological Father not be Handfasted to the biological Mother, he should be given deference as the Father and be bound for financial support for the Child.

When a Coven assumes to undertake the Great Rite, it is responsible for the Child, even should the Parental Elements, in their employment, be forced to quit the Covendom. The Child then should spend some time with the Home Coven during vacations and holidays from school to be with his/her "Aunts and Uncles" maintaining the ties.

The Parental Elements have a moral and ethical responsibility not to withhold the Child from the Coven which has provided the financial foundation for its birth as well as the spiritual, emotional, ethical and moral atmosphere for the conception of the Gods' Child.

The Coven Council, in its collective wisdom, will provide whatever legalities would be necessary for the prime consideration of the Child in the event of incapacitation, moral or physical, of either, or both Parental Elements, allowing the Child to have as normal a childhood as possible.

As many Covens as are able, should opt for the Great Rite, in order to provide a sufficient number of Gods' Children to step forward into the Future, so that, should any one Gods' Child not live to maturity, a number can carry on.

It will be the duty of the Coven Council to provide for any contingencies as time goes by. However, the requirements as stated above, for Parental Elements will be adhered to without deviation or exception.

In the due course of time, it will be from a generation of Gods' Children, under the direction of the Oracles and Queen Mothers of the Craft, who will provide the vessels for the Incarnation of the Wiccan Avatar.

NOTATE BENE: It is realized that the Stranger, and some Coveners, may view this as genetic, physical and spiritual manipulation, taking away an individual's free choice.

There is historical precedent, that certain persons were conceived and raised for the Temple, or special roles in life, such as royalty. Therefore, sufficient numbers of Gods' Children should be raised, educated and disciplined according to the Craft, so that those Children, by free choice and volition, may elect to participate in the further selectivity elevating the Human Species.

These Children are not to have cloistering or censorship from the world at large and are to be allowed access and exposure to any and all philosophies and/or theologies, in order to guarantee their decisions be of free choice.

In the event the Gods' Child/ren are in sibling role with other children of the Parental Elements, the wisdom of a "Solomon" would either be applied to prevent them from being treated differently due to the special circumstance of their conception and their relationship with their "Aunts and Uncles" of the Coven. They should not be allowed to become "smart-alecs" nor "scapegoats."

It would be the responsibility of the Parental Elements and the Aunts and Uncles of the Coven to always place an attractive example before the Child/ren. Let the Coven look to its own conduct.

IT IS WITH FULL REALIZATION OF THE SERIOUSNESS OF THIS RESPONSIBILITY, FOR ALL CONCERNED, THAT THE ELDERS REVEAL THE TRUE ARCANUM ARCANORUM OF THE MEANING OF THE GREAT RITE. ONLY THE BRAVEST AND MOST UNDAUNTED DARE TREAD IN SUCH WATER.

My children, I never promised a rose garden. Who ever said the Craft was easy?

RITUAL OF THE GREAT RITE

WHOSEOVER UNDERTAKETH TO PERFORM THIS RITE, OR THE COVENS WHICH SPONSORETH SUCH, DO SO WITH FULL UNDERSTANDING OF THE RESPONSIBILITY BEFORE THE GODS. IT IS NOT TO BE DONE LIGHTLY. SEEDS SOWN IN LOVE AND JOY, WILL PRODUCE AFTER THEIR KIND. THAT SOWN IN WOE AND MISERY WILL BRING A BITTER HARVEST. THE LAW OF COMPENSATION IN CAUSE AND EFFECT WILL NOT EVER BE ABROGATED. WITCHES, LOOK TO THY WAYS.

After Midsummer Sabbat, if the Great Rite is to be performed, the Altar is removed from the Circle area and set aside in the Ritual Chamber near the Sanctum at the North Wall. The Circle area is to be cleaned and swept.

In the centre of the Circle a dias is laid out and decorated with living flowers to represent the Garden of the Goddess.

Around the Circle, at the Four Quarters, are candles to represent the four points of the Cosmos: one of blue for the East, one of red for the South, one of green for the West and one of black for the North.

At the North of the dias rests a tray bearing a Sacred Chalice of the richest red wine and sweet cake with nuts and spice.

The Parental Elements will take the part of God and Goddess in the course of the Ritual.

The Covenstead, other than the Sacred Flame in the Sanctum, is to be in darkness. All Coveners have departed, including the High Priesthood. Before departing, the High Priestess will have taken a votive and lit it from the Sacred Flame and left it outside the Ritual Chamber for the needs of the Rite. As the last Covener departs, the Covenstead is sealed from the inside by the Couple to perform the Rite.

They bathe and perform the proper ablutions and anointing with a mystic Love Oil made and blended for this purpose by the High Priestess or Queen Mother of the Coven.

She may wear whatever flowers or garlands as would be appropriate for the Goddess in the height of Summer. Otherwise, she is skyclad.

He may bear only his Athamé to cast the Magic Circle of the God. Otherwise he is skyclad.

She enters the Ritual Chamber and assumes a languid and enticing position upon the dias among the flowers. She says:

I am Goddess. I am the cool verdure of the fertile earth. Let the Lord of Light ignite my Being.

He lights a taper from the votive left by the High Priestess and then snuffs out the votive as he says:

I am God. I am the fiery paternity of time and space. Let the Lady of Life quench my passion.

The Goddess calls:

Lord, thy time be at hand. Descend to me in loving embrace. Join me in the realm of matter. Languish among the fragrant essensces of life in matter.

The God responds:

Lady, thy pull is strong and I must limit myself in time and space lest I scorch the things I most love in fire untamed.

He enters the Ritual Chamber, sealing the door behind and goes to the North candle and lights it from the taper and says:

Spirit and Matter conjoin in this Sacred Place. Blessed be.

He moves deosil to the East candle, lights it and says:

Illumination of inspired purpose guides this Sacred Rite. Blessed be.

At the South candle, while lighting, he says:

Strength and Power liven all in joy. Blessed be.

Lighting the West candle, he says:

Love calls forth the beauties of Creation. Blessed be.

From outside the circle of candles, he points the tip of the Athamé at the floor and treads around widdershins from West to West again creating a Circle with the Goddess enclosed within.
She says:

Lord, thy Magic Bond is strong and a Cosmos is created to provide a solid form for thy Fire and Passion. Lay aside thy weapon and enter the Garden of thy Lady's desire.

He sets down the taper at the West beside his Athamé after entering by creating an arch in the wall of the Circle and sealing it back up behind him. He approaches the Goddess on the dias.
She offers him a taste of wine and a bit of sweet cake and says:

The Fruits of Life I offer to thee. From thee through me they flower forth in all of Creation's abundant wonder.

The two of them recite together:

God and Goddess to embrace in joy and delight,
creates the vortex that swirls in flight.
Bring through our passion burning fierce and intense.
A Child of the Gods from Rarified Realms to this plane most dense.

The couple consummate this Rite in acts of love and intercourse and spend the night together in Circle.

In the morning, she carries the Chalice around the Circle deosil to banish the magical barrier. Nothing further need be said, for the Mysteries of the Gods will manifest in their own due time.

The High Priesthood return to the Covenstead and all is made as it was.

This Ritual is placed in the Section of the Works of the High Priest, because he, as Minor Hierophant, would be guardian of this Doorway from Tomorrow and bring it forth only under the direction of the Coven Council.

In ancient times, the Sacred King was sacrificed to help elevate the entire Clan or Tribe. In this Age, it is the sacrifices made by the collective of the Coven in giving of their substance to call forth a Gods' Child that is of importance.

The Gods' Child is raised to help elevate the species as a whole and pass on through him/herself something of the Nature of the Gods. Sacred Kings are no longer sent to the Gods, they come from them.

The Minor Great Rite
Ancient Celebration of Life
The Consummation of Midsummer Sabbat

(An optional Private Rite for the High Priesthood)

After Sabbat Meal has been shared and all Coveners have departed to their various homes, the High Priest and High Priestess clear all remains of the Sabbat celebration from the Ritual Chamber.

The Altar is placed against the North Wall and covered with a black cloth. One red flower is set in the center of the Altar with a ruby colored votive lamp burning before it.

When all is cleared away and the Altar thus arranged, the High Priestess enters the Ritual Chamber skyclad. She then sets out a mat in the center of the floor with its head to the North. She places a yellow votive candle to the North, a blue votive to the East, a red votive to the South and a Green one to the West. The door to the Ritual Chamber is closed.

She then goes to the niche of the Sacred Flame and lights a taper. Ringing the bell thrice, then six times, then nine times (=18) to summon the attention of the Great Mother she Prays:

O great Creatrix and Ancient Womb of Life,
be with me now and witness this Rite.
Blessed be, O triform Goddess,
Sacred Mother of all that is.

She then takes the taper and lights the candles deosil from the North as she purifies the Chamber thus:

The path of the Solar Orb passes southwise
through the heavens, blessing the Earth as it goes.
Thus do I banish all that would be adverse to this Sacred Time.

Once the four votives have been lit, she begins to move widdershins around the circle with a feminine gait and seductive gestures as she holds the taper before her. She chants:

Goddess of Virginity, Goddess of Fertility,
Goddess of the waning tide,
attend this celebration of love.
As High Priestess
and regent of the great Mother on Earth
I become the Altar of her Sacred Mystery.

After she has circumambulated the area thrice, she puts out the taper and lays it by the votive in the North. She then assumes a supine position on the mat in the center of the Circle with her head to the North. After a short silence the High Priest knocks on the door of the Ritual Chamber five times to summon the God.

The High Priest then opens the door and enters the Chamber. He is skyclad and carries a tray containing a Chalice of red wine, a dish with a small cake, a Thurible with burning Incense, a small absorbent towelette across which the sword is laid.

As he enters he says:

The Ancient God of sky and sun descends to Earth.
The Great Rite is begun.
Accept these gifts from your ardent one.

He proceeds to the Altar and sets down the tray. Taking up the sword he proceeds to draw a Circle around the ring of candles circling the High Priestess widdershins. He says:

We build a place between the worlds.
A land of no time, yet containing the seeds of times to be.

After passing around once with the tip of the sword drawing out a Circle, he moves to the South and reaches into the Circle and lays the sword crosswise at the High Priestesses feet (tip to the West).

He returns to the Altar and takes up the Chalice of wine and standing in the West he sprinkles a few drops of wine upon the High Priestess as living Altar and says:

Lady of starlit bower and languid night,
accept my love and bask in my sight.

After a short pause, he places the Chalice at the western edge of the circle.

From the Altar he takes up the Incense and moves to the Eastern rim. He lifts the Incense thrice as he looks across the Circle and says:

Sacred Altar of the Great Earth Mother,
I give you the sweet savour of life and love.

Setting the Incense at the Eastern rim, he returns to the Altar and takes up the dish of cakes and the towelette. Moving to the North he sprinkles a few crumbs of the cake toward the High Priestess and says:

Blood and seed are the sacred mysteries from of Old.
They manifest as the Mother's fruitful bounty.
These we share with all creation. Blessed be.

He sets down the dish of cake at the North and moves to the South. There he stands looking down at the High Priestess holding the towelette in his hands. He says:

Lady of Ancient Mystery
permit me to worship at your Altar. Blessed be.

The High Priestess then responds:

Enter Lord of Sky and Sun,
embrace and bless this Garden of Earth's delights.

Make us one.
Blessed be.

He steps into the Circle and sets the towelette beside the mat. They both recite:

Life to the strong and power to the wise,
thus the Midsummer's Sabbat cries.
May this Sacred Celebration of Love and Life
bring us closer to the God and Goddess.
In the cycles of universes unfolding,
may our works continue the traditions
of the Ancient Craft.
Blessed be.

The Great Rite Has Begun

The High Priest and High Priestess make love in circle.

After they have finished, she takes the towelette and cleans off both of their bodies. The towelette is then sequestered away by the High Priestess. (In other words, she keeps it in hiding as a magick link. See *The Women's Mysteries* in *Book III, Sec. II: Works of the High Priestess.*)

They then share the cake and wine and spend the rest of the night together in circle if possible.

In the morning they join hands and make a deosil circumambulation of the Chamber to banish the Circle.

They then go to the niche of the sacred Flame and together say prayers to the God and Goddess, dedicating their actions to life's eternal expression.

They then declare:

Heaven bears witness and Earth declares that the Great Rite has once more been consumated. May the next Midsummer Sabbat bring us once again into the embrace of the Gods. Blessed Be.

They then leave the Chamber after all objects have been put away.

Autumn Equinox

This Sabbat commemorates the reaping of what has been sown, or invested into this Cosmos. The Law of Compensation in Cause and Effect, and the paying of the Piper for our thoughts, deeds and actions is what is marked and celebrated at this time. The Harvest symbols remind us of the return and just rewards for our efforts as Human Beings. It is Cosmic Justice, rather than subjective Human Justice, that is advocated by this Sabbat.

The Annual Coven Dues are also to be attended to at this time. Each Covener carries an envelope with the dues in his/her cinch cord.

The Incense should be cinnamon and clove, or other sharp spices. The Altar would need, in addition to the High Priest's set-up, an Autumn Symbol of wheat or ears of corn in a pleasant arrangement. It is called the Autumn Hen and stands for the last gleaning from the fields.

There would also be a large basket of seasonal fruit with small plates for each Covener participating in Circle.

When the Time for Sabbat is set, the High Priest casts the Circle with Air and Fire.

The High Priestess carries a Tambor decorated with Autumnal ribbons.

To begin, the High Priest says:

The potency of life ebbs at this time. We see the dark times looming before us. Would that we have laid in store sufficient merit and spiritual prosperity with the Gods to tide us through and lead into the better times beyond.

Witches, retrospection and introspection are the keys to this sombre Sabbat. How have we stacked up on the cosmic scale of things?

If we sought abundance, did we sow joy?
If we sought justice, did we act fair?
If we sought blessings, did we plant love?
Raise the cone and call the God,
we must face Him as we now surely are.

The High Priestess begins to beat a steady, somber rhythm on the

Tambor as she begins to move widdershins to start the Circle Dance. The step is to be steady, heavy and determined. It is not a light-hearted time. The Coven chants:

See the Old Lord downward sinking.
The ebb of life begins us thinking.
The Dark One comes and will give us our due.
Our rewards in life may be plenty or few.
What we as humans have been willing to give,
is the measure of our merit to have and to live.
Blessed be the justice of our God and Goddess.

When the High Priest feels sufficient power has been drawn, he motions for silence. Each Covener then meditates on his/her own compensation as a Human Being before the Gods. The High Priesthood pass out plates of the Harvest Fruits to each and all. The Coveners slowly eat as they commune with the Gods.

The High Priestess places the Tambor at the North Quarter of the Circle and each Covener places his/her Dues into it one by one.

The Circle is closed by Water and Earth and the Sabbat is over.

There is no need for a lively party, as this is the time of sober reflection by each and all.

The High Priestess secrets away the Autumn Hen for use after Candlemas. (See *Section II.*)

The Incenses For Solar Sabbats

The censer of the High Priest should be of the type that swings on a chain. In casting the circle with Air and Fire he censes by swinging the censer with his right hand as he proceeds to the Altar and circumambulates it. While he is constructing the circle he swings the censer thrice to each Quarter as he carries it around widdershins.

From that point on, no further incense is required at Sabbat Ritual for the Works of the High Priest unless it is otherwise specified, such as in Firing the Temple prior to Summer Solstice.

The High Priestess, however, uses mainly an open thurible that is carried by hand and can have more incense easily added as the Terrestrial Sabbats require (see *Book III, Sec. II: Works of the High Priestess*).

The Solar Sabbats presuppose a solar incense. Frankincense has traditionally been found to give the best Solar vibration to any ritual associated with the Four Stations of the Sun.

At Winter Solstice a mixture of 1/3 Frankincense and 2/3 Myrrh would give the heavy vibrations needed for that time.

The Vernal Equinox seems to call for a mixture of 1/2 Frankincense and 1/2 Lavender Buds and a small bit of dried rose buds and petals.

The Summer Solstice should be spicy and sharp, even acrid. Therefore 1/3 Frankincense, 1/3 Cinnamon and 1/3 Clove would be good.

At the Autumnal Equinox 1/2 Frankincense and 1/2 Patchouli would seem to bring in the Autumn Tide.

These are but suggestions and the High Priest may use the incense with which he feels the most comfortable. Other suggestions may be:

I. Pine in Winter, Flowers in Spring, Spice in Summer and Orange, Lemon or Apple in Fall. (Herbal essences may also be Autumnal.)

II. Woodland essences for Winter, Herbal essences for Spring, Flowers for Summer and Spices for fall.

On Creativity in Ritual

The High Priest may wish to compose his own original invocations and chants to be used in the Sabbat Rituals. This book offers a yearly liturgical theme, which may be embellished or enlarged upon. All things in the rituals have been simplified as much as possible to leave room for individual interpretations of the basic themes of the Great Cosmic Drama.

By keeping "The Times" the High Priest establishes a harmony with the Divine Verities the Sabbats symbolize, to which the Terrestrial Sabbats of the High Priestess respond and reflect. The Song of the Sun and the Ode of the Earth are the great rhythms of Life the Craft has ever celebrated from of Old.

This *Book of Lights: Works of the High Priest* should be read and studied by both the High Priest and the High Priestess of any Coven who elects to use them. In other words, she should read his book and he should read hers (*The Book of Lights: Works of the High Priestess*). In that way, each would know and fully understand how the yearly rule of both the celebrants at the eight Wiccan Festivals are properly divided.

Each will then be able to support and assist the other in equal balance throughout the cycle. Some Coven Traditions have divided the year down the middle or crosswise, as some 'authorities' have suggested. Such, however produces an unbalanced effort. It is not Nature's way. The God initiates, The Goddess responds.

It has been the experience of this author to have seen High Priestesses presiding at Solar Sabbat, High Priests invoking the Terrestrial aspect of Godhead. Such can be done successfully, but the vibrations from such a ritual leave something to be desired.

The man must serve and invoke the God aspect of Deity, and the woman must serve and mediate the Goddess forces of Nature. This is what the Great Rite means and tries to harmonize.

These two volumes of *The Book of Lights* along with *The Book of Esbat,* which is Coven magical practices, and *The Book of Beginnings,* which give the Wiccan Traditions of Initiation, will give a complete system of the Ancient Faith of the Wise for contemporary times. Our Faith does not make tyrants of men, for only in love and harmony of common effort can the Magics from of Old be worked. It is in keeping with that Spirit these Rituals are for the first time made public. Blessed be, O Children of the Wise Ones!

If these tomes provide a guide, then this writer is fulfilled.

Section II

Works of the High Priestess

These be the Rites of the Mater Magna, the earthly representative of the Gracious Goddess, Sybil and Seeress, Mother of the Coven. She be the one who observeth the Seasons.

The term "Mother of the Gods" describes the High Priestess. It is basically her duty to perpetuate the Craft.

As the tenets declare, each man and woman is a potential "God or Goddess." The High Priestess assumes the responsibility of providing the most conducive atmosphere in which the spiritual progression of every member of the Coven is aided. She nurtures their acquisition of knowledge and guides their evolutionary development. She must ever be gracious and understanding. Never should harsh words, or criticism of Coveners be voiced by her in public. She knows that each individual is at the stage of development where he or she needs to be at the present moment.

When acting in official capacity during Sabbat and Esbat or other ceremonies, she must always smile and beam of light and love.

She must consider how the "Gracious Goddess" would look upon an individual and act accordingly.

As "Keeper of the Sacred Flame," she is the heart of any coven and by her actions of good will and confidence in each and every one, she will get that in return.

If individuals must be admonished, let it be done privately and with intelligent forethought.

Her duty as Warden of the Ancient Lore means that she should be adept at some form of psychic divination - astrology, tarot, mediumship etc. She must also be an authority on herbal lore, both for healing and magical purposes. The High Priestess should also be an accomplished spellcaster, be able to work candle magic and be knowledgeable in most traditions of Spellcraft.

Her studies should have included all available works pertaining to the Old Religion. She will come in contact, in the course of time, with persons from other traditions and she should be able to see the essential unity in all faiths of the esoteric Wisdom Religion.

The High Priestess should be a woman of mature attitude between the ages of 25 and 50. By 50 years of age, she should have more than one coven organized under her sponsorship and thereby becoming eligible to become a Queen Mother.

As the High Priest is the teacher in the Craft and conducts and supervises the classes in Craft lore, leading to initiation, it is the High Priestess, however, who decides and determines what Craft lore is taught.

She, being of the feminine nature, has a more highly attuned intuitive level. She should then meditate upon each and every aspirant and let her intuitive faculty guide what the High Priest is to present in his classes.

By discussing the level of evolution and character of each person accepted into a class on Wicca, both the High Priestess and the High Priest would be able to best determine the spiritual needs and orientation of each of their students.

The Craft is better served by not giving all knowledge to one who might abuse it, or who could never comprehend it. In this way the Craft of the Wise preserves its integrity and adapts itself to the level of each person's present spiritual station, while helping him or her advance.

The High Priestess acts as officiant at the four terrestrial Sabbats known as the "Seasons Between the Times." These are the four great Earth Rites that marked the life cycle of our ancient ancestors.

At Hallowmass she conducts the Dumb Supper and works in the divinatory ritual to proclaim or obtain the coven Watchword.

The Watchword will then be required for all coveners of the fourth level of initiation (First Degree) in entering any Esbat circle for the working of the coven's magical ceremonies, along with their grade signs.

She will instruct the Summoner to see that the Watchword is also given as each Covener arrives for Esbat ceremonies. Only grade signs are required to be given at Sabbat, as no magics are worked, unless the High Priesthood require Watchwords for Sabbat, as shown in *Section I.*

Candlemas Sabbat is the time the High Priestess celebrates the tide of the waxing light. She mystically renews the Earth and prepares her for the renewing of life.

At Beltane, the High Priestess burns out Winter and welcomes the May. She celebrates a rite marking luck in love and life.

Lammastide is when the High Priestess blesses and breaks bread with the coven to celebrate the first fruits.

Her robes for this Sabbat cycle should be seasonal. It is suggested that she wear black or purple for Hallowmas, blue for Candlemas, rose or mint green for Beltane and dark green for Lammas. However, more flexibility is given the High Priestess in vesting for the seasonal themes and these colours need not be arbitrary.

Her altar cloths should reflect the seasonal themes also. The Earth herself is so rich and varied in her seasonal vestments that she might be copied as far as colours are concerned.

The High Priestess should possess a set of altar tools that she uses only at her four Sabbat ceremonies. These are not used by the coven in general at Esbat and other rituals. They should be the property of the High Priestess. They are as follows:

One silver chalice to contain water that she uses to erect the temple and carries in procession.

One stone or pewter chalice that she uses as a Quaich in giving coveners to drink (like the second chalice of the High Priest — see *Works of the High Priest*.)

One crystal bowl, small and round to contain salt and/or earth, which she also carries in procession.

One earthenware or pewter small round tray for offering bread to be shared with the Coven.

One three-branched candlestick to represent the three aspects of the Goddess. These always burn only white or black candles depending on the Sabbat ritual. (ie. Hallowmass and Candlemass will be black; at Beltane and Lammas, they will be white, unless a particular ritual stipulates otherwise.)

This she will add to the two pillar candles of the High Priest at Esbat and other ceremonies where they co-celebrate. (see *The Book of Esbat*.)

Unless the rubrics of an individual ritual specify otherwise, she should wear her silver cinch cord or cingulum and witch jewels and crown at all Sabbats.

Her broom, even if it is not used, should at least occupy a position either leaning against the altar on the west side or be placed at the door to the circle at the North quarter to be stepped over by all Coveners entering the Circle.

Her Thurible is of the dish type not on a chain.

Altar of The High Priestess

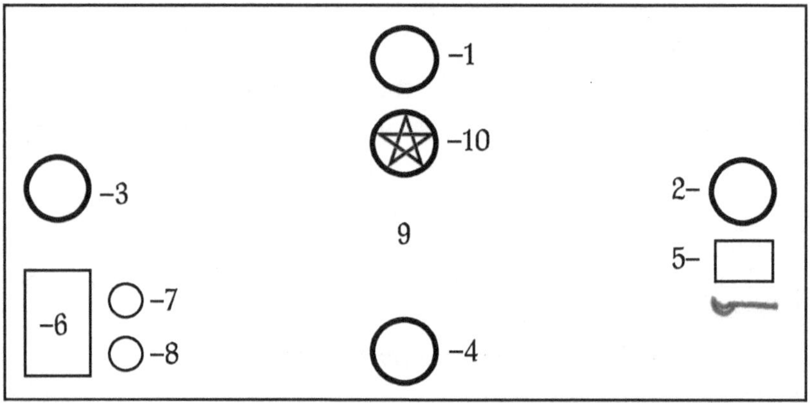

Altar Arrangements for the Terrestrial Sabbats

1. Three Branched Candlestick holder
2. Thurible
3. Chalice for Water carried by the High Priestess in processional to the Altar
4. Small Votive candle lit from the Sacred Flame
5. Extra Incense and spoon
6. Ritual Notes or Book
7. Hand bell
8. Sacred Oil
9. Center Space to hold objects for any Ritual at hand
10. Pentacle to hold a dish of Salt or Earth carried to the Altar in processional

The three-branched candle holder (1) represents the Moon phases of the Mother Goddess and indicates the Light of Life as seen from the Terrestrial viewpoint, as it flows or ebbs.

At Hallowmas, the three candles in it will be black or purple, to show the Season of Death. At Candlemas, the candles could be two white and one black to show the waxing light. At Beltane there should be three white ones to show life in force. At Lammas there could be two black and one white to show the growing days of darkness, unless kept standard, as mentioned above.

The Chalice (3) should be of silver. It will hold the Water that the High Priestess carries to the Altar to begin the Casting of the Circle with Water and Earth.

In addition to the silver Chalice, she should have a larger one of pewter in which Sabbat wine is blessed and shared and/or libations made to the Earth.

The Pentacle (10) holds a dish of Salt/Earth , which she also carries to the Altar.

When the High Priest sets and consecrates the Altar for her, prior to Sabbat, he places her Chalice of Water and Pentacle with salt before the Door of the Ritual Chamber for her to have as she moves into the Ritual Chamber to begin Sabbat.

She should have taken a flame from the Sacred Flame in the Sanctum for him to consecrate the Altar and he leaves that upon it (4).

In other words, fire for the Altar set for the Celestial Sabbats of the High Priest is set outside the Chamber as per the section on consecrating the Altar (see *Works of the High Priest*). For the Terrestrial Sabbats of the High Priestess, that fire is used in consecrating the Altar, but left burning upon it.

The High Priestess in her Sabbat Cycle has more freedom of expression in colour and/or dress in order to reflect the seasonal themes of her Sacred Celebrations. The Altar may be more decorative and/or festive than for the Works of the High Priest. The Sabbats of this cycle are not so somber and should be made joyful and light-hearted from Candlemas through Lammas. Hallowmas, however is a serious and sober Sabbat, but it also takes on a festive mood during its second part.

The Terrestrial Sabbats respond to the Times set and observed at the Solar Sabbats of the Solstices and Equinoxes. They are the seasonal reflections on the mundane level of the forces in motion from the Solar Cycle. The God initiates and the Goddess responds.

To Cast the Circle by Water and Earth

This is the method employed by the High Priestess to create a Sacred Grove for the worship of the Goddess. Her Sabbat Cycle is not as formal as the one for the High Priest. She erects a circle but not a formal psychic barrier that may not be crossed.

At times, during the Sabbats for the Goddess, Coveners may have to step in and out of the Grove in the acts of leaping the cauldron, and at times the Altar may have to be moved to provide space for the movements in and around Circle. The Goddess' Sabbats are light-hearted and spirited celebrations of joy and communion with the seasonal theme.

It is suggested that the Altar be placed at the North rim outside the Circle area directly before the Sanctum, to allow enough space in the Circle for the Coveners to move around. As the High Priestess officiates, she would be standing within the northern area, at the Altar.

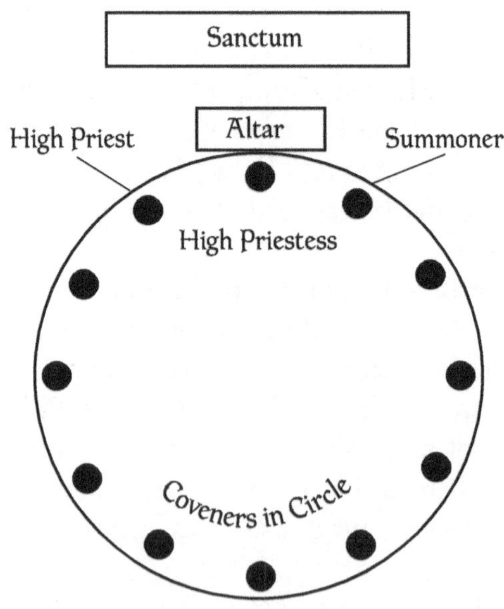

The center space in the Goddess' Grove is for the cauldron and other items as may be needed for the Terrestrial Sabbats.

The High Priest will have set and consecrated the Altar for the Works of the high Priestess. All other necessary prerequisites as explained in *Section I*, for Summoner and Grade signs, et alia, as a general format, will also be familiar by now.

When the High Priestess steps forward to begin Sabbat, she will at all times be and act the "Gracious Lady" whom she represents, as much as is possible. All, all, all, coveners should be looked upon by her with warm and loving smiles. Never is a frown or cloudy expression to pass her face before and during Sabbat. She should be able to bless each one with her mere radiant presence.

Notate Bene: What say ye, Witches, hast thou ever been in Circle and seen a so-called High Priestess throw a temper tantrum? Hast thou been given dirty looks because something was amiss? We are all the Gods Children and not perfect, that is why we are here. It is to be hoped that by treading the Round in the spiral nebulae of the Ancient Gods, that we can elevate to more perfect planes of consciousness. Our earthly representatives of the Old Gods should be an inspiration and aid us as they can. Immaturity and childishness retard our progress.

When everything is ready, the High Priestess takes her silver Chalice of Water and her Pentacle holding Salt/Earth and steps to the Altar. The High Priest follows her and the Coven in order of seniority follows suit.

The Coven assembles outside the Circle area until the Circle has been cast and the Goddess doth bid them enter.

To begin, the High Priestess sets the Pentacle down in its place and lights the coal in the Thurible and sets some incense to burn. She lights the candles in the three-branched holder from the votive (4) sitting on the Altar. She says:

It is Sabbat. the Sacred Light of the Gracious Goddess illumines our hearts as it lights our Circle and Grove. Blessed be.

She is still holding the Chalice of Water and passes the flame of the third candle to be lit over it as she says:

May all our cares and woes be purified and blessed and set aside. The waters of the Goddess bring us joy, life and love. Blessed be. (She sets aside the candle back in its place).

She moves widdershins from the Altar toward the West from the Altar in the North, sprinkling water from the Chalice in small droplets as she treads around the Circle area. As she moves, she says:

Matrix of Creation's Being, cleanse this Sacred Place most pure; a recepticle of love in the gracious Goddess' sight.

Passing from North to North, sprinkling as she goes, she makes a final sprinkling toward the Center of the Circle area and sets the Chalice in place on the Altar.

Taking up the Salt/Earth she again moves widdershins around the Circle, North to North, sprinkling grains as she goes. She says:

Matter of Earth; the Goddess' form. be our solid and firm foundation and prepare this Grove to receive the Gracious One whom we call. Blessed be.

The Salt/Earth is replaced and the High Priestess stands in the Pentagram Position and prays: (she is facing North across the Altar)

Lady of Life; Lady of Love; Lady of Abundant Wonder, attend to us at Sabbat Rite. Enter in thy Sacred Grove and commune with us in our hearts most bright. Blessed be, O Mater Magna.

She continues:

I am the Star Goddess. I am the Great Mother. I am the Lunar Tide. Come my children, gather to my side.

The Summoner bids all Coveners enter the Grove at the Northeastern point. They move in by order of seniority and take positions around Circle. The Summoner enters last but does not seal the door.

The Circle has been cast by Water and Earth and the Sabbat Celebration will proceed from this point.

To Close the Circle by Air and Fire

After the main body of the Sabbat Rite has been concluded, the High Priestess faces North across the Altar and places a bit more Incense on the coal in the Thurible. Taking up the burning Thurible, she (ouch!)... Taking up the Thurible burning the Incense, she says:

The Sabbat of the Goddess has been kept. Let this Sacred Element now conclude the Rite and banish the Grove till cross-quarter next.

She circumambulates the Circle area deosil, carrying the Incense around from North to North.

Replacing the Incense, she takes up the Three-branched candlestick and moves deosil around the Circle behind the Coveners standing in Circle. As she moves, she says:

As this fire goes around, sink this Circle beneath the ground. Blessed be.

Back at the Altar, she prays: *Gracious Goddess of love and life, we have given thee of ourselves this Sabbat night. Live in and among us this season through. Blessed be. Sabbat is finished.*

The Coveners may now step out of place and clear things away and change from robes.

A seasonal party to commemorate the theme of the Sabbat may now begin.

Ritual of the Sacred Flame

This is the yearly regimen of the High Priestess in tending and keeping the Sacred Flame in the Sanctum Niche.

Prior to Midwinter, the High Priest puts out the Celestial Fire at the observation called the Entering in of Death. For the next few days there is no Sacred Flame in the Covenstead.

At Midwinter Sabbat he produces the Earth Fire and gives it over to the High Priestess.

Before he begins to erect the Circle for Midwinter Sabbat, the High Priestess sets the Sacred Flame for her to take fire and consecrate the Altar when she sets it prior to Midwinter. He must therefore delay slightly his beginning of Sabbat to allow her to take the flame from the Earth Fire and consecrate the Altar. (See ritual format for *Midwinter.*)

When the flame is given over to the High Priestess she installs it in a glass encased candle in the Sanctum with these words:

Spark of Life from the Earth Mother's womb, burn in our midst as a link with the Gracious Goddess. Blessed be.

Thereafter, she will keep the flame burning by lighting a new candle each week from its flame.

When the Celestial Fire is given over to her after the Firing the Temple before Midsummer, she will install that in the Sanctum and bless it thus:

Light of this world from the Celestial Orb, be our link with the power of the Good God. Blessed be.

Lighting a taper from the Earth Fire, she touches the flame to the already burning wick of the Solar Fire, combining the two flames and snuffs out the taper.

The Earth Fire is now allowed to burn out and the Celestial Fire will be kept going till Midwinter.

Whenever a Sabbat, Esbat, or lesser Magical and/or Occult works need be done, a spark of this flame will be used to light any and all candles and incense coals used throughout the Covenstead.

She keeps a hand bell beside the Sacred Flame and rings it once, or thrice as a ritual may stipulate, whenever a spark is removed from it for whatever purpose.

Once a week the Sanctum should be dusted and kept clean.

Concerning Privacy

In keeping with the traditions of *The Sacred Pentagraph*, the High Priestess will oversee the functioning of the Scribes and Summoner.

It may be that member of the Coven have friends or relatives who may wish to attend Sabbat ceremonies as observers.

They may only be invited by an official invitation sent by the First Scribe calling them to the Covenstead on the appointed time and day.

It then becomes the duty of the Summoner to be sure that any observers to the Coven Sabbat Ceremonies are at least of the I° in the Craft from a valid tradition.

For this, the First Scribe and the Summoner are responsible to the High Priestess.

We of the Ancient Craft of the Wise, in no way wish to exclude brothers and sisters from Gardnerian, Alexandrian, Welsh or Celtic traditions, however, we must be certain that they have been properly initiated in the degrees of the Craft.

The Summoner is to stand by the door when Coveners arrive for Sabbat Ceremonies and ask for their grade signs to be shown upon entering the Covenstead. Visitors and observers must present their invitations at that time.

When all have properly assembled, the Summoner is to inform the High Priestess of such, and then may seal the door of the Covenstead.

NO observers or visitors will be allowed to attend the magic working of the Esbat circles, as well as anyone below the rank of Covener. For participation in Esbat Circle, the Summoner will require all to give the Watchword (see Hallowmas Sabbat) before entering the Covenstead.

It has been the experience of members of the Craft who have disregarded the Craft creed concerning privacy, that much notoriety is raised about the neighbourhood of the existence of a Covenstead. Such has caused difficulties for the coven members.

Therefore, let the High Priestess exercise due caution in allowing any observers or visitors to the Covenstead. Misplaced trust has been the cause of much unnecessary pain.

The social pendulum swings both ways. Each era of freedom and tolerance is followed by one of bigotry and bondage. It behooves each Covenstead to be ready to disappear overnight, so that the Children of the Ancient Craft of the Wise may not be sought out by the Inquisitors of Church or State.

Let them engain the Sorcerers, Black Magicians and Wizards if they will.

Therefore, each High Priestess should keep her finger on the pulse of the times, in order to best judge how open or public her coven is to be.

Let each Covener heed the charges in their Neophyte and Probationer initiations concerning discretion and good taste. These the High Priestess must ever keep before them, as a watchful mother hen would guard her chicks.

Hallowmas Sabbat

This is the most Sacred Night of the entire Craft Tradition.

Hallowmas ends the Cycle of both the Celestial (Solar) Sabbats and the Terrestrial Sabbats with a ceremony marking the Season of Death called Dumb Supper, to commemorate and commune with those who have Crossed the Veil. It also has a second part to begin the Witches New Year by casting a Divination for the Coven as a whole.

The Divination is boiled down to a one or two word phrase and used as the Coven Watchword for the coming year, which will be required by the Summoner at the following Midwinter Sabbat and each Sabbat, Esbat and Coven Council meeting held until Hallowmas next (Watchwords my be required to enter Circle, should the High Priesthood wish. They would be required to enter the Covenstead, as a bare minimum for official ceremonies and meetings.).

The High Priestess will not cast the usual Circle for Hallowmas, as she would for the other Terrestrial Sabbats. Since this is both the Beginning and the End, it takes a special format.

At least two weeks prior to Hallowmas, each Covener who will participate in Dumb Supper must deliver to the High Priestess the name of the Spirit of the deceased relative or friend he/she would wish to invite and commune with at Dumb Supper.

This will allow the High Priestess at least a two -week spiritual period to meditate on the names of the Spirit Guest nightly in order to open a channel to those realms and give the Ritual a good chance for success in calling forth the Spirits.

Dumb Supper is a minor act of Necromancy conducted in Love to call the Spirits and invite them to share a meal and commune with the people in Circle. It does not constrain the Spirits against their will. A channel is opened and fellowship offered. Conjuration to "visible appearance" is not the object.

There have been Dumb Suppers where at times a Spirit drawn by the closeness of a loved one in Circle uses the thick incense smoke to assume a temporary form, so as to be seen by the Sensitives of the Coven. However, such is rare and very fragile. The invited Spirit Guests are normally felt rather than seen.

The meditative bond established by the participants and their Spirit Guest can at times be strong and during the meditation, participants may be seen to reach out across the area toward the felt presence, or they may weep for joy, having truly felt the nearness of the Spirit. Each is allowed to privately commune with his/her Guest in silence and in his/her own heart.

Although Time and Space as we know them, do not exist in the Realm of Spirit, one stipulation, however, is to be considered. The Spirit Guest invited by a Covener, must have been on the other side of the Veil for at least a Year and a Day.

Any Spirit needs a period of Adjustment to the Other Side and may be unduly and unwittingly sorrowed by being summoned to a Dumb Supper too soon after Crossing.

Should a Covener have a friend or relative recently Crossed Over, he/she may wish the High Priestess to light a commemorative votive for that period as stated above. Hallowmas next would be fine.

In *Diagram I* (pg 223) is an arrangement for a coven to hold a Dumb Supper privately for its own members in Circle.

Standing TV trays and chairs would be set around the Ritual Chamber, or place-settings could be set upon the floor, upon a clean cloth spread.

In *Diagram II* (pg 224) one can see a larger arrangement for a coven to use when it wishes to host another coven, or invite witches from other Traditions in the Craft. The Stranger, no matter how psychic, or adept at Mediumship, or involved in Occultism, is not to be included at this most Holy Day. Sabbat worship ceremonies are for Witches and Witches only.

The Ritual herein to follow, will be for the smaller and simple method for the Coven in private. The larger method may be elaborated once the basics have been mastered and understood.

This takes much preparation and forethought and should be planned well in advance. Last minute slip-shoddiness should not be tolerated and in that event, it would be better to forego the Sabbat altogether, than bring a rush job before the Gods. By falling down on this Sabbat, the entire system would be out of kilter. There would be no Watchword produced for the other Sabbats, Esbats and Coven Council meetings.

In other words, nothing worthwhile would be expected from poor efforts. The Gods would not be honoured, the Craft would not be properly practiced, and such a Coven itself would have its motivations and commitment to the Old Ways suspect.

One need not have the full number of Coveners (12) to practice the

Sabbat cycle, but those that do practice should be dedicated and the Coven will grow as it should. Only Time produces quality. The Initiation Ordeals of Book II would have weeded out the unworthy.

The Altar would be draped in black or purple and set in the manner of the High Priestess beforehand. In space 9 would rest a Skull and Crossbones, either real or artificial, to represent the Death Theme of this Cross-Quarter. Before it would rest a list of the names of the Spirit Guests to be invited, and a branch of a tree as a Wand.

The Incense should be Patchouli for the Altar, but Mace, Benzoin and Storax for the two cauldrons in the center of the Ritual Space.

The High Priest would act as Host for this Sabbat, allowing the High Priestess the pre-ritual seclusion to gather her thoughts and be in the correct state of mind for the ceremony.

The Hand Maiden and Practicus would assist him in the necessary duties for the Supper.

On the TV trays, or, place-settings in their places around the Circle, should be two settings opposite each other. Each setting would have the name of the living Coven participant on a place card at the outside setting and the name of the Spirit Guest he/she wishes to invite at the setting on the inside.

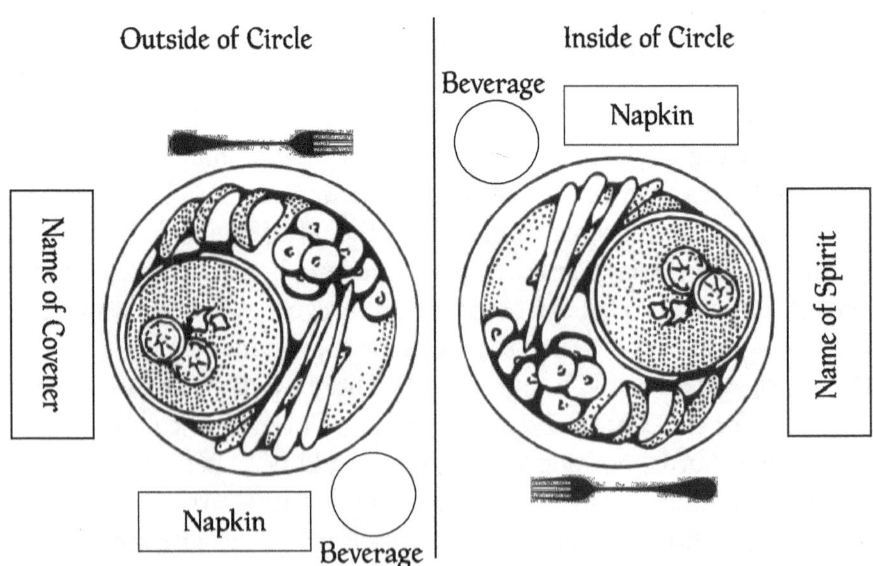

The Names of the Spirits are to be the same as those on the list placed on the Altar before the Skull and Crossbones.

The list of the Living participants and the invited Spirit Guests are to be firmly set no later than one week prior to Sabbat. There will be no changing of the seating arrangements immediately prior to the beginning of Ritual. The Spirits are summoned in order around the Circle and set at their proper places opposite their friend or relative who invited them.

Coveners who wish to sit next to each other must see to it before the Guest List is set.

This prevents a Covener from changing seating places and forgetting to change the Spirit name card at the table and at the Altar on the List. One would not want to summon one's friend or relative from beyond and have him/her set opposite a stranger at the Dumb Supper Table.

Dumb Supper is a serious Ritual and light-hearted frivolousness should be avoided.

On each plate, both for the Living and the Dead, are sprigs of bitter herbs, such as endive or romaine, a sharp spicy sweet and flat bread such as Pita. There may also be figs, dates and nuts to garnish. A simple beverage such as Cider would also be appropriate.

The Hand Maiden and Practicus should see to the setting and proper placements. They would have all plates with food set out in place before the Coven enters the Ritual Chamber.

There is to be as little light in Chamber as possible. The glow from the Sanctum and the glow from the Altar would be all that is needed for this simple observation. However, for a large group, more candles would be used as per *Diagram II,* (pg 224).

All should be set and ready at least 15 minutes before Midnight. About 11:55 p.m. the High Priest will guide the Coveners in and seat them at their respective places; each at the place with the right name card. Each opposite the name of the Spirit Guest he/she has invited.

The Summoner carries the Hand Bell and rings it when the Ritual calls for it. He/she enters last before the High Priestess.

This is the beginning of the Season of Death, this is the High Solemn Celebration of the Most Holy Night.

From the time of entering the Ritual Chamber, each Covener is to maintain strict SILENCE throughout the entire Ritual. Each Covener is there to commune with his/her own Spirit Guest and must not be disturbed by any other. We honour the Spirits of the Deceased on this Holy Night. They are the true Guests of Honour, not ourselves. We honour them by keeping the Silence of the Grave.

At the Stroke of Midnight, the High Priestess appears at the door of the Ritual Chamber carrying the Water and Earth. The Summoner rings the bell 11 times slowly and mournfully.

She silently steps to the Altar and places the Chalice and Pentacle in their respective places. She says:

The Season of the Dark Lord of Death spreads across the land this Sabbat night. Let us honour and commune with those we knew and loved who have slipped beneath the veil of the Goddess in times gone by.

She moves to the center of the Circle and takes up the Broom from the floor as it lays over the Great Wand between the two cauldrons for Incense. With the Coven Broom, she steps to the West of the Circle and moves widdershins all around on the outside of the chairs for the seated Coveners walking backwards all the way around chanting as she goes:

Red Spirits and white, black Spirits and grey,
mingle, mingle, mingle, ye who mingle may.
Around and around, throughout and about,
all good come in, all ill keep out.

As she moves backwards, she sweeps with the Broom. By so doing, she creates a proper psychic barrier around the area containing the seated Coveners.

Continuing backwards all the way around, she replaces the Broom and moves to the Altar. The High Priest may need to place more Incense on the coals in the cauldrons and on the Altar at this time. He would do so quietly and retake his seat.

She takes up the wand from the Altar and taps thrice upon the Altar with it as she says:

Let us open the portals to the Nether Realm and invite our Spirit friends to commune with us this Hallowmas night.

She gives the Necromantic charge:

By the Sacred Rites of Hecate,
by the mysteries of the Moon,
by the watery realm of the Goddess,
come forth from beyond.
At the smoking cauldron's call,
by the skull and bones of death,
through the barrier of wand and broom
come forth from the beyond.
By the love and light of the Gracious Goddess,
by the kinship we feel for thee,
by the ringing of the bell,
come forth from the beyond.

The High Priestess will then call out each name of the invited Spirit Guests one by one in the order that they will be seated as the Summoner strikes the bell once for each name. (Twelve times in all for this private Coven observance, but more if needed for a ceremony with a larger number of participants.)

When the names have been called and the bell struck for each one, the High Priestess will bow low at the Altar and greet the Guests thus:

Welcome. Welcome in the Old Gods' love. We greet thee this Holy night with bonds of fellowship and love. Commune with us and share our meal to keep this Ancient trist between spirit and matter as from ages of years and times before time. Blessed be.

She takes the wand twig and moves to the empty chair before the place of the Summoner (see *Diagram I*, pg 223). She taps thrice upon the chair with the wand and pulls the chair out to offer a seat for the Guest and announces the Spirit's name and sets the chair back in place. In other words, she seats the Spirit Guest in place (however, should the guests be seated upon the floor, she taps with the wand at the proper place-setting).

This she does all around the Circle for each and every place setting reading the name of the invited Spirit Guest from the place card set at each plate.

She seats her own Spirit Guest last and takes her place.

All Coveners participating in Circle then begin to slowly eat the Supper in silence as each communes with his/her own Spirit Guest in quiet meditation. Each Covener will experience something from the other side in his/her own capacity to comprehend.

Should the Coven Mediums, if there be any, receive messages for anyone of the Coven, he/she should keep silent and discuss such after the conclusion of the ceremony so as not to disturb the meditations of others.

The High Priestess will feel when the time is over and the energy of the meditative period is waning. 20 minutes is usually sufficient for the communion with the Spirit Guests for inexperienced Coveners. With time and practice, a Coven may have longer periods as each participant over the years becomes more adept at meditative communion.

The High Priestess will then take up the wand twig and move to the back of the chair of the last Spirit Guest seated (her own), tap once on the chair/place, speak out the Spirit's name and move the chair out and back in. Thus taking the Spirit up from its place. She moves around repeating that at each place back to the Summoner's place. In other words, she removes the Spirits in reversed order of seating.

Back facing West across the Altar, she gives the Spirits the License to Depart:

Thank thee, thank thee, thank thee all. Return to thy place in time and space. Let peace exist till Hallowmas next. The veil be drawn. The portal be closed. Love and light be thy guide evermore. Blessed be..

She replaces the wand as the Summoner strikes the bell 13 times to cleanse the atmosphere in the Ritual Chamber. Dumb Supper is finished and the silence may now be broken. The Coven may discuss what was experienced and/or felt.

The Dumb Supper things are cleared away and the preparations made for the next section of Hallowmas Sabbat.

NOTATE BENE: She did not cast the circle, nor did she need to light the Altar candles. Those were lit beforehand by the High Priest when he and the Hand-Maiden and Practicus were setting the Chamber. The High Priestess would have provided a spark from the Sacred Flame for him to use before she retired to prepare for the ceremony.

In *Diagram II* (pg 224) a more elaborate method is shown to celebrate with a larger group. The Ceremony may be adapted to suit as the basics are properly mastered.

WEST
DIAGRAM I
IF DONE IN CIRCLE,
FOR THE SINGLE
COVEN.
(ALTAR SET FOR THE HIGH PRIESTESS)
THE ALTAR FOR HALLOWMAS
HIGH PRIESTESS
SUMMONER
BELL
HIGH PRIEST
SOUTH
SANCTUM IN NORTH
CHAIRS ON THE INSIDE FOR THE SPIRIT GUESTS
CHAIRS AROUND THE OUTSIDE FOR THE PARTICIPATING COVENERS
2 Cauldrons for Incense
Great Wand
Broom
STANDING TV TRAYS
(or, place settings on the floor)
PATH OF THE BACKWARDS CIRCUMAMBULATION
EAST
Hallowmas Ritual of Dumb Supper

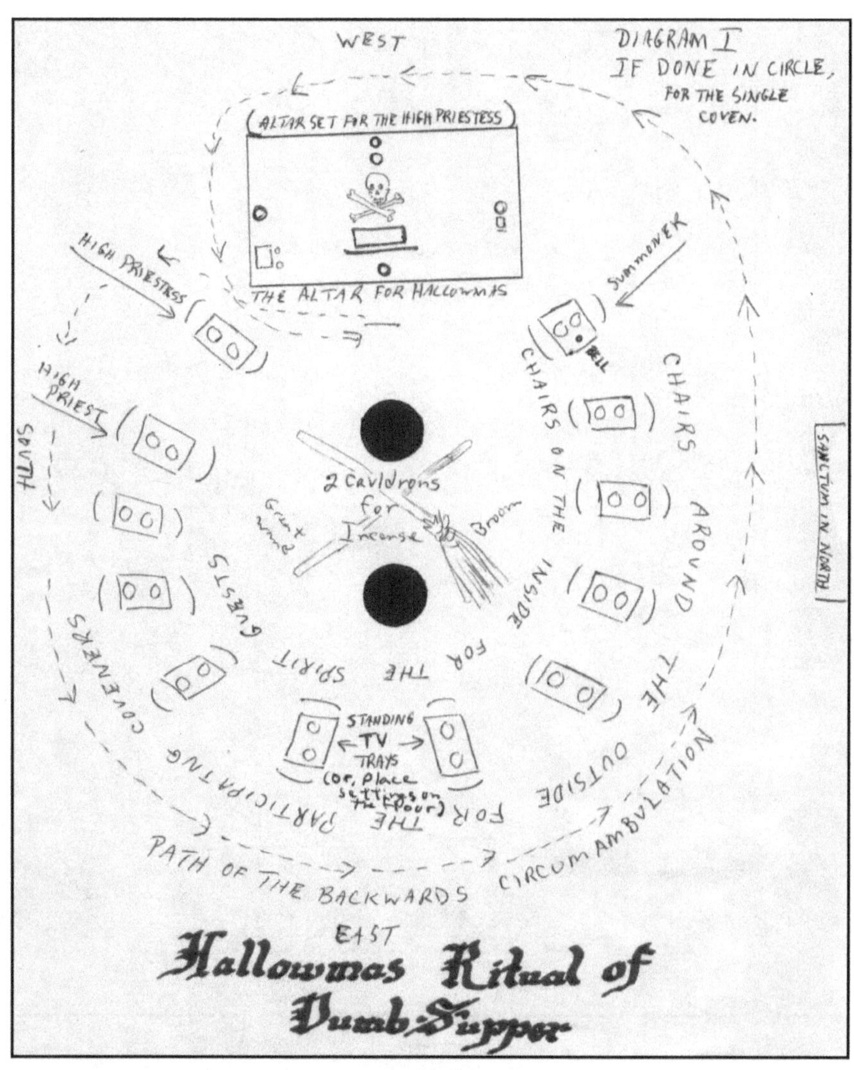

Diagram I

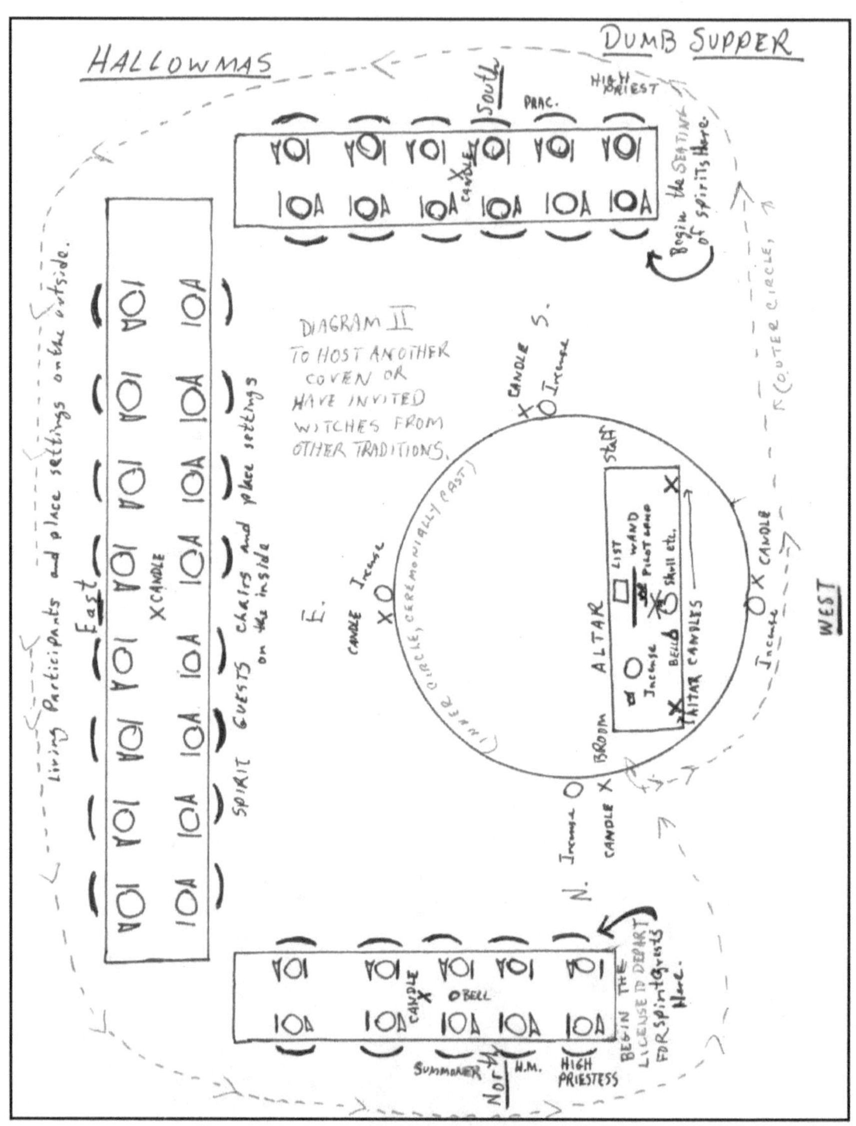

Diagram II

This is a Convenient arrangement wherein a hall or banquet facility, with tables, is available for the evening.

In this simple ceremony no tight Magic Circle is drawn on the Astral Realm, because the Power of the Gods is not invoked, nor are any negative forces conjured to be attracted to the area. It is a Rite of Love and Spiritual Communion offering friendship to the Spirits of the Departed. We need not deal with them from behind strong Psychic Barriers.

The second part of Hallowmas Sabbat now deals with the New Year ahead. All traces of the Dumb Supper are cleared away. The food set for the Spirits should be collected to be silently disposed of properly per proper disposal instructions given earlier.

The Altar is to still be draped in its dark colour, but a white candle set to burn on its East side. One cauldron of Mercurial incense should be set to burn to the East of the Altar on the floor. (See *Diagram III,* pg 227.)

Three Witches will conduct the coven Divination to procure the Watchword for the coming cycle of the year till Hallowmas next.

Traditionally it should be done by the three levels of women in the Craft of senior status if at all possible. An Oracle would be the part of the Hag aspect of Luna and conduct the Divination proper as would be her right as the most senior Witch woman present. The Queen Mother would be the part of the Matron as the Full Moon aspect of the Goddess and the High Priestess would be the Maiden form of the Goddess.

However things may be in a particular coven, perhaps a Queen Mother would need to be the Hag with the High Priestess being the Matron , or a Hand Maiden being the Matron and an Artisan II° as the Maiden, depending on the grades represented in any individual coven. Order of seniority would prevail, so each coven may work this out for itself..

The type of Divination is left to the ability at these Arts by the most senior woman participating.

A few suggestions may help. Perhaps a coven Horoscope could be cast for the coming year and the transits and aspects read for the collective as a whole (coven dates of centering the Cone from the Covenant).

Perhaps a Hexagram from the I Ching could be cast by coins or Yarrow stalks. Perhaps a Tarot reading could be done for the coven entity itself. Maybe Runes by sticks or stones could be read etc. etc.

Whatever method is used, the woman taking the part of the Hag aspect of the Goddess casts the Divination. The prognostication would then be boiled down to a one or two word phrase as the Watchword for the Coven.

One thing, however, to remember, is that in Divination, failure to disclose the truth of a vision or prognostication is a violation of Witch Law. The portends may be positive or negative as the case may be. Do not sugar coat it. The Watchword for the coming year is as it will be.

When all is ready for the second part to begin, the coven comes to order and stands around the Altar area.

The one taking the part of the Maiden Goddess carries some seasonal flowers or autumn floral arrangement steps up to the Altar.

She sets the flowers on the South edge and steps widdershins around the Altar three times as she says:

New Year's blessing I bring to all.
Portends of the Goddess now deftly call.
By Maiden, Matron and Hag, let the casting fall.

The one taking the part of the Matron brings a crystal ball to the Altar and sets it on the North side. She also circumambulates the Altar widdershins as she says:

By Rites of Hecate on Hallowmass Night
the Mother Mild descends from flight
to lift her veil by candlelight.

The Hag then steps forth carrying the things she will use in the process of Divination (Bowl of Water, Tarot Cards, Runes, Horoscope etc.). She sets them in the center of the Altar and steps around widdershins as she declares:

Thus the Dark Mother comes to speak.
She giveth thee what thou doth seek.
It may be good, it may be dire,
it may be ill or thy heart's desire.
She speaketh forth as it shall be.
Gather to Her and thou shalt see.

The Hag takes her place facing East across the Altar with the Maiden to her right and the Matron to her left. They all join hands and invoke the Goddess:

Three Witches come to Hallowmas Sabbat
one as a deer, one a raven and one a
speeding bouncing rabbit.
They came to call the Lady from the sky.
Upward to Heaven their thoughts didst fly.
Goddess young and Goddess prolific, Goddess
ancient and mature.
Mater triformis we seek thy decree
lift up thy veil that we may see.
A word, a rede, a portend of light
we accept thy will of joy or fright.

The three witches then meditate slightly on the coven as a whole. When the Hag is ready she performs the Divination.

The results the three decide among themselves as to its meaning for the coven and boil it down to a one or two word phrase and announce that as the coven Watchword for the coming year.

The Matron thanks the Goddess and the Maiden claps her hands thrice to break the spell of the atmosphere.

The coven then may engage in a party of Psychic Readings where the coven Psychics and Mediums read for all Coveners who wish.

Divination From the Altar

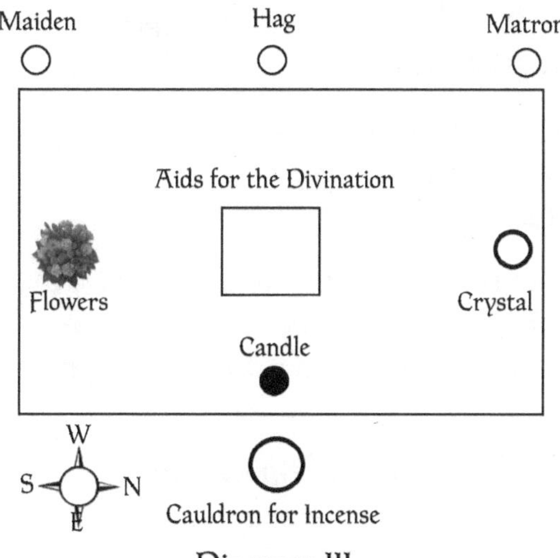

Diagram III

Blessing the Altar Equipment

Prior to Midwinter Sabbat (see *Section I*) the High Priestess participates in the preliminary Rite of Entering in of Death.

The Ritual Chamber is stripped and left dark and bare for the three days prior to Midwinter.

During that time it is the duty of the High Priestess to exorcize and bless the Altar equipment and see that all is clean and fresh for the coming year.

The Sacred Flame has been put out by the High Priest, so she should have taken a spark from that flame to keep and use during this time beforehand. It is not to be kept in the Ritual Chamber, but someplace else in seclusion.

All candlesticks, Chalices, Pentacles etc. and Altar Linens the High Priestess must wash and clean. The women of the coven should also aid her in this rite where they can.

This rite should be done enough in advance so that by Midwinter Day the High Priestess can re-set the Ritual Chamber and dress the Altar for Sabbat.

All coven Altar equipment should be set on a table with the flame secluded from the Sacred Flame and a cup of salted Water and a burning coal of Pine and Myrrh Incense.

She moves around the table deosil and sprinkles each item with a few drops of the salted Water as she says:

Goddess of the Waters, Goddess of the Earth,
cast out the dross of old times past
and make all pure from first to last.

The items may then be re-anointed with a Witches Sabbat Oil of Rosemary and Verbena.

Then she passes the flame over and around all Altar equipment with these words:

This Sacred Flame from Old Times gone will also soon from this plane depart. Let it bless our Tools and Hallows as a link to our Ancient Past.

She then passes all items through the rising Incense smoke with these words:

May we dedicate these Hallows to times ahead. Let them serve and bless our Covenstead. Blessed be.

The spark from the Sacred Flame is snuffed out by the High Priestess and the Incense allowed to slowly die of itself.

The Ritual Chamber is to again be cleaned 6 months hence prior to Midsummer Sabbat, but this ceremony need not be repeated. (See *Section I.*)

Blessing the Yule Log

In this tradition the Yule log is the Center Piece for the Festive Table at the dinner following Midwinter Sabbat.

This dinner the cove takes together in common with all the Old World style food and drink. There should be fun and games and a lot of healthy Pagan revel and good cheer. There should not be a somber note at this occasion. Yule is the Season for Joy, Warmth and Loving Kindness.

A small log decorated with pine cones, holly and mistletoe with six candle sockets affixed to it holding red and green candles sits in the center of the Festive Table. It should be surrounded with the Yule-time foods.

After the Midwinter Sabbat has been concluded and all have changed out of formal robes, the coven gathers around the table.

The High Priestess brings a spark from the new Sacred Flame to the table.

She stands before the Yule log and says:

Good cheer to all Wiccan Children bright
the Gods bestow their love and light.
The Wheel doth turn from time to time
as we advance on the Spiral one day at a time.
May this Coven of __________ *prosper and*
grow in love and fellowship. May the Gods bless
each and every one of the Witches gathered here.
Lords and Ladies, Witches all, let yuletime cheer
warm this hall.

She lights the candles attached to the Yule log and says:

The Child of Promise is in our midst.
The Gods be upon us.
Good Yule let the Festival of the Season now begin.
We bid thee eat, drink and be merry as
the blessing to all, blessed be.

The Midwinter revels should continue throughout the night. In the Morning, as many as are able should go out to greet the Dawn and praise the symbol of the New Born Sun.

Candlemas Sabbat

This is the Sabbat that honors the Goddess in response to the returning of the waxing light that began at Midwinter.

The womb of the Goddess is symbolically prepared to spring forth with all the joys of creation.

All the things the High Priestess has been secluding from the other Sabbats of the Celestial Cycle will be brought out for use in the cauldron: Some of the dried twigs from last Vernal Equinox; the dab of wine and crumb of bread from Midsummer; the Autumn Hen from Autumnal Equinox and some pine needles and mistletoe from Midwinter.

These serve to act as a symbolic link from the Solar Festivals of the God, which will go into the cauldron of the Goddess and be the compost to fertilize the Terrestrial Cycle of the Sabbats for the Goddess.

In addition to these links, the Ritual calls for some seeds, bulbs or roots to be planted after the Sabbat when the coven women conduct the Rites of Cybele.

Also each participating covener will bring a handwritten petition to place in the cauldron as his/her "Seed of Thought" or the resolves he/she wills to accomplish in his/her life over the coming year.

There would be a large black candle and small black ones for each participant. The cauldron should be empty in the center of the Circle.

The High Priest will set and consecrate the Altar for the High Priestess. He will have the links and all other needs for the Ritual (9) on the Altar as per diagram on page 208 (HPS set-up). The Incense should be of a grassy or light floral nature.

When the time for Sabbat strikes, the High Priest has seen that all is ready and the Summoner does his/her duty for Watchwords and Grade signs.

The coven has assembled inside the Ritual Chamber.

The High Priestess enters and casts the Circle by Water and Earth.

When the coven has assembled inside the Circle, the High Priestess begins the main body of the Candlemas Sabbat by invoking the Goddess:

Hail the tide of the waxing light,
the Mater Magna cometh forth from repose.
Be with us here in thy Garden Grove
to illumine our lives and bring forth the bud.

She lights the large black candle from the center candle on the Altar and says:

Thou art the Light in darkness, Lady. thou art the Light that faileth not. Out of slumber we awaken thy Womb to bring forth all creation's bounty.

The High Priest passes out to each Covener participating one of the smaller black candles.

The High Priestess steps around to each and lights his/her candle with these words:

The Star Goddess, the Great Mother, the Lunar tide bringeth love and light and blessings to thy side.

She sets the large black candle in a holder and places it next to the cauldron on the floor.

Each Covener steps forward and drops his/her written petition into the cauldron.

As each is doing so, the High Priestess prays:

Gracious Goddess accept the thoughts we give to thee.
Let them be the seed of good resolve we wish to bring
forth into manifestation in due course of time as thou
bringeth forth the bud which matureth into thy bounty.
Blessed be.

When all have done so, she takes the seeds or bulbs and roots along with the links from the Solar Sabbats down to rest beside the cauldron on the floor.

She places the seeds, bulbs and/or roots into the cauldron and then sets the twigs from Vernal Equinox on them. The dab of wine on cotton and the piece of bread from Midsummer goes on top of that. Then she sets the Autumn Hen to sit on top of everything else in the cauldron. She then sprinkles the pine needles and pieces of mistletoe from the Midwinter Sabbat over everything else in the cauldron. She says:

The Mother's Womb is now prepared.
By seed of thought and seed of deed,
with compost from the old
and wishes for the new
raise the Cone and call forth the Mother's miracles of life.

The High Priest begins to lead the Coveners in the Circle Dance moving widdershins. The step should be lively and airy. It is a joyous time to call forth the Spirit of Life.

He begins the Chant and all Coveners take it up:

Spirit, Light and Seed,
all we have to seal the deed.
Mother of Creation's flower,
we summon thee at candlemas hour.
Spring forth, bud out, manifest thy joy.
All mysteries of life employ.

We giveth thee the planted seed,
return to us the accomplished deed.
Goddess of our heart's desire,
we quicken thy Womb by candlemas fire.

The High Priestess stands with the large black candle held high above the cauldron as the Circle Dance wends around and around. When she feels enough power has been raised, she shouts:

PEACE, BE STILL, THE LADY DOTH AWAKE!

All Coveners then sit down and concentrate inward toward the cauldron and meditate on their private petitions as the High Priestess prays:

We bless our Mother's Womb of Life. We charge this Cauldron to bloom and flower. Gracious Goddess hear our pleas and grant the resolves we store with thee. Blessed be.

The High Priestess then closes the Circle by Air and Fire.

The dressed cauldron will be used later at the Rites of Cybele. Each Covener takes his/her candle home to burn later for a blessing from this time of year.

The Sabbat regalia is cleared away.

MYSTERIES OF CYBELE

Sometime between Candlemas and the Vernal Equinox, better if it were in the Month of February, the High Priestess and at least two other women of the coven go to the spot where all these things are hidden. No men may participate in this ritual.

Some of the coven women have secluded sperm from their male mates or lovers onto dabs of cotton at various times during the previous year. Some of the coven women have secluded menstrual blood from the previous year also onto dabs of cotton. These they bring with them to this Rite.

The stub of the large black candle used by the High Priestess at Candlemas is needed along with the cauldron containing all the things she placed in it at Candlemas.

The oldest Married Woman in the coven is the Officiant for this

Rite, not necessarily the High Priestess.

She who officiates bears the special title: Dame "Good Wyfe." Hers is the duty to prepare the Virgin Goddess to conceive.

All women attend at the Covenstead in formal robe with cingulums of rank. The High Priestess, if she be not the Officiant, will carry the candle stub and a Chalice of Water. Dame Good Wyfe carries the cauldron and the other women carry the dabs of cotton with blood or sperm and bouquets of flowers and ribbons.

The women form a procession with the High Priestess leading followed by Dame Good Wyfe and the others. They walk from the Covenstead out into Nature to some secluded spot singing songs of Spring and joy to the Goddess. (Perhaps they need go by car out of the city, but then a procession into the fields or forest can be made.)

At the chosen spot, the flowers and ribbons are set around to form a circle as a bower for the Goddess. The cauldron is placed in the center with the Chalice of Water nearby along with the candle stub.

Dame Good Wyfe, with her bare hands, begins to furrow and mold a small trench in the earth and shape it to form a vagina. It should be deep enough to be able to hold all the items from the cauldron.

As she furrows the coven women chant:

Life is woman's most precious gift.
Only she can bring it forth.
From the Womb of the Goddess its head doth lift
in the west, the south, the east and north.
Let man toil, let man fight, but woman will
guard her precious light.
We furrow, we delve, we prepare the womb.
That the lady of life may bring forth the bloom.

When the trench is ready the women circumambulate it widdershins dropping the dabs of cotton with blood and sperm into it as they chant:

Seed of man and blood of woman are the matrix of creation's love.
As the cosmos, so the earth, God and Goddess must unite.
Lay we in creation's womb to bring forth joy and belie the tomb.

Dame Good Wyfe then places all items from the Candlemas cauldron into the furrow; seed, bulbs or roots, twigs, wine and bread, the Autumn Hen, pine and mistletoe and the written petitions.

When all things have been placed into the earth, Dame Good Wyfe pushes the dirt back over the trench to cover it.

Taking the Chalice of Water she stands above the spot and says:

Demeter, Astarte, Cybele from of Old,
Lady of Life, corn and wheat fields of gold,
receive thy honour given with love,
and smile on our works brightly from above.
Sustain thy children, man, beast and bird,
work thy wonder of fertility for nations,
crops and herd.

Dame Good Wyfe libates the water onto the spot and says:

Lady, receive thy Lord as He cometh in joy.

She sets down the Chalice and takes the candle stub and sets it in the ground in the center of the buried trench. She says:

It is done. The Great Mother liveth, for all creation's wonder, she sprigeth forth eternal. Blessed be.

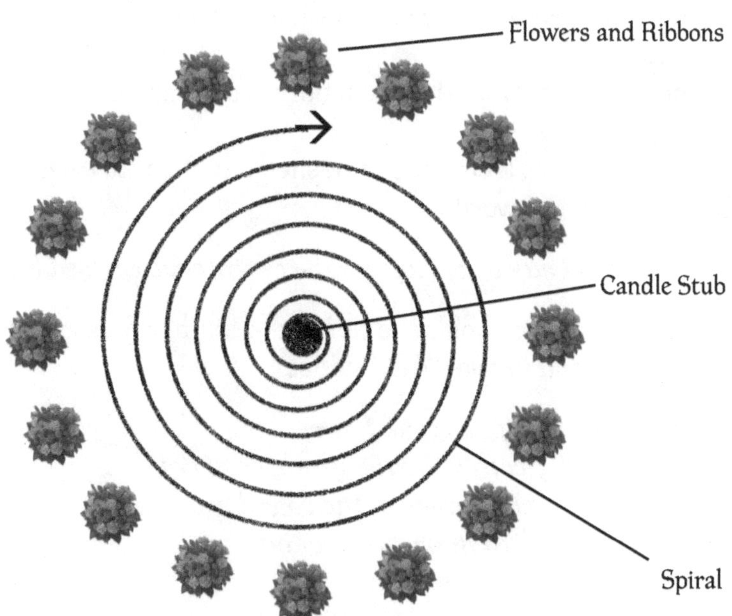

Beltane Sabbat

This is the Season of Wine and Roses, for communion with Life and the Maiden aspect of the Goddess. This Sabbat is directly across the Wheel of the Year from Hallowmas and the Dark Days. Beltane celebrates all living things.

The Spirit of this Sabbat is to be joyful and happy looking ahead to the Bright Tide and the flowering forth of that planted at Candlemas.

The High Priest sets the Altar for the High Priestess with everything in white and with spring flowers in abundance.

The Altar candles should be white or rose pink and the Incense should be a fragrant floral scent.

The cauldron sits in the middle of the Circle half filled with sand and a metal bowl of Lamp Oil resting in the center of the cauldron in the sand. A long taper of wood or wax will also rest upon the Altar for the High Priestess to ignite the cauldron.

(Beltane may be conducted out of doors weather permitting.)

When the Time of Sabbat be ready and the High Priest has seen to all the needs and the Summoner has attended to his/her duties so the coven stands ready in the Ritual Chamber or area, the High Priestess appears.

She steps lively into the midst of the coven and casts the Circle with Water and Earth.

Taking flowers from the Altar, she gives them to each participating Covener with the words:

The joyful Lady of Spring embraces thy soul. Blessed be.

As each Covener holds the flowers to his/her breast, she steps back to the Altar and invokes the Goddess:

Maiden of the springtime flowers
washed and cleansed by the gentle showers,
attend to us who gather in the round
with all that doth in nature abound.
Maiden of the May most fair
bring love and luck and life with care.
By marigold, violet and rose,

the song of spring thou dost compose.
Maiden of the Virgin Earth,
come with gladness, joy and mirth.
Abide with us this season through
in fields of green and skies of blue,
blessed be the Maiden Goddess.

The High Priestess then says:

Good Coven of ________, the Lady dwelleth in thy midst. Raise the Cone and bid her welcome.

The High Priest begins the Circle Dance moving widdershins and begins the chant as all follow suit and take it up:

Need fire, new fire, bale fire burn
blaze up, flare up, brightly churn.

(The High Priestess takes the long taper from the Altar and lights it from the center candle in her three branched candlestick and sets the lamp oil in the metal bowl in the cauldron ablaze.)

Turn, turn, the Wheel doth turn
and on it souls like candles burn...
yet turning, yet burning and so 'round about.
Love and luck and life with cheer
gifts from the Goddess we hold most dear
cometh to us this season of Beltane
and so among us forever remain.

The Dance and chant continue as the coven turns around and around the blazing cauldron until the High Priestess feels enough power has been drawn into the Circle. She then shouts:

Up Witches, up and away!
Leap the Cauldron for luck and life,
by joyful heart we burn out strife,
leap the Cauldron to life! to life!

With the High Priest and High Priestess leading, all Coveners two by two circle around and taking a running start leap over the cauldron as many times as each feel necessary to go up and through the Goddess' purifying fire.

There should be much laughter and shouts of joy and encouragement as each twosome leap. (Should the coven be robed, make sure the skirts are hiked up to prevent catching in the flames.)

When all have passed through the fire the High Priestess calls the coven back to order and takes her place before the Altar. She prays:

Gracious Goddess, our Mother, while the Spirit of Sabbat is with us now, we ask that the Spirit of Fraternity and Sorority and affection dwell with us always.

Thou to whom all are equal, and before whose judgement all must bow, look upon the Sacred Flame of love in our midst. Let it ever kindle in our heart love for all thy creation with unity of spirit and purpose.

As our will, so be it done. Blessed be.

All Coveners respond: *Blessed be.*

The High Priestess then banishes the Circle with Air and Fire.

Beltane Sabbat is short to allow time for any Wiccan Handfastings among the coven.

Afterwards each may go a-Maying as he/she sees fit.

Lammas Sabbat
Returning the Gift

Just as Hallowmas was worked in the Name of Hecate, Candlemas was an impregnation of the Earth Mother, and Beltane invoked the Maiden Aspect of the Goddess, Lammas celebrates the fruitful Matron with the blessing of the first fruits of the Summer Season.

This Season is the high point of the Goddess' love. Her bounty shows the fulfilled promise of maturity.

She must be thanked for Her gifts and part of them symbolically returned to Her, assuring Her eternal cycle.

The Lammas colours should be deep greens, yellows and rich oranges and browns. The Incense should be grassy or woodsy such as pungent redwood.

Notate Bene: Many of the details in these final Sabbats are left to the participants themselves to work out. By now proper care and ritual purity should be second nature to you.

The High Priest will set the Altar and Ritual Chamber for the High Priestess. He will have her large Pewter Chalice filled with a rich red wine and a plate of home made bread on the Altar in space 9.

Lammas may also be conducted out of doors weather permitting.

When all is ready for Sabbat, the High Priestess casts the Circle with Water and Earth.

To begin she places her hands over the wine in her pewter Chalice and the plate of home made bread and blesses thus:

She of the Corn, She of the Seed, She of the Green Fields, She of the Great Loaf, be present here and bless our gifts to thee.

Taking up the Chalice and plate in her hands, she stands in the center of the Circle and says:

Good Witches, attend at Lammastide. raise the Cone to the Goddess sublime.

The High Priest begins to lead the Circle Dance widdershins and start the Chant. The coven picks it up with him:

Fruit of the Earth
and fruit of the spirit
fruit of labour and fruit of love
thus be blessed from beneath and above.
Blessings abound at Lammas Tide,
love's labour flourishes at our side.
See the wheat fields ripe for harvest
let us share what the gods have blessed.
First from the fields;
the Lammas Bread,
given by the Goddess with arms outspread.
Blessed be the first fruits of summer.

The High Priestess standing in the center with the two Elements, feels the power being drawn in by the Dance. When she feels it is at its height, she says:

Peace, be still before the Great Mother. (The Coveners stop and rest.)

She passes to each Covener in turn offering a sip of the wine and a crumb of the bread as she says:

Commune with Her as thou takest of Her bounty.

Each accepts a sip of wine and a bit of bread.

Each participating Covener then spends a few minutes in quiet meditation with the meaning of the Lammas Sabbat and the Spirit of the Goddess.

When all have been communed, the High Priestess, followed by the High Priest and the entire coven in procession, go out of doors from the Covenstead into a spot out in Nature, not far away.

The youngest woman of the coven then prepares a furrow in the Earth to receive the symbolic offering to the Goddess.

Into the furrow the High Priestess places the remaining crumbs of the Lammas bread. She says:

This we do to ensure our Lady's bounty will return ever to Her.
That which She so freely bestows on us must never be diminished.

Handing the empty plate to the High Priest, she stands above the spot with the remaining wine in the Chalice and says:

O Ancient One, as from of Old, the nectar of the fruits of the Earth is thine. Take this libation as we comemmorate the resolves we planted seasons ago. May it transfuse our prayers as we deliver it unto the Earth. As we will, so be it done. (The High Priestess pours the wine on the spot.)

Each Covener meditates on his/her own petition and as to how it has matured since Candlemas, as the High Priestess buries the bread and wine.

Then the procession wends its way back into the Circle in the Covenstead.

The High Priestess closes and banishes the Circle with Air and Fire.

A seasonal party celebration may then follow.

Only the basics of Sabbat themes are herein given to allow each coven to embellish them with any additional rites as would be in keeping with the Spirit of Sabbat.

The traditional foods served after the Ritual as part of the festive gathering would be left to the devises of the coven cooks. There are many Old World cookbooks that may offer suggestions for dishes in keeping with the seasons.

Addenda Odds and Ends

As you can see from the Sabbat formats, it is a closed system where each ceremony carries something over to the next in the Celestial cycle. It all comes together at the Candlemas Sabbat.

The only way on to the Wheel of the Year is at Vernal Equinox. That is both the entrance and exit from the Sabbat Rounds.

Those choosing to adhere to *The Sacred Pentagraph* System must do so at that point.

One would therefore have to provide an Earth Fire from flint and steel to act as Sacred Flame until Midsummer Sabbat. Then the Sacred Flame can be properly kept from the Sun in June and from the Earth in Winter.

Also one would need to provide for the first Watchword. Perhaps something suggestive of New Beginnings until the correct one can be obtained at Hallowmas.

The credence table mentioned in the Vernal Equinox Sabbat to hold items for the Initiation of Neophytes and Probationers should be set with the necessary items according to the needs outlined in *Book II* for those respective Initiation Ceremonies. Always remembering, however, that when a coven is growing, as it should, there will be years when both Neophyte and Probationers will be initiated at the same time. Therefore the credence table needs be large enough to hold items for both.

Neophytes and Probationers are in the Outer Portico of the Temple and not yet of the Craft. They may only be brought before the Altar, but not given anything directly from it. The credence table may be set as festive or kept as plain as the initiating Covens so desire.

At Hallowmas, when Spirits of friends and relatives, who have Crossed the Veil are called, it has been found effective by some groups working this system to provide "links" for the Spirits. They may be small, personal tokens or pieces of property that once belonged to the Deceased which would sit at the place setting for the Spirit. Those are provided by the Covener, wishing to invite that Spirit to attend on

Hallowmas. Such things as a favourite knick-knack or comb or book etc. etc. may be set at the place setting to link the meditating Covener with the Spirit of the deceased.

The Lammas Bread can be of any kind and from any ethnic tradition as long as it is home made bread. Several groups have found that the Challa bread of Jewish tradition for the Schabbas on Friday Nights works well and looks festive.

At the Mysteries of Cybele, to be traditional, Dame Good Wyfe may use a digging instrument to furrow the Earth of a natural non-metallic substance, such as a large wooden spoon or stick.

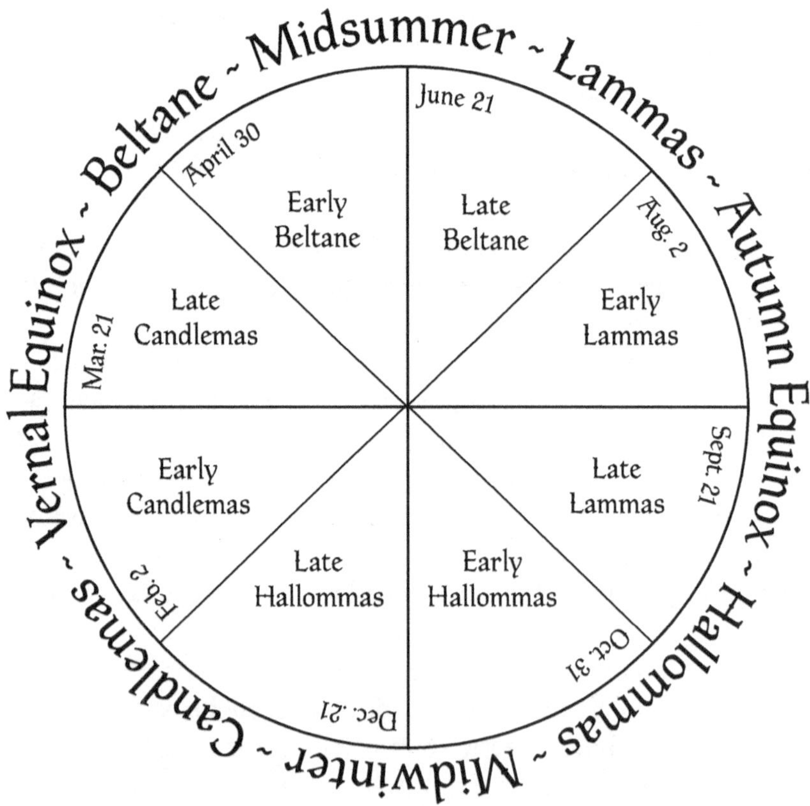

To be correct, no dates have been given in the system of the *Sacred Pentagraph* for the Sabbat Celebrations. Some vary from year to year.

From an Ephemeris, compute the time of Midwinter for your own locality to the Day, Hour, Minute and Second. Then add up the total amount of time in Days, Hours, Minutes and Seconds until the Vernal

Equinox. Divide that exactly in half and you have the time of Candlemas.

The exact time for each and every Sabbat may then be computed. The Solstices and Equinoxes may vary from year to year, back and forth within a day or two of the traditional time, but the proper day should be adhered to if at all possible.

However, the convenience of the coven group must be considered. It is proper and allowable to celebrate the Sabbat within the Octave of the Season; that is within the eight day period from the calendrical date, or exact time, but no later.

The Solstices and Equinoxes set and establish the Times, but do not celebrate a Season. The Cross-Quarter Days establish the Seasons.

For instance, from Hallowmas to Midwinter we have Early Hallowmas. From Midwinter to Candlemas we have Late Hallowmas. This gives four seasons divided in half by the Times.

Another thing to consider is the employ of the system in the Southern Hemisphere below the Equator. When those in the North celebrate Vernal Equinox, those in the South hold Autumnal Equinox. The system is reversed and the South Polar Cap is the direction of facing across the Altar, as the North is in this Hemisphere. In the South, Hallowmas would be celebrated when the North holds Beltane, etc. etc.

Section III

The Manual of Exorcisms

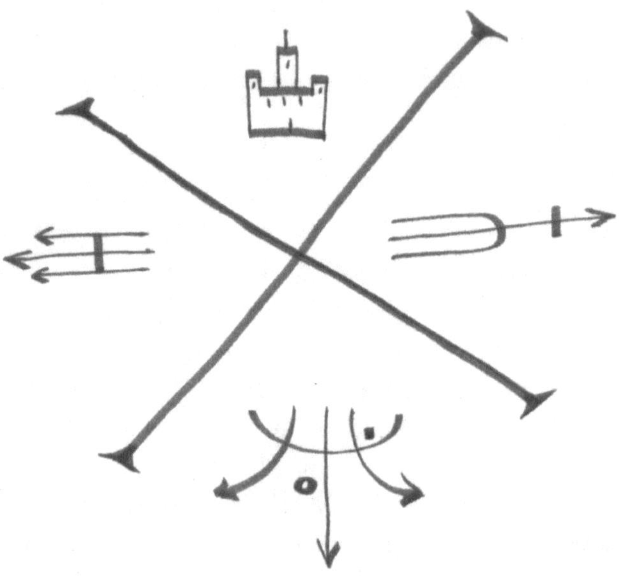

Recommended to those in the Craft of at least Artisan II° status to be employed as part of their work for and in the positive aspects of the Psychic and Metaphysical Arts.

Ritual of the Barriers

At one time or another, each Witch comes under the ill will or psychic attack from either other Witches or practitioners of the Materia Magica Negra. At other times, rabid bigots may rant and rave invective and hate upon a Brother or Sister in the Craft. Such negative energy needs be cleansed away.

When the creeping malaise and bad luck generally associated with negativity becomes apparent in one's life, it is time to seek out a Priest or Priestess of the Ars Magica of the Craft in the Way of the Wise.

For a proper Spiritual Cleansing, seek out an Artisan II° in the Craft or higher of the same Gender. (Ethics of modesty and good taste are to prevail.)

Bring to the Priest or Priestess a white candle, Frankincense and Myrrh to burn on coals, a Sacred Anointing Oil of Lotus or Jasmine, and a packet of Bath Crystals of yellow colour and almond scent. Also have a change of fresh clothing, recently laundered.

Explaining to the Priest or Priestess what has transpired to cause the negative build up in your life, or what has brought on the crossed conditions resulting in negative manifestations, or simply the fact of wanting to be cleansed of the effects of a confrontation with hate-mongers from less evolved Faiths.

The Priest/Priestess will then perform the Ritual.

The Subject is sent to bathe in a tub of clean hot bath water to which the Bath Crystals have been added.

As he/she bathes, this prayer is to be said by him/her:

God and Goddess, I come before thee to rid my being of the evil put upon me by someone of a lesser self possessed. I declare my innocence to thee and seek to make things right as they were before the darkness came upon me.

Let me look beyond revenge and hate. Let me see only thy perfect light and plan for all humankind.

Let any malice on my part be purged into this thy sparkling water and drained away, to be recycled in thine own good time...transmuted to ultimate good. Blessed be.

(The Subject bathes and meditates for 15 minutes.)

While the Subject is bathing, the Priest/Priestess sets a small Altar in white. The candle is lit along with a coal to burn the F&M (Frankincense and Myrrh) Incense. The Sacred Anointing Oil is blessed and set before the candle.

The Priest/Priestess would be Informally Robed (see Modes of Coven Apparel) and standing at the Altar awaiting the Subject.

The subject comes skyclad before the Altar as the Priest/Priestess takes up the burning candle and Thurible of Incense.

He/She circumambulates the Subject seven times with the Fire and Air symbols as he/she recites, moving deosil:

Banish all thoughts of ill.
Banish that which giveth the chill,
away from thee to lodge in nill.

Let not evil it's plan fulfill.
Break the power of negative will.
Keep it locked outside until,
the Gods into love its works distill.

The candle is handed to the Subject to hold and the Thurible of Incense is placed on the floor between his/her legs to smoke upwards covering the Subject in the scent of Frankincense and Myrrh.

The Priest/Priestess places both hands upon the Subjects head and prays:

God and Goddess, descend to us and keep this thy child in thy love. Lend power to my hand as I draw the barriers to hate and malice. Blessed be.

Taking up the Sacred Anointing Oil and placing a dab on the strongest hand, the Priest/Priestess anoints a barrier cross on each ear, eye, the nostrils, the mouth, the belly button, the genital area, the buttocks, and the small of the back on the Subject's body.

With each spot anointed these words are spoken:

The Lord and Lady of life triumph in thee.
Evil magics and malice of deed and thought
dash against thee and come to naught.
Blessed and blessed be.

The Subject blows out the candle after the anointing and dresses in the clean garments.

The candle may be taken home and burned the rest of the way as a reinforcement of the Ritual one week hence.

All ritual items are cleared away and the Subject is free from the negative affects and may go freely abroad and start life anew.

Should the perpetrator of the evil be known, bring the matter before the Coven Council and let the collective of the Coven deal with them in concert according to Craft Tradition.

To Quiet a Restless Spirit

Although Ghost-Hunting is not a prime consideration in the Craft, there are times when disquieting or disturbing conditions in a house or at a place are brought to the attention of a Coven.

If the High Priestess herself is not a Medium, there should be at least a person of II° in the Craft in each Coven who may deal with these matters. The Medium may be either Male or Female, but for the purposes of the Ritual we will assume that the High Priestess takes the part.

No Coveners below II° should participate, as it would be assumed such have not had sufficient experience in Craft Lore to be effective in dealing with Psychic Phenomenon. However, it may be that a person of accomplished Psychic Development has joined a Coven and may yet be in I° Status. Make the distinction that then Coveners I° may participate if such is the case. Craftsman I°, however, may not.

The High Priestess will carry her Coven Broom, the High Priest his Great Wand. A Practicus or Handmaiden will carry the Sword and the Artisans will carry a Bell, A Chalice of Salted Water and a Censer to burn a coal of Sandalwood Incense. All are formally robed. A large white candle is also carried by the High Priest.

The group of Witches gathers outside the house or place with the disturbance, on a Night of the Full Moon. (The rest of the Coven would remain at the Covenstead to hold a simple Esbat.)

At the appointed time, the Practicus or Hand Maiden steps up to the door or entrance and raps loudly thrice with the hilt of the Sword. The High Priest opens the door and raps the Great Wand once loudly and sharply on the floor and says:

Peace be unto this house/place. We come in the name of the Lord and Lady of light and love. Blessed be.

He lights the candle and the coal for the Incense and then leads the group into the center of the house or place. The manner is forceful and direct. Discarnates are not of this plane, therefore they may not injure, but only frighten and disquiet the less knowledgeable. Witches will have none of such fear.

In the center of the house or place the Great Wand and the Broom are laid cross-wise in the center area. The Medium/High Priestess will sit down in the North space within the crossed Wand and Broom. (See diagram to follow.)

The Practicus or Handmaiden will sit facing her to the South with the Sword placed across his/her knees. The Chalice of Salted Water, the Censer and the Bell will be placed around her in the other spaces in the cross. The Candle the High Priest will set directly in front of the High Priestess in the center of the cross.

He sits down directly behind her as the rest of the group form a circle and sit around joining hands with the Practicus or Handmaiden in the South and the High Priest in the North.

In this manner the Medium is enclosed within a proper Circle and may not be directly touched by the entity which may communicate, but not be able to possess the medium.

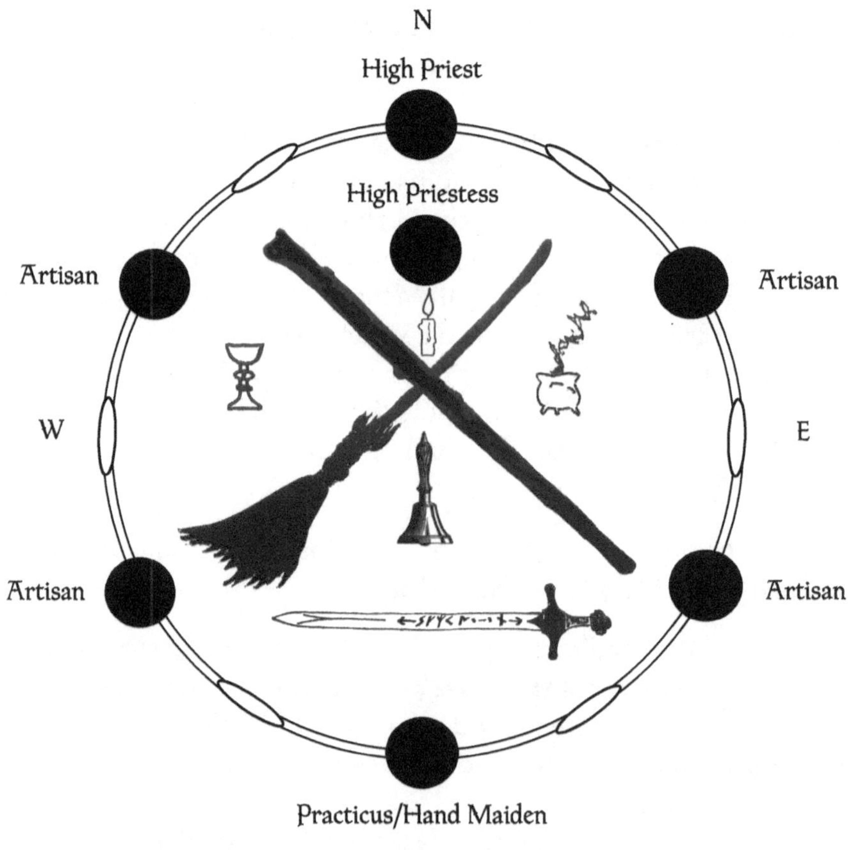

A bit of Sandalwood is placed on the coal to burn before the joined hands close the Circle.

When all is ready the High Priest summons the Spirit or the entity responsible for the adverse phenomena:

Ye who hath not found rest, ye who disturbeth the peace of this place,
ye who wander and art lost, come forth!
Thou who art disquieted, thou that art in pain, thou that rageth and shaketh, come forth!

The participants then go quiet and meditate in silence allowing the Coven Medium to sense out and link up with the entity. The silence must be kept by the Circle of Coveners no matter what disturbances may begin to happen around outside the circle. The participants keep their backs to it and concentrate inward to the medium.

NOTATE BENE: This writer has had the experience where walls scratch and creak, windows rattle and cold breezes blow across the room. However, nothing must be allowed to break the concentration of the circle nor the composure of the participants.

Should the entity speak through the Medium, listen to what it says and let it speak its peace.

The High Priest may question it and try to find out what the reason is for it making itself know through disturbances and disquieting phenomena.

Perhaps it will not speak at all, and the Medium only able to feel it and describe it.

If a discarnate entity needs something done for it to help it find its rest and peace and be able to enter the Inner Planes, the Coven should agree to do so.

If an Exorcism is in order, the Medium will be brought back to him/her self by gently stroking the upper arms upward to stimulate circulation and allow him/her to shake off the influence of the entity.

The group will take up the tools from the floor and step to the farthest room back from the front door. In each room in order, proceeding toward the front, the exorcism is performed.

The Bell is sounded in each room 13 times as the Salted Water is sprinkled and the Incense offered to the Quarters Deosil.

The Sword is held up and a large Banishing Pentagram drawn in the air in each room is made while the High Priest and High Priestess say:

By Lady of Heaven, by God of Light, banished be from this world's sight.

The Candle is circumambulated Deosil in each room.
Back at the front door a barrier cross is made with the Sword.
The place is then to sit in silence cleansed of the negative influence.

Ceremony of Major Exorcism

(Practice restricted to the High Priesthood and Elders)

Coven of Seven – Ritual of the Seven Elders

Very, very rarely are those who walk the Way of the Wise ever plagued with 'demonic activity'. Those persons with mental imbalance, inadequate preparation, and faulty command and application of ceremonial methods, however, at times, can be the victims of negative entities.

In times of old, when most persons outside the Craft had faith in the magics of the Holy Church, the Wise left such problems to those who were masters of the Roman Ritual Rite of Exorcism and allowed the specialist of the Church to deal with manifestations of the 'Devil', since the Church had called such a monster being into existence with its own morbid thought-forms, to begin with.

In this day and age, many of those outsiders have lost faith in the rites and rituals of the Clergy and no longer even perform the simple occult practices the Church prescribed for psychic protection; such as prayer before sleeping, a sacred symbol over the bed, and in extreme cases a sprinkling of St. Johnswort and Blessed Thistle around the sleeping quarters, etc.

It may happen a case of 'demonic possession' be brought to the attention of the High Priesthood concerning a member of the Craft. The High Priesthood should investigate only if called upon to do so by members of the distraught family. They would decide whether such a matter could not better be handled by the medical and psychiatric specialist, or better handled by the Power of the Craft, if the medical establishment has relinquished the case as beyond its ken.

Above all, the High Priesthood is not to seek fame and public approbation as "Experts" or Banishers of Demons. However, after every conventional method has proven to no avail, to release the unfortunate from his/her private 'Hell', the Ritual of the Seven Elders may be tried.

It is the view of those in the Way of the Wise, so-called 'diabolic possession' is due to a gross imbalance in an individual's spirit. Such an imbalance manifests either as, or a foreign entity which displays and projects hateful and chaotic emotions to all those in the world around.

Whenever the emotions of love and goodwill are blocked, hate will always appear in their place, for the vital energy of human consciousness can not be denied. Thwarted in its natural channel of expression, it will seek exit from the mind as its opposites. Chaotic entities of a negative personality are then attracted or manifested.

With this key, seven Elders can then proceed to transmute hate into love.

If such a case, concerning a member of the Craft, comes to the attention of the High Priesthood, they should both discuss the situation with as many Elders as they can find, either in the Covendom, or out of the Covendom, should there be other respected Elders in the District or area. If five Elders feel the situation is real, rather than a case of emotional hysteria, they may suggest this Exorcism:

Signs of Authentic Possession

The High Priesthood and the five Elders must agree the manifesting entity has displayed the following signs:

1. Actions degrading to the spiritual well being of the victim in his/her normal self.

2. Displays of psychic phenomena beyond the normal ability of the victim.

3. Projections of hatred to all other persons and contempt for the victim's own religious belief and sacred symbols.

4. Knowledge of the darker realms of spiritual being spoken or shouted at other persons when hatred and chaotic emotional outbursts are displayed.

5. Delight in emotional torment of relatives and friends or even psychic and/or physical attacks upon them.

6. Periods of normal consciousness marked by remorse and

embarrassment for the chaotic actions.

7. Comments by the victim relating to the 'other thing/person' that comes and resides within, or comments by the 'thing' expressing contempt and destruction for the victim's normal self.

If the situation meets the seven signs, the five Elders and the two members of the High Priesthood must obtain permission of the victim's family to apply the Ritual of the Seven Elders. (In the event the victim has no family, but is a member of the Craft, his/her High Priestess should give permission.)

The Gods have not given the inhabitants of the darker realms of the being any spiritual authority over Humanity.

We are beings composed of four elements in harmony, existing on the seven planes of spiritual light within a Universe of Order and Cosmos.

The negative manifesting entities come from a Universe of Chaos and do not have the four elements in balanced harmony within their natures, nor do they exist on all seven planes of spiritual light.

They seek entrance to the Cosmos through the vehicle of one whose own depressed and hateful though processes correspond to their natures, in order to spread disorder and chaos in the Cosmos.

Therefore, the Ceremony of Major Exorcism stands as a bastion at the gates of our Universe to keep the portals sealed against Chaos.

The Exorcists must realize a human being is master of his/her own soul and the chaotic entities have no power over Humanity, except that which a human being, out of fear or mental affinity allows them.

A major exorcism is never a pleasant thing and may last for days. Persistence is the key. It must, however, be conducted with all due seriousness.

If the entity proves difficult to dislodge, the exorcism must continue for at least 16 hours per day, allowing the victim 8 hours rest before it is taken up again.

The possessing entity wants control of the physical vehicle of the victim in order to spread hate and chaos throughout our world. It must not be allowed such freedom and be thwarted at every turn.

Eventually it will conclude it is no match for the combined Wills of the Seven Elders and will depart this world, restoring the victim and allowing Nature's healing processes to work.

The Elders and members of the High Priesthood conducting the exorcism should always hold in mind that they are masters of the situation and the 'Demon' must obey.

Never are they to enter into dialog with the entity nor engage in any exchange of conversation with it.

Sometimes such beings can read one's mind and will scream out the deepest secrets and privacies from within one's soul for all to hear. This can be very disconcerting for a person inexperienced in such matters. However, take heed, if the 'Demon' can cause the Exorcist and/or the assistants to falter in thought and action, it can spring up and take command of another person present.

An Exorcism is a battle of Will Power on spiritual planes. It will be felt and can cause physical discomforts, but the combined will of the Seven Exorcists being hard as iron and firm of purpose, applied with persistence, will prevail. In the end Chaos must give way to Cosmos!

PREPARATIONS

The Exorcism should be conducted on a Night of the Full Moon most convenient for the five Elders and two Members of the High Priesthood. It may have to continue through the waning phase of the Moon.

The family or friends of the victim are to make the following arrangements before the Elders arrive:

The room used for the Exorcism should be square or rectangle and be a place quite familiar to the victim in his/her normal life.

All items and furnishings must be removed from the room, except the chair or bed for the victim.

On the wall facing the victim should be a large Upright Pentagram which stands for Spirit over Matter.

No objects of any shape other than square or round are to be allowed in the room during the Exorcism. Especially not anything of a trapezoidal shape, as it is suggestive of a Universe of Chaos. This is a Universe of Cosmos, and the entity, being of a chaotic nature, is to be sent out of the Cosmos and returned to its own chaotic realm.

The room, if possible, is to be draped in purple and all participants must wear a purple robe, or garments of that colour. Purple represents spiritual authority and aggravates chaotic elements with its vibration.

At least two strong persons will be needed as assistants in order to hold the victim, firmly preventing the entity from attacking anyone in the room. (In extreme cases the body of the victim may have to be tied down with strong restraints.)

The assistants must be told to expect anything and not to allow any psychic phenomena, they may see, feel or smell, to distract them from their duty.

Evil imbalance does not give way lightly and may take considerable time and effort to overcome.

The assistants must at all times heed the instructions of the High Priest, as Exorcist, and not allow any ravings from the entity, no matter how shameful, profane or true, to force them to release the restraints and hold upon the victim during any periods of psychic agitation that may be brought on by the Exorcism.

No Swords or ritual blades; Athames, should be worn or carried by any of the participants during the Exorcism. (Should the entity/victim break loose and snatch a weapon away from the one who carries it, great damage could be done, obviously.) Forewarned is forearmed.

When all has been thus prepared and the foregoing noted by all participants, the Elders and the High Priesthood gather first at the Covenstead to prepare for the ceremony.

On the Day of the Full Moon selected for the Exorcism Ritual, the High Priestess sets the Altar for the making of this special Holy Water for use in a Rite of Major Exorcism.

She places an unlit purple candle in the North center of the Altar, which has been draped in white. Before the candle is spread a purple cloth upon which is put a vessel containing about ½ a liter of the purest water (rain water, if possible).

Next to that is placed a plate of Salt.

The seven Elders gather around the Altar and sit in prayer for spiritual strength. The prayers must last about 15 minutes to ½ hour as each breathes deeply and slowly, meditating on gathering strength to defeat and overcome Chaos.

The High Priestess stands up and faces South across the Altar, as the High Priest faces her across from the South, looking North. The five Elders each stand and move into the Altar on the East and West.

The High Priestess goes to the Sanctum and procures a flame from the Sacred Fire with the purple candle from the Altar. She sounds the hand-bell once to firm the Will and then sets the lit candle back in place upon the Altar.

All then place their hands over the objects on the Altar in an attitude of blessing, as the High Priest prays:

Gods of perfection, Gods of love,
guide us in this hour of need.
We go to free one of our own
bound by phantoms of endless woe.
Strengthen our resolve to victory
and bless this work of power.
The will of the gods of harmony
and love shall ever prevail!
Blessed be!

He takes out his Athame and strikes the Altar with it as the signal for battle and places it between the Water and the Salt.

All join hands and begin to circle the Altar widdershins, concentrating on activating the Water and Salt as they all chant:

Spirits of the waters deep
rise up from thy liquid sleep.
Soon thou wilt enter the dragon's lair,
to free the soul entrapped there.
Power from the Gods infuse thee!
Power of the Wise Ones wills enflame thee!
Power of the cosmos fills thee!
Salt the sacred, salt the blessed, pure and white
in the Mother Earth's true light.
Fight back the foe thou soon shalt meet!
Drive it like the wind and sleet!
Mix with water as the ancient sea brine pure,
to form our will for victory sure!
Blessed be!

They continue to circle and chant until the chant has been repeated five times for the War God Mars and courage in battle.

Then the High Priest pours the Salt into the Water with a banishing pentagram motion of his right hand.

All then extend their hands over the mixed Salt and Water, as he takes up the Athame and stirs the Water and Salt, in a deosil motion with the blade. He continues to stir as all pray:

Gods of the Ancient Faith, hear us.
Bless this water to banish evil.
May it cast out all that is adverse
to our world of order and form.
Let it be like our ancient Mother the Sea
who first brought life to this planet fair.
May her power of love do battle
to deliver one of her children
from the foe of chaotic night.
As the power of our will, so be it done!

The High Priest strikes upon the Altar with the Athamé blade and says:

Elders of the way of the Wise,
we go to battle chaos.
Let not passion rule they mind,
but firm thy will with calm assurance
that we, with our Gods of harmony,
shall deliver one of our own from
hatred's malice into love's embrace.
Blessed be!

The seven participants; five Elders and two of the High Priesthood, don their purple robes.

The special Holy Water is taken up from the Altar and a sprig of fresh herbs, such as Verbena or Periwinkle to be used as an aspergill is set with it for transport to the place of exorcism.

The implements needed for the ritual are as follows:
1. A large purple candle
2. A hand bell
3. The Holy Water
4. A chained censer for the Exorcism Incense; a Solar Blend
5. A large silver Pentagram

6. A purple binding cord about the same length as the victim is tall
7. This Book of Lights and a Sacred anointing Healing Oil

Also a brass brazier, either round or square, to be placed near the door in the room of the Exorcism.

Each of the seven carries and applies one of the implements. The High Priestess sprinkles the Holy Water, as the ritual stipulates and the High Priest carries *The Book of Lights* held flat with the Vial of Oil resting on top of it.

At Sunset, still at the Covenstead, the implements are placed upon the Altar, as the seven gather around to charge them with spiritual power and authority.

The Elders and High Priesthood place hands over the implements and pray in unison:

Southwards to the west!
Northwards to the east!
Banishes the power of the beast.
Be gone, be banished be sent away!
In this world of order, thou canst not stay.
Chaos is as chaos does,
but solar charms disspells its harms!
Charged be the Witch's tools to combat evil and close the gate.
In realms of love, there be no hate.
Candle, Bell and Water Holy,
banishes what manifests so drolly.
With Censer, Star and Cord to bind,
keep this world safe for humankind.
The Book of Lights and Sacred Unction,
will rob the beast of its horrid function.
Banish all evil, banish all woe,
as along with sol, southward we go!
Blessed be!

The Elders continue to circumambulate and chant until it is felt they are fully charged. They are then taken up and the Seven Exorcists depart the Covenstead and repair to the place of Exorcism.

At the place for the Exorcism the victim is restrained by the assistants, if necessary, and the brass brazier is placed inside the room by the door.

At the appointed hour the Seven gather outside the room to pray, as the High Priest leads:

Hear us, Ancient Ones and Watchers from the Times of Old!
Send to us the spirit of compassionate strength,
that with it we may face the chaos and subdue disharmony.
We pray for the soul of the unfortunate one tormented by
the entity of woe from the dark realms.
Fortify the victim's soul that it may once again take up residence in its own vehicle. So be it done.

The Elders spend a few moments in silent communion together. The purple candle is lit with flint and steel (cigarette lighter), the Incense is also set to burn in the censer.

The door of the room is faced and the High Priest pounds loudly upon it three times. It is opened and the Elder holding the candle high proceeds in first.

They walk in procession: The Candle, The Bell ringing loudly, the Holy Water being sprinkled, the Censer being swung and burning a Solar Incense (Frankincense and Myrrh and Cinnamon), the Silver Pentagram held high and the cord carried by its Elder at heart level.

The High Priest follows with the *The Book of Lights* held out flat before him upon which rests the Vial of Sacred Healing Oil.

The procession of Elders begins to move around the victim, who has the two assistants on either side of him/her. The circumambulation proceeds around widdershins seven times as the Elders and High Priesthood all chant:

Invoked be the God and Goddess.
Invoked be a balanced harmony.
Invoked by the Solar and Lunar powers.
From the north to the west, from the south to the east,
we invoke the Gods to still the beast.
Draw in, draw in the Circles' forces
that this power of harmony for sure endorses.
Full be the moon, the Goddess Triune,
with the Will of the Seven
and the God, makes eleven,

we open the sacred seal of heaven.
Come, O come, the power of the Witch's Will,
with love to heal, a tormented soul to fill.
From spheres of chaos, the enemy to block,
we work the Magic of the Ancient Mind Lock.

After the seven invocatory circumambulations, all stand and face the victim. The High Priest forcefully says:

Spawn of Chaos, give place to the Gods of Order and Harmony!
Restrained be thy ravings, for the Gods compell thee!

The candle is held high, as the bell is intoned 13 times (9 for expansion and 4 for the Elements).

The High Priest continues:

The Sacred Matix of Humankind compells thee!
The August Solar Order ordains it!

The victim is liberally sprinkled with Holy Water, by the High Priestess, and the Elder with the censer, censes the victim with the Solar Incense.

The High Priest continues:

See, O Spawn of Darkness, the symbol of the light of man!
prepare to be bound back in thine own dark realm!

The Silver Pentagram is touched to the victim's chest and the cord is touched to his/her head.

The High Priest takes some Sacred Healing Oil on his thumb and says:

With this Sacred Unciton, we, all as one,
banish thee from the world of light!

He anoints the forehead of the victim with a banishing pentagram. Then opening *The Book of Lights*, reads the Exorcism:

Spawn of chaos, conjured and constrained be!
By the might and potency of the God of the living and the dead,
creature of darkness, be enfolded in the love of the Gracious Goddess and transformed into peace and harmony.
The God of Light compells thee!

The Goddess of Love transforms thee!
The balance of this Cosmos binds thee!
The wisdom of the Ancient Ones seals thy access to this realm!
The combined will of this Coven of Seven prevents thy ravings!
By the authority of the Gods of Old, we command thee depart from the body, mind and soul of (name of victim),
as cosmos reclaims its own!
In the name of Sol Invictus! (Cross[1])
By the power of cosmic order! (Cross[1])
By the Sacred Elements Four! (Cross[1])
Be thou overcome and vanquished!

At each indication he draws a Banishing Pentagram over the body of the victim with the right hand. He continues:

In the name of Anaphaxaton, (Pentagram) *begone!*
In the name Primenoumaton, (Pentagram) *be vanquished!*
In the name Athanatos, (Pentagram) *depart!*

At this point he also draws a banishing pentagram with the oil on the victim's forehead . He then prays:

Hear us, O Ancient Ones, and bless the soul and spirit of (Name victim) *whom we here encircle with love.*

Send us strength and let us work against the force of disharmony. Restore our brother/sister of the Way of the Wise and the Ancient Craft. Send forth thy love to aid us and save one of our own from the night of dark chaos.

Blessed be.

During the reading of the Exorcism, should the entity begin to rave and thrash around, the assistants must restrain it.

Each time the ravings start, the High Priestess will douse the victim with liberal sprinkling of Holy Water and the Elder in charge of the censer will profusely cense the Solar Incense toward the victim/entity.

Any comments or insults from the entity are to be ignored by all present. It would be best if all present fill their minds with silent prayers to the gods, as the High Priest reads the Exorcism.

1 Making the Druid's Cross. See *Book V.*

The reading of the Exorcism is to be repeated seven times. After the seventh repetition the Elders set down their tools/symbols onto the floor back away from the entity/victim and then gather into a circle around him/her.

They all join hands and begin to move deosil as they chant:

Banished be thy chaotic power!
Begone, begone, this very hour!
Deosil motion,
Holy Lotion,
salt and water
of the Sacred Ocean,
seal thee from this world of man
and spoil they dark forbidding plan.
Let thy ravings all be still,
banished in this Witches mill.
The Earth, the Air, the Water and Fire,
cause our Will to grow ever higher!
Motion, motion, out and away!
The power of the dragon these Witches slay!

The seven Elders/Exorcists continue to circumambulate deosil until the High Priest feels sufficient banishing energy has been drawn in.

He then stops the others and they all kneel down beside the victim and place their hands on his/her body as they all concentrate on infusing love and harmony into the victim.

The High Priest prays together with the High Priestess:

(Name of victim), *the Gods of Old enfold thee in love.*
The Elders embrace thee in the Ancient Wisdom.
O Ancient Ones, bless and preserve this Wiccan soul.
Establish him/her in balance harmony and let the combined Will of this Coven of Seven bring in power of spirit for love and light.

The Elders all join in:

Blessed be and blessed be and blessed be.
Love enfolds thee. Light sustains thee.

They repeat this phrase over and over again for at least ten times. They then step back and take up their tools again.

Oftentimes there is a break at this point, the infused love of the seven Elders sitting and holding the victim, causing the entity to depart. However, at times it may not.

Should the ceremony have to proceed further, the High Priest must compel the entity to reveal its name. That is accomplished by tormenting the entity with Holy Water and suffumigations until it reveals its identity.

No other conversation will be taken up with the entity. No matter how it should try to evade the question or change the subject, it must be persistently pressed to reveal its true name.

He or she calls the entity by name and say:

(Name of Entity)! We bind you from the mind of our brother/sister.

A Knot is tied in the cord, and again for each of the following points:

We bind thee from the eyes
We bind thee from the ears
We bind thee from the mouth
We bind thee from the nostrils
We bind thee from the throat
We bind thee from the arms
We bind thee from the heart
We bind thee from the intestines
We bind thee from the loins
We bind thee from the hips
We bind thee from the extremeties
We bind thee from the spirit and soul

As each knot is draw, the bell is sounded once, the candle placed near the head of the victim and the Silver Pentagram held near the face, before the eyes.

Should the entity begin to rave and protest, the Holy Water and Censer again come into action to silence it, along with a strong adjuration from the High Priest for it to be silent, in the names of the Ancient Gods.

The Elders with the Cord and Candle, then step over to the brazier by the door, after the thirteen knots have been drawn. The Candle is touched to one of the knots to sit it afire, as both Elders chant:

Knots be burned,
let the beast be turned.
By this cleansing of fire,
we rid this world of chaos dire.

The knot burning must continue until all thirteen knots have been consumed in flame and the ashes dropped into the brazier to smolder away.

When the entity departs, its leaving can be readily felt, as the atmosphere in the room will considerably lighten.

As it departs, the Elders must shout after it as it goes:

Spawn of chaos, return to thine own!
Be forever shut out from this World!
Harm no living thing of Cosmos as thou goest!

The health of the restored victim must then be looked to with all due concern and everything needed to aid a speedy recovery.

After such and Exorcism all ritual tools must be cleansed and re-blessed before they can be used for any other ritual or ceremony. Such a blessing for the tools can be found in the section on the Works of the High Priestess.

(A large magenta candle may be used in place of a purple one, if such can be obtained. In that case, the binding cord should also be of magenta colour.)

It may be that the physical control of the victim must be left to medical and psychiatric authorities.

However, the ritual may be applied in proxy upon a tag lock from the living victim and the Exorcism done "psychically" by the seven participants. Something to ponder.

Section IV

The Book of Elders
The Ancient Craft in the Way of the Wise

This small tome is given as an Addenda to *Book III: The Book of Lights,* due to many requests from Witches who have read the Covenant.

They wish to know how true Craft Elders keep the faith and see to its proper validity in the Way of the Wise, of the Ancient Order of Bell, Book and Candle.

Never before have the works of the inner circles of Craft Elders been given out. However, in order to facilitate a divine directive to give the Craft a common liturgical guideline and a complete way of life for the Wiccan Tradition, the Elders at the Circle of Starmeadow of A.O. of B.B.&C. now authorize the dissemination of *The Book of Elders.*

This gives the workings of the Council of Elders and the occult magics of the Defenders of the Faith in the inner core as the Mystic Coven of Seven.

True Craft Elders will never publicly identify themselves as such, but you will surely know them by their works.

Tarostar V°
Magister Sacrorum,
Circle of Starmeadow,
Ancient Order of Bell, Book and Candle

By their rites shall they be known.
The higher the standard and quality,
the greater demads for perfection
on those who would practice them.
– W.G. Gray

These are the works of the Elders of the Craft in the Way of the Wise of the Ancient Order of Bell, Book and Candle.

The Elders of the Craft are the true "Defenders of the Faith" and their works consist of maintaining peace and harmonious fellowship among all Covens and Traditions in the Craft. They work for that end and endeavor to offset adverse publicity and attacks upon the Craft by the ignorant and the uniformed.

They also gather to work the Magics of the Craft of the utmost importance on non-physical levels.

This they do in the Mystic Coven of Seven, which is the deep inner core of the Craft, the Sanctum Sanctorum of all the best of ancient knowledge in esoteric and occult wisdom.

An Elder of the Craft, in the Way of the Wise, will always be known by the white robe with black cingulum or cinch cord. Such is the dress of the V°.

A Magister Sacrorum will have in addition to that, a purple sash across the breast and over the right shoulder attached at the waist on the left side. It will bear a silver Pentagram for each of the Coven groups he has formed, hived off, or helped to function. A Magister will have at least two, never less.

A Queen Mother will wear a green garter on the right leg up near the knee. It will also bear at least two silver Pentagrams for the same above reasons. Her robe will, therefore, have a slit up the right side. When she enters a Ritual Chamber, or a Covenstead of other than her home Coven, she will have the hood up over the eyes, so her exposed right knee will let all know the rank of the imposing personage in their midst.

A Philosophus will wear, on his black cinch cord, a curved blade of a scimitar shaped knife in its bejeweled sheath.

An Oracle will wear her Moonstone Pendant about the neck for all to see.

An Elder will never appear in public among the Craft with hood down. Such would be done only in his/her home Coven. In that way, an Elder maintains an air of polite aloofness from the internal affairs of other independent Covens. He/she will only be drawn into the workings of functional Covens as stipulated by *Book I: The Covenant,* where he/she may be called upon to assume the office of the High Priesthood on a temporary basis, and to act as necessary trustee for Coven properties, or may act as a visiting Officiant for any Sabbat or Esbat when invited to do so by the regular High Priesthood of a functioning Coven.

At Initiations raising those of III° to IV° (High Priesthood) the Elders will attend in full regalia but with hoods up, unless the one being elevated comes from the Elder's home Coven. Then the hood of that Elder may be down as a gesture of familiarity.

At Initiations elevating persons to V° status (as Elders) however, full formal anonymity will prevail, to designate such as an official act affecting the Craft as a whole. The member of the High Priesthood becoming an Elder, thus becomes a potent force capable of imprinting his/her influence on the Craft in general.

Therefore, it is in keeping with the best traditions in the Craft that Elders exercise care in whom they elevate to V°. Only those who have worked for the greater glory of the Gods, rather than any self-aggrandizement may be considered.

Even those of the High Priesthood, who have successfully hived of a second Coven do not automatically become eligible for Elder status unless all Elders in the District or Covendom feel they would, by becoming Elders V°, enhance the fostering of the Faith as a force for good.

Imperium Deponere
Elevation to Elder V°
(Eighth Level of Initiation)

This ceremony was lifted from *Book II, The Book of Beginnings,* to be included with all matters pertaining to Elders of the Craft in the Way of the Wise.

When a High Priest or High Priestess has persevered and overcome the tremendous obstacles in Coven organization in having built a Coven entity which has been successful in hiving off another Coven, which has also grown to full stature and has elevated at least one III⁰ person to IV° status; the Elders will grant V⁰ status to that High Priest and/ or High Priestess. Such would have been earned. That is the purging of the soul in Fire.

By being that difficult, it is assured - only the best and the strongest Witches attain Elder status of the Craft in the Way of the Wise.

Having undergone such and Ordeal, one would have developed the strength of Spirit and understanding of Human Nature to such a degree as to make one almost like unto the Gods in their infinite Compassion for the Human Species. It is only to souls such as those that the leadership of the Craft should be given.

Only on the Night of the 13th New Moon, will the Elders meet to elevate a High Priest or High Priestess to V⁰ status. (Remember, Hallowmas is the Craft's New Year. It would be on the 13th New Moon following that Sabbat.)

The 13th New Moon represents the total completion of an entire cycle. Elder status is the fifth and final degree in Craft.

The member of the High priesthood to be elevated comes before the Elders in full ceremonial regalia, having been summoned formally by the Scribe of the Council of Elders and told to make or purchase a hooded white robe and make the black cingulum. The home Coven would have borne the expense of making the insignia of rank. (The purple sash or the Green Garter.) The insignia are given over to the Elders before the ceremony.

Standing alone before the Elders, the High Priest or High Priestess represents the full authority of the Craft in all its ceremonial pride and power.

The Elders stand facing the one to be elevated as the Scribe of the Council of Elders speaks for all.

Scribe:

Thou hast been summoned here to set aside thy regalia of rank and all the pride of rulership in Coven affairs. Art thou willing to give up authority in the High Priesthood and accept the simple garment of an Elder, whose only weapon is the sanction of moral values and the works of mind on non-physical realms?

Art thou willing to work in common for the benefit of all, foregoing status of rank and privilege?

The High Priest/High Priestess:

Lord/Lady Elder, the symbols of earthly pride are as nothing to a true adept of the Ancient Wisdom. I do and will cast them aside.

The one being elevated then lays his/her Coven Great Wand or Coven Broom upon the floor, places the right foot upon it and says:

I divest myself of direct Coven rule.

He/she takes off the Amethyst head band or the bejeweled tiara, sets it aside and says:

Let this Crown of Attainment pass on to others. Having been the first among my brothers and sisters, I now become the least among the Elders.

Taking off the gold or silver cingulum he/she says:

This has been a heavy yoke of responsibility in guiding the seeking souls of the Gods' children. As I wore it with dignity, let me freely set it aside to be a momento of work well done.

(All divested gold and silver cingulums are kept by the Council of Elders in a special rack, so that, with time the collection will grow and grow.)

Now standing before the Elders in only the black formal robe, the divested member of the High Priesthood says:

Lords and Ladies, I stand as nothing before thee. Let the Gods make of me what they will. Blessed be.

Scribe:

Thou hast freely laid aside all pride of place. Thou art empty of ego and arrogance. Thou art the nil point from which Cosmos doth come forth. Let the Gods fill thee.

If the one being elevated is male, the Magisters and Philosophi among the Elders take him into a side room. If the one being elevated is female, the Queen Mothers and Oracles do the same for her. The Initiate is now to receive the Zodiacal Anointing from head to foot.

Standing in the midst of the Elders of the same gender, the Initiate slips out of the black Formal Coven Robe and stands with head high.

The most Senior of the Elders in the room conducts the anointing. Taking a dab of specially blended oil of Rose, Jasmine and Sandalwood upon the strongest thumb, the Elder will draw the zodiacal sign on each place on the Initiate's body as indicated and give the Charge of each sign as it is drawn:

m–At the forehead: *Will Power and Force of Mind.* Aries
n–at the Throat: *Tenacious Steadfastness and Stability.* Taurus
o–on each Forearm: *Works of Skill and Agility.* Geminii
p–on the Breast: *Love of Life and the Pool of Compassion.* Cancer
q–on the Back of the Spine: *Strength and Uprightness.* Leo
r–on the Abdomen: *Exactness of Purpose.* Virgo
s–on the Hips: *Fairness and Justice.* Libra
t–on the Pubic Area: *Self-Transformstion and Rebirth.* Scorpio
u–on the Thighs: *Spiritual Guidance and Self-Knowledge.* Sagittarius
v–at the Knees: *Pursuit of Goals.* Capricorn
w–on the Shins: *Friendship and Humanity.* Aquarius
x–on the Feet: *Contemplation and Reflection.* Pisces

The Elder giving the anointing then places his/her hands upon the Initiate's head and says:

Thy Work in the Craft hath brought two full Covens into being with the potential of a third. The Athanor of Affliciton hath tempered thy soul and brought thee to this 12-fold blessing. The God and Goddess have found their expression in thee. Blessed be.

The Elders in the room dress the Initiate in the simple hooded white robe and lead him/her back into the outer room before the rest of the Elders.

The Scribe of the Council of Elders takes the black cingulum and says:

Thou hast been anointed and blessed by the Gods. Recite now the resolves of the V⁰.

The Initiate:

As I become an Elder of the Craft in the Way of the Wise, I hereby resolve to defend the Faith at all times and at all costs. To arbiter fairly according to the accepted laws of the Craft. To seek harmony and good will among all beings my life may touch. Blessed be.

The Scribe then girds the black cord around the initiate as all Elders point their index fingers of their right hands at the Initiate and shout in unison:

Adepthood is assured thee. Thou art Elder V⁰.

The insignia of rank are given and put on without ceremony.

The newly elevated Elder may then take a place of equality with all others at the Council of Elders and in the workings of a Mystic Coven of Seven.

The newly elevated Elder may keep his/her Great Wand or Coven Broom as a token of his/her service to the Craft. The High Priest's Headband or the High Priestess Tiara should be given back to the home Coven, who made, paid for, or commissioned its making to pass on to those who will follow in the High Priesthood of the Craft.

The cinch cord remains in the possession of the Council of Elders to link the newly elevated one to them.

The newly elevated Elder, will, from that time on, not discuss with others in the Craft of lesser rank what transpires in a Council of Elders or in a Mystic Coven of Seven.

Concerning the Council of Elders

The Council of Elders meets yearly at the Full Moon of July in the place used for its Ritual Chambers at a Covenstead in their District or

Covendom convenient for all attending.

As outlined in *Book I: The Covenant, Sec. E, 6* and *7* and *Sec. L,* the Council does not act as a legislative body passing Laws or rules and regulations with which to pontificate and dominate the autonomous spirits of the various Covens, but is a clearing house for Craft related matters. Covens who feel they may benefit from the advice of the Elders associate under the Council of their own choice and volition.

The Council of Elders receives yearly reports from the active High Priesthood as to the state of affairs of their respective Covens in the Covendom or District. The Elders will at all times uphold the dignity and honour of those of the High Priesthood. They will not publicly side with those of a lesser degree to oppose or degrade the High Priesthood.

Should a member of the High Priesthood display a swollen ego, or be overly dictatorial and arbitrary, he/she must be privately admonished by the Elders to change his/her ways so as not to cause internal strife and tension in Coven Circles.

The Elders will not be prey to complaints about the inner workings of Covens by petitions from single Officers or Coveners.

The Council also accepts written petitions, as The Right of Appeal, from the three Coven Officers of each Coven Council when the First Scribe along with the Second Scribe and Summoner feel that something is drastically amiss in Coven affairs.

Only when the three Coven Officers petition the Council of Elders in unison and have signed the same Document of Petition, will their grievance be considered. In that way the Elders will know there is a serious matter in coven problems needing their attention.

The Elders will discuss all reports and/or petitions and return their decisions as to what is or is not in keeping with the best of Craft Tradition.

The Elders will not openly side with the High Priesthood in conflicts opposing the Will of the individual Coven Council. They will always admonish all to work out their problems in the nature of democratic process, seeking what is best for all concerned, in the majority Will of the Coven Council.

The respective Coven Councils will then work out their own problems and implement the Elders decisions as they see fit.

Should a Coven be unable to work out its differences and be racked with strife, the Elders will withdraw their sanctions from such a group and recommend the High Priesthood void the Coven. Such would be better than trying to worship the Old Gods in a Circle where members hold rancor in their hearts for their fellow beings.

Democratic Government and Freedom of Choice and Conscience are the ideals of the Craft espoused by a Council of Elders. However, once a choice is made, it is to faithfully abide.

In a Council of Elders, the words of a Philosophus and/or Oracle will carry much weight and be listened to with respect. Such ones have devoted their life's work to the Craft, so their sage advice should not be lightly taken.

A Magister Sacrorum or Queen Mother will be elected by the Council of Elders to act as its Scribe.

The Council itself will be composed of all members of the High Priesthood in the Covendom or District, as junior members, and all Magisters, Queen Mothers, Philosophi and Oracles, there may be in any respective Covendom or District, as senior members.

The Scribe of the Council of Elders will answer all petitions sent to the yearly meeting and all reports by the High Priesthood given to the Council.

These answers would offer what suggestions the Elders may have for any of the High Priesthood to incorporate into their rule and offer whatever solutions to problems the Elders have for petitions of grievance from the Coven Councils.

The Elders do not dictate Coven policy or orientation. They bring the pressure of democratic ethics and moral sanctions to bear.

The Scribe of the Council of Elders will sign and affix his/her name and seal to the answers in the name of the Council of Elders for the Covendom or District, but only upon authorization of a majority of the Elders in the Council. Never will he/she act as an individual in the name of the Council.

The Scribe will also act as Officiant in any ritual procedure conducted in the presence of the Elders.

Copies of these answers will be kept in the possession of one of the Elders, so that, over the years, the decisions of the Council of Elders will grow into a Codex of Craft Tradition for the benefit of future generations. The sage advice of all Elders will then be handed down to posterity and prevent another dearth of Craft Lore, as resulted because of the persecutions of 'The Burning Time'. The manuscripts and memoirs of the retiring Elders will also be added to the Codex for the edification of younger Witches.

Questions concerning incompatibility may arise from time to time as mentioned in *Book I: The Covenant, Sec. G, 1-4* and *Book II.*

Some will say let unprepared persons split off if they will. The Elders, however, see that as wrong. It is their duty to validate the High Priesthood.

Incompatible II^{0} and III^{0} persons, having advanced that far in the Craft would be given over to the High Priesthood in the Coven from which they wish to depart so that the High Priesthood may train them as rapidly as possible to be able to qualify for IV^{0} status. They will then be brought before the Elders at the appropriate time for Initiation to IV^{0} and allowed to make a valid Hive Off.

The reason behind such a way is that it provides good discipline for all concerned, both for the High Priesthood themselves and for the II° and III^{0} persons wishing to remove themselves.

It would be suggested, however, that the incompatible ones not participate in the Coven Esbat works in order to assure harmonious results from the activities of the rest of the Coven.

In such a manner the Elders can see to sending a valid High Priesthood forth into the world.

Some traditions in the Craft abound with individuals who have only a smattering of Craft Lore, having had a few lessons from some groups equally lacking in the depth necessary to teach the Craft. The Elders of the Craft in the Way of the Wise will never sanction such as valid.

It is at the yearly meeting of the Council of Elders that III^{0} persons are elevated to the High Priesthood. (except as stipulated by the Covenant and *The Book* of Beginnings.)

Such would be done only after all other business of the Council has been concluded for that year. The Hand Maiden or Practicus to be elevated High Priest or High Priestess would not see nor participate in any of the deliberations of the Council. They would remain outside the Ritual Chamber until the meeting is finished and their respective sponsoring High Priesthood come to fetch them before the Elders.

No format or ritual procedure is given for the Elders to conduct in the meetings of the Council. Such would be at the discretion of the Elders of an individual Covendom themselves. Some may wish a strict formal ceremonial method to conducting the meetings, while others may wish an informal atmosphere, resembling a social club.

Any other matters pertaining to a Council of Elders may be left to the Elders themselves to add or work out as time goes by.

Concerning the Mystic Coven of Seven

A properly cosmated Circle of Elders is necessary to work the Will of the group on the Astral Levels of being. An intense thought vibration must be implanted in the Universal Ether and repeatedly intensified by strong visualization and meditative emotional desire.

A Coven of Seven brings the pressure of linked minds to bear upon a situation or a circumstance that needs to be changed for the better in the best interests of the Craft.

It is composed of an Oracle, a Philosophus, a Queen Mother and a Magister Sacrorum, as the participating Elders and a High Priest and a High Priestess to conduct the ceremonial Invocations for the Mystical Seventh member, the Gods.

The two members of the High Priesthood do not participate in the astral work of the Elders themselves, but supply the channel to the Gods through their Sabbat practice and Esbat works.

The High Priest and High Priestess are drawn from the collective of the High Priesthood in the Covendom because they are junior members of the Council of Elders. Therefore these two ceremonial participants may be from any of the Covens or each from different Covens as the Elders see fit, allowing various members of the High Priesthood to work with the Elders as part of their own training and development.

No specific format can be given that would be standard among all Covendoms at all times and all places.

However, a method can be recommended that has been found effective by many Elders over the years.

A Coven of Seven is, for all intents and purposes, a Spiritual Circle of advanced Occultists who work their will from the inner planes of being in order to affect the World around them. There is no Temple or Ritual Chamber, nor Altar needed.

The Elders decide among themselves as to how and in what way their Inner Temple of Light is to be furnished. They determine what their Altar would look like and what trappings would exist in their own Astral work.

Outwardly, all that is seen is a small group of people sitting in a circle within the symbolic Four Elements (as per diagram).

The Inner Temple of Light is entered by the Elders as they project onto the Astral Levels of being and conduct whatever ceremony or ritual as would be necessary to bring about the change according to the collective will of the group.

From this Inner Temple the good works of others in the Craft may be aided by though forms of success and prosperity, healing energies can be sent, and pressures causing discord and strife may be nullified and relieved.

All constructive matters pertaining to the advancement of Craft interests can be fostered by the Elders through their inner works. Also, the enemies of the Craft may be bound and tethered by the collective will of the Elders. Always remembering, the Gods do not strike enemies down by force, they send a 'Jupiterian' blessing to increase a particular set of circumstances. Their sting then has lasting effect. The Gods admonish by their chastisement, they do not kill.

Tempting as it may be to use the inner power to punish, the Elders will at all times try as much as possible to be like unto the Gods in their responsibility to fellow beings. It is Cosmic Justice that is dispensed by an Inner Temple of Light, not necessarily mere human justice.

Following the proper tides of the Moon, the Elders would gather for the Mystic Coven of Seven in a bare place devoid of all magical trappings and paraphernalia. To the North would be placed a Pentacle bearing a Pentagram. To the West would sit a Chalice of salted water. To the South, a Sword would rest and the East a Thurible burning and Incense appropriate to the rite.

The Elders would stand facing inward within the Circle thus laid out. They would join hands and begin to move steadily widdershins as the High Priest standing outside the Thurible and the High Priestess, standing outside the Chalice invoke the Gods. The light of a single candle standing in the center of the Elders would be the only illumination. It may be white or black depending on the needs of the reason for the working.

The Invocations themselves should be personal to the ceremonial participants, the High Priesthood. They work regularly at Sabbat and Esbat to draw in the nature of the Gods and would have invocations they know to be effective.

Theirs is the duty to continually, during the rite, keep a vivid thought form of the God and Goddess firmly in mind and to be attentive that no distractions are allowed to affect the Elders while they are out of body on the Inner Planes.

As the Elders steadily step the Round to draw in the Gods, the invoked power will grow and grow. When it is felt to be firmly present, the High Priesthood will go silent and sit down in place.

The Elders will bow toward the center of the Circle and also sit down in place.

At this point the Elders will project onto the Astral Level and enter their Temple of Light. They will then proceed to influence astrally whatever matter has drawn their concern.

The rite will last until the Elders return to themselves on this plane.

When the Astral is firmly and emotionally imprinted, the physical will begin to be moved into conformity. The rite may have to be repeated and reinforced as often as necessary to accomplish the group will.

Once the rite is over, the Elders will rise and shake off the meditative affects. The High Priesthood will rise and speak forth a farewell to the Gods as the Elders join hands and step deosil to disperse the energy.

Then the High Priest will stamp firmly upon the floor or ground and the High Priestess will clap the hands several times to astringe the atmosphere and bring all back to normal time and space.

The tools or Hallows are gathered up and all leave silently to never speak of the rite. The Mystic Coven of Seven has worked its Will.

In this manner, the simple format allows the Elders of any particular Covendom to set their own procedure and ritual observances to build the Inner Temple of Light. Each individual has his/her own mental and emotional power to contribute.

The concerted effort of mature minds linked in common purpose to work the group will is sure of success. Such is the Ancient Craft in the Way of the Wise.

Appendix I

Section I: Works of the High Priest

What is offered as suggestions in this appendix will be alternate charges and invocations and prayers for the High Priest to use, in order to provide variety for the ceremonies as he sees fit. They can be worked into the liturgy in place of those already given, or used in addition to the ones in the ritual formats.

Erecting the Temple

(Cast the Circle with Air and Fire)

The ceremony, which follows, is the preliminary to any Celestial Sabbat ritual. The High Priest represents the God, or the masculine force of Nature. He casts the Circle with the two masculine elements of Air and Fire. These elements always stand for the High Priest and are the active parts of any ritual invoking the God.

When the hour for the appointed ritual strikes and the altar is ready, a bell may be sounded thrice to clear the air and announce the beginning of Sabbat.

The High Priest stands in silence outside the Ritual Chamber with the lit Pilot Lamp in the left hand and the burning Censer in the right.

As silence falls upon the group, after the ringing of the bell, he proceeds to the Altar and passes widdershins around it still maintaining silence.

After one circumambulation of the Altar, he stands facing North across the Altar and places the Pilot Lamp and censer in their places. (See *Diagram I, Section I: Works of the High Priest* – pg 223)

Taking the two Altar Candles into his hands (the black in the left and the white in the right) he lights them both simultaneously from the Pilot Lamp as he pronounces:

Holy art Thou, Powers that be.

Then the Altar Candles are replaced in their proper positions (or back in their respective holders) and he draws either a Solar Cross or and Invoking Pentagram over them with the right hand.

He then kneels and kisses the Altar. After the kiss, he rises and takes the Sword. (A Stang or Staff may be used instead. It always lays on the floor before the Altar laying to the East and West. A Sword may stand against the Altar on the East Side.)

Carrying the Sword in the salute position (Upright with both hands on the hilt and held before the solar plexus so that the blade rises up and goes before him.)

He proceeds to the North Quarter, bows to the North and turns the tip of the blade down to touch the floor. He then says:

The Path (we/I) tread is Holy. The Temple (we/I) build is Sacred.

The High Priest then proceeds to draw the Circle on the floor with the tip of the Sword blade moving widdershins from the North back around to the North again. He does this in silence, and draws the circle large enough to contain the Altar and all persons who will participate in the Sabbat Ritual.

He bows again to the North Quarter and carries the Sword back to the Altar and replaces it.

Taking up the Censer he returns to the North Quarter and censes thrice to the North as he says:

Thee (we/I) invoke, O Ancient One. come to the Sacred Song Io Evoh Heh!

He then proceeds widdershins censing thrice to each Quarter and repeating the words until he returns to the North where he bows again. Returning to the Altar, the Censer is replaced.

Taking up the two Altar candles from their holders, as before, he steps to the North Quarter and holds the two candles high before him, he says:

(We/I) call the Ancient One of our Fathers and Mothers. draw nigh and consecrate this Holy Temple. Bless (us/me) from the four corners of this world.

Holding the two Altar Candles high above his head, the High Priest kneels down on the left knee, bringing the Candles down to about his hip level on the left side. Then standing up he lifts the Candles to about shoulder level on the right side. He passes the Candles straight across to the left side at shoulder level and then kneels down on the right knee passing the Candles diagonally down to about hip level on the right side. He then stands up passing the Candles back to their original position high above his head. Thus he completes a large Invoking Pentagram.

The High Priest carries the Candles high above his head as he passes around widdershins repeating the invocation and Invoking Pentagram, thus described, at each Quarter returning to the North. He bows to the Quarter and passes back to the Altar and replaces the two Candles in their proper places.

He then assumes the cruciform position and reverently recites the Charge of God as follows:

The Living God blesses us.
The Mighty God protects us.
The True God inspires us.
The Ancient God fathers us.

The High Priest kneels before the Altar. All present should do likewise. He continues:

There is a Power, which creates the Universe.
There is a Love, which fructifies the Earth.
There is a Spirit which inspires Wisdom.
It is the duty of mankind to read his word.
It is carried on the rush of the wind,
inscribed of flame in stars of fire,
reflected in waves of the rushing sea,
and embodied in form as our Mother the Earth.

The High Priest bends forward and kisses the floor as a gesture of reverence for the Earth. He stands up and reassumes the cruciform position. All stand as he continues:

The God charges us to go forth into this world of form.
There, to see His works and seek His wisdom.
All experience from which we learn are His precepts.
All joys, which elevate our consciousness, are His rituals.
Hear, O Children of Man, and live each day in love and harmony

with all that is, and the blessings of the God will rest upon you!

The High Priest turns deosil to face all persons present and draws a Solar Cross toward them with the right hand and blesses them thus:

Blessed be all who worship the Ancient One! Again I say, blessed be!

All persons present should respond with these words:

The Ancient One indwells His Holy Temple. Blessed be.

The Circle is complete. The Temple has been erected once again. The Sabbat Ritual may now proceed from this point. All Coveners enter the Circle and show grade signs.

Closing the Temple

(The banishing with Water and Earth.)

The following brief ceremony must conclude all Celestial Sabbat Rituals. It is designed to banish the Circle and send out the blessing raised by the Sabbat Ritual into the world at large. All power and energy collected by invocation must be sent to accomplish its intended purpose. Under no circumstances may the banishing be omitted. Energy that has been invoked and then left trapped within a Circle, can go stale and cause the Ritual Chamber to become a very uncomfortable place in which to be.

The High Priest now takes the two feminine elements of Water and Earth to banish the Circle. In so doing, all the mystical elements have been employed, thus making the erecting and closing acts a balanced whole.

The closing proceeds in this manner:

After the main part of the Sabbat Ritual has been concluded, before anyone leaves the circle, the High Priest faces North across the Altar and exclaims:

The Ancient Rite is ended for another season/time. (we/I) now close the Holy Temple.

Taking up the Chalice of Water, he raises it to his lips and speaks upon the surface of the Water thus:

Blessed be, O Water of Life. be thou a healing and holy blessing to all where thou art cast. Carry love and light and banish all that is adverse to God's Holy Purpose.

He carries the Water to the North Quarter and sprinkles a few drops to the North. He then proceeds to tread the Circle deosil sprinkling and saying as he goes:

Bless our Works, O God of Life and give love and light to all of this world. Carry our Sabbat blessing to all our kith and kin. Blessed be!

Returning to the Altar and replacing the Water, he takes up the dish or Paten of Salt or Earth. Lifting it to his lips he says:

Blessed be, O Earth of form. Solidify our Works in our lives and hearts that the blessing of God remain with us in all ways.

Proceeding deosil, as before, he casts Salt to the four Quarters and all around the Circle. As he goes, he says:

May the Positive Power of God be manifest in all that we do. Blessed be.

After circumambulating deosil, he returns to the Altar and replaces the Salt. He claps thrice with the hands and says:

This Holy Temple is closed. May the next happy season bring us together again.

The Candles are snuffed out. The High Priest takes up the Pilot Lamp and the Censer and proceeds out of the Ritual Chamber. All Coveners present may now quit the Circle.

A bell may be tolled thrice to clear the air.

Midwinter

At the Entering in of Death prior to Midwinter Sabbat: When the High Priest puts out the Sacred Flame, he may use this prayer:

Blessed be, O Flame of Life. All through the year's bright tide thou hast burned and kept constant thy witness to the tide of light. The hour of greatest darkness now approaches.

The Death, known as King Winter, knocks on the very doors of this Holy Temple. He must come in, He will have His due. His chill mantle will soon drape our lives and still our hearts.

The High Priestess opens the door to the Ritual Chamber and allows the cold to come in. She taps the bell with her Athamé blade and bows in silence. The High Priest continues:

He has entered. His time is now. Death triumphs over life in this barren season. Farewell, O Flame of Life, thou goest to spirit on inner planes. We keep thee ever locked within our hearts, for the victory of Death is but a day. Sleep now and we shall call thee forth on the great day of return, when thou wilt live again as our Child of Promise! Io Evoh Heh! Blessed be!

Presenting the Sacred Flame deosil to the Four Quarters, he says:

See, O Mighty Ones and Watchers from the Times of Old, the tide of life has run its course. Death's stark silence reigns supreme.

Banished be the time that was! Invoked be the time to come!

Accept this symbol of our world, this Sacred Flame, and keep it safe 'til we call it forth again. Blessed be!

He snuffs out the flame by placing a small dish over the flame to smother it out.

Prior to Midwinter Sabbat, as the Coven assembles outside the Ritual Chamber, to produce the spark of the Sacred Flame, and the Altar has sat in darkness and silence for three days, this may be used:

The High Priest raps thrice on the door of the silent Ritual Chamber and says:

King Winter's thrall is the harshest of times. All Nature sinks into icy slumber. The Great Mother's abundance and flowering beauty have vanished. This world of man stands abandoned to the heaviness of the black hours of freezing night.

The Dark Lord rides on the storm wind's blast, killing and chilling and taking his toll.

The light of this world is faint and dim. We stand in the midst of the tide of darkness, cold and shivering children in the night of time. Helpless before King Winter's whim.

Only if our spirits lag do we succumb to his cruel authority. Then does he hold sway over us.

Yet the seed of life lays hidden. It is not his to rule.

We have hope, that on the morn the dark tide turns. the spirit of life quickens this world, as we raise our spirits and call forth the tide of the waxing light.

From this point the producing of the spark and the regular chant may continue (see *Midwinter Sabbat*).

As the High Priestess leads the Circle Dance to raise the Power, this chant may be substituted:

Come to the round where the path is trod, earth and water, fire and air.

Ama Aima Aradia, with Io Evoh Heh create our world, this planet fair.

Light makes life and spirit, matter, from of old to endless time,
let life's spiral ever climb.
Bring us blessings of renewed life
and still cruel winter's tempest and strife.
Raise up our hearts in this circle of fire,
for the tide of light is the Mother's desire.
Bring to us all joy that can be,
O blessed re-occurant mystery!

Vernal Equinox

As the High Priestess leads the Circle Dance, the High Priest may authorize this chant in place of the one in the format:

Light and life in perfect poise do stand,
at Equinox, at Equinox!
Balance, harmony and love, watchwords proclaimed throughout the land,
at Equinox, at Equinox!
Fresh spring breeze and warmth of sun,
at Equinox, at Equinox!

Announce nature's handiwork has begun,
at Equinox, at Equinox!
Joy springs eternal to the human breast,
at Equinox, at Equinox!
Bringing hope for all that's best,
at Equinox. at Equinox!

Prior to closing his Circle with Water and Earth to end the Sabbat, the High Priest may wish to recite this Benediction[1] on the Coveners:

Whether in Coven or at home, the art of worship is an inner adventure.

'Tis the personal practice of the presence of God.

Outer symbols create the atmosphere and mood of worship –the Altar, the Candles, the silent sanctuary before Sabbat begins, the benediction before you depart for your homes.

But as you go forth, remember that worship – the presence of God – is much more than the mood that we have created as we gathered here today.

It is meditation and prayer expressing the soul's sincere desires.

It is resting our weary hearts and minds in the knowledge of the everlasting goodness of our God/Goddess.

It is emptying and cleansing our minds of fear and worry, jealousy and envy – that the gods may fill the vacuum with their goodness.

It is being quiet and relaxed that we may experience the inflow of that perfect peace profound which passes all understanding.

It is counting our many blessings and giving thanks for the power to grow, to serve, to conquer ourselves and to discover the sublime values of the life of the spirit.

It is the inspiring realization that this is the Gods' world, that all life pulsates with the Gods' eternal purpose and that we are a part of that divine pattern and plan.

It is envisioning, high and lifted up, all that is heroic, great, good and beautiful in our common life.

It is realigning our lives again with the laws and principles of the Gods, that we may move forward, with our brothers and sisters, on the pathway to perfection.

1 The Benedictions are from traditional pastoral tracts adapted for Wicca.

It is the renewing of our noblest dreams and aspirations that we may rise above defeat, failure and discouragement and have another try at making the most of our lives.

It is climbing to the spiritual mountaintop of conscious oneness with the Gods, that we may light the candles of our spirit and return as newly-inspired individuals to the valley of our work.

With blessings and peace surrounding you, go forth and walk with your hand in the right hands of the Gods. Blessed be!

Midsummer

At the preliminary Rite of Firing the Temple, the High Priest may wish to substitute these words when the New Fire is brought to the Altar:

Hear, O Mighty Ones and Watchers from the Times of Old!
I bear the light of this world, celestial gold,
drawn in the ancient manner, from the solar orb.

At solstice tide in winter's thrall, this happy temple is cleansed by the silence of the grave. But, in this happy season, before midsummer's longest day, we cleanse with Sol's Holy Fire.

Behold thy Lord, the vivifier!

As the High Priestess leads the Circle Dance to raise the Power, the High Priest may authorize this chant:

Those who follow the Wiccan Way
are filled with power on this day!
Midsummer's Fire flames in our hearts.
Those who follow the Wiccan Code
are filled with strength from the Gods of Old!
Midsummer's Fire flames in our hearts.
Those who follow the Craft of the Wise
celebrate summer out under the skies!
Midsummer's Fire flames in our hearts.
Air and Fire, Earth and Water,
make us sons of the God and the Great Mother's daughters!
Midsummer's Fire flames in our hearts.
Upward on the spiral flow

to states of perfection we go!
Midsummer's Fire flames in our hearts.

The High Priest may wish to give this Benediction before he closes the Circle:

To get the most out of life, we must take time to live as well as to make a living. We must practice the art of filling our moments with enriching experiences that will give new meaning and depth to our lives.

We should take time for good books, time to absorb the thoughts of poets and philosophers, seers and prophets.

Time for music that washes away from the soul the dust of everyday life.

Time for friendships, time for talks by fireside, and walks beneath the stars. Time for children that we may find again the kingdom of the gods within our hearts. Time for laughter and letting go and filling the heart with mirth. Time for travel, time for pilgrimage and festival, for shrine and exhibit, for rockbound coast and desert, mountain and meadow. Time for all of nature, time for flower gardens, trees, birds and sunsets. Time to love and be loved, for love is the greatest thing in the world. Time for people, time for interplay of personalities and the interchange of ideas – not in an argumentative fashion, but for the enrichment of our creative mentality. Time for solitude, time to be quiet and to look within. Time to give of ourselves, our talents, abilities, devotions, convictions and the sharing of our tables and our earthly gain, which we may contribute to the upgrading of our culture. Time for worship, time for opening our lives to the God's infinite springs of vitality that we may live more abundantly. In all ways let us make our moments glow with life, and let us pray that we not allow ourselves to die before we have begun to live. Blessed be!

Autumnal Equinox

The High Priest may wish to engage in a short responsive litany with the Coveners to express the meaning of this Sabbat. After he has erected the Circle, he may lead the litany thus:

Once again we stand in the balanced time.

A balanced time in the tide of darkness.
Heavy night draws closer with each passing day.
Soon will the Great Mother repose in silence
and the Lord of Death will rule the land.
Companions of the Ancient Craft, what have we stored up against that time?

All Coveners then respond:

True, the light grows ever dim, yet never are we totally abandoned.
As Dame Nature keeps the spark of life deep within her bosom during cruel winter's tide, she also provides her ripened bounty to keep us 'til she smiles again. Blessed be the Harvest time!

To which the High Priest asks:

That is the Harvest of the Great Mother's love.
But what of the Harvest of our souls?

All Coveners respond:

The God's Spirit plainly teaches; nothing comes from nothing. What is sown must also be reaped. This is the season we receive our due. No more, no less. For we ourselves are the Harvest of the God's intentions. may we ever aspire to be the wheat and not the chaff. Blessed be the Perfect Plan!

The High Priest continues:

In this equal time of light and dark let us balance the best against the worst within ourselves and ask the God to grant us rightly what we are due.
O God of balance and measured time,
let that which is sown on Earth be reaped in higher realms, and that which is sown in the Spirit recompense us on Earth.
Let the tenets of the faith: balance, harmony, perfect love and perfect trust, along the path of rebirth guide us by thy law of compensation.
Blessed be, O God of Perfect Justice!

A suggested blessing for the Harvest Fruit:

O Wisdom of the Wiccan Way, teach us to be prudent with what we earn. Let all our works lead us to maturity of Spirit. We abide in expectation to grow as divine beings and to exist on higher realms. But as yet we are not ready for that great Harvest of our Spirits. Until that time, Mother Earth's mature and fruitful bounty are our symbols of that Spiritual state to which we will one day be gathered.

May the God of Justice and the Goddess of Abundant Goodness bless these Harvest fruits to our well being of body and spirit. Blessed be!

A suggestion for the Circle Dance Chant may be:

Down, down to the grave we go.
Shadows grow long and the cold winds blow.
Reaped is the Harvest and ripe is the corn.
Frost in the field is felt in the morn.
Stocks from the meadows and sheep in the folds.
The trees are displaying their reds and their golds.
The larder be empty, the larder be filled.
The southering birds in the sky have trilled.
Down, down to the grave we go,
witnesses at Summer's outgoing flow.
But 'ere the season of cloud and snow,
the Autumn sun is still aglow.
Come to us, O Spirit of Harvest,
of all the year's times, thou are the best.
Blessed be the season of reaping!
Our lives we give to the Old Gods keeping.

Before closing the Sabbat Circle, the High Priest may wish to read this Benediction for the Coven:

The path of life is our stairway to the stars. We are all members of the human race struggling to get to the top. Aiming for the top is our insinctual way of striving toward our mutual destiny, for we are all destined for eventual perfection and at-onement with the Gods.

But in order to become perfect, we must learn by our human experiences. Let us affirm that we are proud to be members of the human race, and recognize, regardless of nationality or creed, man's destiny is our destiny, and that only as we learn to live together harmoniously, can we move forward together.

Accept life as it is and go along with it, bravely trying to change what needs to be changed and serenely adapting to what can not be changed.

Realize that no experience in human life is alien to us, and that our responsibility is to meet whatever happens with fortitude and courage.

Admit that being human we are bound to make mistakes, but try to make as few as possible, and avoid making the same mistake twice.

We must recognize the frailties and foibles of human nature and try to be everlastingly patient, forgiving and understanding, just as the Gods understand and forgive us.

Let us promptly forget slights and insults and hope that others will not hold against us the winged arrows that may escape our lips in anger and irritation.

Let us share courage and hopes with others and keep our fears, heartaches and disappointments to ourselves.

Let us go our ways quietly and humbly and not worry too much about mysteries we cannot explain. If we do our best here and now, the future will take care of itself.

Be grateful for the precious gift of life with its limitless possibilities. Glory in the power of humans to rise to great heights and to outdo themselves in miraculous works of creation, in imitation of their Creator/Creatrix.

We must understand that the goodness of the Gods can only be known through human goodness; that when we express our highest and best, we express the Gods.

Even though, being human, we often fail to live up to our own philosophies and expectations, we must nevertheless keep trying. Be kind to one another and may the Gods watch over you. Blessed be!

It is hoped these few suggestions can give the High Priest more scope and latitude in prayers, charges and chants for his Celestial Sabbat Ceremonies.

Appendix II

Section II: Works of the High Priestess

Here is offered some alternate suggestions for the High Priestess to use in fleshing out her Terrestrial Sabbat Cycle and her minor rites and ceremonies.

It is generally the duty of the High Priestess to oversee the serving of the Sabbat Meals after a major ceremony.

When all have gathered at the table, before the meal begins, she speaks a blessing on the repast:

The High Priestess lifts her arms to the Heavens and all Coveners bow the head and place their hands over their eyes as she prays:

Blessed be this Sabbat Meal, by the power of Sky and Sun.
Upon it we place our Ancient Seal (Draws Invoking Pentagram)
To a work well done.
Blessed be this Sabbat Sup'
the gracious Goddess smiles on both plate and cup.
O God and Goddess of our timeless faith,
join this company and dine with us.
Bring thy gentle blessings and enliven our fare to our well-beings both of body and mind.
Blessed be this Sabbat Meal; a shared communion of common bond; a labour of love with purity of heart.
A wish that forever, we never shall part;
that this Circle shan't be broken on earth and beyond.
blessed be this Coven of___________.

All seated at table respond: *Blessed be!* A plate is set in the center of the table and each person places a portion from his/her own plate in it for the Gods. This food may go into a composting heap, or be buried in the earth; A tradition from Lady Raven of the Oddyseans, at the Wiccan Church of Canada.

After the meal has been shared, the High Priestess takes a cup of the beverage and gives the Dismissal Toast:

Good Brothers and Sisters of the Craft, let us thank the good God and the gracious Goddess for this happy hour.

Let this final toast to this warm circle of friends, so fill our hearts that we go our separate ways blessing all with whom we meet.

She draws a Banishing Pentagram and all respond: *Blessed be!*

Blessing the Yule Log

Blessed be this family circle. Let the Yule Log proclaim the joyous season.

Into our company this night the tide of light returns. As in days of old and times forgotten, the Sacred Fires have shown the way.

Happiness and good cheer rule in our hearts this Sabbat Night of midwinter. May they bless us all through the year ahead.

As the Yule Log blazes forth, Coveners and Craftsmen gather around. Sound the Ancient Call and bring the Season's Blessings on us all!

As she sets the lights to the Yule Log, all chant:

Blessed be and Io Evoh Heh!

She prays, as the Yule Log's candles burn:

Hear us, O Gods of our Ancient Faith!

See the Yule Log burning bright. Bless the Coven of ______ and make it strong of purpose. Keep us all in thy Sacred Love.

Blessed be, O manifold existence!

Blessing of the Tools

In cleansing the Ritual Equipment with the Four Elements of the Wise, the High Priestess may wish to use this formula:

Sprinkling with Water:
Wash away, wash away, wash away do.
Cleanse these tools and make them new.

Sprinkling with Salt:
Scatter sand and scatter salt,
Scatter matter and leave no fault.

Censing with the Incense:

Cense it up and cense it down.
Cense it across and cense it around.
Let these tools be fit and sound.

Passing the Fire over them:
Fire be quick and fire be fast.
Bless these Sacred Tools in the future, the now and the past!

Prayer over the cleansed tools:
Purity and holiness encompass these Sacred Tools of the Art and Craft. May they always be fit and proper to bring before the Gods. Blessed be!

Erecting the Temple

(Cast the Circle with Water and Earth)

Before any Sabbat Ritual the Altar is set thus:

In the center on the North side, stands a three branched candlestick with three unlit candles (Black for Hallowmas and Candlemas and white for Beltane and Lammas , unless a ritual stipulates otherwise).

Before the candlestick the space for the crystal bowl of Earth/Salt is empty.

Slightly in front of that stands the green votive candle as a pilot, which the High Priestess lights from the Sacred Flame when the Altar is set.

On the West side, the station for the Chalice of Water is empty.

On the East side the Thurible stands already burning a seasonal incense.

Between the Ritual Notes on the Southwest corner and the snuffer and taper on the Southeastern corner, will rest any objects to be used by the Sabbat Ritual of the Season.

At the four Terrestrial Sabbats, the Coveners have already gathered in the Ritual Chamber and are awaiting the High Priestess.

She enters the chamber carrying a Chalice of Water in the left hand and the bowl of Earth/Salt in the right.

As she steps into the room she says:

Blessed be all Works of the Goddess!

To which all persons present respond:
And triply blessed be our High Priestess.

She steps to the Altar and circumambulates it once in silence widdershins. She smiles all the while at all Coveners present.

Setting down the Chalice of Water and the dish of Salt in their places on the Altar, she takes up the Broom or Besom and proceeds to the North Quarter of the Circle area.

She bows and raises the Broom to the North as she says:

Hear me, O Great Ones from of old!
Rid this Sacred Grove of the Goddess of all that is impure.

She puts the broom to the ground or floor and draws the Circle around the ritual area large enough to serve all participants from North to North.

Returning to the Altar, she sets the Broom down and kneels.

She makes three raps upon the floor or ground and whispers the Sacred Name of the Goddess. This she repeats twice more after a short pause.

Then cupping the Pilot Lamp with her hands so that it is only faintly seen, she says:

Blessed be, O Great Mother. Awake and arise.
As it was from of old, as it is now, and as it ever shall be, the Ancient Mystery of life comes forth from the darkness.

Standing up and releasing her hold upon the Pilot Lamp, she takes the center Candle from the three-branched candlestick and lights it from the pilot.

She then lights the other two Candles with it from left to right. Then she draws an Invoking Pentagram over the Altar with the flame of the center Candle before replacing it in its holder.

Extending both hands over the three flames she says:

Maid, Mother and Hag. Virgin, Matron and Crone. Birth, life and death. measure for measure all that we have sown.
She is the reciever and the renewer.
O tri-form Goddess the ever changing yet eternally static, come to us we pray.

Be renewed and renew in us life's flowering strength.
Blessed be O multi-formed bounty.
Sacred Mother of all Creation.
(replenish incense)

The High Priestess takes up the Chalice of Water and proceeds to the North Quarter.

Bowing, she then sprinkles thrice to the Quarter as she says:

(We/I) bless this Sacred Grove of the Goddess. Let all that is pure and holy be witness.

Walking widdershins she repeats these actions and words at all Quarters and makes a slight bow at the North.

Returning to the Altar, she replaces the Water and takes up the Earth or Salt.

Again at the North Quarter she bows. Holding the dish of Earth/Salt high before her she says:

(We/I) consecrate this Sacred Grove to the Works of the Goddess. Come O Sacred Mother and dwell with (us/me) Ama Aima Aradia!

She then draws a large Invoking Pentagram thus:

With the Earth symbol held high she kneels down upon the left knee, bringing the Earth or Salt to about hip level on the left side. Standing up she brings the Earth or Salt to level with the right shoulder. Then she passes it straight across to be level with the left shoulder. Then kneeling upon the right knee, she passes it diagonally down to level with the right hip. Then she stands up and brings the Earth symbol back to its position high above her head.

Proceeding widdershins around the Circle, she repeats the invocations and actions at each Quarter and gives a final bow to the North.

Returning to the Altar, she sprinkles a few grains of Earth or Salt upon it as she says:

Be this Sacred Altar of the Earth Mother forever our hope and home. blessed be!

Replacing the bowl of Earth or Salt she assumes the Goddess or

Pentagram position and recites the Charge of the Goddess thus:

There is a Mother who gives us birth.
There is a Mother who provides our needs.
There is a Mother who cradles our hopes.
The Great Mother gives us form.
The Great Mother builds us up.
The Greatest of Mothers recieves us to Herself again.
As She is renewed each cycle, so we, Children of Light and Earth, return each generation to bear Her witness.
Thus speaks the Great Mother, the triple Goddess of Form and Works:
O beloved Children, hear these words!
By an act of Love you were created.
With Love you are sustained.
Unto Love you will be called.
I am the Goddess of Form.
I give that all may live.
I build up and I tear down.
To bear my form is travial, but into this Universe of Being I send my joy that your journey may be lightened.
Be kind to all creatures of this world, they too have their purpose.
Respect the Earth on which you walk, ravage her not, nor make her barren.
Love one another for I dwell in each and every one from the grossest to the most etherial.
The tides and the seasons I send upon you.
You are the seeds I plant and the Harvest I reap.
Eternal life of experience in form is what you are and what you ever shall be.
Thrice blessed is the Great Mother.

She then places her hands in her grade sign position and turns to face all Coveners as she says:

Now the Circle is complete.
In the Grove of the Goddess let us meet.
Blessed be.

All Coveners then enter the Circle and show their grade signs. The Sabbat Ritual proceeds from here.

Closing the Temple
(The banishing with Air and Fire)

After the main part of the Sabbat Ritual has been concluded, the High Priestess faces North across the Altar.

She places some incense upon the coal in the Thurible and says:

Fragrance of the Goddess fair, engulf this Circle and fill the air.

Taking up the Thurible, she steps to the North Quarter where she censes thrice as she says:

Withdraw from here, O Ancient Powers.
Let our Hallowed Rites bless the World of Man.
The peace of this Sacred Grove goes with you.

She then walks around the circle deosil censing and repeating the words at all Quarters, and finally bowing to the North.

Returning to the Altar, she sets down the Thurible and places her hands above the flame of the Pilot Lamp, she then says:

Light of the Goddess' starry night, Circle around this Holy Site.

Taking up the Pilot Lamp, she moves to the North Quarter and holds the flame high as she says:

Flame blaze and Flame burn
as each Quarter is passed in turn,
the walls of this Grove you shall erase
and leave all things with tranquil space.
Blessed be.

Passing around to all Quarters deosil she holds the flame high and repeast the words. She then gives a final bow at the North Quarter.

Once again standing at the Altar, she replaces the Pilot Lamp and claps her hands thrice. She exclaims:

Sabbat Circle closed be. Let us meet again next season happily.

The High Priestess snuffs out the three Altar candles in reverse order of lighting.

Taking up the Chalice of Water and the dish of Earth or Salt, she recesses from the Ritual Chamber with all Coveners following.

The Sabbat party in then enjoyed.

Hallowmas Sabbat

The High Priestess may wish to use this invocation to summon the Shades to Dumb Supper:

Only in the Goddess' name do we open the Portals between the Worlds.

To give a cleansing and banishing before invoking:

Tempests of the airy sky, banish all that does not inspire our minds.
Flames of the fiery force, guard us with benevolent power.
Waves upon the churning sea, form a barrier and mediate our needs.
Strong craigs and mountain vastness, encompass us and manifest our desires.

Invocation to begin ritual:

Spirits of the Earth's departed,
harken to this Ancient Rite.
Draw nigh and cross the portals wide
and greet us on the living side.
Spirits of our friends and kin,
hear this call and enter in.
Spirits red and spirits white,
spirits of sound and spirits of sight,
spirits of black and spirits gray,
spirits of night and spirits of day,
attend this Circle with us we pray.
Above and below, around and about,
all good come in, but all ill keep out!
God of the wildwood, God of stones,
behold the skullface and crossed bones.
Winter's Lord and keeper of the realm of shades,

'ere this midnight hour fades,
release the spirits of those we call,
Wiccan souls, one and all.
Hecate, Hecate, Hecate,
hag of lonely heath and moor,
old woman of the dark moon's night,
be present here and work this Rite.

Invocation of the shades:

By these works of Hecate (bell gong or tap with wand on Altar)
Work the powers of the Witches Will ("")
deep mysteries from beyond and back ("")
bring shades from spirits vapourous realms. ("")
In silence they come, in silence they go ("")
conjured and costrained be ("")
spirits from beyond the sea ("")
the dark moon's power sets thee free, ("")
to commune with us this Hallowmas night. ("")
Cross the portal to this world of light! ("")
As our Will, so be it done! ("")
Spirits come and answer thy name.......

She calls each Spirit's name and sounds the bell once for each.

A necromantic charge:

Black gates swing wide and part the veil!
Abbadon, constrain the foe!
Appolyon, loose the key of time!
Fortisson, illumine the path!
Welcome, welcome to the world of man.
Blessed be in the Goddess' sight.

License to depart:

Go, go by the dark moon's way!
In this world thou mayest not stay.
Fortisson, sound forth the horn!
Appolyon, seal up the gate!

Abbadon, smooth over the veil!
We license all depart to their proper place.
Thricefold we thank thee. love and peace we send with thee.
We bid thee farewell, 'til Hallowmas next. Blessed be and blessed be!

For the second part of the Hallowmas celebration, the invocations for the divinations may be such as these:

Goddess of enchantments, Lady of dreams, Mother of the tide of life, wisest of all Mothers,
give us thy wisdom and we shall take heed.
Give us a sign, for we seek a rede.

Or:

Intuition comes on the Goddess' wings
and knowledge with wisdom of sacred things.
We seek a rede, we seek a rune.
Gracious Goddess, grant us this boon!

A Dismissal:

The signs are given, the omens read,
be they warm as fire, or cold as lead.
The year's full measure has come and gone away.
On the morrow is a brand new day.
Another year stands at the gate and knocks.
The portends of time our fate unlocks.
Thank thee, Goddess for this hour,
the cycles and seasons are in thy power.
Keep us in thy warm embrace,
as we depart from this Hallowed place.
It is done. Blessed be!

Candlemas

These suggestions the High Priestess may use during the blessing of the Candle and preparing the Cauldron to plant seeds of life and seeds of good resolve:

The Festival of Waxing Light has come around again. This is the

time the Virgin Earth is prepared to conceive.
Light waxes and glows
fire sparks and spirit grows.
The tide of life warms the great Mother's heart.
Joy and gladness it doth impart.
Let us now bless the light...
Thou are my lamp, O gracious Mother.
The Lady will lighten our darkness when the night falleth.
Behold, thy Candle, dear Lady, shineth upon our heads;
and by thy light we tread through the darkness.
Yea, the darkness is no darkness with thee,
but the night is as clear as day.
The darkness and the light to thee are as one.
Blessed be, O manifold existence. (blessing the candle)
Out of the night we call thee.
Sacred Mother, hear us we pray.
Accept the petitions of those who worship thee in the Ancient Way.
As we place seeds in the earth with assurance thy master will
bring them to flower, so likewise do we give thee the seeds of our thoughts.
Hear, O Great Mother, the prayers of thy children!...

(Placing petitions and seeds in the Cauldron)

Consecrate, O Great One, these our gifts and bless them to the good works of life's labours.
Blessed be, O tri-form Goddess, from infinite beginning 'til time without end!
The earth is renewed and receptive.
The seeds of life, the seed of thought.
Bring forth the bud and the flower of deed.
Accept the gift of life, O Triple Goddess,
and bring to us the harvest of our needs and desires.
Blessed be!
Blessed be, O Liquid of Life.
The gentle rain will come and refresh the Goddess.
Together with earth and seed it brings life's mystery
to full fruition. (Libations from the Chalice)

Suggested chant for Circle Dance:

Candlemas, Candlemas, high and low,
around the Circle see the light go.
Candlemas, Candlemas, low and high,
lift up our praises to the sky.
Seed takes root and root makes flower,
thus we abide in the Goddess' power.
Round the Circle, round the way,
draw in the force of this Holy day.
Candlemas, Candlemas, down to earth
call we the miracle of the Lady's rebirth.
Blessed be the Ancient Mystery!

Final Benediction:

O spirit of maternal affection, love's bond that holds creation in place,

as we planted life in the soil, descend to us and plant seeds of love in this Hallowed ground, the richest earth there is; our human hearts.

May all Covens of this Ancient Faith be held in love's pure light.

May they ever be true to the Ancient Wisdom in the Way of the Wise.

May their love and light so shine before mankind that they always be a beacon in a dark world.

May they always live with illumined minds and quickened hearts, inspired by the ever waxing light of our Candlemas fires. Blessed be!

Beltane

This suggestion is offered for the High Priestess to use in lighting the fire in the Cauldron:

Burn out winter, burn out the ill.
Burn away the frost from meadow and hill.
Banish the barren, banish the lack,
behold how the Goddess ever comes back.
Begone, begone, the Witches say,
make room for the Goddess on the eve of May.
Suggested chant for the Circle Dance:

Up, Witches and jump for luck! the Cauldron has been fired.
Beltane balefire, see it blaze,
burning bright in the Goddess' praise,
brings us luck in life with prosperity,
thus we worship without temerity.
Beltane, May Eve, Walpurgisnacht, Witchy names to call the hour,
this Sabbat with magic doth empower.
leap up, leap over for love and life,
as the Goddess and God play the harp and fife.

Final Benediction:

O Goddess of the May,
be with us from this day.
Bless this Coven Circle as it keeps the Ancient Way.
Let the ashes from yesterday's cycles bless our homes as they are cast about.
Let them bring in gladness and keep sorrow out. Blessed be!

(Ashes from the fire given to Coveners to take home and scatter in yard or gardens.)

Lammas

The High Priestess may wish to incorporate these forms of prayer and invocations into the ceremony:

Welcome in the Goddess' name. May all your Works bear fruit at Lammastide.
Maiden fair and Mother mild followed by the Hag most droll.
Virgin pure and Mother fertile bring the Crone bearing time's heavy cares.
Thus the tri-form Goddess fares.
Blessed be, O tri-form wisdom!
Of all life's blessings thou are the sum.
We invoke thee, Matron mild and Mother fertile,
draw nigh to us and abide awhile.
The Great Mother blesses us all. The God grants us perfect justice.
For that which in our lives came to manifestation, we give thanks.

For that which we failed to accomplish, we accept our responsibility and resolve to make the next cycle more abundant.

Goddess of life's rhythmic cycles, God of eternal motion,

Supreme One, hear us pray.

We come to bless the first fruits of thy living bounty.

May they bring into this Circle love for our fellow beings with good will in all that we do. Blessed be!

Hear us, O Gracious Goddess and send the spirit of abundant increase among us.

We bless this first fruit of the Earth Mother's sustenance and charge it enliven within us our life's labour to succeed in the Great Work of spiritual advancement.

(Blessing the Bread and Wine.)

Ensoul thy power and love into this Coven Circle and let thy fruitful maternal spirit ever keep us. Blessed be!

The final Benediction outside when libating the Bread and Wine:

O Great Mother, hear me!

We come to give thanks for thy rich bounty.

What we take from the Earth, must of necessity return to her.

As she shows her love for us with the richness of life,

let us return that love by libation of clear crystal wine.

What we are given belongs ever to the giver, for all gifts of the Goddess are but love.

Blessed be, dear and great Matron of the World of Man.

Let this libation of love and gratitude bless this fair world and all its many beings. Blessed be, O Lammastide.

Thus ends the works of the High Priest and High Priestess. It is hoped these appendices have been able to offer a wider variety of practice and depth in the Sabbat Cycles.

The Sacred Pentagraph

Book IV

The Book of Elders

Introduction

The books of The Sacred Pentagraph, I, II, III and V were composed and the system implemented while the original Elders were alive and working in organizing the Tradition.

The Coven organization, Sabbats, ritual methods and teaching guides were brought forth as their group effort, in the 1970s through the 1990s. However, over those years some passed the veil, but the remaining Elders continued to implement the system. Most of the early work was done in the Las Vegas, Nev. area. Witches and Pagans in and about the old Bell, Book And Candle Shop made up the first practicing this Tradition.

Book IV; The Book of Esbat, was only in a rudimentary state in barest outline. Through most of the later years; 1990s through the early 2000s, Tarostar and Lady Laura discussed the fleshing out of that volume and he was able to call upon the resources of The Wiccan Church of Canada and its Toronto Temple, at the old Pagan Palace of 109 Vaughn Road, to organize and perform the rituals therein offered to the Craft.

At the behest of the High Priesthood of the W.C.C., Tarostar became auxiliary clergy at the W.C.C. and was called upon to hold Craft Circles and rites at various Times over the years.

The New Moon and Full Moon Esbats in *Book IV* are the fleshed-out results from the original outline.

Lady Laura passed in the early 2000s and Tarostar has carried on as the last of the original founders of the Tradition. This *Book IV* of the *Sacred Pentagraph* is hereby given to the Craft to perform and carry forward.

Blessed Be!

Books of The Sacred Pentagraph

Book I: The Covenant:

The Eunomia: Herein are all the Tenets and Redes of the Faith with the Laws of Wicca and Coven rules.

It expresses the conditions under which one enters the Faith and is accepted into the Craft and Coven.

The Covenant also contains the rubrics of Coven Worship.

Upon entrance into a Coven, all new members will read, sign and seal their names therein.

Therein is also The Log where all important Coven ceremonies and magic works are recorded. It also contains The Tree, which is the genealogy of the members and vital statistics of the Coven.

Book II: The Book of Beginnings:

Herein are the Initiations where the ancient ceremonies of rising in the Degrees of the Craft are explained and given for use. All spiritual ceremonies that mark the beginning of a new phase in the total life experience of a Covener are found therein.

Book III: The Book of Lights:

Section I: Works of the High Priest – Herein are the Coven Sabbat worship for the four Solar/Celestial Sabbats of the year.

Section II: Works of the High Priestess – The Coven Sabbat worship for the four Terrestrial Sabbats of the year.

Section III: The Manual of Exorcisms – Rituals to banish negative entities.

Section IV: Book of Elders – Concerning the Council of Elders and the Mystic Coven of Seven.

Book IV: The Book of Esbat:

Herein are all the Coven Magics in full ceremony. It contains all the Full and New Moon Esbats.

Book V: The Cornucopia:

Herein are all the Low Magics with the Arts of Spellcraft and Divination along with the basic study course outline for teaching the Craft and development of the powers of the mind for aspirants to the Craft.

The Moon

Being the closest of the astrological bodies to Earth, the Moon acts directly upon the rhythms of the life cycle in shedding Her powers both for good or ill.

First Quarter - Waxing. The right portion of the Moon is illuminated. When She waxes the life energy on Earth increases. This phase is used to activate, vitalize or increase.

Full Moon - Exact opposition to the Sun; total illumination.

Last Quarter - Left portion of the Moon is illuminated. When the Moon is waning life energy decreases. This phase is used to banish, conclude or decrease.

New Moon - Sun and Moon are conjunct. No visible Moon.

For Craft Esbat purposes, it is the New Moon which is the most important as far as spellcraft is concerned. It is used to bring something into being and to begin.

The Full Moon phase is used for the opposite idea in magical works.

The Moon is a signpost which indicates the prevailing direction of the life force, the reproductive energy that animates all living things – mineral, plant, animal and human.

She has a different affect at different times, depending on the Zodiac Sign in which She is passing, and the nature of the element expressed by the sign in which She passes.

To that we add the influence of the Planetary Day or Night and what aspects She makes to the other planetary bodies.

The Moon's vitality is either boosted, thwarted or channeled into specific areas of life, or away from them – all depending on Her position in the heavens.

It would be best for the Coven to have competent astrologer among its members to be able to advise the Coven Council as to the correct nature of the day or night for a particular magical work. Exempli gratia; Should a New Moon fall on a Night of Jupiter, waning Moon in Cancer, trine Saturn, opposite Neptune, what would be the primary vibration effecting a spellcasting astrologically? This is why it is important to do magic works with the most beneficial astrological energy flow possible.

In keeping with the tradition of *The Sacred Pentagraph,* this fourth volume in the series offers the Coven group Magics of both the New and Full Moons with full ceremonial.

This gives the methods in which a Coven can work its collective Will to cause situations and circumstances to change according to that Will.

However, the way the magic works is through the group being in total "one accord", as to the reason and application of the magic.

It is stipulated in *The Covenant: Book I,* that the Coven Council determines the orientation of the Coven's magical works. That is why it is imperative, to truly express the inner essence of the Craft and/ or Wicca for the entire group to be responsible for its own works and magics.

In ancient times, the temples of the old Gods incorporated within the daily ritual of sacrifice that the blood of the slain bullocks and rams be sprinkled upon the altar and then upon the community of assembled worshipers. That incorporated the worshiper within the sacred drama and made it a shared responsibility. The group enjoys the blessings forthcoming, and also shares the karma/compensation for the act. All willingly share and accept. That way the price asked for any expenditure of energy by the Cosmos is met by all and does not fall heavy upon one, or a few.

All action creates karma. Every action, either positive or negative, produces after its kind.

Every expenditure of energy, causing change in and on the etheric, must pay a consequence, also after its own kind.

Not many, today, understand these mysteries. Nor would they be willing to pay the price demanded by the Gods for their blessings and their power. Not many, today, do we find truly committed to a total religious life style in Wicca.

That is why any workings of the magics of the Craft have to accompany the adherence to Wicca as a religion and not just once every six weeks as a lark for a party.

That is why systems like this one require so much preparation and demand so much effort from the initiates.

If the correct amount of time and dedication can not be given, it is best for the Coven not to practice the Esbat cycle.

That is why these works must be determined by the Coven Council, so that all participate and share the blessings and the consequences of the use of Craft power.

New Moons of each month are only one half of the Esbat cycle. The Full Moons give us the other half. Together they present a system where, twice each month, the Coven may come together to apply its magical intention in group spellcraft, or shared community effort.

New Moons are the times for enchantments and spellcasting. Most magic practiced by a Coven is of a positive and constructive nature. The time of the New Moon is to begin projects and to promote the increase of anything desired. Health, financial increase, love, power, blessing, etc., etc., are some of the things undertaken by a Coven at a New Moon Esbat.

There are many forms of Coven magic that can be worked on a positive level at this lunar phase; cord magic, healing, making and charging talismans, in fact anything of a beneficial nature, both for individuals and groups.

The New Moon Esbats are the actual working circle of the Craft. They are where true Witches' Power is evoked and employed in spellcraft and magic.

We know that a dedicated Occultist sees the unity of mankind and recognizes all persons are aspects of the divine whole. *The Working of the Power for a positive result* should be more important than any personal feuds or personal differences between individuals.

The Craft has always been a religion of comfort and for service to Humanity. We progress in our spiritual evolution by the amount of positive energy we expend in helping other human souls lead better and happier lives. If at all possible, individual Coveners, working in a circle, must feel the same way. As Coveners,we should be universal enough, in our thinking to understand all people are part of ourselves.

A Witch must comfort, heal and bless wherever these things are needed. He/She may then quit this world leaving it better than it was.

If the Craft were not a religion of service and comfort, it would have long ago died out on the gibbets and in the flames of the "Burning Times". The fact is it did not and its services are needed more than ever today.

Mankind has a need for a religious faith which allows it to create a better life for itself and fill a spiritual vacuum created by materialistic society.

The mind of man is the creator. It creates the circumstances which manifest in our lives. A religion must uplift the spirit, solve our problems and lead us to higher truths. Then it will make of us better persons.

This the Craft in its most positive aspects can do. Hence it abides, for its essence is the soul of the world.

The Full Moon Esbats constitute the other half of the lunar cycle. However, the Full Moons are celebrated in somewhat of a different vein. Whereas New Moons are used for initiating, beginning and fostering magical themes through spellcraft, the Full Moon cycle is used to bring matters to conclusion, banish and deflate or impede.

Also, many of the Full Moons represent themes consistant with the Season determined by the Sabbat Cycle.

Some of them can be used for the mythological drama of seasonal celebrations. Not always will there be magical spells to do on a Full Moon, but mytho-drama, for the ritual cycles of the God and Goddess can be played and expressed by Full Moon themes.

The Full Moons allow us to connect with the old myths of the Gods and express those in our lives through sacred theater. I will offer some themes for the Full Moons and also give a few suggestions for magics which may be used by a Coven, if and when there may be a need.

However, it is the New Moon Esbats which take precedence for positive Craft magical works. Known authorities in Craft lore describe an Esbat as a gathering of witches for magical works, but rarely give procedures and methods.

Generally, Esbat is held and claimed as a gathering "to frolick", from the old French. Such a meaning should give a hint as to what witches would do at an Esbat.

In the old lore and in the tomes of the witchburners, usually the Full Moon Esbats are mentioned, notably by the Craft's enemies. They have been made sinister and given "satanic" intent, being a celebration outside of and uncontrolled by "Official Religion".

The High Priesthood may use these times to instruct in more advanced methods of spellcasting, or teach by hands-on practice, having the Coven participate and perform.

We are not trying to make everything binding upon the High Priesthood and a Coven Council in these matters, but offer suggestions which can be used as examples, allowing a Coven and its High Priesthood to adapt and embellish as they see fit. An "ideal" is offered, knowing full well inspiration and spontaneity are much a part of Craft works, especially at Esbat.

Esbat group working has been used by some in the past to raise the power and then allow each individual participating to use it by willing or concentrating on personal needs, each, his or her own. Such can be done, but it drains off the power and scatters effectiveness.

It is much more useful for the group to work on one problem at a time, thus combining the collective effort to bring to bear on the matter at hand.

Magic Work of any kind, other than stage theatrics brings a responsibility under the Law of Compensation. When a person sets out to strongly impress the Ether with his/her intense desire and firmly held visualizations he/she becomes a minor Creator/Creatrix of life. One must then be willing to accept the consequences and bear the responsibility thereof.

The Supreme Being/God and Goddess, bear the responsibility for the Universe as it is.

Individuals also create their microcosmic parts of the Whole, as they are.

Negativity and Dark Magics work very quickly and can leave a strong. imprint on the victims. But their effectiveness is short lived.

Positivity and Works of the Light are more difficult to bring about, but they last much longer in their after effects.

On the whole, the Universe is a positive Cosmos and a negative happening is seen vividly like causing ripples in the flow of a stream, which disrupts, but the flow eventually re-establishes itself and flows again normally. That is why evil magics eventually go nowhere and are a waste of time and energy.

The Coven entity itself must determine the type of magic spells to be cast by the Esbat Circle. The collective of the Coven Council in its wisdom is the only authority to decide the orientation of a particular working. It must be unanimous in its resolve to cast a spell by the group mind.

Only then is one-accord able to work the true Witche's Will in the Cone of Power.

In this way the whole group shares the Law of Compensation (Karma) and bears responsibility for its works. Thus, no one person or small group of Coveners will allow emotionalism to run rampant and be tempted to cast negative magics at whim. The Family is responsible for its members and the member is responsible to the Family.

There will be times when a Coven must employ the dark forces in extreme cases. The Coven Council, as determining agent, must then be in unanimous accord and willing to do so. The negative backlash will be shared by all and not fall on one alone.

Be aware that the Gods would grant the request for such, but always demand a comparable value to be given in return. Only when the benefits derived from a negative spell outweigh the price, and when the Coven Council is of one mind would such ever be done.

It would take a vote by Black Ball in the Coven Council; one white would forbid the Coven taking a negative position. (See *Book I, The Covenant*).

Acceptable Money-Making Activities Utilizing Craft Powers

- Psychic Readings for remuneration from the Public such as Crystal
- Bail, Palmistry, Tarot etc.
- Making of Talismans and Amulets.
- Psychometry, Billet Reading and Ghost Hunting, which would require Initiates of the Third Degree, or above.
- Finding lost articles by the Divinatory Arts, Water Witching and other Dowzing methods.
- House Blessings and other Blessings for Donation.
- Mediumship within the bounds of good ethics.
- Herbalism, Psychic and Unconventional Healing Practices such as Reflexology, Massage, Accupressure etc., however not to exclude conventional orthodox medicine where it would be indicated.
- Artistic Creation of Robes and Tools of Art for Craft purposes.

At least 10% of all proceeds derived therefrom should be given to the Practitioner's Home Coven, wherein he/she first learned the Craft and first developed the Psychic ability, for deposit in the Coven Common Funds. If the Home Coven is no longer active, he/she may donate to an active Coven in the District where he/she, worships at Sabbat, or where directed by an Elder of the District who would know of an active but needy Coven deserving of a Sponsor or Patron.

Uses of Psychic and Craft Power Not Permitted and Which May Bring Censure by the Coven Council

- Setting oneself up in the. Business of Sorcery.
- Casting Personal Spells for unseemly profit.
- Use of Negative or Diabolic Magics for vindictive purposes.
- Setting up shop as a. "Spiritual Adviser" utilizing notorious scams and unethical practices.
- Using the Power of Suggestion to frighten others for personal gain or to force a person to do one's bidding.
- Cursing, hexing or binding other persons for trivial reasons.
- When it is necessary to bring pressure to bear upon a person or a place, the matter should be brought before the Coven Council and possibly have the matter handled at a special Esbat
- Ceremony for that purpose, by the entire Coven.

Esbat Ceremony Format

The points of order for a correct application of magical ceremony have five steps just like the points of the Pentagram.

I. Cast the Circle: This section consists of the usual ceremonial way the High Priesthood choose to use for a casting. In this system I offer a co-celebration of High Priest and High Priestess to erect a Cosmated Circle. This section should, after the circle is cast, also contain an invocation of the God-Forms and a Statement of Purpose for the ritual working, which includes the rational justification for the magic, or an expression of the need.

II. Combining the elements: This section is the actual magical act for casting whatever spell or work of magic to be done. For instance, it could be the application of candle work for a love spell, a healing, a charging of a talisman, a casting for money or whatever problem the Coven is working on at this Esbat. The ingredients used will suit the case.

III. Circle Dance: Raise the Cone of Power. This section is where the Coven circumambulates the Altar, or the central area of the circle where the magical act and intention have been acted out or put together.

There should be a chant embodying the idea of and for the spell or ceremony.

To invoke power, the dance, to a chanted beat, should move widdershins, as an invocatory gesture.

To banish, or impede, the dance should be deosil, also to the beat of the chant.

Both II & III could be combined at once, to have the power being raised, as and when the magic act/spellcasting is being performed.

The rhythm and tempo of the chant and dance should pick up and grow louder and faster until it reaches a fever pitch, or until the Officiant feels sufficient energy has been drawn in and is present.

IV. Discharge: This section collects the raised energy through the combined will and concentration of the Coven and through the agency of the Officiant by decree or statement/affirmation of aiming the power toward the subject of the working. The power is allowed to drain.

V. Closing: Then the circle is closed in proper ritual manner and all participants may leave the area.

The Cosmated Circle

In the Sabbat worship outlined in *Book III, The Book of Lights* of *The Sacred Pentagraph,* the High Priesthood officiated and assisted each other, The Esbat cycle, however, consists of works of group Will determined by the collective of the Coven. It is cocelebrated by two officiants, male and female.

It may be the High Priest and High Priestess together, or the Practicus and Hand Maiden together, or a High Priest and Hand Maiden, or Practicus and High Priestess. Whatever the case, a two parent symbolism needs be used. Nothing in the Manifested Universe comes into being without a masculine-feminine, or positive-negative polarity to contribute to its existence.

In this system much of the work of setting up the Altar and officiating at the ceremonies could be delegated to the Practicus and Hand Maiden as part of their training to eventually aspire to the High Priesthood.

In that case, the High Priesthood would attend and supervise, but allow the Practicus and Hand Maiden to conduct the activities with and for the Coven group. In the ceremonies which follow, the parts stipulated for the High Priesthood could be done also by III° persons.

It may be that the High Priesthood itself would take the parts relegated to the Hand Maiden and Practicus so they could assist the III° persons officiating. Use the Esbat cycle as a training ground as much as possible. That way, should a Practicus and/or Hand Maiden ever be called upon to officiate at a Sabbat, they would have some practical experience at the Altar of the Old Gods.

After all, their Initiation to III° makes them Acolytes to the High Priesthood. (See *Book II*).

Ideally a proper Cosmated Circle would alternate male-female all around the Circle area. With most new and recently formed Covens,one gender or another seems to predominate. Be that as it may, strive with time and effort to eventually build the group up to be able to cosmate a Circle properly. The Ideal of an Esbat Circle will be given herein. Covens will need to work out their practice as best they may. Some groups may meet only for Sabbat and do not hold Esbat, however, they are urged to worship the Old Gods at Sabbat and work magics at other times.

Some Covens may wish a. formal ceremonial approach to Esbat, while others would prefer a less strict practice. For that reason, knowing groups are composed of diverse individuals, no absolute and arbitrary regulations ought ever to be imposed. Magic must flow from the combined spontaneous expression of the participants acting in consensual one accord to affect the matter at hand.

Therefore, the observances described in this *Book IV* serve to offer a skeletal framework for the Coven choosing to work the Esbat Cycle. They may be employed as they are, added to or rearranged as the exigencies of a situation may warrant.

The Esbat Rites are designed to raise the Cone of Power. I will give examples as to how it is then applied.

The Coven Council will decide which Rite to use for what purpose, depending on the Tide of The Moon and the positive, and/or negative needs of a situation.

Here follows the method to erect a. formal Esbat Circle and its proper banishing. This is for the times and groups which would call for a strict observance. However, some may wish to dispense with it altogether and allow the meat of the Rite to create its own Circle as the Cone is built. See sections to follow:

The Cosmated Esbat Circle

The formal Esbat Altar would be a combination of the symbolism of the Sabbats. in so far as the Altar Candles are concerned.

The Black and White Altar Candles from the Works of the High Priest would sit in their respective places. The Three-branched Candlestick from the works of the High Priestess would occupy the center of the back of the Altar between the two Altar Candles to signify Esbat as a co-celebration.

However, the Three-branched Candlestick is the focal point of the Rite, as it represents the Triform aspect of the Lunar Power. Luna, of all Astrological influences, affects the Earth most directly. We work by Her Tides.

The candles in the Three-branched holder could be of the color most corresponding to the reason for the Rite: (red for strength, green for fertility and abundance, etc., etc, as per standard color correspondences).

The Altar Cloth may be light or dark or colored to suit the nature of the working. Individual expression is allowed in Esbat, whereas more strict standards are applied in Sabbat. (See *Book III.*)

The Thurible, Chalice and Pentacle to hold Earth or Salt and the candle holder may be from the High Priest or High Priestess, whose

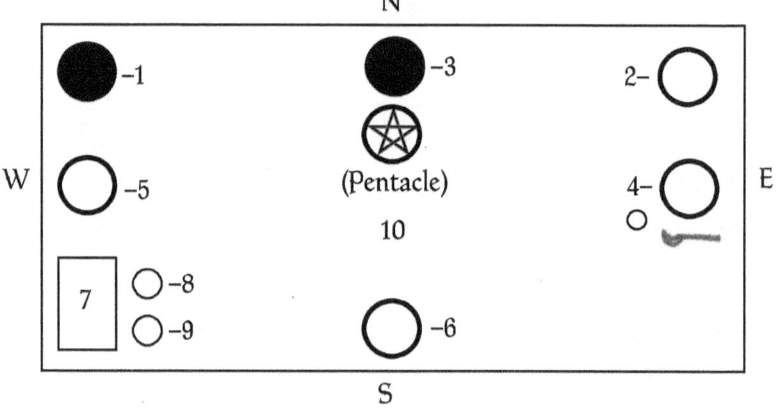

Esbat Altar

1 - Black Candle
2 - White Candle
3 - Three-branched Candlestick
4 - Thurible with coals, incense and spoon
5 - Chalice of salted water
6 - Votive from the Sacred Flame
7 - Ritual Book
8 - Bell
9 - Oil
10 - Center space to hold needs for the Rite and the Cakes and Wine

Hallows are used at Sabbat, or the Coven may have a separate set of Hallows for Esbat. In that case, the Chalice should be silver for Luna.

Prior to Esbat the Hand Maiden and Practicus should set up and consecrate the Altar as per ceremony in *Book III*.

Per the diagram, positions in the circle of #1, 2, 3 and 4 are those for the High Priesthood, Hand Maiden and Practicus (should the HM and Pr be allowed to officiate, they will occupy positions #1 and 2). Position # 12 is for the Summoner, as Circle Door Warden. The other numbered positions are for the Coven members.

At the Time for Esbat, as each ritual will state, the officiants and their assistants take their respective places in the Circle area. All Coveners participating wait outside the area.

The Altar had been previously set with Incense burning.

The Besom and Staff of the High Priesthoods were handed to the Summoner as they entered the Circle area at the North-East.

The Practicus at the East Quarter, representing the Element Air, begins by moving to the Altar in the center and taking up the Thurible burning incense. Moving back to his place in the East, he steps around the edge of the Circle area widdershins, East to East saying:

Motion makes for space and time.
It is the cosmic force most prime.

Having circumambulated the Circle, the Practicus then replaces the Thurible in its position on the Altar and steps back to his Quarter in the East.

The High Priest, at the South Quarter, moves to the Altar and takes up the lit Votive Candle at the South edge and moves with it to his Quarter and steps around the edge of the Circle, widdershins, South to South with these words:

Fire comes from motion's flow.
With it the cosmos then doth glow.

Setting the Votive Candle back in its place on the Altar, he returns to his Quarter.

The Hand Maiden, from the West Quarter, steps to the Altar and takes up the Chalice of salted Water. Moving back to her Quarter, she steps widdershins West to West, sprinkling as she goes, saying:

Cosmated Circle

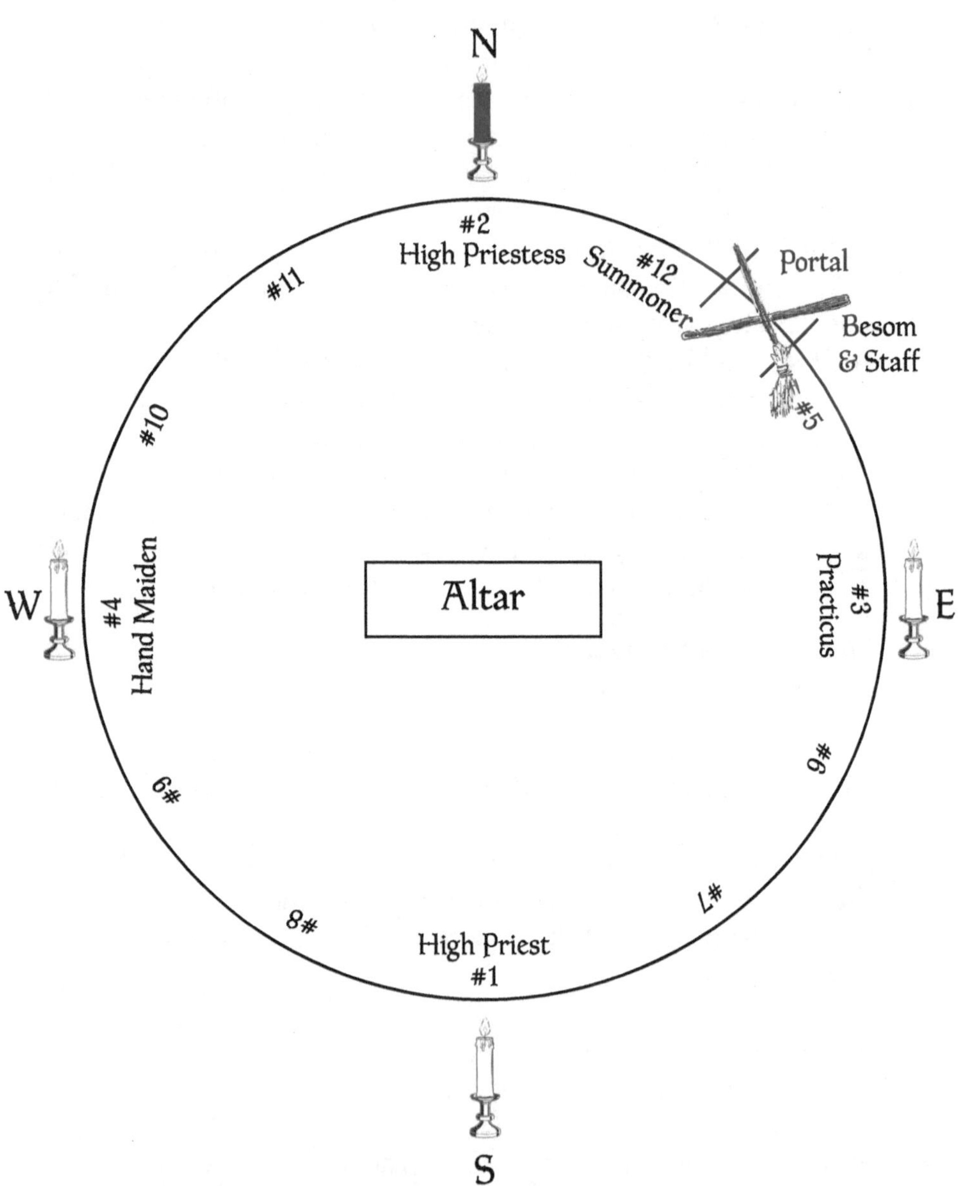

The Officiants take their stations and the rest of the Coven alternates around, male or female, as best as possible.

Water makes the cosmos cool,
So stars and worlds together pool.

Replacing the Chalice on the Altar, she returns to her Quarter.

The High Priestess moves to the North edge of the Altar and takes up the Paten bearing salt or earth. Returning to her place, she moves widdershins, North to North, sprinkling salt or earth, saying these words:

Solid then becomes all matter.
Across the cosmos it doth scatter.
Within which what we contemplate,
becomes our will most consecrate.

Placing the Paten back on the Altar, she takes her place at the North Quarter.

Then, the Summoner opens a portal at the North East of the Circle area with his/her Athame and bids all Coveners, attendees and participants to enter.

When all are assembled inside, the Summoner places the High Priesthood's Besom and Staff on the floor, cross-wise at the North East.

The Esbat Rite proceeds from this point.

Blessing of the Cakes and Wine

At the end of the Esbat Rite, before the Closing of the Circle, The High Priest takes up his Athame' and the High Priestess takes up the Chalice of Wine and the plate of cakes.

He lifts the blade point downward and lowers it into the Chalice with these words:

Words of Will,
thrice spoke, then still,
bind the blessing of lady and lord
bringing joy, health and concord.

He repeats the words thrice as he lowers the blade into the wine.

Then he says nothing and allows each Covener, in silence, to wish whatever private, personal need for self.

After a slight pause for the personal meditations of the Coveners, he places the flat of the blade above the plate of cakes, held by the High Priestess.

She speaks these words:

Gifts of the Gods through the bounty of earth, allow this circle to expand its girth.
Keep us well in our wiccan ways
all the remainder of our days.

She repeats the words also thrice and then pauses to allow each Covener to commune with the Gods in the silence of their inner being.

Both the High Priest and High Priestess then say:

Good Coveners in the circle of______, accept the blessings of Lord and Lady.
To each according to Divine Will,
let thy beings with the Gods now fill.
blessed be and blessed be!

Each Covener is given to taste and to drink.

After the Circle has been closed in proper order, the High Priestess takes the remaining crumbs of the cake and the last of the wine in the Chalice out of doors and scatters them to the Four Winds with these words:

God and Goddess of the Ancient Way,
bless us by night, bless us by day.
In thy magics of the lunar tide
doth all thy goodness yet reside.
Blessed be!

(Author's Note: The Hand Maiden and Practicus may be allowed at times to perform this rite as part of their training. However, it should normally be done by the High Priesthood as the Coven parents. This may also be a short rite by itself for a communal meditation with the Gods either at a New or a Full Moon.)

Closing the Cosmated Circle

The Summoner takes up the Besom and Staff from the floor and stands to the side.

This Circle is closed in reverse order of casting.

The High Priestess again takes up the Paten from the Altar holding salt or earth and moves deosil, North to North saying these words:

Lift the foundations here laid down.
Let them rise from toe to crown.

Back in place, she sets the Paten back upon the Altar and stands in her Quarter.

The Hand Maiden again takes up the Chalice from the Altar and steps deosil, West to West with these words:

Wash away this circle's form.
Peace and quiet become the norm.

Replacing the Chalice upon the Altar, she steps back into her Quarter.

The High Priest takes the Votive Candle from the Altar and moves deosil, South to South, cupping the light with his free hand so it isn't brightly seen, speaking as he goes:

Darkly burns the fire stout,
to dim and flicker, then go out.

Back in place, the High Priest snuffs out the Votive Candle and sets it back upon the Altar and returns to stand in his Quarter.

The Practicus moves to take up the Thurible from the Altar and may need to replenish some incense to burn, as he steps deosil, East to East, saying:

Scatter upon the winds of space,
leaving neither spur nor trace.

Setting the Thurible back upon the Altar, he moves to his Quarter and announces:

It is finished!

The Coveners then leave the Circle area, as the Summoner hands the Besom and Staff back to the High Priesthood.

A Circle, such as the one on pg 19, would be cast on the Esbat nights when Magics or Ceremonies would be performed. When one of the playlets in the section later on is enacted, no Circle would be necessary.

However, in some of the following rites, the Cosmated Circle may not be necessary. Each Coven should work out its own preferences in that respect.

New Moon Esbats

There has been a tradition to never celebrate the New Moon Festivals on the actual Night of the calendrical New Moon. There is none to be seen in the Sky on those nights. Gathering for Esbat on the night Her first sliver of light may be seen was the measure, since the ancestors went by physical appearances, not having precise calendars. The Moon is then definitely on the increase and the Coven may work its Magics one or two nights after the calendrical New Moon.

However, in recent Times, the actual time of the New Moon can be used.

For the rituals and ceremonies which follow, the High Priesthood use them as suggestions and may opt to use rituals and rites from other traditions to variate their yearly liturgies as long as the rites are in keeping with the purposes of a New Moon.

The Ancient Rite of Turning the Silver

(For this rite a Cosmated Circle need not be done.)

- 14 white candles
- 1 bottle All Purpose Oil
- 1 large silver coin.

On the Night of the New Moon for this Coven Esbat, those who have a need to increase their financial base will gather around the High Priesthood for this Rite.

The High Priestess will light one of the candles from the Sacred Flame and the High Priest will carry the oil and the coin.

The group repairs out of doors to stand under the silver sliver of the Moon as She appears at Moon Rise. (If She has already risen, so much the better.)

Forming a circle around the High Priestess, the Coven takes up its positions and chants:

New Moon Goddess of blessed increase
we come before thee to seek thy peace.
Grant us the favor of this boon,
oh, gracious Goddess of the Moon.

The High Priestess hands the lit candle around the Circle, so that each Covener present places his/her silent intention and wish for material and/or financial increase upon it. The candle moves widdershins around and back to her hand.

The High Priest then anoints the brow of the High priestess with the oil and says:

We keep this ancient tryst with Luna
that she may bring forth our bona fortuna.

Look upon our Priestess as we pray
and let thy blessings with us stay. Blessed be.
(He passes the coin to her).

He then begins to lead the Coven in a widdershins motion around the High Priestess, as she stands in the center of the Circle holding the lit candle. The Coven chants:

Lady of this New Moon night
bring to us what is so right.
We need thy power to increase our worth.
Gracious Goddess to our word give birth.

The chant and the movement continues around as the power is built in the cone; center of the Circle. When the High Priestess feels it is at its peak, she says:

Stand and adore thy Goddess of Light,
she is with us this New Moon night.

The Coven stops in place and intently concentrates on their individual needs as the High priestess lifts the candle aloft with her right hand and begins to turn the coin over and over in her left as she says:

Lady, as thy light doth grow,
abundance upon us bestow.
Increase our worth as we ask of thee,
oh, mover of the Primal Sea. Blessed be.

She turns the coin and repeats the words nine tines for Luna.

Then the group returns into the Covenstead and she places the lit candle upon the Altar. It is to burn itself out. Each night thereafter until the Moon stands full, she lights another one to burn out.

When faithfully kept, this old tradition is said to bring abundance and prosperity to any Covenstead and/or individual in need.

The Janus Ritual

New Moon in January

Performed January 1996 and 1997 CE at the W.C.C. Temple in Toronto, Ontario.

- 2 Coveners, adept at divination, to give the readings.
- 1 length of cloth to wrap around both readers.
- An incense of Benzoin, Cinnamon and Mugwort.
- 4 white or yellow candles; one placed at the left and right of each reader.

One reader would have a deck of Tarot and the other a sack of Runes, or stones.

The readers sit back to back and the cloth wrapped around them at the waist area, allowing their hands free for the castings, or card dealing.

The officiant for this rite could be either the High Priest, or the High Priestess. He would use his Coven Great Wand/Staff, she would use the Coven Besom to cast a Circle around the readers.

The Summoner assembles the Coven in the Ritual Chamber and closes the door. He/she stands close by to open it when the officiant indicates.

The readers are in place, back to back and bound together by the cloth.

The Hand Maiden, or Practicus would set some of the incense to burn and circumambulate the readers, thrice with the thurible and replacing it on the Altar.

Then, he, or she would light the four candles, sitting at the left and right of each reader.

When ready, the officiant motions for the Summoner to open the door of the Ritual Chamber.

The officiant invokes:

Janus, keeper of the past, seer of the yet to be!
Let us acknowledge the portals at the waxing of the year!

He/she simulates casting a spear through the doorway. The door remains open during the rite.

Taking the Great Wand, or Coven Beson, the officiant circumambulates the readers, tracing a circle on the floor widdershins and saying:

Gods of fortune, Gods of sight,
be our helpers, here tonight.
As the times do wend and wane,
delve the depths and make it plain.
To these readers lend thy power,
that visions and portents forth may flower.
Blessed be.

The officiant steps back, away from the readers, as a Coven Bard provides a soft musical reverie.

Each Covener, two at a time, may step forward and sit before one of the readers and get a personal prognostication for the year ahead.

More incense can be added to the thurible and the Hand Maiden, or Practicus would be attentive to the readers needs.

The readings are short three or four card spreads, or a casting of three Runes, drawn from the sack at random, so as not to consume a great deal of time, allowing each Covener, who wishes to be read by one, or both readers.

When all those who wished have received a read, the officiant steps forward and circumambulates the readers deosil to close the rite. He/she says:

Gods of fortune, Gods of sight,
we thank thee for this esbat night.
A we lift this psychic veil,
let normal time and space prevail!

All may leave the Ritual Chamber and have a post-ritual social.

Casting the full ceremonial Esbat Circle is not necessary for rites involving psychic skills employed by members of the Coven.

However, should the High Priesthood wish to do the full ceremonial, the Altar may need to be set near the Northern rim of the Circle area, allowing space for the rite to be done in the center before it.

Witches Works of spellcasting and the employ of the Art Magical would rightfully suggest usage of the full Esbat Circle to contain the raised energy and invoked, or evoked power, until it is released and sent to accomplish its intention. Works of the psychic don't require one.

Each ritual should be well thought-out in advance and perhaps even practiced, by the officiants before hand, to make sure everything will run smoothly, with minimum problems.

New Moon Ritual for Financial Need

(Could be done for any Month of the Year as needed)

On a Night of the New Moon, or during a waxing Lunar Tide passing in an Earth or Water Sign on a Wednesday or Thursday.

This ritual calls for an even number of participants, either all of the same gender, or alternating male/female around the Circle.

- Ingredients needed:
- 2 bowls; one with water.
- Change from the pockets and/or purses of all participants.
- A green jumbo size or glass Novena "Money Drawing Candle."
- An Ace of Pentacles from a Tarot Deck.
- One Rose of Jericho; Resurrection Plant.
- t-L. C.

These ingredients would rest in 16, as per Altar set-up.

The incense to cast the Circle could be Ginger, Lavender and Sandalwood, or a traditional Money Drawing compound.

The Circle is cast and the Coven group admitted by the officiant to stand around the Circle area.

The Officiant begins by charging the green candle drawing an invoking Pentagram over it with the Athame blade and these words:

Powers of the Lunar tide,
bring thy blessings to our side.
Burn this candle to draw our need,
as we work this witchy deed!

He/she lights the green candle from the Altar votive and places the Ace of Pentacles under it, saying:

Initiate the powers of money and well-being.
According to our spelling and seeing.

More incense can be placed on the burning coals as needed.

The Officiant then places the change into the bowl with the water and takes up both bowls and steps into place around the Circle with the other. participants.

He/she pours the water and change from the one bowl into the other with a chant such as:

Luna, as thou doth grow and swell,
hear my call, clear as a bell.
From the ethers and nebulous space
bring thy fertile financial grace.
We need the money, we need the cash.
Bring it here on the dash.
Money to swell, money to spend,
money to put to lack an end.
Money to grow with thought as seed
is what we invest in this witchy deed.

Passing the two bowls to the right, the Officiant hands them to the next Witch in place around the Circle.

The next person pours the water with the change into the empty bowl and repeats the chant, and then passes them to the next person on the right.

Thus the pouring and chanting continue around the Circle until each participant has poured and chanted three times.

The bowls move widdershins around the Circle three times in all, as each participating Witch chants, pours and invests the water and coins with his/her clear visioning of the resulting better cash flow for the group.

After the last time around, the Officiant takes the two bowls back to the Altar and sets the empty one aside.

Setting the Rose of Jericho into the bowl with the water and change, to open and spread as it will, the Officiant says:

Charged water and coins of wealth
bring to us all blessings and health.

Increase our silver, increase our gold,
As we have worked with vision so bold.
Blessed power of the lunar tide,
bring the results quickly to our side.

Then the Officiant proceeds to close the Circle in the usual manner.

At that point the Rose of Jericho in the bowl of water with the change along with the burning candle can be set on the floor next to the Covenstead door as a drawing charm.

After the candle has burned out, take the water from the bowl with the Rose of Jericho and coins and sprinkle it around the Covenstead as a blessing.

Place fresh water in the bowl and keep the Rose of Jericho moist and fresh until the financial boon manifests.

During that period after the casting of the spell there will usually ensue discussions of ways to budget and better employ the group's finances and ideas and opportunities will present themselves for bringing the needed cash flow.

The discussions are not "negative", but a healing catharsis to help the group better handle the financial needs; a healing crisis.

The ritual shakes up the group lethargy and gets the ball rolling to a better and brighter financial future.

Running a Coven, especially in this Tradition, can be rather expensive. High Priests' robes and jewels, supplies, Coven expenses, Sabbat and Esbat meals, etc., etc., should not be expected to be the burden of the High Priesthood alone.

Coven dues are provided for, as seen in *Book I, The Covenant* and various other money making activities can be employed by the group.

This is why financial spells, from diverse traditions are offered to use as an Esbat Rite, when needed.

Naturally, all accumulated funds from Coven activity would go into the Coven Common Funds and be accounted for by the Second Scribe, as that office is required to do, per The Covenant.

A Witch's Reading

by Tarostar

New Moon Esbat. A rite to gather psychic insight from the Coven.

Sister witch and brother too,
Tell me what I am to do.
I seek thy redes, I search thy runes
To find my Coven's precious boons.
Scry my face and scry my form
That knowledge in droves to thee may swarm.
Witches know and witches show
The omens which upon the wind do blow.
By "the pricking of thy thumbs",
Tell me of what here comes.
By the candles burning bright,
Give thy word unto the night.
By the incense of mystic scent,
Tell me of the Gods' intent.
Oh, brother witch and sister too, I seek the Wiccan Way so true.

A Witch's Reading

Suggested for February New Moon

On a night of the New Moon, gather for esbat and cast the Circle in the usual manner.

To open the heart of the ceremony, after all Coveners have assembled inside the Circle, have a small cauldron burning coals and mugwort.

Place around the cauldron nine white candles anointed with Moon Goddess or Gardenia Oil.

Have one Covener, the one to be read, sit facing North before the cauldron in the center of the Circle.

All other Coveners sit semi-circle around the one facing to the South, looking directly at the one Covener to be read, through the misty mugwort fumes.

Both the High Priest and High Priestess chant:

Witches all do gather around.
Cogitate without a sound.
Read thy (brother/sister) here,
giving thy insight both good or drear.

All Coveners then chant:

We see, we see, we truly see, that which comes on wings of air,
that which comes both ill or fair.
We tell, we tell, we truly tell, be it blessed or be it fell.
Let the Gods illuminate our mind,
that in our reading truth we'll find.

All then silently sit and focus on the eyes of the Covener being read, or on a part of the body, or on the space or wall behind him or her.

Slowly, out of the silence, impressions will come. Each one is to verbalize the impressions as they press upon the mind.

No doctoring, nor rationalizations should be allowed to change the immediate first impressions.

Each witch present should speak out the impressions as they are urged into the consciousness, freely, without any attempt to impress or appear knowledgeable. It is a free association of the vibrations for the one being read.

There can be an order to start, such as going from one side of the semi-circle to the other, allowing each witch to verbalize his/her psychic impressions as they come.

However it is done, it is a psychic reading giving the individual the benefit of the group consciousness, freely, without cause to try and impress any specific ideas onto the one being read. He/she must be allowed to interpret as he/she will.*

The impressions can be written down by each witch receiving them, to be discussed later and entered into the log.

Impressions come in short phrases, or in simple ideas, which may appear to have no rhyme or reason. They are symbols from the psychic.

That is why it may be necessary to have a discussion period to allow all input into interpretation along with the one read, after the circle is closed.

When the energy feels to be on the wane, the High Priesthood together will chant:

Thank thee, thank tree, thank thee all.
Let normal time and space here fall.
The veil doth close and seal the channel shut.
By this chant the lines be cut:
New Moon by thy sliver so white,
we thank thee on this esbat night.
For thy gift of the second sight,
we bless thee as thou groweth in light.

The Ceremony of The Cakes and Wine would then follow to bless the rite before proper closing of the Circle.

This New Moon Esbat can be done whenever a Covener has a serious need for the collective input of the entire Coven for a heavy problem.

Highly effective it is when only the officiants know what the Covener's problem may be, but the rest of the group do not.

That way the true insight of the collective group mind comes to bear. However, it should only be done Saw once a year for any individual Covener. That way, one Covener does not hog the lime light and become a center stage attraction, depriving others of the benefit at other Esbats.

* Attempts to propagandize, or influence a person to a specific mode of action or belief, by any conscious directing of the impressions by anyone, High Priesthood or Coven Officers, or individual Coveners, will void the rite, as it deprives the Gods of an open channel. That will bring its own consequences in their own good time.

Wishes in the Flame

A Ritual Chant by the Author
(Could be used in the rite to follow.)

Oh, burning candle of the Moon,
Short thy life and gone too soon.
Dressed with oil of the Lunar Tide,
Burn to bring wishes to my side.
Lit to blaze an the New Moon's Night,
Disspell all darkness by thy light.
I wish upon the candle flame,
And ask for blessings in the Goddess's Name.
An increase of love, an increase of joys,
An end to an enemy's plots and ploys.
Things to wish into the Things to wish into the fire
Are all the wealth of thy heart's desire.
Burn for me, as thou art lit,
Bringing my wish as The Lady sees fit.
Oh, burning candle, so tall and white, '
I ask only what would be right.
I wish, I wish, I really need
This thought I set to become pure deed.
Thoughts are things which wander and wend.
But very potent, when with flame I send.
I vision in thy flame, brightly burning,
The World according to my Will new turning.
I see my wish as very real.
All thereto will now congeal.
Oh, burning candle, flash and flicker.
As thou burneth away, my wish becometh thicker!

Wishes in the Flame Ritual

New Moon Esbat for February after Candlemas

One white candle inscribed with a Moon Crescent, a Pentagram and a symbol of the Element for the purpose: Air, Water, Fire, Earth.

Use a Moon Goddess or Lotus Oil for anointing and charging the candle.

Vision the wish clearly as the oil is rubbed on.

The Officiant casts the Circle as per usual method and assembles the Coven inside.

The officiant recites the chant above as he/she dresses and charges the candle. He/she sets a bit of Sandalwood incense to burn and lights the candle, set in the center of the Altar.

The Coven begins to circle the Altar widdershins if the wish is to attract a boon, or deosil if to banish a negative.

The Officiant repeats the chant or a shorter version of it over and over, faster and faster as the Coven's circling heats up, each member concentrating on the wish being fulfilled in the Present.

When the power drawn in feels to be at its height, the Officiant calls to order and all repeat:

It is done!

The Circle is then closed in the usual manner after the Cakes and Wine.

A Witch's Tarot Spread Ritual

New Moon of March

(Any standard Tarot Deck favored by the Officiant)

A casting of the cards in four pentagrams for a reading of the planes of being that most concern individuals and circumstances.

Arrange the Altar to face North and set up the candles, chalice of water, incense and Earth symbol as shown in the diagram that follows.

A red candle will stand near the West edge of the Altar representing Fire of Spirit. A chalice of clear water rests between it and the blue candle as a symbol of mentality.

In the center is the Thurible to burn a Mercurial Incense. To the right of the Thurible stands a green candle for emotional health. Next to that is the symbolic Earth Element; the Altar Pentacle or a small dish of salt. A brown or yellow candle completes the Altar set up representing the physical plane at the East edge of the Altar.

The Reader/Officiant stands at the South of the Altar facing North. The pack of Tarot Cards rests near the Southern edge of the Altar directly in front of the Reader. A small candle lighted from the Sacred Flame in the Covenstead Sanctum sits to the North of the Tarot Deck.

The Esbat Circle is cast in the normal way the Coven uses for Esbat.

When all is ready, begin the reading thus:

Knock five times upon the Altar to summon the forces of impartial Justice; X X X X X.

Light the four candles from the small candle at the South of the Altar and the coals in the Thurible and say:

That which seers mark as fate,
that which deals with love or hate,
that which may be small or great,
let this rite now illuminate.

Sprinkle some of the Mercurial Incense on the coals and continue:

The planes of being summoned here,
forces from the nether world,
neatly in the cards appear.

The small candle at the South is put back in place.

The Reader consecrates the Tarot Deck for this rite thus:

He/she sprinkles the deck with a few drops of water from the Chalice and touches the deck to the Earth symbol, the Altar Pentacle or the dish of salt as he/she concentrates on cleansing them of any previous associations. Then, the deck is passed thrice through the incense smoke and once over each candle on the Altar as he/she dedicates the deck mentally to the work at hand.

The Reader then recites this prayer while holding the deck above the Altar:

Powers of impartial truth, divinitory elements show forth we pray, to our enlightenment, that which, for us this day/night, in honest decipherment, an answer is given, as the cards fall where they may. God and Goddess, Supreme and Supernal head of all, read the innermost needs of our thoughts and show us a sign. come to our call . . .

He/she meditates on the question or circumstance upon which illumination is sought for a full sixty seconds. Then, passes the cards thrice again through the incense smoke and once again over the candles on the Altar and says:

I, _____________, Priest(ess) and Witch, do open this Sacred Book of seeing. Let my hand be guided by the spirit of impartial truth.
So be it done!

He/she shuffles the cards and mixes them well maintaining silence until time to read and interpret.

When the cards are thoroughly mixed, one is laid to the North of the red candle face down.

The second to the South-West of that candle. The third to the East of the candle. The fourth to the West of the candle and the fifth to the South-East as shown in the diagram that follows. They must be dealt from the top of the deck.

The remaining cards are mixed and shuffled a second time and the same done around the blue candle in the exact order as before. They are shuffled and mixed a third time and arranged around the green candle. This is repeated a fourth time and placed around the brown or yellow candle. This gives five cards arranged around the four candles on the Altar, 20 cards dealt out.

The Officiant shuffles and mixes the remaining cards concentrating on obtaining the final answer to the lay-out and then places the twenty-first card to the South of the Thurible standing in the center of the Altar. The remaining cards are set back in place from the start.

Beginning with the five cards around the red candle, they are turned over in the order 1 through 5 being careful not to reverse them from the way they have been dealt out. They are read and interpreted from a spiritual standpoint.

Moving to the cards around the blue candle, repeat the process reading them for their meaning in the mental realm.

Those around the green candle are read for their illumination and commentary on the emotional level affecting the question, or the circumstances involved.

The last set of cards, around the brown or yellow candle are read as to the results and consequences of the previous three sets and effect on the physical plane.

The twenty-first card is turned up and read as the final results and answer.

If the cards are approached and handled this way in a respectful manner, they will give serious answers

This spread is for questions of great import to individuals or Covens and should not be used for frivolous matters where one of the less complicated spreads would do.

The date and phase of the Moon and card sequence should all be recorded for future reference.

After the reading and interpretation are given and recorded, the Officiant holds his/her hands over the candles on the Altar on both sides of the Incense Burner and says:

The spread has been read.
Rune and Rede,

stone and card,
the Ancient Book we are bound to guard.
I__________, Priest(ess) and Witch close its leaves
and lay it to rest.
Let the spirit depart from its pages blest,
to come again at our behest.
Blessed be O Sacred Tarot.

The Officiant claps the hands thrice to clear the air and takes up the cards in reverse order of spreading. The cards are then put away and the candles on the Altar left to burn themselves out.

The Esbat Circle should be closed in the usual manner.

Ascent From Hades

Performed at the W.C.C. Temple in Toronto in 2000 CE

Suggested for New Moon in March. No Circle needs be cast for this rite, as it is more of a playlet for the Spring Season.

Ideally, the participants should be able to channel the God-forms they portray. However, those acting the parts could also use conventional methods of divinitory reading if not channeling the God-forms directly.

The ritual chamber is set thus:

At the North-West is a throne set for the person embodying Hades. It is dark and somber. One assistant sits on the floor beside the throne with a deck of Tarot, if the person portraying Hades is not a channeler.

At the South-East is a throne for Persephone decorated with Spring flowers. There is also an assistant with Tarot for the same reason as stated above.

The male reader personifying Hades sits on his throne with the female reader personifying Persephone sitting in his lap, both in an embrace.

One member of the Priesthood leads the Coven into the chamber, telling them:

You are summoned to the Court of Hades this night.

The Coveners take places standing around the area in a wide circle.

The Altar stands in the center of the area between the two thrones, decorated with Spring florals and burning a floral incense.

The Priest or Priestess says:

We come to celebrate Spring . . .
We mark a joyous time . . .
But our Lady is not here!

A female Covener personifying Demeter enters the chamber and stands beside the throne in the South-East. She extends her hands imploringly to the throne of Hades in the North-West.

Priest/ess:

Dame Nature bids and Great Zeus has commanded that our lady be released from cold death's embrace.

Hades! Death bringer! Transformer!

Stern one, yet of tender heart, set the world at right. Release our joy in life!

The Coven Bard begins a musical reverie or someone could sing a calling song for the Goddess. (The Celtic style *Come Lassie Come* may be appropriate.)

A female Covener as Hecate, holding a lit candle in each hand enters the ritual chamber and proceeds to move widdershins thrice around the Altar in the center of the area, symbolically descending to the Underworld to retrieve Persephone. Reaching the throne of Hades, calls Persephone to arise.

Hades and Persephone release their embrace and she stands, bidding farewell to Hades as she follows Hecate around the Altar thrice deosil, symbolically ascending from the Underworld, as the music and song continue.

Hecate delivers Persephone to the Priest/ess officiating and Demeter, who moves forward to greet her daughter. Persephone removes her dark robe and dons a robe of floral colors.

Demeter and the Priest/ess escort Persephone to her throne in the South-East and seat her there, then they both step behind her throne and stand.

The Priest/ess says:

Hail, Bright One! We rejoice you are back among us!

Hades has pulled the hood of his robe to cover his brow and sits looking dejected.

The Priest/ess says:

Coveners! New life sits among us. Go before the one who may answer your query. If your need be light go before Persephone. If matters are serious, go before Hades.

The bard plays soft music as the Coveners, one at a time, directed by the Priest/ess move to sit before Persephone or Hades.

If the Tarot is to be read, the assistant at the foot of the throne shuffles the deck and fans it out so the querent may select three cards at random, which are laid on the floor before the feet of either Persephone or Hades.

The readers personifying the Deities then read the short spread as the selected cards indicate.

Should experienced channelers be personifying the Deities, he/she speaks out the channeled impression received for that person, in which case, no assistants would be required.

After all who wish have been read, and the Priest/ess perceives the energy waning, he/she indicates to Hades, who stands up and says:

> *Persephone, as you are in life, I am in death. I await in darkness for your return with the Autumn. Take all and leave this place!*

He turns his back on the group and stands with head bowed in sorrow as Persephone leads the group from the ritual chamber, where a party celebrating Spring may commence.

A Megalesia for the Goddess

A New Moon Esbat for April

So many times Coveners come before the Gods with personal petitions and requests for themselves and others. This is a time to honor the Goddess and offer thanks.

The Goddess is invoked and offered gifts and entertained by the Coven through its own expended energies. No questions, nor petitions are asked of Her.

This is a night for drums, music, dancing in wild abandon and feasting in honor of the Goddess.

The High Priestess, or Coven Medium, can act as vessel for the Goddess.

A roast suckling pig with breads and vegetable dishes could also be offered and some white, or rosé wine.

If the High Priestess is the medium, either the High Priest, Hand Maiden, or Practicus could be the officiant.

Two male Coveners take the part of Galli, priests of Cybele, dancing and brandishing and clashing two swords each.

The incense should be sharp, pungent, uplifting and fiery.

No Esbat Circle needs to be cast, as the dancing and wild abandon create their own atmosphere.

When all is ready, the incense is already burning in the Ritual Chamber and a throne set for the Goddess' vessel. She is escorted in and enthroned.

The officiant motions to the Summoner and he/she allows the Galli to lead the Coveners in dancing to drums and music.

The Galli give high-pitched wails and whistles brandishing and clashing their swords as they lead the Coveners around the vessel, as to raise the energy level as many times as felt necessary.

Coveners continue to dance around the vessel, until the officiant feels enough energy has been drawn in. He/she motions for silence. The music stops and the Coveners come to order around the vessel.

The officiant recites the *Orphic Hymn To The Mother of the Gods*

(The Hymns of Orpheus; Hogart; Phanes Press, 93, ISBN 0-933999-41-0, pg. 78).

The officiant then says thrice:
Great One, Goddess of all good blessings,
be with us now and accept our gifts!

He/she allows a pause for the vessel to trance and channel the Goddess.

Should the Goddess wish to speak, the Coven should be attentive. She may have messages for individuals, or words of blessing.

Should she simply manifest her presence upon the vessel, the officiant motions for the drums and music to resume, but in a more subdued manner.

The Galli have taken a position behind the vessel, where they sway back and forth, clashing their swords to the music. They are continually providing energy projected at the Goddess' manifestation. The Coven continues to dance around the Goddess and her vessel, while the officiant has the Hand Maiden, or Practicus bring the food offerings into the Ritual Chamber.

They are presented to the Goddess and she may partake, as she sees fit. Wine to drink can be offered.

The Coven sits down to also engage in the repast and libations.

Individuals and/or couples may come forward to dance or perform for the Goddess.

The Galli pick up the pace to the music, swaying, howling, clashing swords and generating energy.

The party in honor of the Goddess continues with good times and cheer.

When the energy is felt to wane, the music should grow slow and faint, allowing all to come down from the high.

The officiant then recites a license to depart:

Thank, thee, Lady, for being our guest.
Leave us now and give us rest. Blessed be our Gracious Goddess!

There should be a pause to allow the vessel to return to her normal self and then the officiant, together with the Galli, lead her from the Chamber.

The party things are cleared away and the Coven may depart.

Those acting as Galli should practice brandishing and clashing the swords in a manner to preclude any accidents during ritual.

Water Gazing as an Esbat

To develop a Coven's concentration, imagination and intuition. New Moon of May.

The Hand Maiden or Practicus could act as Officiant for this rite.

- A large clear glass chalice or bowl, 2/3 filled with water.
- One yellow and one blue candle
- A Moon Mist Oil, or a Hermes Oil.
- Burn an Incense of Jasmine and Ginger, or one of Mugwort and Mastic.

Divide the Coven into couples, gender not an issue.

It would be best if all participating had a ritual bath beforehand with salted water and oil of Camphor or Fennel. Enter the ritual area robed and anointed.

Cast the Esbat Circle in the group's usual manner.

Anoint both candles with the oil and place them to stand on either side of the chalice or bowl of water. Light them.

Set some of the incense to burn on coals.

The Officiant intones:

Luna wax, or Luna wane; Luna dark or Luna bright,
bring us mystery, or bring us light.
We seek thy gift of the second sight.
Moon which grows, or Moon which fades,
loose the visions of lingering shades,
which fleets or flashes or boldly parades,
lady, who sets the portends of the sky,
grant these visions 'ere this night doth die,
as we breathe upon the waters and attempt to scry.

Touch the rim of the chalice or bowl with the fingers of both hands as the above is chanted thrice. With the last recitation, inhale. Place both hands over the surface of the water and exhale upon its surface to make it ripple.

Scry in the water for 5-10 minutes and speak forth what is shown, whatever betide.

Each couple comes forward on opposite sides of the chalice or bowl and takes turns scrying for each other, speaking forth what is shown. When all have finished, *Close the Esbat Circle* in the group's usual manner.

Allow a discussion group for what may have been seen.

Dispose of the water out in Nature by casting it into the air to fall where it may, or into a running stream.

Spell of the Magic Rod

Suggested for the June New Moon with a Circle casting being optional.

The Staff is the symbol of the High Priest in the Coven. It is his rod of authority in Coven affairs. A powerful tool, when properly charged, it is used to impose the collective Coven Will on persons, places and things.

An all purpose ritual for the Staff can be employed at any time by the Coven group working in unison and in one accord.

Need, not Season, or astrological times,would determine the use of this spellcraft, but best at a New Moon Esbat.

A cauldron of fresh earth is placed in the center of the Ritual Chamber, or center of the Covenstead.

Burn an Incense appropriate to the nature of the intent of the Rite itself: Rose/Lavender/Lotus for love. Mace/Nutmeg/Dill/Anise etc., for luck. Frankincense for healing. Orange/Saffron/Sandalwood for power and influence, etc., etc.

Have a red or black candle for each member of the Coven participating in the ritual. Light them all before the rite is to begin, so that the Coveners carry the candles into the Circle area with them.

The High Priest stands forth and holds his staff high, as he announces the nature of the Spell to be cast: Love, Luck, Healing, Binding etc., etc.

He then drives the staff deep into the earth in the center of the cauldron.

Each Covener steps forward in turn and touches the staff and adds his/her intention for the rite to it and his/her candle in the earth around the staff.

All joining hands, they begin to circle widdershins as they chant:

Powers of the Wizard's wand
draw in forces of the beyond.
Into this world of space and form
bringing flash of light and wind of storm.

Might and power to charge this rod
we work in the name of goddess and god.
Around the cauldron of earth and fire
set we the influence of total desire.
(each concentrates on the intention)

The chanting and the circling should grow louder and proceed faster and faster as the group circles the staff in the cauldron. When the point of exhaustion is reached, the High Priest shouts:

Peace! Be still! In the Silence of Naught. our magic doth work! It is begot!

The coven comes to order and silently sends the idea and intention of the rite to the subject or object or victim, as the case may be.

The group circles thrice deosil to unwind the knot of energy and send the idea.

The staff is taken by the High Priest and carried thrice around the person or object of the spell to bind the collective Will upon it.

How that is accomplished is up to his ability and ingenuity.

A Mind Lock has been created and set in motion.

Words of Will and Witches' Petitions

A New Moon Esbat for July

This is an out of doors rite, The High Priest acts as Officiant.

- Small fire with cauldron of boiling water.
- Holy Oil of Jasmine or Gardenia.
- small hand bell.
- copy of The Book of Esbat held flat as a tray for bell and oil.
- packet of herbs; Mugwort, Wormwood and Mullein.
- packet of gums and resins; Frankincense, Myrrh and Mastic.
- Parchment papers and pens for the Coveners petitions.

In the center of the ritual area the fire burns with the cauldron boiling water, The Staff of the High Priest rests on the ground beside it.

When it is Time for the Esbat to begin, the Coveners assemble around the fire in a circle.

The High Priest, carrying the Book of Esbat, upon which rest the hand bell and Holy Oil, herbs and resins, steps to face North across the fire.

He pours a few drops of oil into the boiling water and rings the hand bell thrice above it and says:

Holy Oil, Book and Bell summon the Will to work this spell!

He sets the Book of Esbat, with the oil and hand bell upon the ground beside the fire and takes up his staff.

The High Priest steps to the North Quarter of the Circle of Coveners. With staff in the left hand, he takes the hand of one Covener with his right. All Coveners join hands around the circle.

He leads them all in one complete circumambulation widdershins.

At the North Quarter, he thumps his staff thrice upon the ground and says:

I place the Wards of the North upon this spot!

He then leads another complete circumambulation, proceeding then past the North to the West and says:

I place the Wards of the West upon this spot!
as he thumps thrice upon the ground with the staff.

He leads them around again in one complete circumambulation, proceeding past the West to the South, where he thumps the staff thrice and says:

I place the Wards of the South upon this spot!

Leading the group another complete circumambulation, past the South to the East, he thumps the staff thrice on the ground and says:

I place the Wards of the East upon this spot!

Moving a final complete circumambulation, past the East, he bows to the North Quarter, thumps the staff thrice again and says:

The Circle is complete. This be now Witches work.

As the Coven stands in place, the High Priest moves to face North across the fire.

Setting the staff back down upon the ground, he takes up the packet of herbs.

Moving widdershins around the boiling cauldron, he sprinkles in the herbs and says:

By herb and root, by gum and oil,
let this cauldron froth and boil!

Facing North again moves widdershins around the cauldron, casting in handfulls of them, saying:

By visions in the water and steam,
enliven both desire and dream!

Facing North, again across the cauldron, he takes up the Holy Oil and moves widdershins around, pouring the remainder into the cauldron saying:

Thrice around the cauldron go,
as time and space ebb and flow.
Into it we put both wish and will,
that the world must now set to fulfill!

Music, with a lively drum beat sounds at this point, as the Coven begins to dance widdershins around the circle area.

Each Covener dances forward, around the cauldron and drops his/her written petition into the boiling water. The dance continues until the High Priest feels the energy is at its height.

He motions for the music to stop and summons all Coveners to move in close around the cauldron. Each concentrates intently on his/her private petition upon the surface of the boiling water.

Any Pagan Song of Blessing may be sung by the Coven, such as:

We give thanks for the blessing already on the way!

Then the Coven turns to face outward from the circle and points either the fingers of the strongest hand, or the Athame blade outward, as the High Priest says:

All the Elements and Gods and Goddesses bear witness to our efforts! Send our thoughts to all corners of the Earth, as each desire and petition seeks its own fulfillment. Blessed be!

Taking up his staff, the High Priest moves to the North Quarter of the circle and steps deosil, where he thumps the staff thrice at each Quarter, saying:

I break all Wards from this spot! Let normal time and space resume!

He rings the hand bell thrice and all Coveners may leave the circle.

The water in the cauldron should be cast upon the Earth, or into a running stream.

Do Ut Des

(I give that you may give)

Invocation of the Pagan Virtues

A High Ceremonial – A New Moon Esbat for August

- 4 Priests - each pair has a list of 10 Virtues (Performed at the W.C.C. Temple 1/14/01).
- 4 Priestesses
- 1 cauldron with several live coals
- 1 Packet of Incense; cinnamon, frankincense, myrrh and sandalwood
- 1 spoon for incense
- Small squares of parchment for Coveners to write what they will to give the Gods.
- Pens or pencils.
- 1 Large Chalice of water
- 1 Bouquet of 40 flowers
- 10 Small white candles
- 10 Small white stones
- 1 Large cauldron in center of the room containing earth
- 1 small amount of methenol

There are four stations set at the Quarters with sufficient illumination for the four pairs of Priesthood to read their lists.

Coveners are requested to write on the parchments what they will give the Gods and told to be sure to fulfill their vows as soon as possible after the rite. The parchments are carried into Circle by each Covener.

The pair of Priests at the East Quarter act as the Officiants for this rite.

The Coven is led into the Temple to any processional chant appropriate. They are arranged to stand between the four stations.

When ready, the Officiants summon the Twelve Olympians:

Priest: *Zeus, Sky Father, the best and the greatest!*

Priestess: Hera, Queen of Heaven, binder of Sacred Oaths!

Both: *Be with us now!*

Priest: *Poseidon, Earth shaker, horse breeder, rage of the sea!*

Priestess: *Athene, Maid of Wisdom, battle Queen!*

Both: *Be with us now!*

Priest: *Ares, bold one, inciter of passion!*

Priestess: *Aphrodite, beauteous one, lovers delight!*

Both: *Be with us now!*

Priest: *Apollo, shining one, truth teller!*

Priestess: *Artemis, fleet of foot, huntress of night!*

Both: *Be with us now!*

Priest: *Haiphestos, maker and shaper!*

Priestess: *Hestia, hearth fire and domestic Lady!*

Both: *Be with us now!*

Priest: *Hermes, swift messenger, market lord!*

Priestess: *Demeter, Lady of bounty and produce!*

Both: *Be with us now!*

A moment of silent contemplation to welcome the Olympians.

One of the Officiants:

We give to the Gods, that they may give to us.
As each gift is given, all will exclaim: Be thou increased!

The other Officiant:

Let us summon all the virtues taught by the Gods and given to human community! (As each Virtue is summoned and explained, a spoon of incense is placed upon the coals and *"Be thou increased"* is recited.)

Priest: *Auctoritas!*

Priestess: *Spiritual authority; the sense of one's social standing built up through experience, piety and industriousness!*

Priest: *Comitas!*

Priestess: *Humor, ease of manner, courtesy, openness and friendliness!*

Priest: *Clementia!*

Priestess: *Mercy; mildness and gentleness!*

Priest: *Dignitas!*

Priestess: *Dignity; a sense of self-worth, personal pride!*

Priest: *Firmitas!*

Priestess: *Tenacity; strength of mind, the ability to stick to a purpose!*

Priest: *Frugalitas!*

Priestess: *Frugalness; economy and simplicity of style without miserliness!*

Priest: *Gravitas!*

Priestess: *Gravity; a sense of the importance of a matter at hand, responsibility and earnestness!*

Priest: *Honestas!*

Priestess: *Respectability; the image one presents as a respectable member of society!*

Priest: *Humanitas!*

Priestess: *Humanity; refinement, civilization, learning and being cultured!*

Priest: *Industria!*

Priestess: *Industriousness; hard work!*

Then the priesthoods at the North Quarter take the lead. As each Virtue from their list of ten is summoned and explained, a drop of water from their chalice is spilt upon the bouquet of flowers at their station and the words; *"Be Thou Increased!"* are intoned.

Priest: *Pietas!*

Priestess: *Dutifulness; respect for the Gods and the Natural Order!*

Priest: *Prudentia!*

Priestess: *Prudence; foresight, wisdom and personal discretion!*

Priest: *Salubritas!*

Priestess: *Wholesomeness; health and cleanliness!*

Priest: *Severitas!*

Priestess: *Sternness; gravity and self-control!*

Priest: *Veritas!*

Priestess: *Truthfulness; honesty in dealing with others!*

Priest: *Abundantia!*

Priestess: *Abundance; plenty, the ideal of food and prosperity for all!*

Priest: *Aequitas!*

Priestess: *Equity; fair dealing by both government and among the people!*

Priest: *Bonus eventus!*

Priestess: *Good fortune, rememberance of important positive events!*

Priest: *Clementia!*

Priestess: *Clemency; mercy shown to all as persons and nations!*

Priest: *Concordia!*

Priestess: *Concord; harmony among the people and among the nations!*

The Hand Maiden, after each set of Virtues has been summoned and gifted, takes the incense cauldron from the East and places it in the larger cauldron in the center and the bouquet of watered flowers from the North and places them also in the larger cauldron.

At this point the priesthoods in the West Quarter take the lead. As each Virtues on their list is summoned and explained, one or the other, or both alternating, light one white candle and set it at their station along with the words "Be Thou Increased!"

Priest: *Felicitas!*

Priestess: *Happiness, prosperity; celebrating the best aspects of society!*

Priest: *Fides!*

Priestess: *Confidence; good faith in all commercial and government dealings!*

Priest: *Fortuna!*

Priestess: *Fortune; acknowledge positive events!*

Priest: *Genius!*

Priestess: *Acknowledgement of the Spirit of a place and its people!*

Priest: *Hilaritas!*

Priestess: *Mirth, rejoicing; to express happy times!*

Priest: *Justicia!*

Priestess: *Justice; through sensible laws and governance!*

Priest: *Laetitia!*

Priestess: *Joy, gladness, thanksgiving after the resolution of a crisis!*

Priest: *Liberalitas!*

Priestess: *Liberality; generous giving!*

Priest: *Libertas!*

Priestess: *Freedom for the arts of civilized living!*

Priest: *Nobilitas!*

Priestess: *Nobility; dignified action in the public sphere!*

The Hand Maiden takes the 10 lighted candles to the center and places them around the large cauldron.

The priesthood in the South Quarter call out and explain their list of 10 Virtues and place a white stone at their station for each one.

Priest: *Ops!*

Priestess: *Wealth; participation in the prosperity of the community!*

Priest: *Patientia!*

Priestess: *Endurance, patience; ability to weather storms; mental and physical!*

Priest: *Pax!*

Priestess: *Peace; celebrate peaceful relations between people and nations!*

Priest: *Providentia!*

Priestess: *Providence, forethought; the ability to survive trials and manifest a greater destiny!*

Priest: *Pudicita!*

Priestess: *Modesty, chastity; to avoid the appearence of moral corruptness!*

Priest: *Salus!*

Priestess: *Safety; concern for public health and welfare!*

Priest: *Securitas!*

Priestess: *Confidence and security in peace and good public order!*

Priest: *Spes!*

Priestess: *Hope for times of great difficulty!*

Priest: Uberitas!

Priestess: *Fertility in the arts of agriculture and husbandry!*

Priest: *Virtus!*

Priestess: *Courage to be a leader within the community!*

The Hand Maiden takes the 10 white stones from the South and places them within the large cauldron.

Officiants: *The hand written vows to the Gods now go into the centre!*

The Hand Maiden goes around and collects the parchments from the Coveners and casts them into the large cauldron. She stands ready with the methenol as the Offficiants say:

Officiants: *Before the High Olympians and all the virtues summoned we give thanks for these blessings and will fulfill our vows!*

The Hand Maiden sprinkles a bit of the methenol on the items in the large cauldron and then picks up one of the candles and casts it in to fire up the contents. As they blaze:

Officiiants: *Be the Gods increased! Be the virtues increased! Be we ourselves be increased! (meditation or song) we thank our ancient Gods as we depart the temple!*

The Coven files out.

The items given may vary as to food stuffs, artifacts,liquids etc., as the Priesthood may feel appropriate for the time or season.

These observances may be done whenever it is felt the community needs an infusion of Pagan Virtue.

(Author's note: Due to the amount of smoke from the incense and cauldron fire, it is suggested this rite be done out of doors.)

Ritual Invocation of Athena

Officiant - Tarostar, Medium - Lady Tamarra, High Priestess
of The Wiccan Church of Canada
Performed April 12,1992, Toronto, Ontario
At The W.C.C. Temple. Attendance: 50
Suggested as a New Moon Esbat for September

This is a rite to bless a Coven through a recitation of Pagan Virtues. The old seven virtues for time-honored ethical codes of conduct praised by the Greco-Roman writers from Ancient Times are very much lacking in our Modern World.

This is a ritual to incarnate them among the Coven.

Tarostar, of The Sacred Pentagraph Tradition, was invited to officiate as guest High Priest at the W.C.C. Sunday Circle.

This rite is offered here for those Covens and Craft Circles who may find it useful to incorporate into their own practice.

Items needed to Invest the Goddess:

- Greek or Roman Helmet
- Spear
- Round shield
- Armlets for the Goddess's wrists,
- Large Pectoral for Her Breast
- Wide belt for Her waist.

The High Priestess/Medium would wear a long Chiton, white and unbelted. Her hair should hang loose and untied.

There should be a chair set in the East of the Circle area for the Goddess's enthronement.

Below the Altar, on the floor should rest a bowl of olives, a Quaich of white wine, a Quaich of Water, a bowl of cakes or bread, a bowl of white or yellow flowers and sprigs of either olive branches, or myrtle, and an open vial or bowl of olive oil. An empty cauldron.

On the Altar should stand a small elevated image of Athena, either plaster, stone or bronze.

There should be one white and one black Altar Candle set at the North edge of the Altar flanking the image, unlit.

At the East on the Altar should rest either a Censer on a chain, or thurible with a burning coal.

The Incense is a mixture of Frankincense, Myrrh, Benzoin, Mace, Mastic, Dragons Blood Resin and Copal Gum, all of equal proportions.

To the West on the Altar should stand a silver Chalice with salted water.

A bowl of salt would rest at the North before the image of the Goddess.

To the South on the Altar should stand a small red candle, lit, and the officiant's personal Athame. Any needed notes can be set where convenient.

Quarter Candles can be lit prior to beginning to demarcate the Circle area.

The Medium must be an experienced High Priestess adept at the arts of invocation and capable of assuming the God/Goddess.

She should take a short seclusion before the rite to center and get into the right frame of mind.

As she is doing so the officiant and any assistants, such as Hand Maiden, Practicus or Summoner see to all necessities and set up.

When all is ready, at the appointed hour, the Summoner calls all Witches attending to order and leads them into the ritual chamber to stand around outside the Circle area against the walls.

The officiant and Hand Maiden stand within the center of the Circle area, ready to begin the rite.

The Summoner remains near the door to process the Lady/High Priestess/Medium into the ritual chamber and Circle area, when the Officiant indicates.

The officiant proceeds to cast the Circle in the manner of the High Priest from *The Sacred Pentagraph, Book III.*

The Hand Maiden, who has been standing within the Circle area holding her Athame and is now enclosed within the Circle along with the officiant, moves to the North-East and opens a doorway in the Circle.

She stands with Athame and challenges all Coveners to give the Coven Watchword before they enter Circle (Perfect Love and Perfect

Trust or what ever Watchword the Coven may use).

As each Covener steps to the Circle door the Hand Maiden asks:

What Gifts do you bring to this Temple?

Covener: *Perfect Love and Perfect Trust!*

As each Covener files into the Circle, he/she moves around widdershins to take a place within the Circle.

After all Coven participants have entered, the officiant says:

Let the Summoner now bring the Lady.

The Summoner leaves the ritual chamber and brings the High Priestess in procession to the doorway at the North-East of the Circle.

The officiant moves to the North-East and greets the High Priestess thus:

Extending his hands to take hers, he says:
Lady, a Temple of the Old Gods,
dedicated in perfect love and perfect trust, stands ready to
receive you. Enter and be welcome.

He leads her into the Circle, as the Summoner follows her and stands always slightly behind her in attendance.

The Hand Maiden seals the doorway and moves to assist the officiant. The High Priestess is lead to stand before the chair in the East Quarter, facing West.

The Summoner stands behind the Lady as her attendant. The Officiant and Hand Maiden stand facing the Lady across the Altar, as he begins the Invocation of the Goddess:

Maid of battle, Maid of will,
Maid of wisdom, Maid of skill,
we shall follow and fulfill.
Hail to thee, Athene! (chant by Lady Tamarra of the W.C.C.)
Bright Jove's daughter, Goddess of wisdom and war, Lady of
stratagems and wiles, be with us now and bless our bite.

As the officiant intones the invocation thrice, the High Priestess trances and assumes the Goddess. When She manifests, the officiant continues:

Lady, assume your attributes and let your virtues illumine our lives.

With the Summoner and Hand Maiden assisting, the officiant begins the investiture of the Goddess with Her attributes.

He places the helmet upon Her head and says:
This represents Rectitudo – right thinking. That which is involved in integrity and ethical social conduct.

Placing the shield upon Her arm:
This is the Jus Gentium–the Law of the Tribe; that which is best for the greatest number takes precedence over the individual. It is our shield and protection allowing the social body to continue and abide as a whole.

Handing Her the spear into her right hand he says:
This is Aequitas–the attttudes or fairness to and for all as the content of individual character does warrant.

Placing the Pectoral around Her neck, he says:
With Gravitas–responsibility, the social peace, the family, the tribe, the city and the nation are preserved.

Placing the armlets upon Her wrists, he says:
By Pietas – respect fop the ancient rites and rituals, we preserve the cosmic order and the stability of civilized society.

Fastening the belt about Her waist, he says:
With Humanitas, we see our duties to custom and act in ethical and responsible manners through all walks in life.

Stooping down, he places the myrtle or olive branches at Her feet and says:

Through all the other virtues we receive Libertas – freedom for things and not from things. the freedom to be and to do, to become and to transcend. blessed be, O gracious goddess.

The officiant, the Hand Maiden, the Summoner and all Coveners in Circle bow to the Goddess. The officiant says:

Lady, speak what you will. Your people await your voice.

All within the Circle sit down in place as the Goddess stands and speaks forth as She will, with what message She may have for the group.

When She has finished Her message, the Hand Maiden helps Her to sit upon the chair as the officiant places the gifts before Her: the bowl of olives, the container of oil, the quaich of wine, the quaich of water, the bowl of bread or cakes, and the flowers.

The officiant says:

Let all who wish draw near the Goddess and receive her blessing, or her admonitions; her instruction or her guidance.

He steps back and allows all who wish to come singly forward, bow before the Goddess and touch one of the items laying at Her feet.

She responds to each and reads psychically whatever message She has for him or her.

This process continues until all who wish have received a personal word from the Goddess.

Then the officiant steps before Her and says:

Lady, the hour doth wane. Lay aside your attributes and receive our gifts.

The Summoner and the Hand Maiden divest the Goddess of the items placed upon Her (Helmet, shield, spear, etc., etc.).

The officiant places the cauldron into Her lap and as he mentions each gift, he places it into the cauldron in her lap:

By the waters of life you sustain us (pours water into the cauldron).
By the wine of life you enliven us (pours wine into the cauldron).

By olive and bread you grant us bounty (puts those in the cauldron).
By oil and herb you heal us (the oil and flowers also)
The sprigs of life we return to you with grateful heart for all your love and blessings (the sprigs of myrtle or olive are laid across the top of the cauldron).

Then the officiant stands before the Goddess and intones the dismissal:

We thank you, O Gracious Goddess for attending our rite. Take our praise, our love and our blessing with you into higher realms. Hail Athena! Hail Athena! Hail Athena! (all respond). He claps thrice loudly to disperse the energy.

The High Priestess begins to come out of trance as the cauldron of gifts is taken out of her lap and the Summoner conducts her from the Circle through the doorway at the North-East, which the Hand Maiden re-opens.

Then the officiant closes the Circle in the manner of the High Priest from *Book III* of *The Sacred Pentagraph.*

The rite is ended and all Coveners may leave the Circle area.

(Author's note: The cauldron containing the gifts should be later taken out of doors and some methenol or Isopropol sprinkled over it and set alight, giving the contents to the Gods.)

The Dionysia – A Roman Farce

To Celebrate The Wine Harvest

Performed 9/26/04 at the W.C.C. Temple in Toronto, Ontario

Performing playlets, a Coven should have sufficient members to fill the cast with enough to also be the audience. Perhaps two or more Covens could combine efforts to stage them.

These were preformed at the W.C.C. Temple, which usually hosted upwards of about 50 or more people for the Weekly Circles.

Props:

Dramatis Personae:. . . . . . . A fan for each cast member set at their places.
Zeus . . . . A Whoopi Cushion for Audience Member
Hera (holding her own fan) . . A Cord for Handfasting
Demeter . . . . A Wedding/Bridal Veil
Semele . . . . Pills and Herbs to sprinkle by Asklepios
Dionysos . . . . Thyrsus for Dionysos
Ariadne . . . . A Mechanical Wine Fountain set to flow
Theseus when turned on. . . . Plastic Wine Goblets
Pindar . . . . A Couch for Theseus and Ariadne
Satyr . . . . Chairs for Zeus, Hera, Demeter and Semele
Maenad . . . . A Guy Fawkes Mask for Zeus
Asklepios
Audience Member
Hera's Attendant

Mise en scene: Mount Olympus looking down on the Island of Naxos.

The Summoner gives usual Charge and impresses upon the audience they are attending at the Court of Zeus and Hera.

The Hand Maiden greets the audience filing into the Temple and seats them.

On stage to begin are:

Zeus, Hera, Hera's attendant, Demeter and Pindar.

The Audience Member comes in with the rest, keeping his prop hidden. He has no fan. He takes a seat not far from Pindar.

Pindar (to audience): *Good people, let us relate the tale of dionysos and ariadne. : . . . . . .*

Many times we have heard the tale of Theseus and the Minotaur, of how the youths and maidens of Athens were paid as tribute to the Beast in the Labyrinth.

We have heard of courageous Theseus, locked in titanic struggle with the Minotaur Beast.

Of beautiful Ariadne, who provided the secret out of the Labyrinth, of how the two of them sailed off from crete and came as storm tossed lovers to the verdant Isle of Naxos . . . . .

Enter Theseus and Ariadne. They proceed to the draped couch and sit and cuddle.

Pindar: *Little did they know this island was home to the Immortal Son of the Goddess Semele, Goddess of the Earth. Dionysos, wild rover, frenzy inducer, God of the wilds and the mountain path . . . .*

Enter Dionysos, skipping arround the area, followed by the Satyr and Maenad.

The Satyr and Maenad make lewd faces at the audience following Dionysos around.

Pindar: *Dionysos discovered the two lovers and became enamoured of Ariadne. he cast a sleeping spell of forgetfulness upon them . . . .*

Dionysos waves his Thyrsus over Theseus and Ariadne. They fall asleep upon the draped couch. He skips off stage followed by the leering Satyr and Maenad.

Pindar: *Knowing, as we do from the story, Theseus was to change the black sails on his ship to white so that his father in Athens could see his return boded success against the Minotaur.*

The Audience Member sounds his prop, the whoopi cushion.....
All cast members blank and stare at him. Theseus and Ariadne sit up and stare.
The members of the cast, on stage begin to hold their noses and act disgusted.

Hera: *Wheeeeuuuuu! My fan!* (she faints in her chair).

Hera's Attendant begins to rapidly fan Hera, while holding the nose and staring disgustedly at the Audience Member. All cast members grab their fans and begin fanning toward Hera also holding their noses and glaring at the Audience Member.

Demeter: *Do something about the poor mortal's windy bowels!*

Semele: *Yes, before we have something else to deal with!*

Zeus and Hera: *Asklepios!*

Enter Asklepios, in medical gear and spilling herbs and powders.

Asklepios: *This better be important. I'm right in the middle of surgery!*

All cast members, holding their noses, point at the Audience Member.
He proceeds to stomp over to the Audience Member and dump his herbs all over the guy's head, he hands him two pills and says....

Askiepios: *Take these pills tonight and sacrifice a rooster in the morning.* (he stomps out in a huff.)

Theseus and Ariadne resume their sleeping position in the bedding.

Pindar: (shocked) *Ummm, to continue ....*
Theseus awoke from the spell, forgetting what had happened, and not knowing Ariadne had departed and set sail back to Athens ....

Theseus gets up, stretches and departs off stage. Ariadne sleeps.

Zeus: *He left her flat. what a cad!*

Hera: *Speaking of cads, husband, how many have you loved and left over the eons?*

Demeter and Semele giggle and hide their faces.

Zeus: *Growl, humph!* (thunder rolls, flashes.)

Hera: *Oh, stop that!* (stomping her foot) *Every time you throw a snit the winds get a workout!*

Zeus: *Snit??? Who drove Io mad? Who persecuted Herakles? You throw enough snits for both of us!*

Hera bats him with her fan and glares at him.

Pindar: (mortified) *I'm trying my best to relate this tale, but it ain't easy!!!!!* (sobs, weeps).

Demeter: *Come on, let's behave and allow the poet to continue.*

Semele: *Yes, this is supposed to be about my son's wedding. I've been planning it for centuries.*

The Olympians straighten up and get serious.

Pindar: (composes himself) *Hopefully, without further interruptions ....* (he glares at the Olympians and at the Audience Member.)

Pindar: *The frenzy God, the mountain rover, Dionysos returns to claim his prize.*

Enter Dionysos followed by Satyr and Maenad with wedding veil.

Pindar: *He awoke the sleeping Ariadn.e. . .and took her for his bride.*

Dionysos waves his Thyrsus over Ariadne. She awakes, stretches and gets up from the bedding.

Satyr and Maenad arrange the wedding veil upon her.

Pindar: Semele, shining Lady in the Heavens descended to Naxos and made a handfasting . . . .

Semele moves to stand before Dionysos and Ariadne and binds their wrists.

Pindar: *To commemorate this joyous occasion, and to lighten the hearts of mankind everywhere, Dionysos made a miracle; He created wine!*

Dionysos waves his Thyrsus over the wine fount and it starts to flow.

Pindar: *Come one, come all to celebrate this day; the glorious gift of wine!*

Dionysos, Ariadne, Satyr and Maenad process around the room leading the dance. The Bard and drummers play . . . "Dionysos, father of the vine" . . . .*

Semele and Demeter help the audience to their feet and urging them to join in the occasion.

The Satyr and Maenad set about serving the wine.

Demeter and Hera help with the wine serving to everyone. Zeus does a glamour and appears like so eone else (he dons his mask) and joins in the party.

Appropriate food/snacks to go with wine may be served.

* The words to this chant:

Dionysos, Father of the vine,
hear the dancers on the hill
singing Evoeh
for the holy wine!
Evoeh for the holy wine!
Evoeh for the holy wine!

From Lady Tamarra of the W.C.C., Toronto, Ontario

Journey to the Underworld

This is a rite of consulting the Sibyl, in the manner of Ancient Times going to the cave shrine at Cumae near the Bay of Naples. Querents would be taken into the caves and presented to the priestess and receive a word or prognostication from her.

The shrine at Cumae became very popular in Greek and Roman Times, so much so that the city itself became a perpetual Psychic fair. It flourished until Marcus Agrippa, friend of Caesar Augustus, and admiral of the Roman fleet, harvested all the forests about for shipbuilding and closed the shrine for eventually becoming notorious. Cumae was transformed into a Roman naval base and the sibyl's voice was heard no more.

This rite is suggested for the New Moon of October and was first performed 11/03/02 at the W.C.C. Temple in Toronto, Ontario. Even though it was first done in November, since the W.C.C. operates with Circles on Sundays, it should be kept in the Hallowmas Season.

There was a large group of participants for that night and they were taken in small groups from the Temple on the second floor, along the hallways and down flights of stairs to the basement, affectionately known as "The Troll Hole".

Groups doing this rite would work out the particulars with their own available facilities.

The Coven gathers in its ritual area and each Covener is given a white candle and a stalk of wheat or barley. The candles are lit just prior to setting out on the journey.

The High Priest acts as the Guide to the Underworld to take the group down, below ground to the place the High Priestess sits as the Sibyl of Cumae.

Before her rest a small cauldron burning incense of mastic and mugwort, a tray for the wheat or barley stalks and another cauldron of sand for the candles to stand.

As the guide leads the group out of the ritual chamber, he will invoke:

Dark night of the Soul, enlightenment is our goal.

Along the path to the place of descent, he says:

Down to the netherworld, the house of persephone. shades of mortal torment and blight,... shades of woe, darkness and fright, shades of anguish seeking the light, we tred your path to the realms of the dead.

Proceeding along, he says:

Step softly along the darkened ways. as the Hell Hound loudly bays. Look not back, nor to the side, lest the Night Hag upon thee ride.

A Covener acting as Cerberus at the door to the descent begins to howl and bark at the Coveners in a foreboding tone.

At the door to the descent, knocking thrice loudly on the door:

Queen of Darkness, stern Lady of Hades Abyss, we come as supplicants to your shrine, we seek the Sybil, Oracle of the Dead!

In silence the guide leads the group down to the place where the Sibyl awaits.

The Guide says to the Sibyl:

Omens for this night in time, as the deep night hours chime. Priestess of our Lady's power, we beseech thee in this hallowed hour.

The supplicants come before her and place their wheat or barley offerings in the tray and their lit candles in the recepticle of sand.

The sibyl speaks to the group, or to each, as the Goddess directs.

When the Sibyl is finished speaking, the wheat or barley stalks are set alight, as the group departs and ascends back up out of the area.

Back in the ritual chamber, the Hand Maiden and Practicus could perform the Cakes and Wine Ceremony and post-ritual refreshments can be served.

Hecate's Court of Dreams

A working by the "Dark Minions"/Coveners themselves.
Suggested for the New Moon in December.

The Coveners stage and perform the rite using the High Priestess or a Coven Woman adept at dream interpretation to channel Hecate.

First performed at the W.C.C. Temple in Toronto 11/02/01.

A ritual for dream interpretation through the power of Night.

A high seat for the vessel of the Goddess Hecate, so she is off the floor, in the center of the Temple Ritual Chamber.

The seat and Vessel face East within a semi-circle of burning black and purple candles.

There should be some white wine for the Vessel to imbibe.

Several bouquets of dark flowers with a white one in their centers set around the chamber.

An incense of Oak Moss, Patchouli and Mastic burning in a small Thurible set at the North of the Vessel.

A Hecate formula Anointing Oil set beside the Vessel.

One female Covener acts as a Hand Maiden for the Vessel to attend upon her needs as prompted.

Since this ritual is organized and performed by the Coveners themselves, the usual Coven High Priesthood participate as mere Coven members.

One is chosen to be the Officiant as "Chief Minion" and all others as "the Dark Minions".

To open the rite, all the minions/Coveners, chant in unison:

Children of the Witches ways, think of those dreams which have troubled you.
Bare them in mind and come before our Lady of the Dark, un-named Daughter of Old Night.
What dreams have made you ponder? What quandries have they posed? She, who is phosphoros will illumune them. Come to the realm of Hecate Chthonia!

All minions sit upon the floor around the high seat and the Vessel.

One of the minions takes up the incense thurible and moves widdershins outside the circle of minions, saying as he/she moves thrice around:

I make a place between the Worlds! I set this space apart!
I open the realm of my Queen of Night! Let all Lords of Light depart, as into the Dark we go!

The Covener acting as Chief Minion steps before the Vessel and invokes:

O Chthonia; phosphoros Enodia! (thrice)
She who passes the Gates of the Realms!
She who guides the Phantasms of Night!
Lady before the Portals of Dawn!
Look kindly on us and read us those dreams found troubling.

Any song in honor of Hecate may be sung by the minions, as the Vessel assumes the Dark Goddess. One minion may chant this invocatory song:

Come, Hecate, Goddess of the Three Ways, who with your fire breathing phantoms have been alloted dread roads and harsh enchantments . . . .
Wings of Night bring Death and despair.
all is foul and nothing is fair.
In the Darkness we summon Your Name;
Dark Goddess, old and lame . . . .
Mormo, Gorgo, Bombo, come . . . .
Mormo, Gorgo, Bombo, come . . . .
Mormo, Gorgo, Bombo, come!

When it is felt the Goddess has arrived, the Chief Minion turns to the others and says:

Those who would have the goddess interpret a dream, hold up your hand. Other minions will see you and present you to Hecate.

One minion takes up the anointing oil and stands beside the Vessel. He/she anoints the nape of the neck of each minion/Covener who comes forward to kneel before the Goddess and guides Hecate's hand to that spot on each person.

The minion/Covener will then tell the Lady/Vessel what dreams may be troubling. She speaks out an interpretation as directed by the Goddess.

Minions may dance and sing songs or chants for Hecate and help others go before the Lady.

Music may play softly, so as not to over-ride communion between the person and the Goddess.

When the hour or the energy wanes, the Chief Minion speaks the Dismissal:

We thank thee, Goddess of the Night!
Be propitious and keep us in thy favor.
May we summon thee again another time,
blessed be and blessed be!

One minion picks up the bouquets of flowers from their vases and moves around outside the Circle area deosil, dropping flowers as he/she goes, as the Chief Minion continues:

Let the Lords of Light return! I close the realm of my Queen of Night, as I bring us out into the world into the Light we go!

Any after ritual festivities may begin.

Authors note: No full moon Esbats need to be done in months that there is a Sabbat.

Changing of the Tide

November, 2nd, 2003
Toronto Temple of the W.C.C.

High Priest Officiant: Antler Crown, dark robe, sword.

High Priestess Officiant: Dark veils, cushions bearing Summer robes and jewels.

Practicus: Light colored robe, .staff of a herald.

Hand Maiden: Dark veils. Assists the High Priestess during Necromancy.

Fawn: Acts as chef, serving tools for meal.

Temple Hand Maiden: Usual regalia, acts as Major Domo to seat the people and direct traffic for

the reads.

Mise en scene:

In the Southeast corner is a seat for the Dark Lord; the High Priest with a coven member as the officiant with a small table bearing Tarot Cards.

In the Northwest corner a seat for the Dark Lady; the High Priestess with a coven member as the Officiant with burning bowl for incense and empty bowl for offerings for the dead.

In the center of the Temple a table containing the feast; beef, vegetables, breads, etc., and serving essentials.

Summoner's Charge:

At this season of Samhain the Dark Lord assumes rule.
The Lady of Light departs into the Underworld leaving us to His cold embrace. The Dark Lord invites you to feast.
Are you worthy of His bounty?.
Have you reaped what you have sown?

The Summoner leads the people into the Temple. The Bard may play a dirge as processional music.

The temple Hand Maiden seats the people around the feast table, keeping a space clear before both the seat for the Dark Lord and the seat for the Dark Lady.

The Practicus, the Hand Maiden, and a coven member acting as the fawn stand by the feast table. The Dark Lord and Dark Lady stand by their respective seats.

The Temple Hand Maiden, once having seated the people, stands by the Summoner, attentive to any needs the people may have.

The Practicus:
Beloved ones, the time of the Lord of Death has come
upon us again. The wheel of life turns around, the tides reverse
and the cycles continuously change.
On this darksome night His power waxes, while that of the Lady
wanes. To this end we prepare to relinquish the crown and draw
deep within that we may replenish the force of love and light for
times to come. So be it.

The Practicus proceeds to cast the Circle all around the assembled people, widdershins, saying:

I conjure thee, O Circle of Power that thou be foremost a boundary
between the world of mortals and the realms of the Mighty Ones.
blessed be that which is purified by ritual summoning of Earth,
water, fire and air.

The Practicus repeats the foregoing at the four Quarters around the assembled people.

Back in place, he speaks to the Dark Lord:

We fear thee, Lord, for one of thy faces is Death yet, Thou offerest
needed rest and repast. The dying fires of the midsummer sun
extinguish in Thy icy breath.
(Dark Lord only nods in silence.)
Turn, turn, the wheel doth turn
and on it souls like candles burn ....
one swiftly, one slowly, one flickers out ....
yet turning, yet burning and so round about.

Practicus cont. turning to face the Dark Lady;

Before the season is upon us, the Lady must grant her charge.

The Hand Maiden goes to the Dark Lady and takes the cushion bearing the Summer regalia and proceeds to lay them near the seat of the Dark Lord in his corner and returns to stand beside the Dark Lady.

High Priestess/Dark Lady:
We place the summer at your feet.
All hail, O Horned One! Ride the wind and in the wild chase hunt the hind. As by the fire we wait the blast and harken 'til the hunt is passed.
O ye, who seek the death of man, pray, spare as many as you can, by sparing with the wind that chills and brings with it the winter ills. Be frugal with the snow and rain that we might fill the earth again and dig the ground and turn the sod.
Be kind to us, O dreaded God!

The High Priestess/Dark Lady seats herself upon her chair with the Hand Maiden on the floor beside her, in attendance.

Practicus:
Lord of Winter and misrule, Thy turn is at hand . . . . we commend ourselves to thy care.
Pray, favor thy Wiccan children.
If it be Thy just decision to take some from among us, this cold and harsh season, we ask that those souls be returned to earth in the fullness of time, to be reborn into a true Wiccan family, among a loving Coven of the Ancient Faith.
We have always been a joyous people, with love in our hearts for all creation for as surely as the sun returns to illuminate each day, and one season follows upon another . . . .
we know that all must rest to be renewed. The sleep Thou givest is but a short watch in the night.

The High Priest/Dark Lord seats himself as the Practicus moves to sit beside his seat and assist with the Tarot reads.

The Hand Maiden stands to face the High Priestess/Dark Lady and says:

Thou art my lamp, O Gracious Mother. The Lady will lighten our darkness. Behold, the night falleth and darkness covers the Earth, but Thy candle, dear Lady, shineth upon my heart; and by Thy light we tread through the darkness.
Yea, the blackness is no fetter with thee.
The night is as clear as the day.
The darkness and the light to thee are as one. Bleseed be.

The Hand Maiden continues, turning to the people:
Good brothers and sisters of the Craft, the Lord and Lady bid you to feast. Partake of the bounty and be well.
Those who would commune with the departed, this eve, take of the raw foods and go to the Lady and deposit that offering.
Those who would seek a word for the season ahead, go to the Lord and draw of the cards.

She returns to sit by the Lady and assist as needed.

The Bard may begin a soft musical interlude.

The Temple Hand Maiden moves to assist the Fawn at the serving table and help direct the traffic flow in the circle.

The Fawn begins to serve up the repast.

At the Lord's place, the Practicus will shuffle the cards for each querent and allow them to draw three cards, which they place before the Lord on the small table.

He reads as they fall.

At the Lady's place, supplicants place the raw meat in the offering bowl and take a small candle, which is lit and placed in a cauldron for the spirit they would call through the Lady.

The feast and reads continue, until the time wanes.

Both the Practicus and Hand Maiden proceed to close the Circle thus:

He moves deosil, she moves widdershins from the North, passing each other in the South and back to the North, saying:

It is done, the power has been released. The Sabbat work is over. Blessed be.

The feast may continue.

January Full Moon Ritual

Hecate's Court of Dreams

A ritual for dream interpretation through the Power of Night.

A high seat for the Vessel of Hecate, so she is off the floor, in the centre of the Temple.

The seat and Vessel facing East within a semi-circle of black and purple candles.

White wine for the vessel to imbibe.

Several bouquets of dark flowers with a white one in their centres. Incense of Oak Moss, Patchouli and Mastic, burning in a small cauldron to the North of the Vessel.

A Hecate formula anointing oil.

Hand Maiden to attend upon Vessel's needs as prompted.

The Summoner assembles the Coven and gives any instructions as necessary.

Dark Minions are coven members: (howls, cackles, shrieks)-enter they and say to the Coven, in unison, as a Greek Chorus:

Children of the Witches ways, think of those dreams which have troubled you. – Bear them in mind and come before our Lady of the Dark; unnamed daughter of Old Night.
What dreams have made you ponder? What quandries have they posed? She, who is phosphoros, will illumine them.
Come to the realm of Hecate Chthonia!

(Howls, cackles, shrieks) they lead the Coveners into the Temple and arrange them to sit in a circle around the high seat and the Vessel.

One of the minions takes up the incense and moves widdershins, outside the circle of Coveners, saying, as he/she moves thrice around:

I make a place between the worlds! I set this space apart! I open the realm of my Queen of Night! Let all Lords of Light depart. As into the Dark we go!

The incense is set back in place and more added as needed.

The Chief Minion steps before the Vessel and invokes:

O Chthonia; Phosphoros Enodia (repeat thrice).
She who passes the gates of the realms!
She who guides the Phantasms of Night!
Lady before the Portals of Dawn!
Look kindly upon us and tell us those dreams found troubling.

Any song in honor of Hecate may be sung by the minions, as the Vessel assumes the Dark Goddess. One Minion may sing the Invocatory Song:

Wings of Night bring death and despair
all is foul and nothing is fair
in the darkness we summon Your Name;
Dark Goddess, old and lame
Mormo, Gorgo, Bombo, come
Mormo, Gorgo, Bombo, come
Mormo, Gorgo, Bombo, come

(The above set to music and sung by a Dark Minion after the Chief Minion invokes the Goddess upon the Vessel.)

When it is felt the Goddess has arrived, the Chief Minion turns to the Coveners and says:

Those who would have the Goddess interpret a dream hold up your hand. The Dark Minions from Hades will see you and present you to Hecate.

One Minion takes the anointing oil and stands beside the Vessel. He/she anoints the nape of the neck of each Covener who comes forward and guides Hecate's hand to that spot on the Covener.

The Covener will tell the Lady what troubles him/her in dreams. She speaks an interpretation as the Goddess directs.

Minions dance and chant a Hecate Song, lowly in tone and help each Covener to stand up and be presented in turn. Music may sound, but not to over-ride the communion between Covener and Goddess.

When the hour wanes, the Chief Minion speaks the dismissal:

We thank thee, Goddess of the Night.
Be propitious and keep us in Thy favour.
May we summon Thee again some other time.
Blessed be and blessed be.

One minion takes up the bouquets of flowers from their vases and moves outside the circle of Coveners and steps deosil all around, dropping flowers as she/he goes, saying:

Let the Lords of Light return! I close the realm of my Queen of Night, as I bring us out into the world into the Light we go!

Lights in the Temple go on. Coveners file out.

Full Moon of May: The Old Whitmast Tide The May Wine Moon Ritual

This Esbat rite is a communion with Deity by the Coven and used to raise psychic consciousness to an at-one-ment with God/Goddess. It does not work any heavy magic, but does open the psychic channels to the Old Gods and places one in their mystic embrace.

The items needed for this ritual are quite simple and easy to set up and accomplish.

The Altar should be dressed in white and be set with May-time Spring flowers. Thirteen white candles should be burning in a row on the Altar.

Upon it will rest a large plate containing 13 slices of the darkest and richest Rye Bread available.

There should also be 13 chalices of the headiest red wine money can buy (twelve for the Coven, one for the Gods).

All participants are to have fasted for 24 hours prior to the ceremony. To get the full benefit from this rite, the above stipulation is essential. The incense used in this ritual should be mercurial, such as benzoin or mastic with a bit of Basil and Mace or ground nutmeg blended in.

That would also help in opening the psychic channels.

It would be best to dispence with the usual method of casting the Circle for this Esbat and just assemble the Coven around the area of the Altar. The twelve participants, forming a closed circle by holding hands around the Altar, would make the proper psychic link.

The thirteen white candles are lit and the incense set to fill the ritual chamber.

The High Priest and High Priestess stand facing North across the Altar, as the Practicus and Hand Maiden join hands with the rest of the Coven and enclose them within.

The High Priest places his hands in blessing over the chalices of wine, as the High Priestess does the same for the bread.

Together they pray:

Hear us,. God and Goddess of our Ancient Faith. Let Thy power and blessing pour forth upon this Coven and at this Wiccan Altar. Reach out to us, as we reach out to Thee.
Thou art God and Goddess; creation's Supreme Being. Thou art God, thou art mankind.
Be what Thou wilt as one.
God and Goddess, bless these elements of wine and rye that through them we may come closer and experience Thy love and light. Blessed be.

The High Priestess passes the plate of the rye around the circle widdershins, each person taking a slice.

The plate with the one remaining slice of rye is set back upon the altar to stand for the Goddess.

The High Priest passes each a chalice of wine around the circle area widdershins so each person takes one.

The last, or thirteenth chalice of wine remains upon the Altar to be for the God.

Both officiants (High Priest and High Priestess) say together:

Come all Coveners and partake of this Whitmastide blessing. as the spirit of the Gods reaches out to bless the world at this full moon, seek ye all in inward communion to be and become as one with them.

All Coveners eat the rye and sip the wine until they are constuned.
The chalices are replaced upon the Altar.
Then the whole Coven recites this Litany of the Gods:

Lady of this full moon night,
bring thy consort; the God of Light. God of Life, our Lord Supreme, bring Thy Lady; Heaven's Queen.
We lift our spirits high to Thee,
from field and dell and shore of the sea. Do not linger so far away, come to this circle and with us stay.
Lift us into Thy power and might, be here on this Esbat night.
Thy children call and cry to Thee. To Thy comfort we shall flee.
Gods of our most Ancient Faith and Way mingle and conjoin and

with us play. We accept Thy Will into our minds. Witchery's way us to thee binds.

After the recitation, the High Priest and High Priestess step into the circle of Coveners, joining hands with them and begin to lead a circle dance widdershins taking up this chant, to which all join in, as the circle dance proceeds faster and faster:

Rye and wine
make this night fine.
We seek our Gods by dance and tune. We read their Will by rede and rune.
They speak in silence and teach by love, bringing inspiration from above.
Rye and wine and wine and rye,
by them let our spirits ply.
Let the power of fast and prayer
the veils of existence rip and tear.
By the ergot, by the wine, by the chant and by the dance,
our heightened minds we do enhance. By the light of Lady and Lord, let channels open, as we implored.
Come, O Full Moon, to the May Wine Feast. Let all vex and stripe be ceased.
Come O Full Moon to this Esbat rite, and bathe us in thy sacred light.

The High priesthood keep the circle moving and the chanting going until it is felt enough energy has been raised and until the wine and ergot begin to affect the empty stomachs of the Coveners.

(The psychic will open)

Then they bring the circle to order and all sit down around the Altar and go into a meditative silence, each communing with God/ Goddess in the privacy of inner space.

As the silence proceeds, let each commune and hold what thoughts impign upon him/her and remember them.

After a good 15 minutes of meditation, the High Priestess can then begin to ask each person what he/she may have experienced.

Allow each Covener who wills to share his/her thoughts with the others. However, do not force one to divulge what may be felt to be a personal or a private message from the God/Goddess.

When the power begins to drain off and wane the High Priest should stand up and say:

Thank thee Lady of the May Wine Moon.
We have seen and heard Thy Witchy rune.
Return to Thy heaven's orb in flight.
We bless Thee on this Esbat night.

The High Priestess then claps the hands thirteen times to dispell the vibration and return normal time and space.

The Altar arrangement may be cleared away and the results of the rite properly recorded.

Proceed into a short supper or refreshment to off set the wine and ergot on empty stomachs.

Full Moon of July Council of Elders

The full Coven does not meet this night. Present are members of the High Priesthood from all Covens which can trace their origin to the work of those in the district, or Covendom, who are the Elders, and those of the V° in the Covendom; a Magister Sacrorum, a Queen Mother and a Philosophus and Oracle, should there be any in the district.

The members of the High Priesthood are IV° and junior members of the Council. There may be as many as the Elders have elevated to the High Priesthood over the years.

There may also be as many of the V° as there are in the district.

With time, the Council will grow to a full compliment of persons.

However, the Council meets at one Covenstead or another, as it sees fit, for ideally, it should meet at different Covensteads on different years.

That way each Covenstead receives the honor of hosting a Council. For the opening ritual to follow, the host Covenstead should perform the rite.

All other members of High Priesthoods attend, but sit around the outer area and allow the hosting High Priest and High Priestess to celebrate the ritual.

The Elders take their seats to the sides against the opposite walls, as per the diagram that follows.

Should there be more than one Elder of the same level, he/she would allow the Elder more closely associated with the hosting Coven to have the seat of honor for the ritual.

On the Altar at the far end of the Ritual Chamber, sits two three-branched candlesticks bearing candles of the kundalini colors. Also will rest there the agenda and notes for things to be considered by the Council.

At the opposite end will be a small table bearing the host Coven's Sacred Flame and two lit white candles, which the High Priestess has lit previous to the beginning of the Council.

The hosting High Priesthood stand beside the small table as the Elders take their places.

The hosting High Priesthood begins the ritual by taking up each one of the two lit white candles from the small table.

The High Priestess says:

We of the Coven of_____ welcome our Lord and Lady Elders and all visiting High Priesthood. Blessed be!

The High Priest then says:

May the blessings of the Old Gods guide the deliberations of this council.

They then move across each other's path to the opposite wall and stand before the seats of the elders. The High Priest before the Philosophus, Magister and Oracle. The High Priestess before the Queen Mother and the two empty seats, which the hosting High Priesthood, themselves., will take later.

They lift up the candles they hold before the elders and say:

In the light of the Sacred Flame, by the power of the Ancient Gods, we call the spirit of justice and equinimity to guide this council in all its serious business. Blessed be!

Then they proceed to the opposite sides of the Altar, crossing each other's path once again.

At the opposite corners of the Altar they light the candles in the two triple-branched candlesticks, from the outside inward, with these words:

May tie fires of the Divine Light and Sacred Energy mix and mingle in this council to give all persons participating true and uplifting divine inspiration. Let all opinions be heard and all facets of questions be duly and fairly expressed. May the good God and gracious Goddess be with us in this hour. Blessed be!

Snuffing out their candles, they set them on the corners of the Altar

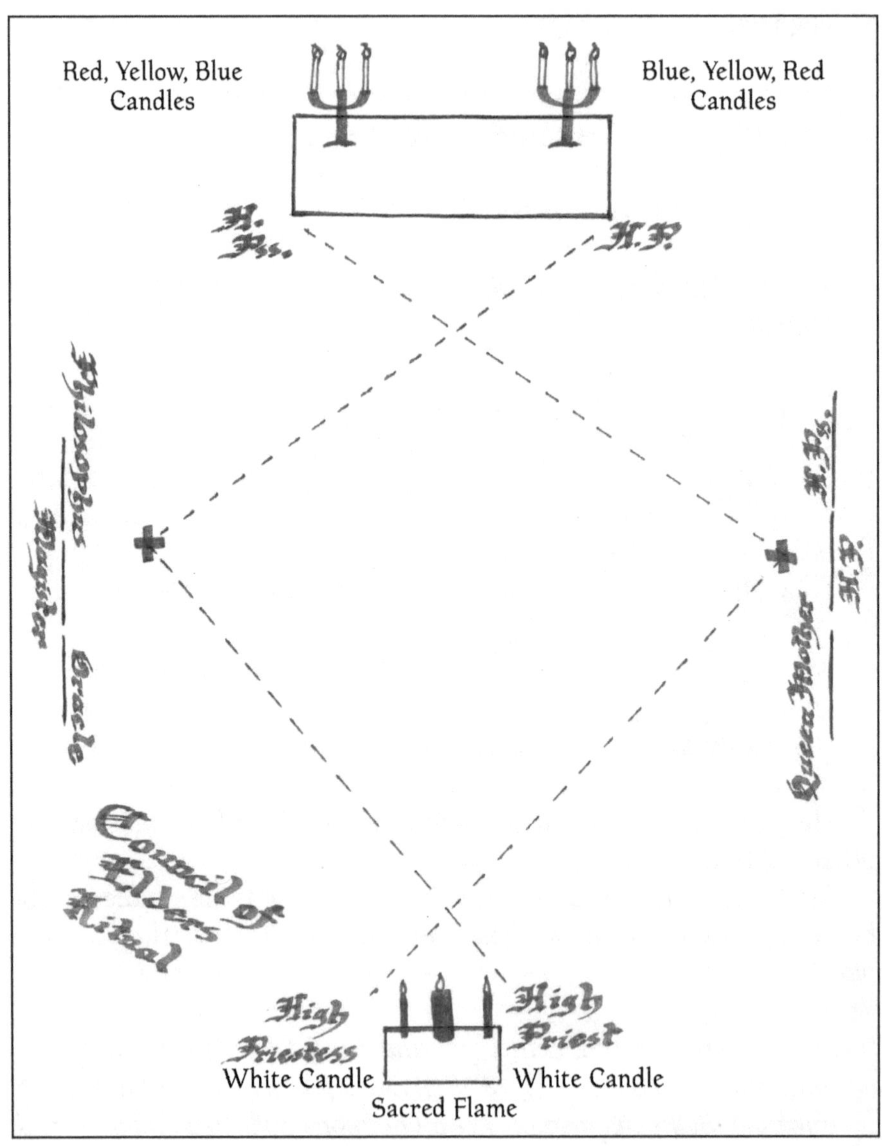
Red, Yellow, Blue
Candles
Blue, Yellow, Red
Candles
H.
Pss.
H.P.
Philosophus
Magister
Oracle
Queen Mother
Council of
Elders
Ritual
High
Priestess
White Candle
High
Priest
White Candle
Sacred Flame

and both walk to their seats beside the queen Mother.

Then the Scribe of the Council of Elders, either the Magister or Queen Mother, stands forth and says:

I, Magister Sacrorum/Queen mother V°, and scribe of the Council of Elders, declare the proceedings of this council for the year ____ in the Covendom of ______ now open. Blessed be!

From this point the Elders and High Priesthood deliberate as is the custom for the Covendom.

(See *Books I, II, & III* for matters done at a Council of Elders).

After the Council meeting the candles on the Altar are snuffed out in reversed order of lighting.

The Cornucopia

Spells, spellcasting, divination and the Arts of Low Magic along with the teaching guides for the true method of training in the Craft.

The Sacred Pentagraph

Book V

The Cornucopia

Introduction

In keeping with the other tomes of *The Sacred Pentagraph,* this volume contains the teaching outline for the High Priesthood to use in bringing persons up to the level of becoming a First Degree.

The *Book of the Wise I* is for the Pre-Initiate to prepare for the taking of the Neophyte level Initiation.

Book of the Wise II is the basic course outline from which the High Priesthood may draw their lectures and reading assignments. Those lessons prepare one to take the Probationer level.

Book of the Wise III is the continuing study for the Probationer to prepare one to take the First Degree Initiation, Becoming a Craftsman First Degree.

Those three levels of Initiation bring one into full status as a Witch. As *The Book of Beginnings, Book II of The Sacred Pentagraph* states, any further advancement in the Craft is optional from that point.

The next section of this tome gives various suggestions for Spellcraft and the Magical Arts within the Craft. Spells and Talismans are offered and suggested for the further advancement in the Craft for those wishing to take the Second Degree level of Initiation, becoming Artisan.

However, that level is sought on one's own without any training or classes held by the High Priesthood.

Responsibility, integrity and self discipline are laid upon the individual him/her self in studying the Ars Magica.

The system of *The Sacred Pentagraph* is difficult and demanding, but it does produce the very best in the line of Students on the road of Adepthood in the Occult Arts and Psychic Sciences.

The ideal is always held up to the Student to try and embody. No form of compromise can and will be tolerated in study and application. To allow otherwise would do the Student and the Craft dishonor.

If you seek an easy way and a less involved method, this system is not recommended. It can only be mastered from the beginning and by working it through to the end. That may not be possible in one life time.

However, if the Perfecting of being is what you seek in The Old Religion, this method can be numbered among the best.

Many will try. Most will fail. But the ideal will still stand. Some will persevere to the end. In that way the Ancient Wisdom Tradition will not vanish from the face of the Earth.

The Book of The Wise I
The Precepts of Cosmic Order

Knowledge and mastery of which lead to
the grade of Neophyte.

Tarostar V°
Magister Sacrorum
Circle of Starmeadow
Ancient Order of Bell Book and Candle, Las Vegas, Nevada.
1986 ce

These are the Redes and Rules offered to the Pre-Initiate in the Why of the Wise, in order that he/she may align his/her spiritual nature toward the life of balance and harmony as taught by the Craft:

I. It is an eternal Law of the Cosmos that there be no effect without a cause. The seed will produce a harvest by the Law of "Like Produces Like".

II. It is the law of Mind that "As a man thinketh–so is he.". Life is formed from the inside out. Thoughts are the transformations one releases in life.

III. It is an eternal Law of the Cosmos that to live is to function. Therefore, work and effort are the result of function. That which does not function must die..

IV. It is the Law of Mind that "Belief is Power." The act of believing is the force that leads to accomplishment.

V. It is the Law of Mind that mental attitude is more important than mental capacity. One can only make others feel that which one demonstrates by attitudes.

VI. It is an eternal Law of the Cosmos that only the fit survive. Therefore, life is a great battle.

VII. It is an eternal Law of the Cosmos that growth and maturity are the goals of all life.

Maturity of body should lead to maturity of spirit. When things stop growing, they begin to die . . . .

VIII. It is an eternal Law of the Cosmos that life is to learn experience. One must learn to live in order to handle any and all things life may bring.

IX. It is the Law of Mind that misfortune is born of the inability to make proper choices. To Man is given the power to choose. Let Him, therefore, choose well, for most of life depends thereon.

X. It is the eternal law of the Cosmos that there is only one supreme and absolute power as the source of all Life. The duality of Nature (the Gods) is but a name for the effect of Source.

XI. It is a Law of Mind that to improve the external world, one must first improve the internal person. One should always attempt self-discovery and adhere to the Dictum: "Man, Know Thyself". For such is the sum of all wisdom.

XII. It is a Law of Mind that one must make contact with the full environment in order to commence living. Therefore, one must distinguish living from mere existing.

XIII. It is a Law of Mind that material things must be kept in proper perspective. They are only tools, or a means to an end. Not the and in itself.

XIV. It is an eternal Law of the Cosmos that one must live life before one can understand it. Not all things in life may be proven, nor may all things be defined. Certain things have their mysteries.

XV. It is an eternal Law of the Cosmos that that which is natural is also simple and of abiding greatness. One must acquire naturalness in all circumstances and forego false impressions. The Wise will ever seek to simplify their lives and cut away complexities.

XVI. It is an eternal law of the Cosmos that all things must flow with life. One must adapt to conditions and not oppose what cannot be changed, but change the things which can be.

XVII. It is a Law of Mind that Mankind is designed for action. Not what one knows, but what one does is that which counts. If one allows the world to go by - it will.

XVIII. It is an eternal Law of the Cosmos that moderation within order is the key to satisfaction in life. One must stay in balance and harmony with one's concept of the Creator, the Gods or Source.

XIX. It is an eternal Law of the Cosmos that that which is used will increase and that which is abused or misused will decrease.

Therefore, one must use all things correctly. The right use of all faculties will increase their. effectiveness.

XX. It is an eternal Law of the Cosmos that change is the only thing that abides. The secret of success is to adapt to things as they change. What becomes an obstruction is flushed away.

XXI. It is a Law of Mind that Man is a creature of habit. Success is a habit as well as failure. What one habitually does is the real person.

XXII. It is an eternal Law of the Cosmos that adversity exists only to be striven beyond. The more opposition one faces, the better are the chances for moving ahead. Only by accepting defeat as a reality is one ever truly defeated.

XXIII. It is an eternal Law of the Cosmos that nothing ever moves without a mover. The Law of Inertia states anything in a state of being will continue in that state whether resting or moving. One must, therefore, use that law to advantage rather than disadvantage.

XXIV. It is a Law of Mind that there is a Wolf in Man. Human nature must be tamed to serve rather then allowed to rule.

XXV. It is a Law of Mind that Man is designed for success. In order to obtain success one mast do more for the world than the world does for one. Then only is success obtained on the physical, mental and spiritual planes.

XXVI. It is a Law of Mind that happiness is created not by how much one has, but by how much one enjoys that which one has. Happiness is joy, which is spiritual prosperity.

XXVII. It is a Law of Mind that responsibility educates and helps to make life better. Man is born into this world to perform His duty. That duty is meeting the day's demands responsibly.

XXVIII. It is an eternal law of the Cosmos that Time limits Man's existence. One should only live one day at a time. The cost of anything is the amount of time spent obtaining it.

XXIX. It is a Law of Mind that one must be ever aware of one's own limitations. Each one's resources and privileges are limited only by oneself.

XXX. It is an eternal Law of the Cosmos that creativity is eternal. Each individual has creative ability. One's Imagination is more valuable than one's knowledge.

XXXI. It is an eternal. Law of the Cosmos that vitality wasted imposes severe consequences. Food and fresh air preserve the body, but right thinking preserves the mind. One must not waste energy on unnecessary fears and worries.

XXXII. It is a Law of Mind that one should ever cultivate the best within oneself. One must ever seek to become more noble and find ones own true worth.

XXXIII. It is an eternal Law of the Cosmos that noble parents have noble children. Heredity and environment make Man what He is..

XXXIV. It is an eternal Law of the Cosmos that to give is to get. One best serves oneself who looks for privileges of service. The universe pays each one according to what is given out.

XXXV. It is an eternal law of the Cosmos that the Law of Moral Worth produces penalties for unmoral conduct and rewards for moral action. Behavior is the mirror which shows one's own true image..

XXXVI. It is an eternal Law of the Cosmos that all needs are met. One must truly distinguish between needs and wants. Wants do not always make for happiness.

XXXVII. It is a Law of Mind that one makes or unmakes oneself.Self-discipline is the tool with which success is forged.

XXXVIII. It is an eternal Law of the Cosmos that prayer brings communion with the Infinite. It is the belief one exercises in the heart that brings results.

XXXIX. It is an eternal Law of the Cosmos that all things show gender.. There must be a union of the heart in order for persons to unite. Otherwise the Law of Sexual Attraction operates destructively.

XL. It is a Law of Mind that life is made or ruined by one's habitual thinking. Proper adjustment to life avoids mental illness.

XLI. It is an eternal Law of the Cosmos that Love cements the universe. There are two kinds of Love: "Agape", that which builds up, and "Eros", that which tears down. One must always strive for the constructive aspect of Love. Love does not explain the Gods, it reveals them.

XLII.. It is a Law of Mind that the sum of experience is stored in memory. Communion with yesterday will enrich today.

XLIII. It is an eternal Law of the Cosmos that all actions and attitudes effect others. "No man is an island unto himself."

XLIV. It is an eternal Law of the Cosmos that Spirit is the power in Man. The greatest contribution one can make is to live at one's spiritual best.

XLV. It is an eternal Law of the Cosmos that Freedom is the natural state of all life. Freedom does not mean license or avoidance of responsibility. One needs freedom for something rather than freedom from things.

XLVI. It is an eternal Law of the Cosmos that all Nature ages. To live is to function and each hour should be made rich with value and beauty. Let not the body die because it is infested with a dying mind. Age should be the most beautiful time of life.

XLVII. It is an eternal Law of the Cosmos that all endings are new beginnings. Life's end is its beginning. All wisdom teaches that nothing disappears without a trace. Nature knows not extinction, only transformation. To die is to gain.*

Such are the Witch's Redes for these days of wrath and anguish. Let them guide the Children of the Good God and the Gracious Goddess into the Future.

Blessed Be!

Tarostar
7/2/82 Luna waxeth in Sagittarius

* Author's Note: In her many visits to the Bell Book & Candle Shop in Las Vegas, NV in the late 1970's, Sybil Leek gave Lady Charmaine a copy of a book called *The Supreme Philosophy of Man.* It was her suggestion perhaps the ideals expressed therein could find a place in the Sacred Pentagraph system.

It was thought appropriate to present those ideals as these Precepts.

The Book of The Wise II

Of The Magical Universe and The Ancient Gods

Teaching plan for the high priesthood
Lessons for the Neophyte in the Way of the Wise
(Leading to the grade of Probationer)

Tarostar V°
Magister Sacrorum
Circle of Starmeadow
Ancient Order of Bell Book and Candle, Las Vegas, Nevada.

As Elders in the Graft, it is not Our intention to impose dogmatic or fast rules concerning the lessons given to Neophytes by established Covens and presently active members of the High Priesthood.

However, certain standards of intellectual capacity and aspects of knowledge should be mastered and displayed by any candidate for advancement in the grades of the Craft in the Way of the Wise.

Levels of Initiation must, first of all, be earned. Mastery of Craft Lore should be taught to facilitate such advancement.

These lessons for the Neophyte are given as suggestions to help augment the classes and information which the High Priesthood should require of anyone seeking to advance into the grade of Probationer.

They are designed to cover one full year of monthly assignments and personal application applied in conjunction with weekly lectures on these subjects given at the discretion of the High Priesthood and/or Artisans II Degree acting as teachers under the direction of the High Priesthood.

The books for reading and research are suggested by the Elders as being the best[1] available which contain the elementary knowledge required for the Neophyte preparing to advance in the Craft.

1 - Best available at the time of writing this manuscript. Since then, more recent books and texts have become available on the market, which those teaching the Craft may apply.

As soon as a person has been initiated as a Neophyte at the Vernal Equinox, he or she must than begin the study for the next stage in the initiatory levels of the Craft.

The Neophyte may research these books in a Public Library, the Coven Library, or purchase them for personal use when available.

The first Month after the Neophyte's Initiation should be devoted to learning about and understanding the Magical Universe.

At the weekly classes there should be lectures concerning the high points of the subject and discussions of the various viewpoints of the authors herein suggested:

Theories of Cosmogenesis: Magic, an Occult Primer; David Conway; E.P. Dutton & Co.; New York; pg. 19-60.
Occult Powers in Nature and in Man; Geoffrey Hodson; The Theosophical Publishing House; pg. 3-87.
The Tree of Life: A Study in Magic; Israel Regardie; Samuel Wiser; New York; pg. 23-101.

A written test on the Theories of Cosmogenesis should be given at the end of the Month.

The second Month should be given over to the study of the nature of the Gods of the Craft.

The Neophyte is taught that all the Gods of Antiquity are but various aspects of the Primordial All-Father and that all the Goddesses of earlier epochs are but the different faces of the Ancient Earth Mother.

Lectures on the ancient Mythologies should be given and readings assigned to augment:

Mytholgy; Edith Hamilton; Mentor Books.
Gods and Myths of Northern Europe; H.R. Ellis Davidson; Penguin Books.
Witches: Investigating an Ancient Religion; T.C. Lethbridge; Citadel Press.

Plus, any of the good books on the Ancient Egyptian Religion, of which there are too many to list, and the old standard by Margaret Murray, *The God of the Witches.*

At the end of the Month a written test should be given to cover general knowledge of Mythology.

The third Month should be devoted to the History of the Craft from earliest times through "The Burning Time" up to the repeal of the Witchcraft Laws. Lectures in Craft History should be supplemented with readings from:

Witchcraft, the Old Religion; L.L. Martello; University Books Inc.
An ABC of Witchcraft Past and Present; Doreen Valiente; St. Martins.
The Secrets of Ancient Witchcraft; Crowther and Crowther; University Books.

A written test should be given covering a general knowledge of Craft early History.

The fourth Month should continue with teaching the History of the Craft since the repeal of the Witchcraft Laws (1736 and 1951).

There should be lectures on the modern Revival of the Craft and contain information about the individuals who have contributed to this revival. Several assignments for reading should be given from such books as:

Diary of a Witch; Sybil Leek; Mentor Books (plus any of her other books on the Craft).

Books about Alex Sanders:
King of the Witches; J. Johns; Coward McCann; N.Y.
What Witches Do; Stewart Farrar; Coward McCann; N.Y.

Books by Raymond Buckland:
Witchcraft: Ancient and Modern; H.C. Publishers; N.Y.
Witchcraft From the Inside; Llewellyn Publications.

Books by the Crowthers:
The Witches Speak; Weiser; N.Y.
Witchblood; L.C. Publishers; N.Y.

Also such books as:
The Anatomy of Witchcraft; Peter Haining; Taplnger; N Y.

Witchcraft, the Sixth Sense; Justine Glass; Wilshire Book Co. (seems to be a rehash of Gerald Gardner's *Meaning of Witchcraft*).
The Grimoir of Lady Sheba; Llewellyn Publications.
Witch; Lady Sheba; Llewelyn Publications.

A written test should be given concerning general knowledge of the works of the modern writers on the Craft, Gardner to the present.

The fifth Month should be devoted to the comparative study of the various Traditions within the Craft.

Lectures should explain the differences and the basic similarities between the Gardnerian, Alexandrian, Celtic, Welsh, Sicilian, etc., groups within the Craft.

One is advised also not to neglect the sister Faiths to the Craft such as the Macumba, the Santeria and the Voodoo. They should also be taught and researched.

The reading assignments are recommended from such works as:

Drawing Down the Moon; Margot Adler; Viking Press.
The Spiral Dance; Starhawk.
The Tree: The Complete Book of Saxon Witchcraft; R. Buckland, Weiser N.Y.
Witchcraft Today; Gerald B. Gardner; Citadel Press.
Mastering Witchcraft; Paul Huson; G.P. Putnam's Sons; N.Y.

(Plus any of the aforementioned books from the third and fourth Month's lessons, and any of the recent publications put out by Covens as newsletters and the magazines such as old copies of *Gnostica* and *Green Egg*).

Macumba: The Teachings of Maria Jose; Serge Bramly; Avon Publishers..
Macumba; A. J. Langguth; Harper and Row.
Santeria; Gonzales-Wippler; Anchor Books.
Romany Magic; Charles Bowness; Weiser N.Y.
Gypsy Demons and Divinities; Charles Bowness; Weiser N.Y.
Gypsy Sorcery and Fortune Telling; C.G. Leland; University Books.
Divine Horsemen: The Voodoo Gods of Haiti; Maya Deren; Delta.
The Complete Book of Voodoo; Robert W. Pelton; Berkley Publishing.
Secrets of Voodoo; Milo Rigaud; Pocket Books.

At the end of the Month an oral test should be given to determine the Neophyte's basic knowledge and familiarity with Craft Traditions.

The entire sixth Month should be taken up by a research project chosen by the Neophyte from any of the reading material covered thus far.

At the end of the Month a basic research. paper should be handed in to the Instructor and a Short talk presented to the class by the Neophyte covering the subject chosen..

The paper should be graded more on the content and the effort put into it by the Neophyte, in his or her research, rather than in being judged for perfection of grammar and/or literary style. Absorption of knowledge is the most important thing to consider.

The first half of the course is complete.

The seventh through the eleventh Month is devoted to the study of basic ESP. It is not the aim of the Grade of Neophyte to master any of the Psychic Sciences in toto. However, a general knowledge of the various fields of Psychism should be the goal.

People develop psychic ability at different speeds and to varying degrees of ability. It is hoped that the course will wet the appetite of the Neophyte sufficiently to study and possibly specialize in one of the psychic fields later on in life.

The High Priesthood and/or Artisan in charge of the Neophytes should hold classes with more "lab work" than lecture during the second half of the course.

The exercises for developing psychic ability may be gleaned from the suggested reading material, explained to the Neophyte and given him or her to practice at home.

Each Month written and oral tests should be held in order to check the progress of the Neophyte in understanding psychic development.

Assimilation of the knowledge and familiarity with the subject material are, however, the prime factors to consider. Rather than expecting the Neophyte to display perfect psychic ability, he or she should be encouraged to seek out the field of psychism that would be best suited for his or her as an individual, always keeping in mind that some persons are not natural psychics and would need considerable time to develop such ability.

There is always a place in the Craft for each person according to his or her own merit.

The development of psychic ability is not a prerequisite to being a Witch. Therefore, the Neophyte should only be presented with the methods to cultivate the different forms of psychism and allowed to seek his or her own level.

The Neophyte should be judged on willingness to experiment with the lessons and willingness to apply the necessary disciplines involved, rather than on success or failure in the display of psychic ability.

Suggested material:

The Astral Plane; Leadbeater; The Theosophical Publishing House.
How to Test and Develop Your ESP; Paul Huson; Stein and Day.
David St. Clair's Lessons in Instant ESP; Prentice Hall Inc.
Astral Doorways; J.H. Brennan; Weiser; N.Y.
Clairvoyance and Occult Powers; Swami Panchadasi; Yogi Publication Society.
Psychic Energy; J.J. Weed; Parker Publishing Co.
Thought Power; Annie Besant; Theosophical Publishing House.
The Psychic Healing Book; Wallace and Henkin; Delacorte Press.
The Complete Illustrated Book of the Psychic Sciences; Gibson and Gibson; Doubleday.
Master Guide to Psychism; Boswell; Lancer Books..
The Art and Practice of Creative Visualization; Ophiel; Weiser; N.Y.
Methods of Psychic Development; Crawford; Llewellyn.
Creative Visualization; Wiehl; Llewellyn.
The Psychic is You; Rhea; Celestial Arts.
Telepathy; Sybil Leek; Collier Books.
The Diviner's Handbook; Graves; Warner Books.
How to Read the Aura, Practice Psychometry Telepathy and Clairvoyance; W. E. Butler; Warner Books.
How to Tell Fortunes; Rod Davies; Pinnacle Books.
Palmistry; Mary Anderson; Weiser; N.Y.
Palmistry: The Whole View; Hipskind; Llewellyn.
The Complete Gypsy Fortune Teller; Martin; G. P. Putnam's Sons.

The twelfth Month should be given over to a research project involving some aspect of the Psychic Sciences and a paper written on one subject covered in the second Six Months.

The Neophyte should then be ready to accept the next level of initiation; the Grade of Probationer.

During this year of study, the Neophyte should obtain his or her set of Craft Tools. Those will be needed for him or her to consecrate as part of the lessons in the Grade of Probationer and to employ him or herself during the initiation ceremony attaining the First Degree status as Craftsman.

Magical Axioms Part I

I. It has been said nothing happens to us we not will to happen. Thus, the witch needs but only to plant a "seed" in people's minds which cause them to dwell upon whatever is to come or upon whatever danger or "ill" has been predicted. Such becomes firmly embedded in the subconscious which in turn directs people's actions to whatever end result the witch presaged; good or bad.

II-A. The name of an object or person contains the essence of the thing or person. To name a substance after a person using the will power to impregnate the substance with thought energy and to visualize an image of the person on the substance, Creates that person's essence within the substance. What is done to the image, is done to the person.

B) In many instances it is better to have a physical link from the subject or victim worked into the substance forming the image. A "tag-lock" of hair, nail clippings, blood or excreta from the body could be employed. Such objects carry the vibrational essence of the person from whom they come, having been in contact with the person in an intimate way. Such an object provides the focal point of concentration for the witch.

C. This is the principle behind the lore of the waxen image; the ancient theory of like to like. That which is done to a replica of a thing is done to the thing itself.

III. The astral plane (gray area) is quite apart from the physical, but names and words have the same vibrational ratios in an archetypal condition. They can serve to link the two planes calling through a "metaphysical" power to accomplish the will of the witch on the physical plane. The gray area encompasses the imagination, and in operating the art magical it is only the personal imagination which triggers powers from the deep mind. If the deep mind has been rightly attuned during the working of a spell or ritual, the subject should feel the effect and show signs thereof within a very few days. It takes time to affect a waking conscious through its own levels of the deep mind via the gray area.

IV-A. The secret of success in working witchcraft rests in whipping up the passions to the correct intensity and at the same time alerting the deep mind by the right degree of concentration and proper numbers of repetitions of the visions and chants.

B. In spellcasting the actual materials used or consumed in themselves are only focal points for the concentration of the deep mind of the practitioner. It is the intent, the force of will and the attitude behind that will which makes a spell effective.

C. For love spells the emotion should be real toward the subject. The desires and even lust must be turned up to the point of orgasm or climax, which releases a bioelectrical energy from the spellcaster.

D. For curses and spells of vengeance the emotions of hatred and violence must be whipped up and sent forth in a repetitious ritual until a point of utter physical exhaustion has been reached.

E. Power manifests where attention is directed.

V-A. By chant, sonically, of a word or name, the higher form of that "idea" can be magically contacted. Each thought, idea or action carried out on the physical plane sets off a sympathetic response on the astral or gray area.

B. When casting a spell, vibrations are set off by the witch's thoughts, words and actions which contact the astral essence of the person on whom the spell is cast, causing a response accordingly. The one affected by the spell will react actively to do things to him or herself as the spellcaster wishes.

VI-A. In order to affect a thing over distances of time and space, one must have intense concentration and be actually "obsessed" with the idea of that which one wishes to affect. The stronger the feelings, the more intense the vibrations eminating from the mind. A state of "frenzy" would be the easiest picture one could give to describe such state of mind.

B) Repetition of the ritual is also important. The more often repeated, the stronger the will power and the subconscious would become.

Magical Axioms Part II

I. All of creation is composed of vibrations which proceed from the unknowable eternal infinite we call God/Goddess. They penetrate the layers of matter from the most rarified and refined to the densest. The reactions of these vibrations upon the matter in the densest layer produce the physical universe. They vibrate through eons of time in all the planes of being in their cycle both from and to whence they came.

II.The being "man" is a four-planed entity. He has a physical element, an astral counterpart, a reasoning mentality and a spiritual core.

III. The astral plane contains man's thoughts, emotions and desires. These attract around themselves the subtle matter of that plane. That matter is plastic and assumes the form of the thought which is projected into it.

IV. The astral plane was called such by the witches of old due to its luminosity having a higher rate of vibration than the physical. It is chiefly this plane the witch deals with in works of the art magic.

V. On the astral a person is seen only by his/her aura; a large pentagram, according to the hermetic philosophy. Most persons thoughts are weak, cling close to the aura of their creator and dissipate after a time. The more intense and more detailed last longer and eminate further afield. They can lose themselves in the aura of the one they are sent to affect, causing, thereupon, a sympathetic response.

Magical Axioms Part III

I. Your word will not return unto your void.

II. Thoughts are things. Thoughts are the stepping stones to knowledge, and knowledge is power.

III. Evil has no power apart from what you give it by believing in it.

IV. Whatever you believe with great emotion, that you will bring into your life by the use of creative imagination. The perfect prayer or meditation is the method to bring this about. For whatever you need, or for that very special need, meditate and give the need to the divine creative intelligence and then forget it immediately. You will receive what you asked for in the form you are prepared to receive it.

V. Creative thought is a mental branding-iron. When you want something for yourself, mentally brand it with your name and it will be yours.

VI. Man is a mental being and mind is primary. Mind is cause and experience is effect. Change the cause and the right experience will follow. Your thoughts materialize as experience weaving the pattern of your destiny.

VII. Before a thought pattern or a creative idea can work in your life, it must be accepted by your subconscious mind. Repetition of an idea conditions the subconscious to accept it. Build by use of picture images in the subconscious those experiences which will later materialize as physical reality.

VIII. Think it, talk it, live it and it will materialize. What you bind in your belief will be bound and what you loose with the same conviction, will be loosed.

IX. Use your mind and your will power. Learn to control and focus your thoughts. Whatever you give your mind and attention to, you will become and whatever you concentrate your will power upon will come into your life.

X. Emotional control and release are necessary in the practice of the art magical. Control for visualizing the effect you want to produce and emotional surge to propel toward the subject of your working.

The Book of The Wise III

The Sacred Tools of The Craft

Study guide for the grade of Probationer leading to initiation as a Craftsman I° Witch.

Tarostar V°
Magister Sacrorum
Circle of Starmeadow
Ancient Order of Bell Book and Candle, Las Vegas, Nevada

The Grade of Probationer is assumed during the initiation ceremony bestowed on the Vernal Equinox one year hence from becoming a Neophyte. Thereupon, the Probationer should begin to study for the next Level of Initiation, approximately Six Months later. The third level grants the individual the actual status as a Witch; Craftsmen First Degree.

As the Probationer prepares for the First Degree Ceremony, he or she continues to attend the classes given by the High Priesthood. This series of study is to cover the basic groundwork in the understanding of magical methods.

The suggested reading material should be digested by the Probationer and discussed in class with the High Priesthood. No written tests need be given. However, the instructors are to tell from the discussions of magical philosophy, how well the Probationer has absorbed the material.

The real work of the Probationer is in the planning and conducting of the brief rituals for the consecration of his or her own Sacred Tools preparatory to employing them during the Ist Degree Initiation.

The High Priesthood assigns reading for discussion from such works as the following:

Philosophy of the Magical Elements and Correspondences:
Magic, an Occult Primer; Conway; E. P. Dutton.
Magical Ritual Methods; W.G. Gray; Helios.

Inner Traditions of Magic; W.G. Gray: Weiser.
The Tree of Life: A Study in Magic; Israel Regardie; Weiser.
The Magician: His Training and Work; W. E. Butler; Wilshire Books.
Incantations and Words of Power; E. Maple; Weiser.
The Practice of Ritual Magic; G. Knight; Weiser.
Occult Exercises and Practices; G. Knight; Weiser.

The traditions of candleburning:
Candleburning: Its Occult Significance; M. Howard; Weiser.
The Magic Candle; C. Dey; Original Products; N.Y.
Candle Magic; Leo Vinci; The Aquarian Press.
Practical Candleburning Ritual; Ray Buckland; Llewellyn.

Preparatory Divination:
Tarot; Connally; Newcastle Publishing Co.
The Devil's Picture Book; Paul Huson; G.P. Putnam & Sons.
A Practicle Guide to Geomantic Divination; Israel Regardie; Weiser.
Magic Mirrors; N. Clough; Weiser.

General theory:
The Complete Book of White Magic; K. Martin; A.S. Barnes & Co.; London
The Complete Book of Spells, Ceremonies and Magic; Gonzalez; Wippler, Crown Publishers.

This series of lessons should consume the six Months following the initiation to Probationer. He or she should read and study the works assigned and be able to answer any quiz or oral exam that the High Priesthood may give in their discussion classes.

In the meantime, the Probationer is proceeding with the practicle application of the rituals which follow. In Other words, it takes a period of 18 Months to obtain the status of Craftsman First Degree and to become a Witch.

The Ceremonies for The Sacred Tools

To Consecrate an Athamé

After the initiation to Probationer level, at which time the Craft tools are presented to the Initiate, he or she must begin to gather the needed supplies for these rituals. (All the Witch's Sacred Tools must he consecrated and charged properly before the Probationer advances to become a Witch by taking the First Degree Initiation.)

Some traditions call for the Athamé to be buried in the Earth for a period of time to receive its consecration. The Way of the Wise, however, feels such is wrong.

Never is anything to be consecrated by burial in the Earth. She is destructive in that She claims everything unto Herself. She will only cause the metallic substance to discharge and begin to oxydize, even if set upon Her for a short while.

Therefore, any Tool of the Craft to be used in "The Art Magical" must be insulated from the Earth Element by a linen cloth whenever placed upon Her to magnetize.

On a Day of Mars as Luna wanes the knife chosen as an Athame is annealed with Fire and Water to "Make it virgin" by being heated to a cherry glow with a blow torch or in the embers of a fire. It is then plunged into a bucket of water to realign its molecular structure.

Out of doors upon the Earth, the knife is placed on a linen cloth with blade pointing North and a small magnet set at both ends for 24 hours. (The waning Moon is best for this work because this is the Witch Weapon with which most banishings are performed and the will of the Witch is imposed upon places and things).

On the following Day of Mars as Luna wanes, this consecration is performed:

A small home Altar is erected and covered with a red cloth.

A Waning Moon symbol is painted on the blade's black handle in white. Any other symbols would be optional.

The Athamé is placed in the center of the Altar, blade to the North. West of it is placed some salted water. To the East is set a dish of burning Martial Incense. North of the blade should be a vial of Sacred

Oil, while to the South stands a lit red candle.

The Altar is circumambulated 13 times widdershins, as these words are spoken:

Athamé, Blade of the Craft, be pure and virgin, blessed by earth.

The salted water is sprinkled thrice upon the blade as these words are said:

Waters of emotional love empower this blade to work for me, blessed be!

The athamé is taken up and wiped dry with a clean cloth and passed thrice through the incense smoke with these words:

Fire and Air command this blade to work my will, blessed be!

A dab of Sacred Oil is placed upon the blade handle as its secret name is whispered over it. (Henceforth, never is that name to be mentioned, or its power will be lost.)

The Athamé is taken up in the right hand and the candle in the left. The blade and candle are held crosswise together forming a barrier cross as this Charge is spoken:

Witches Blade work for me.
Never blood of man you'll see.
Pure and true you banish all evil
and astral phantoms of the mind primeval.
Rule all elements of this world,
to impose my will as a banner unfurled,
blessed be!

The barrier cross composed of knife and candle is then circumambulated thrice around the altar with these words:

Banish adversity, banish all woe.
Impose my will as around we go. Blessed be!

The blade and candle are set back down upon the altar and the candle allowed to burn out. The Athamé rests there for 24 hours.

The blade is then wrapped in linen and placed away for future use.

The Athamé will first be employed by the Probationer when called upon to cast his/her own Magic Circle during the First Degree Initiation Ceremony.

The Lore of The Blade

In Magical Tradition the Witch's Blade is used to impose Will upon things and places in time and space. It helps to erect Psychic barriers and create astral thought forms placed upon the Etheric Realms by the mind and Will of the Witch or Wizard. Much practice goes into developing that ability.

Practice by placing a spot on a blank wall about eye level. Stand before it about four feet away and concentrate on the spot. Bring the blade up to stab the center of the spot without touching the wall.

In other words, be able to stick the point of the blade forcefully into any form seen held in mind. Drive the blade to the heart of the vision held in mind. The flow of the gesture should be quick and decisive. With practice, the blade can flow to its astral target without hesitation or conscious effort.

Next practice drawing and imposing Invoking and Banishing Pentagrams in and on the Ether of space before you. The flow of the blade should be quick and fast, leaving an astral impression, held in mind, of a Pentagram Symbol in space before your eyes.

An invoking Pentagram sets up a widdershins force flow of energy to bring in the Magical Powers or Entities called upon.

A Banishing Pentagram turns the astral or Etheric in a deosil fashion to drive out or away any force already there.

With practice, the gestures will become second nature and be done without effort.

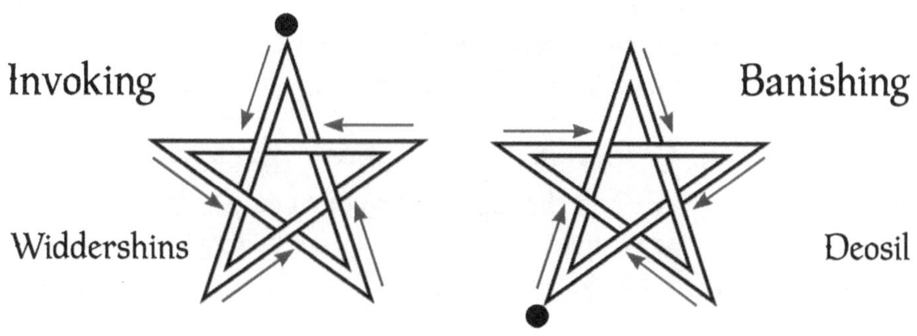

Ritual to Consecrate a Witch's Chalice

The Chalice is consecrated on a Day and Hour of Venus; during the waxing phase of the Moon.

The altar is set with a green cloth and a lit green taper candle set at the North edge.

Set a Venus Incense to burn at the East edge of the altar with a cup of salted water to the West. Set a dish of salt to the North next to the candle.

When this has been done, bring the Chalice to the altar, raise it high to the North and bow. Sprinkle it silently with a few drops of the salted water as you think of it being washed clean of all previous associations. Then wipe the Chalice dry with a clean cloth.

Next pass it thrice though the incense smoke as you silently dedicate it to your works of magic.

Take the Chalice in both hands and hold it to your heart as you proceed to walk 7 times widdershins around the altar humming a lullaby to the Chalice, as though it were a Human Child. (The lullaby should be either one from your own childhood, or one made up on the spot as long as it has happy emotional connotations.)

Then take the dish of salt and sprinkle a large circle in the center of the altar deosil. Then make a smaller widdershins circle within that. Set the Chalice within the two salt circles.

Extend your hands above it in the attitude of blessing and say:

Womb of Mystery, Cup of Life,
bring happy emotions and block out strife.
Be my symbol of the moving sea,
to rule the waters along with me. Blessed be, O Emotion's Frame,
encompass love in the Goddess's name.

The Chalice is left to stand in the center of the altar for 24 hours within the salt circles and the taper left to burn out.

It should then be wrapped in linen and placed away for future use, first during the First Degree Ceremony.

The Lore of The Chalice

The Chalice standing for the Water Element has come to be associated with the mysterious Holy Grail. It rules the desires and the emotional realm in Magical Tradition.

It also is associated with Psychic fluidity and acts as the Magic Mirror for the Art of Scrying.

In order to develop the rudimentary Psychic ability, it is necessary to train one's mind to attain a calm, unemotional state of hopeful expectation. From that center point in consciousness, concentration on a question or problem can bring visions and impressions to the mind.

The Astrological force called Mercury rules the Psychic and it is during the times of mercurial influence that one may obtain better psychic impressions. For purposes of scrying, use the Days or Nights of Mercury, as the Moon waxes in an Air sign to read visions and impressions seen in the water of the Chalice.

Ring the Chalice with 8 candles of yellow or light blue.

Set a pleasant incense of Benzoin or Sandalwood to burn.

Light the candles around the Chalice of Water moving widdershins, counter-clockwise.

Calm the mind and concentrate on a specific question, without straining or effort. This will help open the Psychic channels to the divinatory powers. Allow the vision produced in the sparkling reflections of the candles upon the water to speak to your inner mind as they will.

With time, adepthood in scrying will be properly developed so as to make one a good Psychic Reader.

The Chalice is also used in works of the amatory nature in casting Love Spells. It is used to conjure visions of the face of the intended lover onto the surface of the water in order to influence him/her on the emotional level.

Fridays as the Moon waxes in a Water Sign would be the best time for those kinds of works. Through a vivid image of the lover, one has access to the deep levels of mind.

To Consecrate The Thurible

An altar Thurible is a small bowl or cauldron holding sand or rocks in order to insulate burning coals and incense from scorching during rituals as they are burned.

Pick a Day of Mercury during the waxing tide of the Moon and at the exact moment of Dawn, which is the Hour of Mercury.

Have these things arranged near an open window facing East, or out of doors, to catch the Sunrise.

A yellow cloth is to be laid out flat on the floor or ground. Upon it place 3 yellow candles as a triangle with its apex to the East. At the West edge of the cloth have a cup of salted Water.

To the South of the triangle place your flint and steel (cigarette lighter). To the North of the triangle set a dish of salt.

The Thurible rests within the triangle half filled with sand (also coals and a Mercurial Incense rest nearby).

At the exact moment of Sunrise, when it lifts its crown above the horizon, light the yellow candles and say:

Greetings Sol, the Earth salutes thee.
Bless this Mercurial Magic at this hour.
The Sacred Elements Four aid me in this
work of power. Blessed be!

Stand up and begin to walk deosil around the objects arranged upon the cloth as you chant:

Sol and Hermes, Appollo and Mercury, Balder and Odin, Ra and
Thoth, names from times forgotten and ages of ages. From children's
fables with dusty pages, praised and sung by the Ancient Sages.
Heat and motion, light and life,
banishes inertia and casts out strife. Magics and auguries and
forecasts dire, the psychic element my soul doth inspire.
In Mercury's tide
shall magic bide
to banish evil

and force it to hide.
Blessed be this sacred time
to the Horned One and the Goddess sublime.

After the objects have been circumambulated 8 times, the salt is taken up and sprinkled around the triangle of candles deosil to form a circle and these words spoken:

Spheres of stars and spheres of cycles, ever onward the ancient duality.
The Circle is our ordered symbol, by it we measure human mortality.

The water is exchanged for the salt and a few drops are sprinkled on the Thurible as these words are spoken:

The sea is love, the sea gives life.
Fluidity added to mentality
makes us strong unto finality.

The Water is replaced on the Altar Cloth. Then the coal and incense are taken up. The coal is lit and placed upon the sand in the Thurible. As a few grains of the incense is cast upon it, these words are said, as the smoke rises:

Fumes and smoke,
fragrance and cense,
to thwart all evil and send it hence.
Fumes and cense,
fragrance and smoke
draw in the good
as blessings be spoke.

The hands are placed above the Thurible in the smoke in an attitude of blessing as the Charge is given:

Censer, censer, incense burner, imprisoned within this salt Circle white.
Give forth your. blessings with delight.

As you stand within this ring, create a Circle about all Magic rites where you are used.
Draw an air of blessings for each and every work of power.
Rule the airy forces by
Mercury's swift and Magic might. Blessed be, O King of Air!

The Thurible is lifted up and presented to the 4 Quarters widdershins beginning in the East and censing thrice to each Quarter silently. A final censing is made toward the Sunrise and the Thurible replaced within the 3 candles. All candles and incense are left to burn themselves out. Then clean the Thurible and put it away for future use.

If this is done out of doors, do not scatter the salt from off the cloth onto the ground. It will kill any living thing and make the Earth barren in that spot. Dispose of it some other way.

To Consecrate The Altar Pentacle
The Craft Earth Symbol

The Pentacle is either a small flat round dish to contain salt or earth during rituals, or a. flat piece of stone, wood or wax, upn which a small dish containing those items would stand.

Consecrate the Pentacle on a Day and Hour of Saturn as the Moon Waxes.

An upright Pentagram should be inscribed on it in either black or silver.

The altar should also be covered with black or silver and bear 10 brown candles arranged in a circle evenly spaced.

A burner with live coal for the Earth Incense (Patchouli, Musk or Kyphi) will set at the East edge of the altar. A cup of salted water will stand in the West.

When the altar has been thus arranged, the Pentacle is taken out of doors into the open air, held high to the North as these words are spoken:

Mother Earth, come bless this shield,
be it a symbol of our Solid World.

A bow is given to the North and the Pentacle taken back to the altar.

It is placed in the center of the unlit circle of candles. Set the incense to the coal in the burner and rap upon the altar 10 times and speak these words:

Summon to me, summon to me,
the powers in the Earth that be,
ten is your number.
I arouse you from slumber.
Blessed be this Earth rite
in the gracious Goddess's sight.

The Pentacle is picked up and passed through the incense 10 times as these words are spoken into the rising smoke:
Fragrance of Earth fill your frame
to shield my Magic in the Goddess's name.

A few drops of the salted water are sprinkled on the Pentacle, as the following words are spoken:

The Earth contains the Sea.
The Ocean floods the Earth.
Cycles and Ages and Eons that be.
You are the Goddes's bejeweled girth.
Blessed be!

The Pentacle is then replaced in the circle of candles and the candles are lit widdershins starting in the North with the traditional "Earth Fire" of flint and steel (modern cigarette lighter).

As the fire surrounds the Pentacle and burns brightly, the hands are held above the circle of candles and the Charge spoken thus:

O Pentacle, O Pentacle, Shield of Magic,
symbol of Earth,
the gracious Goddess gives you birth.
Safe within the Earth Fire's womb
you mark the times
and the Earth's silent forces you disentomb.
I charge you to rule the kingdom of

the Crystal Forces, the rocks and elements of
solid things,
all which solidity and stability brings.

Ten more raps are made upon the altar and the candles are left to burn themselves out.

The Pentacle rests there for 24 hours, Then wrap it up and put it away for the future.

The candle wax and incense ashes must be scattered on the Earth at that time.

The Altar Pentacle

SPELLS OF THE CORNUCOPIA

Dedicated and recommended to those aspiring to Artisan II° status as, Priest/Priestess of the Ancient Craft in the Way of the Wise. The spell, or the consecration of a Talisman to be performed in full Coven by the Candidate to II° status, may be chosen from any collection and from any tradition of the Occult Arts. These, the Cornucopia, are offered as suggestions.

INTRODUCTION

A Covenstead is the center of our group religious expression. It is the Temple, the Ritual Chamber, the hearthfire of The Old Religion.

We will not concern ourselves with what Covens may or may not have done in previous Centuries and Ages. In many instances, continuity of practice can not be clearly traced and established beyond doubt, due to the dearth of evidence allowed to filter down to Modern Times.

All we can say for sure, is that people have adhered to the old ways of popular religious practice above and beyond and outside of the "Official Cult", which, in the Western World, is Christianity, since times long past.

The Humanism of the "Pagan" Past is in resurgence in this time period. The Official Cult, maintained by Government, State and Church, no longer holds sway over intelligent hearts and minds.

The Old Religion, therefore, seeks the light of Religious Freedoms secured by Law and ancient practice. It may now bring forth more of its inner light and Wisdom Religion.

This section, *Spells of The Cornucopia,* is designed to give a more accurate picture to the observances and rites conducted by a well run Coven in the ideal of Wicca/Old Religion.

It is to help Witches/Pagans, observing the true essence of Wicca, have a set of Temple Ceremonies, of a minor order, to practice, which with time, build up a reservoir of vibrational energies, making the Covenstead very spiritual and potent as well.

Ritual purity can not be over-stated in The Old Religion. Rites performed for periods of time, over and over, as necessary, impress upon the spiritual ethers an identifying code, so to speak, which helps attract the Orders of beings above the Physical and the Nature Entities as well.

They would attend, on the inner planes and lend their force and powers to the Rites, Ceremonies and Magics engaged in by a Coven. They must not be ignored, nor forgotten.

They are recognized and given a small offering before major Sabbats. Consider them the "Penates" of Classical Times. It is for them, these minor rites are performed to preserve the potency of the Ritual Atmosphere in a Temple or Covenstead. Neglected, the life, the inner feeling of religious observances, is not there.

It is a spiritually vibrational feeling these minor Covenstead Rites are designed to create and maintain within the Ritual Chambers of The Old Religion. It had that feeling in the Ancient Past, and would strive to re-create it today.

A place becomes consecrated by its habitual use, not by "Holy Words" spoken by some priest or Hierophant. A true Temple of the Old Gods would give one that special consecrated feeling by merely walking into it.

It is very important in Ritual Work to have the correct atmosphere for the power of the Gods to manifest and work its blessings in and upon those who seek their Light and Love.

Used wisely, the Old Religion will speak for itself.

Preparation Time

Many books are written on Spellcraft and Magic and offer various kinds of procedures to follow. However, very little space is devoted to the most important aspect of success in the Occult.

Some read a spell and jump in trying to do it on the drop of a hat. Some have created such powerful occult and spooky reputations for themselves by impressing the impressionable, that they feel they can dispense with necessary preparation time altogether.

Does any star or professional entertainer refrain from rehearsal? How many hours of private rehearsal go into a public performance of any kind?

The same is of the utmost importance for works of Magic.

One must first decide what type of Magic Ritual or Spell would be needed for a particular situation and then calculate the most propitious and corresponding astrological configurations for it. One must know when the tides are right, in order to have the flow of the Cosmos/ Universal Flux, going with, not against nor transverse to, one's magics.

Hypothetically, let us say it is a Waning Moon, Day of Mercury, Moon in an Earth Sign.

The Occult Shop Apothecary probably is not doing much in the line of business, so, he/she tells a customer: "Oh, yes, today is just fabulous for a Love Spell! You will need ...." , just to make any sale possible.

The customer, if not up on astrological knowledge, would buy and work it and wonder why nothing happened. Wrong tide, time and day! Go ahead and swim upstream, if you will, but by working with the flow, in proper order, success will come with less effort.

By setting the proper time in the future, from a good Ephemeris or an Astrological Calendar, one has days to set about gathering the needed ingredients for the Spell or Ritual.

One then thinks it out clearly, lives it in mind, stages it in one's consciousness, thinks it, feels it and knows it to such a detailed degree, that when the Spell or Ritual act is finally performed on the proper day or night, the ceremony is but the climax - release - for and of all the steamed up energy built in and during the preparation time. The Magic then has every omen for positive results.

If you think you can just flip your finger and have Magic happen, you have been watching too many movies!!!!

If you think you can prance around in a Magic Circle and scream at the Gods and demand your Will be done, you've missed the boat somewhere along the line. Yet, that is often what we see "Magickians" trying to do. They attempt to overcome lack of preparation by sheer expenditure of energy.

God/Goddess are Principle, not Personality. You could not influence them, nor insult them, no matter what you did. The Course of the Cosmos will not change. However, one can cause changes in situations according to one's Will, which is Magic, when one works with the Astrological Tides, set by the Godhead.

The Gods manifest through the principles of what we know as Astrology. Calculate the most favorable transits and aspects for your

Magics. That is why Preparation Time must not be ignored. To do so is folly.

Traditionally, the Astrological Forces of the Planets imprint an essence or a "vibe", if you will, to the days of the week. Each day of the week bears a personal association with the Planet which governs it. The Planet rules certain aspects of Human physical and spiritual activities.

SUN	Sunday	Honors, Wealth, Health, Advancement, Good Fortune.
MOON	Monday	Peace, The Subconscious, Emotional Affinity, Illusions.
VENUS	Friday	Harmony, Friendships, Love, Beauty, Artistic Expression.
MARS	Tuesday	Strife, War, Justice and Defense. Sex and Passion.
MERCURY	Wednesday	Psychism, Divinations, Luck, Gambling, Business.
JUPITER	Thursday	Expansion, Prosperity, Fortunes and Magnanimity.
SATURN	Saturday	Lessons, Karma, Limitations, Restrictions.

The positive or the negative applications of those main qualities affect the individual day.

With the Waxing Moon, and with the Planet in favorable aspect to Her and to other Planets, brings out the positive side of the Planetary Nature. The Waning Moon and/or adverse aspects of the Planets to Her and to each other, would allow a negative or a stressful situation to affect the day.

Also the Nature of the Zodiac Sign in which the Moon passes mutates the vibrational energies and affects them either positively or negatively. The Element of a Sign would cast a specific quality onto the day: Fire, Water, Air or Earth.

Magic has been, for millennia, associated with the Power of the Lunar Tides. Her influence has the most active and direct bearing on the type and kind of Magic to be cast on any particular Day.

The Covenstead should have a competent grounding in Astrology to be able to apply the qualifying astrological associations in working Magic.

One must know the nature of a Waxing Moon in each and every Sign and in aspect to the Planets as they transit. Obversely, the affect of the Waning Tide must also be studied as the Moon passes in Signs and in aspect.

Then, favorable days can be calculated upon which the Coven could work Spellcraft and conduct Ceremonial Ritual. Every Coven should have one or two persons well versed in Astrology.

The astrological calculations would be one of the first steps in the total over all Preparation Time invested in any work of Spellcraft.

A Natural Zodiac Wheel for the Heavens can he drawn for any day and the Transiting Planets placed in the proper Signs, so that the mutating affects of the Moon, in waxing or waning phase, can be seen. This map of the Heavens would show, by study of the interconnecting influences of the Planets and the Moon, how the particular day/night would stack up for particular works of Spellcraft or Ritual.

One just does not decide to do a Spell and ignore the important powers exerted by the Astrological Configurations and expect to have success. The flow of energy and the flavor of the Tide must be taken into intelligent consideration. At least, those of the Craft do so.

The Witch's Candle Blessing

It is in the best of magical traditions to bless candles before they are employed in a Spell or Ritual. The reason being, they are composed of natural substances which catch and hold a magnetic charge from the minds and attitudes of those around them.

Candles sit around factories, truck loading docks and for long periods of time on Occult Shop shelves. They will assume the "vibes"/ influences from those persons who are habitually around them and from those who pick up and handle them.

One would want to ensure the candle has a state of virginal purity before one would apply it in a magic working of any sort. The candle must be dedicated to the Witch's or the Practitioner's Magic Will alone.

For that reason, candles should be ritually blessed to cleanse and purify them of any previous associations, once they are bought and brought to the Covenstead for use in Spellcraft.

This minor blessing is good ritual practice and should be done to each fresh batch of candles to be used in Magic.

Light a white candle and place a Goblet of water next to it. On the other side of the candle set a sweet Incense to burn.

Place the candle(s) to be blessed to rest before the burning white candle.

Set a dish of salt before the candle(s).

Take up the candle(s) to be blessed in the strongest hand and with the mind, see all negative associations fleeing from you and the candle. Say:

In the Name of the God and Goddess, I cleanse, purify and cast out any adverse conditions which may linger here. Blessed be!

Pass the candle(s) right through the flame of the white candle and pass it/them then through the Incense smoke.

Then, with the candle(s) still in the strongest hand, sprinkle some water out of the goblet onto the candle(s) and also cast a few grains of salt onto it/them. Say:

I bless, consecrate and ratify this/these wax candle(s) to the Magic Work of this Coven. Blessed be!

Set the candle(s) down upon the Altar or work space and place both hands over them in an attitude of blessing and say:

May the Powers of this Coven's Magic be the only force absorbed by and worked through this/these candle(s).
Blessed be!

The candle(s) may then be locked away out of sight to be kept for future use as needed in Spells and Rituals.

That is the general format for taper and jumbo sized candles. Those in the glass jars should be washed outside and around the inner rim of the glass with isopropal alcohol before being blessed. That clears away any excess wax drippings on the glass jar.

One must present one's best efforts to the Gods/Astrological Forces as valuable attention to detail in magical purity. Haphazard or sloppy attitudes and neglect of correct procedures only tells the Forces that be, that one is not putting out one's best efforts to gain the request/ prayer, Spell or Ritual. One would only get same from them in return.

The Circle of Art

The Witch's Magic Space, wherein the acts of Spellcraft are done, has traditionally been associated with what has come to be called the Magic Circle of Art.

It is somewhat different from a Sabbat Circle for Worship and from an Esbat Circle for Coven Magics. This Circle deals with the forces of Magic which the individual Witch/Practitioner conjures and/or evokes just for his/her own personal Spells and Rituals.

It contains the energy the Witch evokes to send and accomplish his/her Will, or it forms a barrier in which the Practitioner of the Arcane Arts summons forces from the Unseen Beyond.

The most convenient Altar Space would simply be a black cloth spread upon the floor or Earth in the center of the work area. The Circle itself would be large enough to allow the Witch room in which to move around, generally 9 ft. in diameter.

The Tools of Art would then be arranged upon the cloth in the center along with the necessary items for the Spell or Ritual at hand.

There would be a Thurible for the Incense corresponding to the Spell standing at the East side, a Chalice of water at the West, a Pentacle for salt or Earth at the North and a small candle for Fire at the South along with the Athamé (or Sword, should the Witch be III°).

Within the center, between the tools, would rest whatever items a Spell may call to use.

At the appointed time for the work, the Tools and necessary items are placed upon the cloth. The candle is lit and the Incense burning. The Witch would then proceed to Cast the Circle:

Taking up the Incense in the Thurible, it is circumambulated around the area widdershins in silence as a wish is made to clear a space for Magic. Replacing the Incense, the blade and candle are taken up and also circumambulated North to North. As the blade is carried around, an Invoking Pentagram is inscribed in the Air at each Quarter with these words:

Powers of the Four Mighty Ones, bless this Work by air and fire. Build my Inner Temple of Art. Be it strong and sound of purpose.

After all Quarters have been thus addressed, North to North, the candle and blade are put back in place.

A firm commanding attitude should be displayed by the Witch at all times which impresses the power onto the Ether.

The Spell or Ritual may then be cast.

Afterwards, the Circle has to be taken down in a reverse manner:

The Chalice of Water is circumambulated around the Circle, North to North, deosil as a banishing Pentagram is inscribed in the Air holding the Chalice firm and upright (the Chalice is used to form the Pentagram). Then a few drops of Water are scattered to each Quarter with these words:

Powers of the Four Mighty Ones, bless this Work by water and earth. Be all forces sent away. Let normal time and space prevail.

The Chalice is then replaced by the dish of salt or Earth and a few grains scattered around the Circle in silence deosil.

The Witch/Practitioner may then depart the Circle area.

This basic format should be learned by rote so that it can be performed for each work of Spellcraft where a Magic Circle is required.

The Herbal Love Potion

This is a work of Venus, Planetary Influence for Love. It should be done on a Friday Night as the Moon waxes. If She waxes in a Water Sign, that is good for emotional harmony, in a Fire Sign, for passion and sex, in an Air Sign for mental stimulation and friendships, in an Earth Sign for the fertile and material aspects of Love.

In addition to the usual Tools of Art, there should be a Chalice of rich red wine, Incense of Rose or Sandalwood and a pink candle anointed with a Lovers Oil. Have a Mortar and Pestle handy.

To that add 1/4 oz. each of Verbena, Spearmint and Jasmine.

The Circle of Art should be properly cast (see *Circle of Art*). The candle used for the Spell is also the candle used to cast the Circle, as well as the Incense called for.

Place the candle next to the Chalice of Wine and begin to grind the herbs together in the Mortar and Pestle with these words:

Herbs of the Venus Power,
upon my lover all delight I do shower.
Let the one who drinketh of thee,
come to love and be with me!

Chant over and over again as the herbs are thoroughly ground and mixed. The entire area should resonate and vibrate to the sound of the chant.

After a good twenty minutes of grinding and chanting, stare deep into the flame of the candle and see the Lover's face in the flame.

When the image can be held in mind, transfer it to the surface of the wine in the Chalice and say:

_____ , Thou art mine to be.
Thy face in the wine I see.
None but the forces of Love consume thee!
Thou canst not resist. Thou art mine forever!

Cast the herbs into the wine and allow them to steep. (Cover the Chalice with a clean cloth and allow it to steep for 24 hours.)

Close the Circle and clear all away. The candle and Incense should burn themselves out.

On the next day, the wine should be filtered from the Chalice and placed into a stoppered bottle to be put into whatever food or drink one would share with the lover at the next opportunity.

Tradition says soon the lover will turn to thee.

King Solomon's Apple Love Seal

(From traditional sources)

If there is to be a Handfasting at the Covenstead, the High Priestess would do this work sufficiently ahead of time to have the necessary tides and astrological forces working to bless the couple.

On a Night of Venus, as the Moon waxes in a Water or Earth Sign, the seal must be scribed in inks of copper brown and reddish pink. The names of the two to be joined in Holy Union by Rite of Handfesting would be scribed on the reverse side.

Seven pink candles are anointed with Lotus Oil and set in a circle around the Seal. A bit of "Love" Incense of Rose and Benzoin would be lit.

She would then burn one candle per night, along with some of the Incense for the seven nights following.

She would chant over and over the seal seven times each night, as the candle burns:

This Seal I bind to handfast these two.
Naught but words of Will will do:
Oyoth, hean, vean, eant!
This couple never shall know want. Wisdom of Sages and powers of ages,
keep secure as the outside storm rages.
Bless this union bound with love,
Holy Lady high above!

At the Handfasting, she will circumambulate the couple thrice and again recite the sealing words. The couple would keep the Seal as a memento of the Rites.

The Arts of Divination

I. Reading The Aura

This is a very ancient method of Divination used by Wizards from the dim past and time immemorial. It requires a sensitivity to the eminations given off by objects that were in close proximity to a Subject for a time.

Make for yourself two strings of beads and pass them through the smoke of an incense of Benzoin eight times on a Night of Mercury as Luna waxes in an Air Sign.

Thereafter, on Days of Mercury, read for people by having them place a piece of jewelry or trinket worn by them into the center of the two stings of beads.

Intently gaze at the item and allow your sensitivity to seek a rapport with the item and read out what impressions thy inner eye receives therefrom.

II. Cartomancy For The Witch

The ability to function at some form of psychic science is the first basic achievement for those who aspire to mastery in the Craft.

One sees numerous "Readers" advertised all over the World. Mostly in the Tarot Cards.

Tarot Is concerned with the spiritual progress of the Querent for whom its arcana are laid.

All one can say is *Caveat Emptor.*

The playing cards do not presume to take such a responsibility.

They show only the three major human concerns; Love, Luck and Money.

One should be well warned not to place a dependency on a professional "Reader" to the exclusion of common sense.

It would be worth the effort to develop a reading ability of one's own.

Be that as it may, playing cards, as tools for fortunetelling, can be the best way to help one develop the rudimentary psychic ability.

When two persons come together for any reason, the electromagnetic fields of each person's auras merge to produce a temporary Over-Soul which is composed of the best and worst of each being. That merger is what allows the flow of psychic energy to pass between both parties. It is also in contact with the consciousness of the entire human race and its reservoir of knowledge. This may sound rather Jungian but it is more scientific than attributing psychism to nebulous "Spirit Guides".

Psychism is a fluid force. Never try to make it fit any pattern. It must have the freedom to be what it is needed to be for any given person seeking to learn what it can show. If the spontaneous flow is made to conform to a pattern, it will appear to dry up.

That is why there is really no set meaning to the cards. Each author can only give his/her personal opinions as to what any card means for readings.

Meditate on the pattern in each card and allow the card to tell you what it should mean.

Write down each impression and boil that down to a few "key" phrases. In that way you become your own authority on the cards.

I offer my interpretations of the cards as a guideline only. You may use these meanings, however, do not consider them absolute. You may find the cards saying things of their own as you read for any given person.

Allow the Querent to shuffle at least thrice, as he/she concentrates on what is to be known.. I find it best for the Reader not to be told so the cards can read only the Querent's situation. The Reader only interprets the cards as they fall. The Querent fits that meaning into his/her own life or circumstance.

Above all, be only a Medium through which psychic insight may channel. Realize that knowledge comes through you, not from you.

Beware of the temptation to act as an Oracle and bask in the adulation others may place on you when your insights prove true. Leave that form of egotism to those who need to display it.

A Witch develops the "Second Sight" to help fellow beings, but only as a stepping stone on the road back to the realms of spiritual perfection. As time goes by, he/she should grow beyond the "Show and Tell" stage of Spiritual Enlightenment.

Do not consider the playing cards any way inferior to the Tarot.

They give practical advise not spiritual. You are functioning as a Fortuneteller, not a metaphysical adviser.

Read the cards honestly, be sensitive to the Querent and keep the mind open to feelings and impressions as they flow through you.

Avoid the situation of allowing a Querent to affix a dependency on "Readings", where he/she would request a Reading almost every other day. Some will be impressed with your ability and wish to ask your advise before (proverbially) going to the bathroom.

Know what power that places in your hands. The Lords of Karma will not be cheated.

A Witch is about the only honest Psychic one can find in these days of wrath and anguish, days of calamity and misery. Be honest. In that way the Arts of Divination are used as they should be, as an aid to help the lost navigate properly through the stormy sea of life. No more, no less.

Suit of Hearts

ACE: "The romantic card." *The promise of joy.* It is the cause for celebration. Love versus sex. Good feelings about the matter. An indication, of good news concerning an emotional relationship or romantic love. A birth or rebirth of spiritual faith and joy. It indicates a better social life. *The basis for happiness.*

KING: "King Solomon." *Prospects for love.* Love and warmth are on the way or may even be present. A man of influence and good intentions interested in the Querent or Subject. An easy going generous masculine influence. *A Protecting individual.*

QUEEN: "The Pink Lady." *The passion card.* It stimulates love situations. It offers joy and pleasure with unqualified love and compassion.. This is action through instinct, not reason. It is friendly and helpful. assistance. *A possible love affair in the future.*

JACK: "The Priest." *A sign of good times and good company.* Loving friends and general good fortune. A carefree interlude with the influence of a confidant. The person with whom one may be involved. *A love affair.* Ten "Castles in Spain". *The wish fulfillment.* The sign of a successful future. A very fortunate romantic card. It is complete fulfillment in an emotional situation. it is triumph against all odds and good luck to any project. It is good news and the reason. to be optimistic. *This is happiness and love.*

NINE: "The Great Nine." *The card of protection.* Spiritual joy in life, with inspirational awareness. It is protection. with the retrieval of losses suffered. There is spiritual well being and inner growth. An alliance with positive life forces is indicated. It is reason for much happiness as there is a positive answer. *This is the wish card.*

EIGHT: "The Party Card." *The card of enthusiasm and gusto.* Friendly reactions from those in the environment. Love and sex are synonymous. Money through love, or a gift which causes pleasure (not necessarily material). It is the formation of friendships with pleasant dispositions. It is the making of the best adjustments. *Good health.*

SEVEN: "Lovers Quarrel." *It concerns romance within the partnership.* A bad omen for marriage. There is an indication of unreliability. Others involved may be apt to change their minds. There is a call for wisdom and reflection to bring calm and serenity to one's surroundings. In that way one can win out over an unpleasant situation. *Love life not stable.*

SIX: "Grace's Card." *Troubles and problems.* An omen of conniving associates. Plans take shape, but others may steal the advantage. It is a sign of emotional disturbances. There is a risk of total failure. No sign of immediate gains or any accomplishment. There seems to be disappointment. *Partial fulfillment of desires.*

FIVE: "Learning of the Truth." *An omen of indecision.* The desire to escape issues. There are regrets, tears and disappointments. Sorrow, however, does not lie deep. An indication of a delightful passing romantic involvement, but not lasting. *There is relief from self imposed bondage.*

FOUR: "The Old Maid." *The sign of stability.* A happy productive and pleasant home life. Happiness through. work and its opportunities. Enrichment of life through service. The stable plan for fulfillment in courtships, engagements and friendships. *Satisfaction where unselfishness is rewarded.*

THREE: "The Lady." *The promise Of increased happiness.* All depends on the Querent's determination. A good idea or heartwarming news. There is fun and friendships and things that are emotionally pleasing. *A happy mental state.*

TWO: "The Falling Star." *The lucky omen of fate and destiny.* The success card. Unexpected good which keeps things moving. (Time Element - 2 days, weeks, months).

Suit of Diamonds

ACE: "The Pot of Gold." *The constructive power.* Sudden news of a lucky nature. Important information concerning business or money matters. An expansive financial endeavor. Good payment for past efforts. *Good luck.*

KING: "King Midas." *The creator or driving force.* Reward, recognition and dignity for services rendered. The dignified male. A good reputation and long standing situations. (Could be legal Counsel.) A dangerous man, ruthless competitor or rival. Bad or deceitful lover. *Better financial gains*

.

QUEEN: "Queen Victoria." *The creatve force.* An opportunity to expand the existing circumstances, or to create new ones. Devise for making money. Tremendous potential on both the material and spiritual planes. The flirtatious woman. An unfriendly situation, possibly scandals. Watch out for trickery. (Time Element - 3 days, weeks, months.) *Progress is made.*

JACK: "The Crossroads of Life." *Improved business conditions.* Gains and profit through friendships. The personality is improved. A self centered person. Bad. *Prestigeous luck.*

TEN: "Fortune's Favor." *The sign of wider horizons.* Escape from narrow confining situations in life. Enjoyment of new experiences. A very good card, success, security and freedom from financial fear. *An omen of tremendous gains.*

NINE: "The Curse of Scotland." *The sign of a new start.* Expanded interests. Self improvement, both material and spiritual. Business profit and protected interests. A new undertaking will succeed with satisfaction and happiness. *Secure holdings.*

EIGHT: "Fortress on a Hill." *The sign of balance.* Opportunities at work behind the scenes. Gains are slow but steady in financial matters. Savings grow. Skill, coupled with spiritual, strength. *One is dealt with. fairly.*

SEVEN: "Dispute." *An omen of distress.* The card of bad aspects. Other people's interests take precedence. An unresolved problem involving finances. Do not gamble. There is bad luck in any enterprise or purpose. *A delayed decision.*

SIX: "A Windfall." *Opportunites bringing gain.* Expansion in work situations and increasing income. A warning against an over reliance on material things. *Accept the good with a little caution.*

FIVE: "Napoleon." *The destiny card.* Things beyond one's control come into play. It may be good or bad according to placement, but usually denotes support from the forces of destiny. There may be a. clash of wills over a business matter. Uncertainty in matters of gambling. *An expansion card.*

FOUR: "The Idealist.". *The insurance card.* There is positive outcome in matters of idealism and wisdom. There is a concrete and measurable improvement and success in the financial concerns. Possible quarrels among friends or relatives. *Beware a betrayal of faith.*

THREE: "Thumbs Down." *Omen of the negative answer.* Stop and think all situations over. The sign of separation. There could be a dispute over finances or an entanglement with a negative outcome. (The following cards will indicate the result.)

TWO: Dynamite." *The wild card.* It blasts old patterns in order to create new. There may be an unexpected offer of money or a business venture *A steady increase.*

Suit of Clubs

ACE: "Hammer of Thor." *The power card.* The card of talent and helpful associates. High hopes and ambitions. Ideas and inspirations. Inventive or innovative changes to attitudes. There is strong energy and imagination coupled with power and emotional strength. An important message concerning the initiation of a new venture. *Good luck, financial success and good health.*

KING: "The Crusader." *Overcoming obstacles.* Good advice and help. News about honors and authority. Recognition that is due the Querent. Strength, knowledge and experience. Faithful friendships. *The power of the moral establishment.*

QUEEN: "Lady of the Manor." *A struggle between: desires and obligations.* Difference between needs and wants. An indication of news and many changes. *There is a responsibility to the past.*

JACK: "Edward, the Black Prince." *Things initiated and sustained.* One must be alert. There are changes involving associates and enthusiastic friendships. An aggressive go getter type. Look into all deals. *Keep in control.*

TEN: "Something in the Wind." *A fresh outlook on life.* A new opportunity. Adapting to new ideas. Successful ventures of all kinds. One gets what one wants out of any situation, either pleasure or pain. It wards off the evil of other influences in the cards. *Strong good luck.*

NINE: "The Trouble Card." *A suprise twist to whatever is going on.* Much talk and little action. One may lose some friends because of one's success. Ambition injured by obstinacy. Unexpected opportunity leads to well-being. *Hard work is neccessary.*

EIGHT: "The Glorious Victory." *A fortunate omen denoting harmony.*

Loyal support-from those in the environment. It shows a need to communicate in order to reach any agreement. The sign of balance, harmony and spiritual quietude. Inner qualities guard against life's vicissitudes. Caution is urged in money matters. *Happiness increases with time.*

SEVEN: "Lords of Karma." *That which is due one in life.* Much social activity and opportunities for meeting new persons. Business changes for the better (unless coupled with Spades). It shows a need to take time to relax. There may have been arguments or weaknesses that need correcting. Finish what has been started. Money is coming. The repayment of a debt. A warning against an unstable effort and an illusionary success. *An increase in value is indicated.*

SIX: "Unfavorable Partnership." *An energy loss.* That which affects the physical co-operation of efforts. Changes in work situations. Wasted energy and losses. A reaction to a poor attitude. Opportunities for a favorable social life. Changes of attitudes and outlook for the better. *Try harder.*

FIVE: "In the Pits." *End of a cycle.* The situation is hopeless and reaches its conclusion. Nothing more can be gained. Possibility of a quarrel among friends. Rivalry, strife or competition and jealousy. A sign that one needs to take matters in hand and become more self-sufficient. *Move on to other things.*

FOUR: "The Devil's Bedposts." *Increased activities.* A strengthening of friendships and social capacities. Unexpected assistance coming. A day by day growth. The possibility of lies. One is blind to the situation. Self-deception. Sudden misfortune and failure of a project. *The thorn rose.*

THREE: "The Four Leaved Clover." *Omen of good luck.* An activity which has the potential of successful growth. Cleverness and ingenuity. Short comings not recognized. Face facts, make amends. *The idea card.*

TWO: "Tug of War." *The omen of direct opposition.* Associates may oppose one's works. Tremendous power and intensity of emotion. Social invitations of important consequences. Just enough money to get by on. It takes a lone wolf to beat this card. *Luck only by fate.*

Suit of Spades

ACE: "The Black Hole." *The complete negative.* Expectations of the worst. Worry, fear, anxiety and doubt. Setback and delay. Complications in plans. One may be trapped by circumstances. Few or no alternatives. Indecision and possible financial debts. Bad news (legal or emotional), but there is force, power and strength. *Triumph only after severe obstacles.*

KING: "Kaiser Bill." *Losses in position.* Complications from a legal figure, or one in a superior role. An enemy, dishonest and opportunistic. *Be on guard.*

QUEEN: "The Black Maria." *A warning card.* Hidden deceit could cause sorrow. Underhanded tactics, or deliberate delay. The duties in life. Disturbances, scandal and deception. *The card of treachery.*

JACK: "Black Jack." *Unwelcome news.* An evil omen for lovers. Betrayal and dissatisfaction. All is not what it seems to be. A pretended friend. Misfortune through a love affair. Lack of character in a lover. Misfortune to friends and associates. *Dissatisfaction with the way things are.*

TEN: "Walking in Darkness." *A dark body of water by night, the situation looks black.* Trouble, difficulty and pressure from all sides. Disappointment, delay, anxiety, loneliness and setbacks. There are walls and barriers. An abandonment of long cherished plans. (It blights good cards and strengthens evil ones.) *The good is nullified.*

NINE: "The Fall of Gibralter." *An omen of catastrophe.* These are the swift destructive forces of evil. Changes through unexpected and unpredictable sources. Sorrow and defeat, failure in general. Adversity ahead. Things not going the Querent's way. Disappointments and unfortunate spiritual experiences. Watch and wait. Need to develop a responsible attitude. There may be tidings of death or illness. (9 and 10 of Spades - the Death Combination). *Complete adversity.*

EIGHT: "A Dreadful Storm." *Disillusionment and opposition*

looms ahead. Disappointment in plans and wishes. An unhealthy relationship. Difficulty in self-expression. There is a reinforcement of energy. Drop all plans and make a fresh start. (If surrounded by other spades, it could mean a health problem.) *Thorn in the flesh.*

SEVEN: "Seven. Devils." *A sign of division.* A reversal in plans. An unhappy anxious period of time. Does not indicate expected satisfactions or rewards. An upset over unwanted changes over which one has no control. Sorrows and losses in marriage and partnerships. Partners could be at a serious disadvantage affecting the Querent. Poor judgment in legal affairs. Tricks and intrigues. A change for the worst. With forcefulness of character touchy situations improved with time. *Let all matters ride until the bad cycle rolls by.*

SIX: "The Beleaguered Castle." *The card of stress.* A depletion of energy and a lessening of intensity around any particular situation. The breaking of bonds, the cutting of ties. Obligations with little reward. Much planning with little results leads to discouragements. Decisions are made by others. Dismay over work conditions. *There is anxiety and suspended motion.*

FIVE: "Pressures." *Making a voluntary change.* Heavy responsibility with grief, sorrow and remorse. Unfortunate in love matters. Success only after much work and many reverses. *Evaluate all aspects.*

FOUR: "Upward Climb." *A pause to renew strength.* There is a recuperation and healing. There is an end to anxiety and strife. A period of minor aggravation. *Temporary reverses.*

THREE: "The Black Trinity." *Interference.* Trouble in the home. Poor rewards for work done. Mistakes slow down progress. An unhealthy mental attitude. Little solution to problems. *Endure and await a better time.*

TWO: "Either/or." *The wild card of ambivalence.* A stumbling block. Abrupt changes in direction. Complete change or separation. A negative material worth. *Halt spending.*

Spreads for Readings

The Horseshoe Spread – For General Readings

Use a deck that has two Jokers. Mark one for a female Querent and one to represent a male Querent.

Set the Joker as a significator to represent the Querent in the center of the table.

The Reader should shuffle the deck thoroughly and fan it out upon the table. The Querent must then select nine cards from the fan and hand them face down to the Reader. The fan should then be gathered up and set aside.

The Reader then deals out the nine selected cards in a horseshoe shape around the significator starting at the left.

The first three are read as the Past, the second three as the Present and the third as the future, thus:

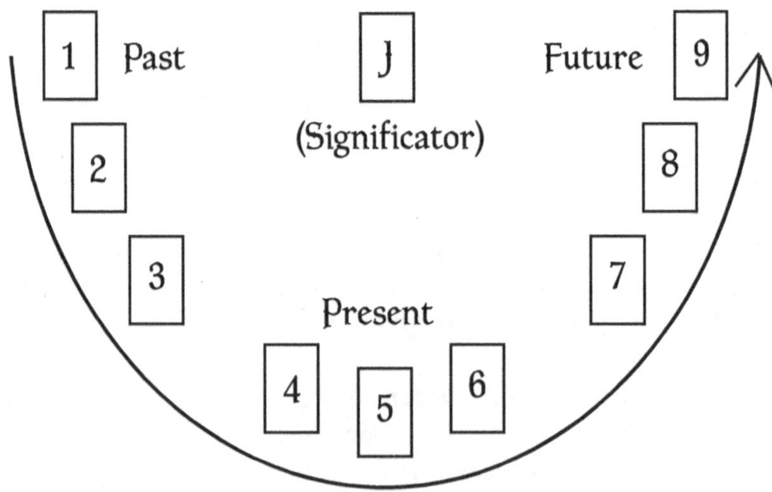

The Horseshoe Spread -- For Specific Questions

The Querent must shuffle and cut the cards. into three piles to the left with the left hand as he or she concentrates on a question needing a specific answer.

The Reader picks up the three piles from the left and deals off seven cards in a horseshoe moving to the left. They are read thus:

1. Past Influences.
2. Present Circumstances..
3. General Future Conditions.
4. Best Course of Action.
5. Attitudes From Others in the Environment.
6. Opposition and Obstacles.
7. Probable Final Outcome.

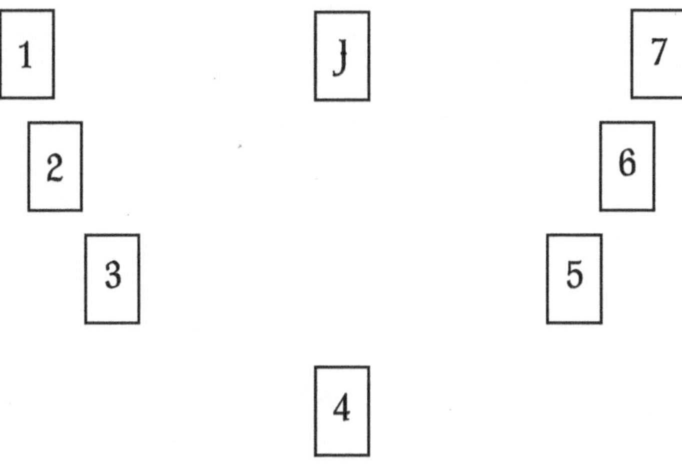

The Seven Card Advice Spread

Have the Querent shuffle and concentrate on his/her problem or concern. (A Joker should already be set as a Significator.) Lay out the cards from the top of the deck:

1 should be read as the events leading to the Present.
2 & 3 are the cards of the most likely outcome.
4 & 5 are the counsel the Oracle offers.
6 & 7 are the cards for the best course of action to take.

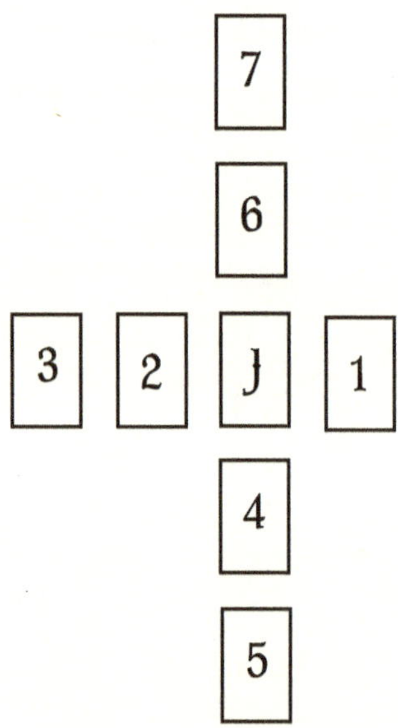

Spread For a Comprehensive Answer To a Very Heavy Question

The Querent should shuffle the cards very well and deeply concentrate on the matter needing a prognostication.

The cards are not cut, but stacked and handed back to the Reader and dealt from the top.

They are laid in the following sequence and read thus:

Card # 1 & 2 are read as the immediate influences around the matter.
Card # 3 & 4 are the forces coining to bear on the situation.
Card # 5, 6, 7, & 8 are the forces in favor of the Querent.
Card # 9, 10, 11, & 12 are the forces of the opposition.
Card # 13 & 14 are the end results portended.

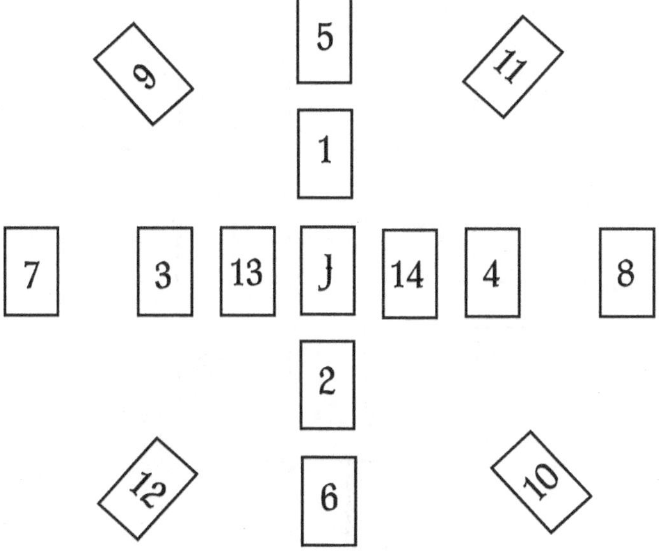

The Seven Sisters -- For a Comprehensive Reading

The Querent shuffles the deck and cuts them into three piles to the left with the left hand.

The Reader draws one card off each pile left to right forming a cluster of three cards. This process is repeated six more times, resulting in seven clusters of three, or 21 cards.

The Reader turns each cluster face up and reads left to right The center card in each cluster is the most important, with those on either side qualifying it thus:

Step 1: Querent shuffles and lays cards in 3 piles

Step 2: Reader draws cards ——›

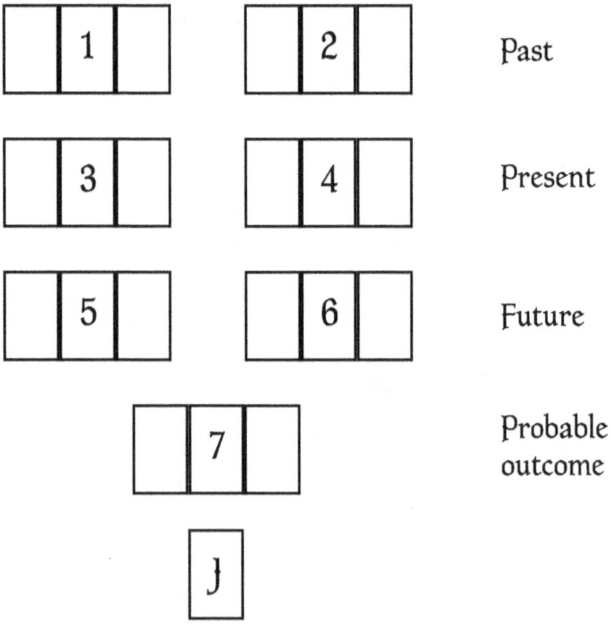

1 2 Past

3 4 Present

5 6 Future

7 Probable outcome

J

Tirage en Croix
(From the French)

The Querent shuffles and cuts the cards into three piles.

The Reader picks up the piles in direct order of the cut, that is, the Querent's first pile ends up on top in the Reader's hands.

Deal out four cards in order three times around using 12 cards in all, or four stacks of three.

Read them thus according to meaning:

Stack # 1 Pertaining to the Self.
Stack # 2 The foundation of the matter.
Stack # 3 The outer world influences.
Stack # 4 The results/La suprise of the Reading.

This gives a general outlook for a Querent's situation.

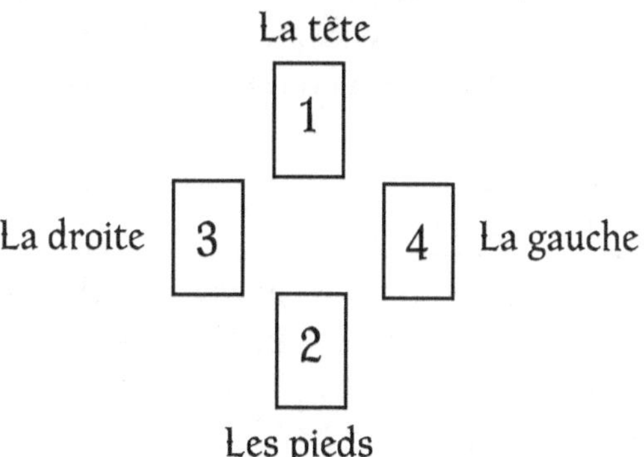

The Three Card "Yes or No" Spread
For a Quick Answer to a Simple Question

Shuffle the cards well and cut into three piles to the left as the question is concentrated upon. Turn over the piles.

The cards on top are then read thus:

2 red means yes.
2 black means no.
3 red is a positive yes.
3 black is an emphatic no.

III Spirit Runes

	The Windmill: Place this Rune over a doorpost to impede evil and protect property from envy. Inscribe it on a Day of Mercury as Luna wanes. A protective influence around the question, not reversible.
	The Arrow of the Dawn: This Rune symbolizes the Will to Success. Reversed, it stands for Failure. A very positive omen in upright position. It deals with the activities of life and one's affect on others.
	The Spiral of Life, Order, Cosmos. This Rune stands for creative motion. Reversed, it means the Ceasing of Effort. The Karma, or the course of life is proceeding as it should and one's efforts are blessed.
	The Tempest. This Rune represents the forces of strife and chaos. In its reversed meaning, it stands for the containment of strife, or peace. There are wild and contentious forces at work. Seek to control the emotions, or chaos will result.
	The Rain God. This Rune is called the Winds of Change. It causes a movement in circumstances. Reversed, it is the force that resists change. Opportunities and benefit on the way, if upright. Otherwise, the status quo remains the same.
	The Wizard's Bane. This Rune invokes the Air Element to lift any curse or ban. Reversed, it lays one upon a person. Enemies afoot behind the scenes, if reversed. Upright, the forces are removing obstacles.
	The Upliftment. This Rune stands for the indomitable spirit in Man.. Reversed, it means submission to contrary forces. One may overcome any adversity along the path of progress.

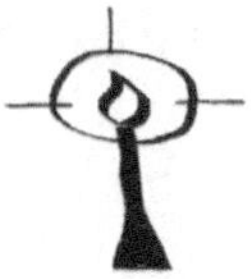	The Flame of Life. This Rune symbolizes spiritual expansion. It is a Blessing Rune and has no reversed meaning. The Light of Heaven shines in the Querent's life and good things are on the way.
	The Trident of Fire. This is a Rune for offence, it means Magical Attack. Reversed, it stands for surrender to such powers. An omen to take the offensive in any situation where action is needed. Reversed, nothing can be done, someone else has the advantage.
	The God's Bolt. In this Rune is the motion of the Life Force. It means courage and power. Reversed, it is the destructive use and results of power. A way will be knocked through any blocks. Reversed, no victory in the long run.
	The Goddess's flame. This Rune stands for spiritual. protection and the tranquil hearthfire. It is a Blessing Rune and may not be reversed. The positive sign of happy and contented home life.
	The Eye of Wrath. This Rune represents anger and rage. Reversed, it is the Star of Harmony and used to calm tempers. The destructive is allowed the upper hand and only ruin will result.
	The Sea. This Rune symbolizes the churning of emotional situations. Reversed, it is called Oil on the Waters, and stands for calmness. Relationships are not clear, but cloudy and uncertain. Not evil, but a caution in love is indicated.
	The Chalice. For happy containment in love and all that love would represent. Reversed, it is The Spilling Out and means the loss of love. The perfect match for love. A very good omen for affairs of the heart.
	The Wave. This Rune stands for the Force of Life in full flow. Its reversed meaning is The Abyss which has no way out. All is happening as it should to the best advantage possible. A mature outlook to the situation.

	The Blessed. This Rune means emotional stability and life in perfect balance. It can not be reversed.. Health and wellbeing is indicated. A good omen of right thinking and doing,
	The Hood. This Rune represents heightened psychic awareness. When reversed, it is the Barb, or evil magics. Sensitivity to life is good. The inner being is progressing well. Reversed, adverse psychic forces at work.
	The Flower. This Rune is the fruit of Maturity and Wisdom. Reversed, it is the Fall, or instability. One's plans coming to fruit as planned. This is the right course to follow. In an ill aspect, the insecure is causing pressures and changes, not for the good.
	The Barrier. This Rune impedes progress and may be used both for offense and defense. The definite NO! Abandon all hope. Nothing will come of this question or course of action.
	The Tree. This Rune stands for life, growth and nourishment. In a reversed position, it is the Spearhead and means death. Upright, the YES and the way to go.
	The Platter And Loaf. The meaning of this Rune is prosperity and abundance. Reversed, it is the Bare Table and brings hunger and want. Money. The sign of positive material worth.
	The Far Horizon. This Rune offers power and dominion. Reversed, it is the Sun Below, and means the loss of property. The positive indication of advancement and opportunity in expanding one's horizons. Better relations on the job and with associates.
	The Shield. This Rune stands for the powers of defense. Reversed, it means the depths of defeat. A time to be on guard and prepared for any eventuality. Upright, one will win out. Reversed, the power rests in other hands.

	Cycles. In an upright position, it represents good over evil. When reversed, it is the triumph of evil. The matter has run its course and the results are as they are. Reversed, only a bitter harvest is due.

The Spirit Runes are not of the ancient lore of Wizardry, but are of this Day and Age. They came from meditation on the Mercurial Power and offer a minor form of Divination such as the Playing cards.

They are not a deep oracle, but give a prognostication into the mundane questions affecting the Human Animal.

As a Witch, people will come to you and ask your insight into their problems and want to know what they should do.

By casting these runes you will be able to get a general insight into their situations and be able to offer an answer.

On a Day of Mercury, as the Moon waxes in a Water Sign, go out into Nature under Wind and Sky and search for 24 flat round pebbles of about two inches across.

Paint them white and inscribe the runes on them on one side only in black paint. The backs of the pebbles should be white, but unadorned.

At night on that Day of Mercury, pass them eight times through the smoke of a Mercurial Incense and repeat eight times over them:

Runes of seeing, Runes of rede,
give the answer one must heed.
What be the doom that we must deem?
Omens of luck, or a Night Hag's scream?
Runes of gladness, Runes of woe,
show us true the way to go.

Then place the runes stones in a small box and put them away for future use.

How to Cast The Spirit Runes

Make for yourself a Rune Cloth of dark blue. It should be no more than one square yard of material, a natural linen, or cotton, or leather or skin would be favored above any synthetic fabric.

You may adorn the cloth either with embroidery or fine paint with any symbols desired that reflect the idea of the Mercurial power or of the old Norse God Odin. Dark blue was His color.

This cloth you would only use for casting the Runes upon, spread out on a table or flat surface. They may also be kept wrapped in the Rune Cloth when not in use.

Cast Runes on a Night of Mercury when He be not Retrograde, but moving direct and best if Luna passes in an Air Sign and waxes.

In that way Rune Casting would be done in the time and favorable influences conducive thereto.

Burn an Incense of Mugwort and Mace which favor the Psychic Powers at such times.

The Spirit Runes are to be read for yourself alone and not in the company of others. You may, however, read that which would pertain to others in consulting the Runes.

Cast the Magic Circle and stand to face East across thy Altar and have the Rune Cloth laid out upon it before you.

Holding the Rune stones in both hands cupped together, pass them eight times through the smoke of the Incense and say:

Hermes, Thoth and Odin art thou known among mankind.
Attend to me in this great need.
Thy wisdom and elucidation I would have.
Lead me to the light out of dark unknown.

Holding the Runes close to your breast, meditate deeply on that question or matter for which you seek an answer for about 8 minutes quietly and intently.

Let the Incense fill the Chamber.

When you feel ready, cast the 24 stones forth onto the cloth and let them fall where and as they may.

You should remove to the side those which fall face down.

Read only those which fall face up from the furthest point from you, moving back toward yourself. The last and closest Rune should be the answer and the others contributory thereto.

Ponder the doom and deem it well. All the Runes pertain to the final one and create the answer you seek.

You can then ask as many questions as needed, but cast them in like manner one question at a time during the course of the night. However, not more than eight castings should be done in one session.

Record your results in your journal and close the Magic Circle and clear all away.

By keeping the Spirit Runes as a personal Oracle for yourself conducted in a ritual manner thus, they become highly charged and attuned only to your employ in the Mercurial works.

You should, at all times, keep them from being handled by any other person, no matter how close.

Should they be handled by others, they must then be re-consecrated in like manner, as indicated above.

Scrying in The Goddess's Name

On Nights of Luna as She waxes in Water Signs, set two violet, blue or white candles to burn beside a Chalice of water. Allow a fragrant Incense such as Jasmine or Sandalwood to lightly scent your Ritual Chamber.

Sit yourself comfortably at a table with the candles and Chalice set before you.

Gather the Coven[1] all around to concentrate and invoke the Lunar Orb from on high.

All in unison then must chant:

Come down, come down
in thy gossamer gown.
Into our circle place thy crown.
Give us thy mystery in water by vision
and knowledge to know its meaning by precision.
Come, O Goddess of the Tide of Life,
bring peace and love and an end to strife.
Come down! come down,
O Lady of renown!
Bring thy smile, belie the frown.
What is thy will? What redes dost thou bring?
Inspire us as we chant and sing.
Witches call thee this night of Luna,
Mater Dea, Bona Fortuna!
Come down! Come down, O Mistress of Night,
answer our plea! Allay our plight!

The Witch then goes into light trance to scry in the reflections dancing on the surface of the water.

He/She speaks out what is given to see. The Seer may be questioned

---

1) Author's note: For a Coven rite, an Artisan II° could be the Seer, or the High Priestess or a Hand Maiden/Practicus III°. However, this may be better suited for the Coven women to perform.

and asked to answer what the visions in the water would say to individuals in the Coven Group.

It would be a violation of Witch Law not to give the contents of a vision thus conjured, be it good or ill. The Goddess will speak as She will.

When the conjured vision begins to fade, or when it is felt the power starting to wane, the Seer blows out the candles and says:

Blessed Lady of the Sky,
bless us before thou doth
upward fly. We thank thee
for thy visions so keen.
We know what to do, we
have seen. Blessed be!

The results of such vision rites should be entered into the Coven's Log.

Scrying in The God's Name

(Author's Note: The same format, as above, can be done with this rite as to the person acting as Seer. But, perhaps the males in the Coven would be better suited.)

On Nights of Mars, as the Moon waxes in a Fire Sign, have procured a tag lock from the person about whom you would know.

Pour a small amount of alcohol (Isopropol) into a metal container of either brass, iron or steel.

Gather the Coven around to link up with the God by this collective chant:

Mars, the warrior, God of Fire!
Heed our call, answer our desire.
Beat the drums and thunder thy roar.
We seek to know what doth go on before.
Come, O tramper and marcher of power!
We call thee in thy rulerships hour.
Burn, burn, the flames mount high!

Come cracking and thundering out of the sky!

As the alcohol is set ablaze, these words are said:

We call thee in thy blazing fire most bright.
Illumine our minds, O God of Light!

The Seer holds the tag lock to the brow or Solar Plexus and concentrates on the individual from whom it came as he/she gazes into the fire and goes into light trance.

Soon visions will be seen in the dancing flames as he/she scrys.

One must then speak out what is seen as this reverie proceeds.

Those in the Coven, most concerned with the Subject's welfare, whereabouts, or doings, may pose questions to the Seer which are answered as the fire reveals them.

As with Scrying in the Goddess's Name, when the conjured energy seems to begin to slack off and wane, the Seer will smother over the fire with a black cloth to put it out and say:

Thank thee, thank thee, God of Light.
We bid thee return to thy orbit in flight.
Pax tibi, pax tibi, pax tibi this night.

The Crone's Blessing

As part of the presentation of a Wiccan Born at the Covenstead (see *Book II* of *The Sacred Pentagraph*) this minor rite may be performed.

The oldest woman of the Coven would bestow this Witches Blessing on the Newborn.

For a male child she would use Air and Fire, that is Incense and a candle. The Incense would be of Frankincense and a white candle would be lit from the Coven's Sacred Flame.

She would circumambulate the infant boy thrice widdershins as she invokes the Gods thus:

Lord and Lady of our Ancient Faith,
bless this manchild and keep him in thy light.
Powers of the God bless this infant by Air and Fire.
Give him strength and manly grace.
Keep him in the wisdom ways of the Old Gods.
Let not the circle be broken,
that the future be assured.
Blessed be, (infant's name), and blessed be!

For the female child, she would circumambulate with a Chalice of Water and a plate of salt with a small piece of bread or cake. These words are spoken:

Lady and Lord of Witchery and Lore, keep this womanchild
forevermore. Bless her with thy mysterious power, to blossom
as a rose of love.
Powers of the Goddess of Life, bless by water, Earth and love.
Keep her in the Lady's ways all the remainder of her days.
Blessed be, (infant's name), and blessed be!

The Crone, at the last line of each blessing, whispers the secret, magical name into the infant's ear, so only the babe could hear it. The name would be indicative of the powers personified by the child either chosen by the parents, or bestowed by the Crone from her own repository of Wiccan Lore.

From that day forward, no one, absolutely no one, will speak that name, nor allow anyone to ever know it.

The Crone and/or the Parents will take that name to their graves so the secret will be safe.

From that time on, no form of adverse Occult Powers could affect the child on through adulthood, not ever having the real secret name.

In Memoriam

Part of the Women's Mysteries in a Coven is to mark the passing of life from this Earth Plane.

High Priestesses, or the women acting as their delegates, would observe a novena in honor of a deceased Covener 30, 60 and 90 days after his/her passing.

It can be done either with Seven Day glass candles burning for 90 days, or a large white candle could be set to burn itself out for the 30th, 60th and 90th day after the passing.

The candle need not be dressed with any oil, nor would any incense be necessary.

We know persons pass on to bigger and better things. Therefore, Wicca does not Egyptianize the fact of death, nor do we expect to put on the public show of sorrow and mourning, as seen in most other faiths.

We prefer to send love and good will following after the dead. That way, the spiritual essence of the deceased is not held back toward the Earth Plane. Mourning can become morbid and affect those who passed in an adverse way.

On the 30th day after a Covener has crossed the veil, the High Priestess will set the candle alight and say:

God and Goddess of our Ancient Faith,
we commit to thee the spirit of_______,
Brother/Sister of this Coven.
Now we set the Memorial Light
to keep the ways of Ancient Rite.
See this candle burning bright,
to speed this soul beyond the night.
Upward and onward to spiritual progression
says our ancient mode of confession.
Never to stop nor make digression,
Universes unfold without retrogression.
Leave the flesh and take to wing

as joyous and blessed thy voice doth sing.
Love and fellowship is the only thing
that the cycles of time around will bring.
__________, may the Lord and Lady receive thee.
As things unfold, as is the plan, mayest thou once
more find a loving Wiccan hearthfire as
thou returnest in a more perfected state
of being. Blessed be and blessed be!

The same is repeated on the 60th and 90th day after the Covener's passing. Ever afterwards is that Covener only spoken of with fond thoughts. Only to be remembered at his/her best.

Such is the Wiccan attitude to death.

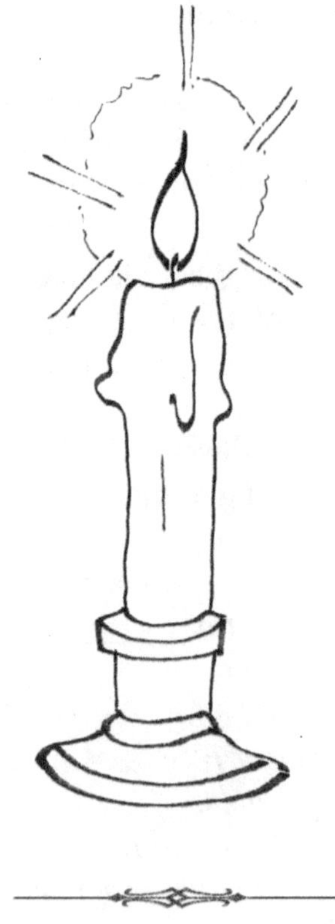

Craft Poppetry For The Witch

The use of Poppets has been an ancient art passed down in the Craft from distant times.

Poppetry operates on the assumption of a Law of Sympathetic Contagion, where an item from a person, or intimately in association with him/her, is acted upon magically, to produce an affect physically and/or astrally upon the person.

The item from the subject/victim may be hair, nail clippings, body fluids or worn garments. It would be termed in the old idiom a Tag Lock. It is somehow woven into the structure of the Poppet to help identify the Poppet, in the Practitioner's mind, as the subject/victim.

The Tag Lock, being a natural substance, would contain the essence of the person from whom it came; his/her astral counterpart, so to speak. What would be done to it, theoretically, would be done to the person. (If pieces of garment are used, be sure they are natural fibers and not of a synthetic substance, as is common in materials for dress in this day.)

The body of the Poppet could be cut out of felt or flannel, or better yet, from a garment of the subject/victim. (However poppets can be obtained, the usual store bought variety is common. Red or black would be the traditional colors for the Poppet.)

Cut out two sides from a doll pattern and sew them together. Leave a small opening in one foot to place in the stuffing and the Tag Lock.

The stuffing should be herbs associated with the reason for the spell in which the Poppet is employed:

Mint, Lavender, Verbena or Rose Petals for works of love.
Sunflower Petals, Marigold Buds and Hyssop for healing.
Dill Seed, Five Finger Grass, Basil or Cinnamon for Luck and Money matters.
Patchouli, Valerian, Mugwort and Mullein for the works of hexerei.

Once stuffed and with the Tag Lock worked in, the last bit of stitching can be completed to finish the Poppet.

It would be best within the Magical Tradition to make the Poppet in a properly cast Magic Circle. Use either the Circle of Initiates from *Book II* of *The Sacred Pentagraph*, or the simple Circle described in this volume earlier on.

Have all necessary items for making the Poppet and for the spell in which it is to be used on the Altar at the appropriate Planetary Day or Night.

Fridays for Love. Wednesdays for Luck/Money. Sundays for Healing, or Saturdays for Binding and Thwarting. Tuesdays for Blasting enemies. Keep to the suggestions as to the phases of the Moon, etc., as already explained.

Cast the Circle, according to the prescribed ritual and then begin to construct the Poppet.

As it is being made, hold vividly in mind the subject/victim and the purpose for the spell.

With each stitch of the sewing needle, chant a ditty to embody the idea, or the reason for the Poppet:

Stick and sew, stick and sew, by the works of stitchery,
I work my Magic Witchery.
Sew and stick, sew and stick, this little poppet doll
becomes the one whose name I call.
By needle and thimble,
with fingers so nimble,
for spells of (purpose), from long ago,
I employ the Witchy Art I know!

Then the Poppet must be identified as the subject/victim by a process of repeating the person's name over it at least three times, using warm breath if the spell is of a beneficial nature and a cold one, if for a negative purpose, by blowing and whispering the name over the poppet thrice:

Little doll, thou art now known
as the one whose name be blown
over and upon thee yet.
Thou art (name), (name), (name),
thou canst bet!

From this point proceed to work whatever spell would be necessary, such as driving a pin into the region of the heart activating love; binding the doll's arms and limbs to prevent or thwart action, impede physical function; sewing up the mouth to stop talk, or by using a pin to place in a spot needing healing; etc., etc.

For whatever reason the Poppet is being used, the emotion for the spell must be felt and experienced as real; love-hate-compassion, etc.

The chants embodying the idea should be from the Practitioner's own composition, as he/she is more personally involved with the case at hand.

It should be a vivid ritual drama to recreate, as clearly as possible, the reason for the spell. The Poppet is emoted over until a point of emotional exhaustion is reached.

Then the Circle is closed.

Repeat the Spell as often as may be necessary to accomplish the task and then dispose of the Poppet in the way appropriate to the purpose of the working.

Necromancy Divination by Shades of The Dead

At the waning of the Moon, in the dark days after the Winter Solstice, when the Sun be in the Sign of the Goat Fish and all sleepeth the great Death at the waning of the year, thou canst summon and question shades....

Necromancy is the Art of communicating with and obtaining information from the Shades of the Departed. It is almost a forgotten form in this modern World.

However, Necromancy has always been a part of any decent Wizard's repertoire, and to do it effectively, serious thought and study must be undertaken.

There are several forms of Necromancy still being used today. One is the Dumb Supper performed by certain Covens of Witches on the Night of Hallowmas, the other form, most commonly heard of, is the seance, held by a Spiritual Medium.

The Medium may think and feel he/she is in actual contact with a sort of "Spirit Guide" which helps bring in the other Shades to be questioned by the sitters in the circle.

True spiritualistic phenomena brings through the actual personality of the deceased individual for all to hear and recognize.

I will give two forms of Necromancy for the Witch and allow him/her to attune the self to the one most suitable to his/her own nature.

It may be good for the Witch to set up his/her own seance group and communicate with the Shades of the Departed who wish to speak to the living, on this side of the veil.

The deeper one gets into this type of phenomena, the more one will see there is really a thin line between the two, and that they on the other side, are not much different than those on this.

First, some pointers to avoid:

Do not use a totally black room. Do not use black cloths on the table. Do not use any heavy incenses.

In a spiritualistic circle, one is opening up to the influences from the other realms. The Dark ones must be left where they are.

Most Spirits are no different than the general run of people. There are good, bad and in between. Leave the criminal element in its own milieu.

It is best to always sit on the same day of the Week, best on Wednesday Nights, at about the same hour each week.

Use a dim room, painted a pale white. Use a white cloth on the table. Use a light fragrant Incense and have flowers on the table and a bowl of water in the center (the flowers could float in the water) to absorb any hostile psychic influences. Flowers give an essence.

Ring the bowl of water with a circle of 8 white candles, which should be the only illumination for the seance.

Have the above arranged and the candles lit along with the Incense at least five minutes before the "Sitting" is to begin.

The Sitting should be composed of a few serious-minded friends or associates, or Coven members, who are interested in Psychic Studies and are agreeable to sitting and developing a Spirit Circle.

They must be knowledgeable enough to know it may take weeks or even months of constant weekly sitting before a clear channel can be established and open to the other side.

For the first several sessions nothing at all may happen. The spirits must be convinced of your sincerity and perseverance before they may wish to attend.

Be skeptical of immediate results. It may be a trickster on either side of the veil.

The number of people should be as even as possible between males and females. They should sit alternating male, female around the table to keep a balance.

With a serious frame of mind, meet each week and allow the group to simply sit around the table and meditate on seeking a rapport with those in Spirit. No specific individuals should be called at the beginning.

After about a half hour, have the group, break the meditation and discuss what was experienced in the session. Have a member act as recorder and keep a journal of the results of each and every meeting.

With time, a channel will open to the other side. Impressions will come through and certain individuals in the group will feel strongly that they must voice them.

Mediums who rock back and forth, gasp and moan and thrash

around are a product of Hollywood movies, and not the norm.

However, with serious cultivation., one in the group may develop into a good sensitive.

Then trance phenomena may manifest.

Do not touch the entranced Medium while it lasts, until the spirit has finished speaking and departs.

You will know the phenomena is real when you afterwards stroke the medium's arms upward to restore circulation. He/she will feel cold to the touch.

Once a channel has been opened, regular sessions will bring through much information.

A "Spirit Guide" may be the main contact with the other side. Do not believe all the mystical hogwash about Spirit Guides some people tell you.

They are not the Mystic Masters of lost Atlantis. They are not great Priests or Priestesses from the Temples of Ancient Egypt. They are not Mahatmas and Gurus of Hindu lore.

They are not Amerindian Shamans. And certainly not Amy Semple McPhearsen.

They are the collective over-soul of the group, itself.

Do not let the overly credulous and the deliberate phonies waste your time and sap your energy.

The Spirit Guide will manifest with each and every session, once serious practice has opened a channel. .

Then, after a considerable amount of experience has been gained by the group as a whole, specific Spirits may be contacted and asked to speak through the group or its Medium.

This form of Necromancy does not constrain or conjure the Spirit against its Will. The over-soul of the group establishes a rapport with the Spirit and invites it to manifest.

Begin by contacting Spirits of people known to someone in the group, so as to have a confirmation of the authenticity of the personality of the being contacted.

When positive results are forthcoming, then "strangers"/non-coveners may be allowed to attend the sessions, so that the group's Spirit Guide may contact those they wish to question.

A reputation for honesty and authentic Spirit Contact will then begin to grow.

A session should begin by having the sitters link hands around the table to keep a closed circuit of living entities and give life to the over-soul of the group.

The meditation should begin and the group sensitives may link up with it.

In the glow of the candles, with water, flowers and light Incense, there is no possibility of phony tricks, as can be done in a totally dark room, so loved by some commercial Mediums.

Keep the hands of all sitters linked through the entire session. That way contact is not lost with the over-soul.

You will have to play much by ear, and allow the group to set its own pace in these matters. I can only give a few hints to help you along.

In questioning the shades of the departed, the matter of foretelling the future usually comes up in the course of time. Do not expect Spirits to reveal the secrets of all the ages to you. They do not know them.

They can, however, see the immediate Astral Influences around individuals, which are about to come into being. No more, no less. They also are fallible, since they were mere Human Beings themselves.

Death, or that state we call such, does not elevate one into the Privy Council of the Most High Gods themselves.

We call such contacts "Spirits." That is really a misnomer for what it is. The Spirit of any departed individual has elevated and gone to its place in the beyond and away from the Earth Plane. Mediumistic Circles can only contact Astral Shells.

Why else do you think I mentioned identifying the "personality" in the explanations above? The shell has a life of its own on the lower planes directly above this one for a period of time after death and maintains its identity and persona, but it is not the real spiritual essence of the departed. It is but a part thereof and a layer of the being that also is cast off, like the body.

The prognostications derived from them, can be useful, but see the Spirits for what they are and do not be mislead by false information.

In this field of the Occult, it is mandatory to keep one's feet on the ground.

Practice Spirit Communication and learn what it can teach, but do not let yourself be carried away.

Concerning the Wizard's Triangle of Manifestation or The Seal of Spirits

It should be made new for each ceremony in which such may be called for. The particulars for its making will follow.

It may be drawn in chalk on the Ritual Chamber floor, or made on a large parchment so the smaller parchment containing the Sigil of the individual Spirit to be summoned can be set within it.

The Sigils of individual Spirits or Powers which the Witch would invoke are the symbols associated with the name of the Spirit or Power itself. These can be obtained from many books on Ceremonial Magic readily available, such as *The Grimoire of Armadel*, by Mathers from Weiser, or *The Lesser Key of Solomon*, or *The Arbatel of Magick*.

The idea being, that the "Force" or Power, which is called a Spirit, is meditated upon, invoked and constrained to enter the Triangle of Manifestation to rest, on or above its own Sigil or Symbol. That is done by use of the proper Incense, number vibration, colors and Words of Power to which the old Grimoires say the Spirit will respond. The Witch will, of course, be within the Magic Circle and conjure the Spirit to attend and enter the Triangle.

From there, the Witch will lay or put whatever Charge or request he/she Wills upon the Spirit to bring about his/her Will.

The Medieval Ceremonial Magicians and Wizards called the Powers Spirits, but they are not really what normally today is meant by the word. They are the lesser Forces of the Divine ALL, which have particular responsibilities in the overall scheme of the Cosmos, both for good, or ill, as we see it. They are neither good or evil in themselves.

The process is one of attracting that particular Force and filling it with one's own Will and desires. As long as the Will or desire corresponds to the particular Province of the individual Spirit, the Will of the Wizard/or Witch can be made to come about, according to the old lore.

In times long ago, when Humanity was more primitive in its thinking, blood of animals, and even, Humans, were used to place beside the Symbol or link for attracting the Spirit.

The "Beings" invoked, drew strength from the essences given off by blood.

Today, the same can be accomplished by using a living essence in much the same way, but not blood.

Beside the Sigil in the Triangle, place a small bowl into which a raw egg has been cracked open, or a flower of the color of the Spirit Force may be set in a small vase with water.

When that is combined with the proper Incense, there is sufficient essence given off to allow the Spirit to draw energy and assume a temporary Astral vehicle in the Invocations.

An egg or flower represents the basic forms of life and would be better than blood, which may only attract beings from the Chaos.

(Traditional sources)

Triangle of Manifestation
Seal of Spirits

Inscribe this Seal outside your Magic Circle at the Quarter from whence, you would summon a particular Spirit.

Scribe the Spirit's name along the three sides of the triangle and set the Sigil of the Spirit

scribed on parchment in ink of Dragons-Blood in the, center thereof.

From within your Magic Circle, burning the proper Incense,

and reciting the proper Invocation, you can summon the Spirit to attend the rite and charge it to do your Will.

You can also scribe this Seal on parchment and surround it with three candles of black or white, and place therein a Crystal Ball to scry the portends of Time and Space.

It is into the center of this Seal, that the link would be cast during the Ritual to follow, so that no Sigil would be needed, when the Spirit summoned is a deceased person and not of other orders of being.

The High Ceremony of Necromancy To Summon Shades of The Departed

(Keeping this ceremony in old idiom, to impress the deep mind.)

Such wouldst thou do only upon great need and in pressing circumstance after much deliberation and deep thought given thereto.

Thou art dealing with the Mysteries from the Beyond and it be a heavy and dire working, dangerous to the unprepared.

In the waning of the year, from the Autumnal Equinox to the Winter Solstice, is the only time thou shouldst attempt to conjure the Shades from the Beyond. The best times would be at the Dark of the Moon on a Night of Saturn as the Sun passeth in the Sign of Capricorn.

However, The Waning Moon Nights of Mercury during the Winter Season from Hallows to Midwinter are also favorable.

That be the Season of Death and the breaking down of Life, preparatory to the deep sleep of Winter. The Spirits are stirring at that time, it is traditionally said, and may be more easily attracted. The veil between life and death is thin at that time.

Thou wouldst not perform this Necromancy in the presence of other living persons, but alone within thy Magic Circle.

Shouldst thou have an apprentice to the Arts of Wizardry or Witchcraft, that thou teacheth and traineth to follow after thee, then he/she may be allowed to sit within thy Circle to observe the Ritual, but not actively participate, nor contribute thereto.

Thy Chamber should be dark and draped in black. Thy Altar cloth and all candles be also of that shade. Thy robe and cord should also be black.

Thy manner and mien shouldst be dark and somber and commanding. Not the forceful commanding manner of a warrior, but the cold, hard, steady approach of one who knoweth dark things. Cold and firm, shouldst be thy bearing. All must be dark and heavy around thee.

Heed well these words of warning and follow them to the letter, or thou place thyself in grave peril. Thou couldst fall into the Abyss of Madness and do great damage to thy sanity and equilibrium, as the Ancient Sages have warned.

Obtain the necessary items and put them together as I instruct thee. Foolhardiness and frivolity wouldst abort the effort.

Decide what information thou require from the Beyond and meditate deeply on it to obtain a clear, precise idea.

Choose the Spirit thou wouldst conjure. It must have been on the other side of the veil for at least a year and a day.

Have at hand a personal item from that Spirit when it was in physical bodily form. That be thy link to the personality thou wouldst conjure.

Obtain Dittany of Crete, Patchouli, Mugwort, Valerian and Black Arts Incense.

Wear a Pentagram of Silver whenever dealing with Spirits, as it is a symbol of mastery in the Occult.

Thou must have the items ready before two weeks prior to the Night chosen for the Ritual.

Two Weeks prior, thou must retire nightly into thy Chamber and light a black candle and hold the link in thy hand. Meditate deeply on the name of the Spirit thou wouldst conjure for about one Quarter of an hour, as thou grind in thy mortar and pestle, the herbs above mentioned and mix them well with the Black Arts Incense.

In other words, nightly, thou must meditate with the link and grind thy mixture picturing the Spirit summoned to thee. Such will open a channel and rapport with the Shade/Spirit so it may more readily be summoned on the Night of the Ritual.

If thou canst not set aside the necessary amount of time, abort thy effort and attempt it not.

On the Night of the Ritual, thy Altar candles must be black, thy four Quarter candles around thy Circle must be black, thy Altar also draped therewith and thy robe and Ritual Chamber also black.

In the center of thy Altar should sit thy Burner and thy Incense mixture.

Thou must face West across the Altar towards the Quarter whence the Winter Sun went down.

Have thy hand bell near thy Incense.

Deep in the night, at the Midnight Hour approach thy Altar and ring the bell 11 times.

Follow thy usual format to cast thy Magic Circle. (Should thy Apprentice be with thee, he/she must sit quietly at the East side within the Circle).

Use some of thy Incense mixture to cast the Circle, and keep a goodly amount handy to use during the Ritual.

Thy manner must be cold and firm. Thy voice commanding and forceful.

When thy Circle be erect and the Ritual ready to proceed, state aloud:

> We come in the Dead of Night, in the waning of the year, to summon the forces of the Beyond.
> Wardens of the gates, swing open the doorway. Send forth the Spirit of the one I call......
> I be the servant of the Nameless One! Amen Selah!

Rap thrice upon thy Altar with thy knuckles loudly. (Remember, thou should have placed a Seal of Spirits to the West outside thy Circle bearing the name of the one to be summoned.

Thou must repeat the words above twice more.

Add more Incense to the coals as needed.

Take up thy Sword or Athame and step to the West side of the Circle and point it down toward the Seal of Spirits. Cast the link, the item belonging to the Spirit when it was in this life, upon the Seal.

Speak out:

> *By thy own do I summon thee! By thine own essence art thou bound to attend upon me!*
> *By thy life, that thou werdst, must thou come!*
> *Conjured and constrained be to do my Will!*
> *I be the servant of the Nameless One! Amen, Selah!*

Thou must here pause and allow a silence to ensue. Things may begin to stir outside thy Circle.

Under no circumstances, from this time on, must anything leave thy

Circle.

Thou must have firm command of all that happens from this point.

Return to stand across the Altar facing West to the Seal of Spirits and add more Incense as needed.

Set thy Sword or Athame back in place and take up thy hand bell once again.

Ring the bell 12 times and say:

At the twelve strokes of time, be summoned to obey!

Allow a silence to ensue again and listen for any sound round about thy Circle.

After the slight pause, speak forth the Necromantic Charge:

By the powers of this dying year,
by the waning of the moon,
by the western shores of life,
by the Night of Time and space,
by the words of Will and might
(Name of Spirit), come forth!
By the works of wizardry and wonder,
by the darkness of the grave,
by the force of Gods and man,
by the summons from the dark,
by the scent of herb and smoke
come forth!
By the Dark Angel's bidding,
by the bounds of living essence,
by the Seal of Spirit manifest,
by the command of the Nameless One,
by dark candle's light,
(Name of Spirit), come forth!
Enter into this world of form.
Clothe thyself in smoke.
Approach the Seal of Spirits.
Pantheon Asyen!
Messyuz!
Sother!....

Emmanuel Sabaoth Adonoy!
Be subject unto me!

Thou should add more incense at this time and take the burner and place it at the western rim within thy Circle, near the place of the Seal of Spirits.

A presence will now be felt to manifest outside the Circle near the Seal. Allow it to swirl and form as it will in the Incense. Lift high thy Sword or Athamé to the West and speak:

(Name of Spirit), thou art summoned to answer my questions truly and without delay! Give forth thy answer!

Now thou must put what query thou wilt to the Shade.

It must be the precise wording for the purpose thou meditated upon during the two weeks prior to this Night.

After the question, allow all to go silent and await thy answer. It may not be an audible voice thou hearest, but a deep impression of words and symbols coming to thy mind.

Remember everything which happens in this long silence. Record it later.

After a good few minutes, the atmosphere will begin to grow light as the power begins to wane. That is the sign that the session is over.

Thou may have beheld a form taking shape in the dim light and Incense smoke during the silence. Study it well, but do not disturb it by any sound made from thyself or thy Apprentice whatsoever.

The Shades are very nebulous and are easily dissipated by vibrations.

It will begin to fade of itself when the feeling of the lighter atmosphere ensues.

Allow the energy to drain away by itself. Then thou canst begin to close the Ritual.

Take thy Sword or Athamé to the West Quarter and holding it high, begin to trace a Banishing Pentagram towards the West with these words:

Close the Veil, banish the Power, seal the Gates!
Spirit of (Name of Spirit), return to thy proper place in space and time. Depart this realm of matter and be at peace! Amen, Selah!

Return thy Sword or Athamé to its place on the Altar and take thy hand bell and ring it 13 times and say:

All Shades and lingering Phantoms be gone and away!

Then close thy Circle in the proper fashion.

When all has been done, then and only then shouldst thou step out of the Circle area.

Burn some Frankincense to cleanse away the heaviness and change the vibrations.

Thou canst then record thy impressions.

In the course of the following days and weeks, thy question to the Spirit will bring an answer to thee in mysterious ways. Be ready and open to everything pertaining thereto, and thy works of Necromancy will bring thee positive results.

If nothing seems to transpire during the Ritual, think not that it worketh naught. Not all are sensitive to see or hear Spirit voices. Thou wilt, however, feel the heaviness of the presence of something outside thy Circle.

It would communicate with thee to answer thy question in the way most conducive to thy psychology and understanding.

The Spirit Realm will give thee a response to the question asked in whatever form thou could safely handle.

The ideas pertaining to the Spirits in the use of communicating in a Spirit Circle, in the pages above, would also apply in the ritual approach such as this.

Do not summon the Dead for light or frivolous matters, but question them only for solutions to problems thou canst not deal with thyself.

Remember, their powers of foretelling the future are limited and can only be accurate in the short run.

(Author's note: The divine names used in the Necromantic Charge are from traditional ceremonial ritual procedures.)

Talismans of The Cornucopia

These minor Talismans for the Planetary Influences are offered in this Book as an example of Magical Procedure and methods of Consecration.

The Covener may use them in his/her Ordeal to attain Artisan status.

Seal of The Occult

(Traditional)

To help one obtain knowledge of ancient and arcane lore.

Scribe the Seal on parchment on a Night of Saturn, as Luna waxes in a Water Sign.

As the Seal is being scribed, chant over it, at least 15 times:

Ancient Spells and Wisdom from of yore,
these things do I implore,
and more....
Knowledge of the Arcana Aracanorum, Mysteries of the past
for my mind's open forum.

Anoint a black candle with Black Arts Oil and set it to burn standing upon the Seal.

Set a Meditation Incense to burn and deeply concentrate on the Seal and any question needing an answer.

Let whatever message come to you as it will.

Keep the Seal on the North wall of your Occult Library.

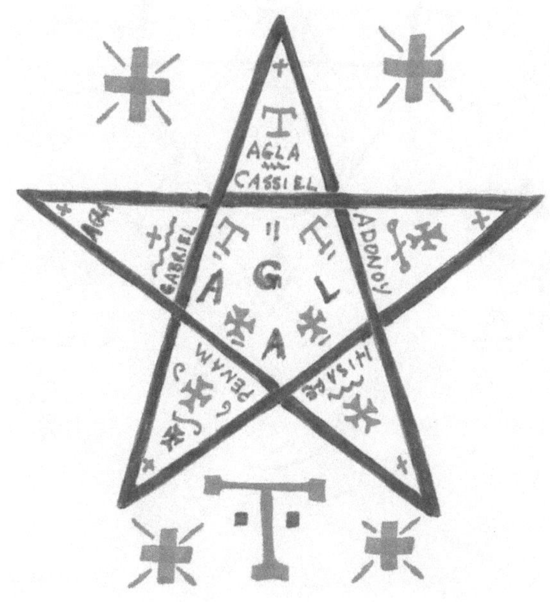

Talisman of The Seven Seals

(Traditional)

The power of the "Mystic Seven Planets of the Ancients."

It takes a full Week to properly make this Talisman. Begin to scribe it on a Day of Sol, Moon waxing in a Fire Sign, by making the Seal of the Sun.

Thereafter, each following day, scribe the Seal for the Planet of that Day.

Then consecrate it by passing it 6 times through the smoke of Frankincense and placing it under a lit 7 Color Candle in glass, on the following Day of Sol.

After the candle has burned itself out, carry the Talisman on your person to attract the positive forces of the Planets.

Seal of Luna

A Moon Talisman is designed to attract the peaceful emotions into personal relationships and establish harmony in the domestic situation when made and consecrated on a Night of Luna as She waxes in a Water Sign.

It may also serve to cloud the mind and weave illusions of uncertainty for an enemy when made on the same night as Luna wanes in a Water Sign.

Scribe the Seal on parchment in inks of violet, gray and cobalt blue. Pass it 9 times through the smoke of Jasmine or Gardenia Incense as you chant:

Luna, Luna, Bona Fortuna, weave thy mystic spell of reflection
upon my wish without rejection.
Calm with peace or cloud with mist,
as I commune with thee in this Ancient tryst.

Meditate on the purpose for the Seal until it is felt it has absorbed the mental charge.

Then carry it on your person to work its intention.

Seal of Mars

A Talisman to take the offensive and destroy the work or Will of an enemy. Scribe on parchment on a Night of Mars as Luna waxes in a Fire Sign, in inks of red, golden yellow, orange and black.

To act as a shield of defense and ward off magical attacks from enemies, scribe on a Night of Mars, as Luna wanes in an Earth Sign.

Scribe the reason for making the Seal on the reverse side and anoint it with Mars Oil.

Pass the Seal five times through the smoke of Dragons Blood Reed Incense mixed with ground Stinging Nettles with these words:

God of war and warrior strong, offence against an evil throng. To fight my cause and win the day, up Mars, up I say!

or:

Shield of strength, defense of power, keep me safe from this hour.
Ward off the attacks of my ugly foe. I stand firm forever, let them know!

As an offensive weapon, it must be buried at or near the enemy's door step on a Night of Mars, Luna waxing.

As a defense, keep the Seal folded in the left shoe when the enemy is afoot and around about.

Seal of Mercury

To gain acclaim in the fields of communications, acting, music or the performing arts. To help clarify one's own thinking and mental abilities, to sharpen the wit. A Psychic's Charm.

Scribe the Seal on a Night of Mercury as Luna waxes in a Water Sign with inks of yellow, blue, purple and black.

To confuse someones thinking and foul up lines of communication, scribe it on a Mercury Night as Luna wanes in an Air or Water Sign.

Carry the Seal in a yellow Charm Bag with Marjoram (Dittany of Crete), a small vial of Quicksilver and 8 pinches of Dill Seed, to attract the positive mercurial benefits.

Burn the Seal and scatter the ashes to the Four Winds to act as an aid in influencing the mind of others.

Consecrate the Seal on the proper nights of Mercury, as above, with a mixture of Storax, Olibanum and Benzoin as an Incense, by passing it 8 times through the smoke as these words are spoken:

Air Sprites and Sylphs and Spirits of Hermes, attend to me on wings of air!
Aid my psychic power and influence, bring the matters of mind to bear.

Silently meditate on the reason for the Talisman until it is felt to be sufficiently charged.

Seal of Jupiter

Scribe the Seal in inks of blue and purple on a night of Jupiter as the Moon waxes in an Earth Sign to help a project or circumstance expand and prosper. It is a good fortune seal for all constructive purposes.

Scribe on a Night of Jupiter as the Moon wanes in a water Sign to cause situations to deflate and dwindle away. Give it as a gift to an enemy.

Compose an Incense of Cinnamon, Cloves, Lavender and Benzoin to burn on charcoal and light a candle of royal blue or dark green, anointed with Jupiter Oil.

Pass the Seal four times through the smoke and say:

Zeus, the royal God of Wealth, preserves my money, peace and health.

or:

All expansion doth here halt, an afflicted Jupiter be at fault!

Set the Seal to rest beneath the candle until It burns itself out. If made for positive ends, carry it on your person.

Seal of Venus

To help increase love and friendship and attract the attention of a loved one, scribe this Seal on a Night of Venus, as Luna waxes in a Water or Earth Sign. Use inks of pink, green and copper brown.

Scribe the name of the intended Lover on the reverse of the Seal and set it to rest between two candles; one pink and the other green, anointed with a Love Drawing Oil.

Burn an Incense of Rose and/or Jasmine with some Sandalwood.

Set seven copper pennies in a circle around the candles and Seal, as these words are spoken:

Seven coins of copper, seven nights of love, seven times seven
times seven times seven.
Such joy in life from the Seventh Heaven.

Let the candles burn themselves out and contrive to sew the rolled up Seal into the hem of the intended Lover's garment.

Seal of Saturn

In inks of black and purple, on a Night of Saturn, as Luna wanes in an Earth Sign, scribe this Seal to impede and restrict the actions and affairs of an enemy.

Pass it through the smoke of Patchouli and Valerian burned on coals. Set it beside a black candle anointed with Black Arts Oil and light the candle to burn slowly.

Speak not a word, but vision the bindings you would impose on the victim, as the candle burns.

Place the Seal and the candle stub, along with Knot Grass and Snake Root on the victim's door step at the Dark of the Moon.

Seal of Sol

For Good Luck, Good Fortune, Health and general Well-being, scribe this Seal in inks of red, yellow, gold and orange, on a Day of Sol as Luna waxes in a Fire or Earth Sign.

Pass the Seal 6 times through the smoke of Frankincense and 6 times through the flame of a gold candle anointed with Prosperity Oil.

Speak these words:

Wealth, good fortune and all life's blessing,
Sol will give for sure without guessing.
Prosperity and finances within my gate.
Sol will deflect all jealousy and hate.

Let the candle and incense burn out with the Seal beside them. Then place the Seal where the rays of the Sun will fall on it for six days in a row. Carry it on your person as a luck charm.

The Basic Robe

This. is the basic way for the Probationer, aspiring to become a Craftsman First Degree, to make a simple robe which is worn in the process of the Ordeal to Craftsman status.

The reason for this robe, is to also help the Probationer in his/her discipline. He/she should be familiar with the old way of doing things.

An object made by hand carries the magnetic energy and charge of its maker. Therefore, a magical robe, where each stitch drawn by hand is pulled with an invocation and ritual intention, becomes a potent tool in the Witch's armory. It becomes more than just a robe for dress-up, but a part of the Witch's persona.

This may or may not be the type of formal Coven Robe. required by the Coven Council for Sabbat Ceremonies, Esbat Works and/or any other ceremony demanding robed attire.

This is the type of robe worn by those of Craftsman status. It does not have a hood.

When Craftsman is called to become a Covener, however, he/she must then buy or make the uniform type of robe with the Coven Insignia as required by the determinations of the Coven Council. Such would have a hood. The Formal Robe would always be black.

Coveners of all degrees, thereafter, during ceremonies of a formal nature, attend in robe with hoods up drawn to hang and drape the eyes. The person is only recognized by the color of his/her cinch cord and the proper grade sign given by hand (see next section).

The Summoner, standing at the entrance to the Magic Circle will see to it that only those showing the proper grade sign of their status and giving the right Watchword will be admitted to the Coven Circle. (The Watchword is determined each Hallowmas as part of the group ritual divination. This word embodies the Coven orientation for the year ahead. See *Book III.*)

There are three easy steps for making this basic robe:

Underside of material

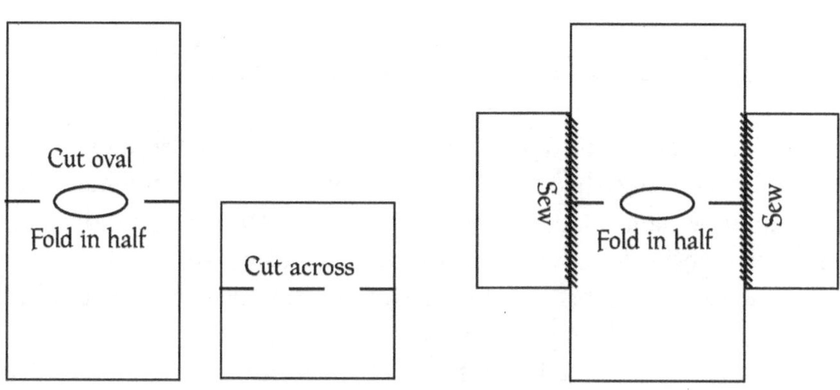

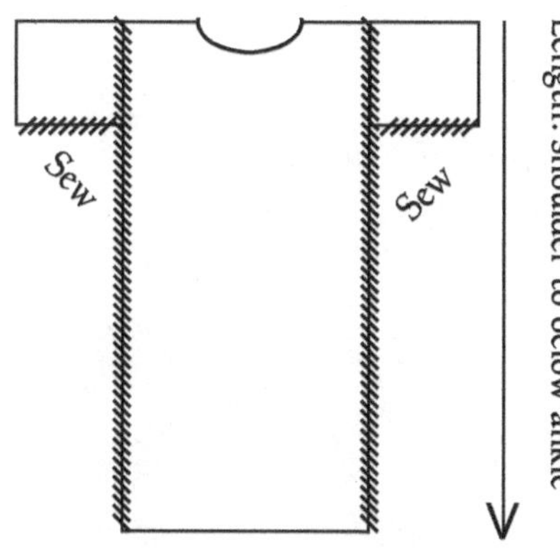

1. Two pieces of cloth; 1 piece is half the length of the other. Cut the oval for the head and cut the smaller piece for the sleeves.

2. Sew the two smaller pieces to the larger one.

3. Fold the robe and sew up the sides and sleeves. Turn inside out.

Sewing chant:

"I sew, I make, I make, I sew.
Sew and make, sew and make,
a robe of art for my Magic's sake."

The Cingulum or Cinch Cord

The cinch Cord is of dyed leather, or cords of natural substances tied and braided together forming the belting for the ceremonial robe.

It should be hand made, either by the candidate for Initiation him/herself, or by others in the Coven for him/her as a gift.

Three strands of cording are required to make the Cinch Cord. They should be all of equal length, at least six feet long.

Three ends are knotted together and the strands carefully braided with this chant as each weaving is drawn:

Wrought by hand, this braided strand,
to show my Grade when Magic is made.

Each status in the Craft has its own color of Cingulum:

Craftsman 1st Degree, blue..

Covener 1st Degree, green.

Artisan 2nd Degree, yellow

Prac./HM 3rd Degree, red

High Priest 4th Degree, gold

High Priestess 5th Degree, silver

Elders 5th Degree, black.

Prior to each person assuming a Degree or status in the Craft, the proper Cinch Cord/Cingulum must be made and brought to the Initiation Ceremony. It will be girded around the Initiate as part of the Declaration of Status by the Initiator. (See *Initiation Rituals, Book II*.)

Craft Grade Signs of Rank

Upon entrance into the Ritual Chamber, or Circle for worship or Magical Ceremonies at the Covenstead, the Summoner will challenge all persons to show his/her grade sign. (Neophytes and Probationers excepted, as they have none and are only admitted by the Summoner and Sponsor at their respective Initiations.)

As each grade sign is shown, the Summoner will give a slight bow to those of higher rank than him/herself. To all he/she will say:

Only Perfect Love and Perfect Trust abide in this House.
What say ye?

To which the one entering will respond: *Blessed be.*

The Summoner will then require the Watchword to be whispered into his/her ear. Only thereupon will he/she step aside to allow the person to proceed into the Ritual Chamber or Circle.

No Covener should show irritation or impatience with the duty of the Summoner. This is to insure that only proper Coveners and those of true rank in the Craft participate in Craft works.

Visitors and those from other Traditions who have the right to attend Sabbat and/or Esbat, must be told the Watchword in order to pass the. Summoner. Perhaps their system does not have grade signs.

The Summoner has the right to forbid entrance to even those of V° status if such are not familiar with the Coven's Watchword. No Summoner should be afraid to enforce this rule.

The security of Craft Meetings is his/her particular domain.

The Signs:

Craftsman I°: Fingers entwined, the index fingers extended to form a steeple; the thumbs forming the closed door.

Covener I°: The same, except the thumbs are crossed, left over right for a female, and right over left for a male.

Artisan II°: Right hand over heart, left hand held high as the Torch of Knowledge.

Practicus/Hand Maiden III°: Slight bow from the waist, forearms extended with palms up; Egyptian Servant Gesture.

High Priest IV°: Thumbs entwined, fingers of both hands extended and laid upon breast; The Phoenix asending.

High Priestess IV°: A triangle formed with the two hands pointing downward over the abdomen; the Water Symbol.

Magister Sacrorum V°: Right arm pointing upward, left arm out pointing earthward; the Tarot Magus.

Queen Mother V°: Both hands under breasts lifting upward; the Many Breasted Diana.

Philosophus V°: A triangle made with the two hands pointing upward upon the forehead; the Fire Symbol.

Oracle V°: Both hands held up concealing the eyes to show that an Oracle is for all without partiality.

Epilogue

Here we have a complete Occult Lodge System for the Craft of Wicca in practicing the Old Religion. It follows the Initiate throughout life from birth to death, giving all necessary rites and ceremonies, both major and minor, for a rising on the planes of being and aiming the Initiate on the Road of Adepthood.

It is a complete way of life for the Wicca and would require a dedicated life's work to accomplish the entire system.

It is a complete path of occult attainment for those seeking spiritual advancement in affecting the Great Work for Self-transformation.

It is not for everyone, nor does the system itself maintain that it is the only way, but it offers a path toward Occult Adepthood which is not complicated, nor abstruse, as some other systems, but difficult requiring sincere effort.

It has been offered for those who feel they can profit and gain thereby, in advancing the Self on the path of esoteric Wisdom. It holds up an ideal for the individual and/or group to strive for and embody as best as they are able.

If the ideas and organizational methods recommended by the Sacred Pentagraph are able to assist and give deeper insight in the Coven and initiatory aspects of the Old Religion, this work is well served.

- Finis -
This is my legacy for the Craft.
Blessed Be!
Tarostar

CRAFTSMAN ~ COVENER
ELDER
HIGH PRIESTHOOD
PRACTICUS / HANDMAIDEN
ARTISAN

www.ingramcontent.com/pod-product-compliance
Lightning Source LLC
LaVergne TN
LVHW041052080826
845145LV00007B/1551

* 9 7 8 1 8 9 0 3 9 9 8 9 4 *